About Pearson

Pearson is the world's learning company, with a presence across 70 countries worldwide. Our unique insights and world-class expertise comes from a long history of working closely with renowned teachers, authors and thought leaders, as a result of which, we have emerged as the preferred choice for millions of teachers and learners across the world.

We believe learning opens up opportunities, creates fulfilling careers and hence better lives. We hence collaborate with the best of minds to deliver you class-leading products, spread across the Higher Education and Test Preparation spectrum.

Superior learning experience and improved outcomes are at the heart of everything we do. This product is the result of one such effort.

Your feedback plays a critical role in the evolution of our products and you can contact us at reachus@pearson.com. *We look forward to it.*

Public Policy

Vighneswara Swamy

Professor of Economics, IBS-Hyderabad
Dean Research of ICFAI Foundation for Higher Education

Suresh K.G.

Assistant Professor of Economics
Indian Institute of Management, Bodh Gaya

Pearson

Senior Editor—Product: Anindita Malhotra
Senior Editor—Production: C. Purushothaman

ISBN 978-93-560-6798-1

First Impression

Published by Pearson India Education Services Pvt. Ltd, CIN: U72200TN2005PTC057128.

Head Office: 1st Floor, Berger Tower, Plot No. C-001A/2, Sector 16B, Noida - 201 301, Uttar Pradesh, India.
Registered Office: Featherlite, 'The Address' 5th Floor, Survey No 203/10B, 200 Ft MMRD Road, Zamin Pallavaram, Chennai – 600 044.
Website: in.pearson.com, Email: companysecretary.india@pearson.com

Printed in India at Sai Printo Pack Pvt Ltd

To my late mother, Mrs. Vishalakshi,
who passed away during the writing of this book.
You are my guiding light, inspiration, and greatest supporter. Your unwavering belief in my abilities and encouragement to pursue my dreams will forever be ingrained in my heart. This book is a testament to your love, sacrifice, and dedication to our family. Your spirit lives on in these pages. Thank you for everything you did for me and for instilling in me the love of learning and knowledge.
I will always cherish your memory.

— Vighneswara Swamy

To my late father, who always supported me in pursuing my dreams.

— Suresh K.G.

Endorsements

Prof. S. Mahendra Dev

Public policies and their effectiveness are important to achieve goals of development: growth, inclusion and sustainability. Many universities and other academic institutions have started courses on public policy in social science and management departments. But, there is no suitable and comprehensive textbook to teach the course on public policy. Dr. Vighneswara Swamy and Dr. Suresh K.G. tries to fill this gap by providing a comprehensive textbook on public policy. Both of them have a lot of experience in teaching, research and collaboration to write this volume. The strength of the book is that it covers theory, policy making, process, implementation, policy reforms and contemporary topics –all of these topics in one volume. The material in the book is informative, analytical, and timely and the style is uncomplicated. It is a valuable resource for students, teachers, policy makers and civil society. This Book is a testimony to the high quality of authors' work and sincerity of their commitment.

Prof. S. Mahendra Dev
Former Director and Vice Chancellor, Indira Gandhi Institute of Development Research, Mumbai
Distinguished Professor, ICFAI Faculty of Social Sciences, Hyderabad,
Chairman, Institute for Development Studies, Andhra Pradesh, Visakhapatnam,
Former Vice Chairman, International Food Policy Research Institute (IFPRI), Washington, DC.
Former Chairman, Commission for Agricultural Costs and Prices, Government of India
Former Director, Centre for Economic and Social Studies, Hyderabad,
Former Member and Acting Chairman, National Statistical Commission, Government of India

Prof. Bhanoji Rao

Ever since the beginning of the liberalization process in the early 1990s, public policy institutions and programmes have grown significantly in India. Up-to-date, comprehensive, and motivating Public Policy textbooks are increasingly sought after.

This text by Swamy and Suresh deals with 'five modules' covering theory, policy making, implementation, India-centric policies and gaps, and latest developments (such as the global focus on Sustainable Development Goals).

The book is very teacher friendly: the clarity of the five modules providing enough scope to structure a course with less or full coverage of the modules; and the structure of the text, with side matter fitting into power point presentations, a boon to the teaching faculty.

Bhanoji Rao
Formerly with the University of Singapore
(Lecturer/Senior Lecturer, 1967-78)
World Bank, (Economist, Jan 1979-Aug 1985)
National University of Singapore
(Senior Lecturer/Associate Professor, 1985-2001)
(Professor, LKY School of Public Policy, 2009-11)

Prof. Pundarik Mukhopadhaya

This "Public Policy" textbook by Swamy and Suresh is essential for anyone interested in understanding the nuances of public policymaking. In this book the authors eloquently unentangled the complex process of public policy making and its implementation for the readers. Here are the key highlights that impressed me in this book.

The textbook is well structured and the explanations are clear and concise. These make this book invaluable for comprehending public policy.

A thorough discussion of recent regulatory changes in India enhances the book's relevance and applicability to public policy practitioners and students.

The value of the book is further enhanced by the inclusion of contemporary issues like data science and its role in public policy.

If you want to learn about public policy in India, this textbook is for you.

Pundarik Mukhopadhaya
Professor of Economics, Macquarie University, Australia

Preface

Public policy is essential for modern governance to address social, economic, and political challenges. It affects the lives of citizens and shapes the functioning of societies worldwide. This textbook offers a comprehensive overview of public policy, covering its theory, process, and analysis. It provides insights into how policies are formulated, implemented, evaluated, and reformed to meet evolving societal needs. The textbook is designed to be a valuable resource for students, teachers, and practitioners seeking to understand the intricacies of public policy. The textbook offers a comprehensive understanding of the policymaking process by exploring the various stages of policy development, from problem identification to implementation. With its broad coverage and practical approach, this textbook is an indispensable guide for anyone interested in public policy.

Module I offers a comprehensive introduction to public policy theory, explaining the essential concepts and principles involved in the field. It covers the different stages of the public policy process, such as agenda setting, policy formulation, adoption, implementation, and evaluation. The module explores policy analysis models, such as cost-benefit and multi-criteria analysis, used to evaluate policy options and make informed decisions. Additionally, it examines the political economy of public policy, including the distributional impacts of policy decisions, the role of interest groups, institutions, and collective decision-making, and the interaction between different levels of government in policy development and implementation. This module provides a strong foundation for those interested in understanding public policy's complexities and impact on society.

Module II is a comprehensive study of public policymaking, delving into the various actors and their roles in policymaking. It covers political parties and their influence on policymaking, as well as the mechanisms of parliamentary democracy, executive decision-making, and the role of the judiciary and bureaucracy in shaping public policy. Students will gain an understanding of the complex interplay between these actors, including their relationships and interactions, and the impact they have on the policymaking process. The module also explores different approaches to policymaking, including top-down and bottom-up strategies, and the role of public opinion in shaping policy outcomes. Finally, this module will provide students with the information and abilities necessary to assess and comprehend the policymaking process in contemporary societies.

Module III of the course delves into the practical aspects of public policy implementation and evaluation. It explores challenges during policy implementation, such as resource constraints, bureaucratic hurdles, and political resistance. The module also discusses the importance of good governance in ensuring effective policy delivery, including the role of transparency, accountability, and citizen participation in promoting good governance. Furthermore, the module emphasizes the significance of evaluating public policies to determine their effectiveness and impact. This includes the measurement of policy outcomes, the identification of unintended consequences, and the assessment of policy costs and benefits. Students will better understand how policy implementation and evaluation can inform evidence-based policymaking and contribute to better governance by examining real-world case studies and evaluation techniques.

Module IV is a dedicated section in the study of public policy in India, which focuses on analyzing the institutional issues that have hampered effective policymaking in the country. The module primarily concentrates on two significant policy reforms, namely police reforms and regulatory reforms. The study of police reforms examines the challenges faced by the Indian police force, including issues related to accountability, corruption, and political interference. On the other hand, the regulatory reforms module analyzes the inadequacies of regulatory bodies in India and the need for reform to ensure the effective implementation of policies. The module seeks to give a complete awareness of the issues that policymakers in India confront, as well as viable ways to address them, through the study of these changes.

Module V is the final module of this book and seeks to offer students an in-depth grasp of current problems in the area. The module covers emerging trends and issues shaping public policy today, including the use of data science in policymaking and current trends in public policy. Through this module, students will explore how data science transforms the public policy landscape and how policymakers can use data to inform decision-making. They will also learn about current trends in public policy, including the increasing focus on evidence-based policymaking and the role of technology in shaping public policy. Overall, Module V provides students with a comprehensive overview of the latest developments in public policy and equips them with the required knowledge and necessary skills to stay ahead of the curve in this rapidly evolving field.

As we poured our hearts and minds into this book, we aimed to create a captivating and honest portrayal of public policy. With a wealth of information gathered from the latest research and analysis from around the world, we aimed to provide readers with a balanced and unbiased view of this complex field. Our ultimate hope is that this textbook will serve as an invaluable resource for students, teachers, and practitioners and a tool to inspire a passion for public policy that will drive them to make a positive difference in the world. We believe that with the knowledge and skills imparted through these pages, readers will be empowered to engage with public policy meaningfully, leaving a lasting impact on their communities and the world at large.

Vighneswara Swamy
Suresh K.G.

Acknowledgements

The creation of this textbook would not have been possible without the support, encouragement, and contributions of many individuals and organizations, and we are grateful to all who have made this endeavor possible.

First and foremost, we extend our heartfelt thanks to our families, whose unwavering support, understanding, and patience have been instrumental in bringing this idea to fruition. Their constant encouragement and belief in us have kept us going through the long and challenging process of creating this textbook.

We also want to express our gratitude to our colleagues, mentors, students, and friends who have provided us with valuable insights, feedback, and suggestions at every stage of the book's development. Their input has been instrumental in shaping the textbook's content and ensuring its relevance to the field of public policy. Without their support, this textbook would not have been as comprehensive and informative as it is.

We would like to extend a special thanks to the Pearson India Education Services Pvt team. Ltd, who worked tirelessly to bring this textbook to fruition. Their dedication, professionalism, and expertise have been invaluable in producing a high-quality resource for students and practitioners. Their guidance and support have helped us transform our ideas into a book we are proud of.

Finally, we want to thank the students, teachers, and practitioners who will read this book. We hope that this textbook will inspire a passion for public policy and equip readers with the knowledge and skills to make a positive difference in the world. We hope everyone interested in public policy will find this book a valuable resource, and we are grateful for the opportunity to share our knowledge and insights with others.

To conclude, we would like to express our heartfelt appreciation to everyone who has supported us in creating this textbook. We are grateful for the encouragement, feedback, and contributions, and we could not have done this without you.

Thank you for being a part of this journey with us, and we hope that this textbook will be useful to all who read it. Thank you all for your support and contributions.

Vighneswara Swamy
Suresh K.G.

About the Author – Dr. Vighneswara Swamy

Dr. Vighneswara Swamy is an academician with over two decades of experience in research, teaching, and consultancy. He is the recipient of several prestigious awards, fellowships, and recognitions, which reflect his contributions to economics and public policy. Dr. Swamy is currently Professor of Economics at IBS-Hyderabad and Dean Research of ICFAI Foundation for Higher Education (a deemed university).

As an accomplished educator, Professor Swamy received the NJ Yasaswy—Apollo Hospitals Best Teacher Award in 2018-19 and the IBSAF Best Teacher Award in 2017. He has also won the IIBF Macro Research Award twice, in 2016 and 2012, and the SANEI Regional Research Award for South Asia twice, in 2015 and 2013. Prof. Swamy was a Sir Ratan Tata Trust Senior Fellow at the Institute of Economic Growth and has been a UGC Post-Doctoral Fellow.

Prof. Swamy has extensive experience teaching public policy to MBA students and has published numerous papers on regulation, supervision, and stability. He teaches Public Policy, Managerial Economics, Macroeconomics, and International Finance and Trade in the MBA program and Topics in Microeconomics in the Ph.D. program. His research provides valuable insights into the challenges and opportunities facing policymakers. In addition to his academic contributions, Prof. Swamy is a prolific researcher with publications in top international journals, including The World Economy, World Development, and the International Review of Economics and Finance. He also writes columns in national business newspapers and other reputed portals.

About the Author – Dr. Suresh K.G.

Dr. Suresh K.G. currently serves as an Assistant Professor of Economics at the Indian Institute of Management (IIM), Bodh Gaya. With a decade of experience in research, teaching, and training both managers and government officials, Dr. Suresh teaches in the MBA and IPM (Integrated Program in Management) programs at IIM-Bodh Gaya, focusing on Public Policy, International Business, Environmental Economics, Macroeconomics, and Econometrics. He is an active member of the Executive Education Committee and the CSR and Social Innovation Committee at IIM Bodh Gaya, contributing significantly to the training of government officials and managers through various programs offered by the institute.

Before joining IIM-Bodh Gaya, Dr. Suresh was a faculty member at ICFAI Business School (IBS), Hyderabad. He earned his PhD in Economics from the ICFAI University, Dehradun, and his M.Phil in Management from the ICFAI University, Tripura. In 2019, he co-chaired the Academy of International Business (AIB)-India Conference held at ICFAI Business School Hyderabad. Additionally, he served as the convener of the Doctoral Thesis Conference held at IBS Hyderabad in 2016. Dr. Suresh's research papers have been published in international peer-reviewed journals such as Empirical Economics, Economic Modelling, Current Issues in Tourism, and Economic and Political Weekly, among others. His articles on contemporary issues have been featured in national dailies such as The Economic Times and The Hindu Business Line. Dr. Suresh is a life member of The Indian Econometrics Society (TIES) and a member of the Academy of International Business.

Brief Contents

Contents

Module I

Public Policy Theory

Module I: Public Policy Theory

This module has five chapters:

Chapter 1 introduces the concept of public policy, its scope, objectives, and characteristics in detail. It discusses the types of public policy in brief. Further, it offers a brief on the public policy life-cycle.

Chapter 2 provides an overview of the public policy process, models, and analysis. It discusses corporate political activities, political business activities and their types, the nine public policy models, and provides an overview of public policy analysis.

Chapter 3 offers an outline of the political economy of public policy. It discusses the role of the state in public policy, forms of government, the nexus between the state and the markets, and the attributes of a developmental state.

Chapter 4 presents a synopsis of the role of institutions in public policy decision-making and describes the decision theory, public choice theory, and rational choice theory. It explains decision-making in legislative bodies and the democratic dilemma.

Chapter 5 discusses the principal-agent problems with elected representatives, political money, and other political resources. It provides an interesting discussion on the three institutionalisms and neo-functionalism.

CHAPTER 1

Introduction to Public Policy

Public policy as a discipline is fairly young. But its practice is as old as that of civilizations. In recent centuries, as democracies have evolved, Public policy has gained greater prominence. Public policy in the recent past revolved around providing equal opportunities to citizens without discrimination of race, gender, cult, or community. Public policy has significantly helped the nations in their progress towards peace, prosperity, and security.

The purpose of this chapter is to introduce the concept of Public policy. As we progress in this chapter, we will discuss first what a policy in general is. Then we introduce the concept of Public policy and discuss its scope, objectives, and characteristics in detail. We will briefly introduce the types of public policy and the Public policy life-cycle.

Section 1: What is a policy?
Section 2: What is a public policy?
Section 3: Characteristics of Public Policy
Section 4: Typology of public policy
Section 5: The Public Policy Life-Cycle

1. WHAT IS A POLICY?

To begin with, let us quickly understand what a policy in general is. A Policy can be defined as a statement of intent for achieving a particular objective. The statement of intent is deliberate and is aimed at fulfilling a specific objective/s. Quite often, a policy constitutes a set of ideas, goals, and plans that offer a base for decision-making. Policies are essentially outlines of rules, values, beliefs, principles, roles, and responsibilities that are intended to achieve something specific or general.

> A policy is a statement of intent guided by a set of rules, principles and regulations.

1.1 Functions of a Policy

A policy does some important functions like (i) reflecting the ideology and value systems of the policy maker, (ii) emphasizing the principles

> Policies guide our actions.

that guide the actions, (iii) helping in proper goal setting, and (iv) providing clear terms of reference and guide program implementation, and (v) help in program evaluation in terms of clarity and accountability.

Policies can be at different levels of interaction – *personal, organizational,* and *governmental.*

Policies can be at the personal, organizational, and governmental levels.

Personal policies guide the decisions and actions of individuals. An example of a personal policy is *"I buy local goods to support local communities."*

Organizational policies are a framework of rules and regulations set by organizations to achieve their goals. Usually, organizational policies are documented in a written format and exert considerable influence on the decisions and actions of the organization. They can be internal or external and guide how the organizations carry out their activities. An example of Organizational policy is *"Our company upholds gender equality."*

Governmental policies are a kind of declaration of the government's intentions and plan to address a particular issue or a public cause. Governments often formulate policies to attain certain stated objectives to benefit the people at large or to solve a prevailing challenge faced by society or the economy. Generally, government policies are often considered more important as they impact the public at large. Government policies are used as a tool to safeguard and ensure better services to the people and society.

A government policy is a guided action of the government that is intended to result in positive outcomes that benefit the community or society.

Governmental policies are broadly classified into **regulatory**, **restrictive**, and **development** or facilitative policies. A regulatory policy aims at accomplishing the government's objectives with the use of rules, regulations, laws, and other policy instruments to better the living of citizens and businesses. An example of a **regulatory policy** is *"Minimum wage for labor."* With this minimum wage policy government intends to ensure the provision of a minimum reasonable wage to the workers in the economy.

A restrictive policy intends to prevent the citizens from the use of what they are doing. The use of tobacco is injurious to health as it contains carcinogenic chemicals. According to World Health Organization (WHO), all forms of tobacco are harmful to humans. Because of this, to restrict the public from using tobacco, the government has brought a **restrictive policy** like *"28% Goods and Services Tax (GST) on tobacco products."* Similarly, the consumption of drugs is detrimental to the health of a person. Hence, the government has announced a national policy on narcotics, according to which, it is illegal for a person to possess, sell, or consume any form of a narcotic drug.

Development policies of the government are intended to encourage constructive activities in the society like encouraging economic and social development. For example, the *"National Health Policy – 2017"* of the Indian government is envisaged to provide universal health care by providing access to quality health care and lowering the cost of health care delivery in India. Another example can be the *"National Intellectual*

Property Rights Policy – 2016" to promote innovation and encourage entrepreneurship in India.

1.2 Importance of a Policy

The importance of any policy lies in its objective. Besides, policies guide on one hand and indicate consistency, clarity, and accountability on the other. The reasons for formulating a policy can be myriad. Change and reform are the only constants in life and society. Accordingly, several needs for change and reforms in life necessitate policy formulation. Such needs can be socio-economic, cultural, organizational, technological, etc. For example, the Insolvency and Bankruptcy Code (IBC), 2016 in India was introduced for a time-bound resolution of insolvency of companies. Essentially, IBC aims to bring balance between the debtors, creditors, and stakeholders, besides speeding up and catalyzing ease of doing business.

Policies are important because of their consistency, clarity, guidance and accountability.

Financial inclusion of the resource-poor is an important requirement to speed up financial development and thereby attain economic development. Given this underlying principle, the Government of India launched the Pradhan Mantri Jan Dhan Yojana (PMJDY) in 2014 with the aim of opening bank accounts for the unbanked besides providing them with a RuPay debit card, and access to social security schemes like insurance, pensions, and other direct benefit transfer schemes. The advancement of mobile technology has greatly helped to bring about the policy of linking Jan Dhan Yojana accounts with Aadhaar and their mobile number popularly called the JAM trinity (Jan Dhan – Aadhaar – Mobile).

2. PUBLIC POLICY

Any policy that is envisioned to benefit the public in simpler terms can be called a public policy. A public policy reflects the collective intent and action of the government in addressing the issues of public concern. A public policy involves the rules, regulations, principles, values, ideals, and cultural ethos of the government in its decision-making. The public policy mirrors the priorities and measures of the government in addressing matters of public interest. In recent times, public policy is embodied in the national constitutions, legislative actions, and judicial pronouncements.

A public policy is set of rules and regulations based on the principles, values, ideals, and cultural ethos of the government in its decision-making to address the matters of public concern.

The study of public policy has gained importance as it focuses on the decision-making of the governments and non-governmental organizations in addressing the issues that concern a substantial number of people and communities. The study of public policy relies on a wide range of social sciences like Economics, Political Science, Public Administration, Sociology, Philosophy, Law, and Organizational Science.

Public policy has multiple dimensions and hence is studied in several disciplines political science, public administration, economics, sociology,

Public policy has multiple dimensions and is interdisciplinary

Public policy as a policy science is normative and value-oriented discipline

and philosophy. Table 1.1 below shows how are these disciplines related to public policy.

TABLE 1.1 Selected disciplines and their relationship with public policy

Discipline	Description	Relationship to Public Policy
Political Science	It is the study of political relationships and processes through which societies pursue the allocation of political power and decision-making.	Public policies are made and implemented through political processes.
Public Administration	Public administration as a discipline studies the management of government and public institutions in attaining the stated objectives of socio-economic development.	Public administration includes the study of public policies, particularly in terms of their effective implementation in ensuring quality service delivery.
Economics	Economics is a discipline that studies the allocation of economic resources to satisfy the unlimited wants for the economic welfare of the people.	Public policy making is often influenced by economic factors like productivity, employment, standards of living, and economic growth. Quite often the economic tools help explain the public policies.
Sociology	Sociology as a discipline explores the structure of social life, causes of social change, and the consequences of human behavior on society.	Society as a group of communities plays an important role in public policy-making as these policies affect the people in the society.
Philosophy	Philosophy as a discipline emphasizes the importance of logic, values, principles, ethos, and ethics.	The tools and concepts of philosophy based on ethical theory, social philosophy, and political theory are useful in public policy making and its enforcement.

Public policy goal is an anticipated situation or a state of affairs in a society or an organization

As a policy science, public policy has evolved as a normative and value-oriented discipline. It is mostly problem-oriented and multidisciplinary in nature because every socio-economic problem has multiple elements drawn from different disciplines.

What is the goal of public policy? In understanding public policy more meaningfully, it is crucial to make a clear distinction between the policy and its goals.The goals are what the policy aims to achieve. A goal is, of course, understood from multiple perspectives. It is often specific and can be understood as an anticipated situation or a state of affairs in a society or an organization. For instance, the eradication of poverty is a specific goal of the state (government). Quite often, public policies are related to explicit goals.

The study of Public policy is quite broad in nature as it affects society at large in many facets. For a proper understanding of Public policy from a theoretical perspective, it is desirable to define Public policy. In the next section, we look at the different definitions of public policy.

2.1 What is Public in Public Policy?

The term 'public' originates from the Latin word 'publicus' or 'poplicus' and is similar to the English word 'Populus' or 'populace' which in general means the people. In understanding the importance of the public in public policy, it is essential to know **the three elements of policy: (i) problem definition, (ii) goals, and (iii) policy instruments** used to tackle the societal problem. Problem definition refers to the public concern. Goals are the specific levels of attainment to meet the aspirations of the public in addressing the problem faced by the public. Policy instruments are the tools and techniques employed by the public authorities to implement the public policies and achieve the set goals.

Public policy is bothered about the public goods than private goods.

Public policy is more concerned with the common good than the private good.The notion of the common good is quite ancient from the times of Pluto and Aristotle. It includes those conditions that satisfy everyone's interests (Douglass, 1980).

The FIVE public elements in a public policy are Public interest, Public sector,Public finance, Public property, and Public law.

Every public policy is crucial in framing the guidelines based on the principles, value systems, and aspirations of society. Public policy is for the public because it is formed out of the collective action of the governments, institutions, and concerned citizens of the society.

The notion of 'public' in public policy suggests that the common life that is not private is much important for public welfare.

The importance of the public in a public policy emanates from the broad five elements of public policy: (1) Public interest, (ii) Public sector, (iii) Public finance, (iv) Public property, and (v) Public law.

Public interest means what is in the general welfare of the public or where there is public stake involved. It includes several areas of public interest such as education, gender equality, child protection, equal rights without discrimination, property rights, poverty eradication, employment, housing, consumer protection, safety, and protection, etc.

The major factors that differentiate the public sector from private sector are public interest, common goods, ownership, and power of policy making.

Public sector involves an economic system in an economy which managed by the government and public organizations. Generally, the public sector in India encompasses sectors like education, national defense, law and order, public health, public infrastructure like railways, public transport, urban development, rural development, etc.

Public finance is the management of government revenue, government expenditure, and government debt through budgetary and non-budgetary mechanisms. The main components of public finance are tax and non-tax collection, government budget, public expenditure, managing budget surplus/deficit, and government debt.

Public property denotes the property that belongs to the public, i.e., government-owned as against the private property owned by the individuals. In simple terms, public property is government property that is meant for public use. For Example, public places, airports, highways and roads, lakes, mountains, forests, dams, and bridges, parks, power distribution infrastructure, historical monuments, museums,

Public law means legislative enactments that affect the public at large. It is a body of law that deals with the powers, rights, and obligations of the government and the public. For example, public laws encompass constitutional laws, criminal laws, and international laws.

Essentially, the notion of 'public' in public policy posits that the common life that is not private is much important for the peace and progress of society. The term 'public' largely refers to public ownership and, or public control for public purposes. It is perceived as a common action that requires government intervention.

The three elements that distinguish public policy are goal orientation, collective actions, and decisions of the government.

What differentiates the public sector from the private sector? According to Andrew Massey (1993), we can list some important distinguishing factors: (1) the Public sector involves complex and seemingly contradictory actions, (2) It faces several challenges in implementing its decisions and policies, and (3) It addresses the concerns of a large number of people with varied motivation, (4) It focuses on safeguarding opportunities for large masses in the society, (5) From the economic perspective, it is bothered about market failure and protecting the economic interests of the people, (6) From the legal perspective, it sets out standards of obligations and commitment, fairness, equity, and justice, (7) It always operates in the public interest, and (8) It mostly engages in activities that are of greater significance for the society.

For a better understanding of the public in public policy, Table 1.2 illustrates the differentiating factors between the public sector and private sector in understanding the importance of the public in public policy.

TABLE 1.2 What differentiates public from private?

Differentiating factor	Public sector	Private sector
Interest	Public interest	Private interest
Power of policy making	Government	Individuals or groups of individuals
Consumption	Public	Private
Investment	Public	Private
Decision-making	Governmental	Private
Provision of goods	Public goods	Private goods
Ownership	Public	Private
Employment	Public sector	Private sector

2.2 Definition of Public Policy

As a concept, public policy is a deliberate action of the public authorities in the pursuit of set objectives which includes a set of decisions, well-defined rules, regulations, and procedures, based on suitability and rationality. While conceptualizing public policy the following three points emphasize the nature of public policy as a policy science. First, public policy is always **goal-oriented**. These policies are designed and implemented to realize the governmental objectives to benefit the public at large. Second, public policies are the results of the **collective actions** by the government. Third, public policies are **decisions of the governments** in the form of laws, acts, ordinances, orders, rules, regulations, resolutions, etc. Logically, the idea of public policy includes all governmental actions of doing or not doing for the public.

Public policy as a policy science has evolved as a branch of social sciences only after the concept of policy sciences was popularised by the renowned political science professor, Harrod Lasswell in 1951. Lasswell relied on the works of well-known pragmatist John Dewey (1886-2016) and others to provide a clear vision for policy science as a multidisciplinary discipline that is problem-oriented and explicitly normative (Dewey, 1927; Lasswell, 1951).

Daniel McCool observes that modern studies on public policy began in 1922 and public policy as a policy science did not spring into prominence during the 1950s and 1960s (Daniel McCool, 1995). According to Daniel McCool, a good theory is essentially based on positivist rigor.

Several public policy theorists have defined Public policy in different ways. Birkland is concerned about no consensus among the theorists on the definition of public policy (Birkland, 2001). According to David Easton, an eminent political scientist, public policy is the representation of the authoritative allocation of values for the entire society (Easton, 1957). Robert Eyestone states that *public policy is a relationship of a government unit to its environment* (Eyestone, 1971).

Public policies in recent times have become all-pervasive.

Thomas Dye, a well-known theorist of public policy provides the briefest definition of Public policy as "*anything a government chooses to do or not to do*" (Dye, 1972:2). Anderson states that a public policy should be regarded as "*apurposive course of action followed by an actor or set of actors in dealing with a problem or matter of concern*" (Anderson, 1975). Lineberry in his book on American Public Policy, states that public policy is "*what governments do and fail to do – to and for their citizens*" (Lineberry, 1977).

Heidenheimer et al. studying the public policies in America, Europe, and Japan, define public policy as "*how, why and to what effect, governments pursue particular courses of action and inaction*" (Heidenheimer, 1990). However, Parsons takes a rational approach in defining public policy as "*an attempt to define and structure a rational basis for action or inaction*" (Parsons, 1995). Nicholas Henry observes public policy as "*a course of action adopted and pursued by the government*" (Henry, 2012).

According to Clarke E. Cochran et al., the word public policy indicates "*the actions of the government and that determine its intentions. In a*

Kautilya's Arthashastra is one of the ancient treatise on public policy in India.

way, it is the results of the struggle in the government over who gets what." (Clarke E. Cochran, et al., 2014).

On the other hand, Guy Peters states that "public policy is the sum of government activities, whether acting directly or through agents, as it influences the life of citizens" (Guy Peters, 1999). Smith and Larimer observe that *public policy is a broad and interdisciplinary area of study and research in the field tends to reflect this* (Smith & Larimer, 2016).

Public policy is a policy science that studies the intentions and actions of the government that affect the public.

One of the ancient documents on public policy is Kautilya's Arthashastra (350-275 BCE), which is a treatise on public policy making in the areas of rajniti (statecraft), Athaniti (economic policy-making), rashtra rakshaniti (national defense), and raj dharma (political science). Arthashastra provides an extensive exposition on public policy making.

To be precise, we define public policy as *a policy science that studies the intentions and actions of the government that affect the public.*

2.3 Objectives of Public Policy

Basic objectives of Public policy are to regulate public behavior, collect taxes, distribute the benefits, organize bureaucracy, protect people and the nation.
a is a policy science that studies the intentions and actions of the government that affect the public.

Public policy is a major area of study as well as practice. As we discussed in section 2.2, public policy has specific objectives that address the concerns of the public. A public policy objective is an envisioned outcome that the policymakers intend to achieve. Generally, public policy objectives include: (1) Regulate public behavior (2) Collect taxes (3) Distribute the benefits (4) Organize bureaucracy (5) Protect people and the nation, and (6) Some combination of the above.

In tackling societal problems and socio-economic challenges, changing public behavior is often a necessity. For example, to prevent people from alcohol abuse, drug abuse, and various other problems, public policy must nudge public behavior. Hence, the objective of regulating public behavior is intended to achieve a state of affairs where all the public lives in harmony. Broadly, Incentives, mandates, bans, Information campaigns, and nudging are used as policy instruments for public behavior change

The basic objective of taxation is to raise resources for meeting public expenditure. We know that taxation is the major source of funding for governmental activities. This objective of collecting taxes for a public policy assumes greater significance as it affects the production, consumption, investment, and distribution of income in the economy.

The equitable distribution of economic benefits is one of the important functions of the government. In this direction, the policy objective of the government is to ensure that the benefits of economic policy reach the needy and targeted public.

The role of the government as a protector of the citizens and its nation, and provider of the necessities to its citizens distinguish the role of public policy.

Governments can play a major role in mitigating poverty and income inequality by proper taxation and distribution of benefits through direct benefit transfers, subsidies, allowances, exemptions, etc.

Managing the government requires various resources and related expenditures. In organizing the bureaucracy for public administration, governments have a clear objective of efficiency and effective implementation of their policies and actions. In this regard, the government has to pay for its employees for which it requires financial resources. Credible and just use of public resources for bureaucracy must be one of the objectives of public policy.

The role of the government as a protector of the citizens and its nation, and provider of the necessities to its citizens distinguish the role of public policy. The objective here is to ensure that its people are protected from violence, wars, terrorism, and foreign invasions. In this regard, it is required to marshal the resources for nation-building.

2.4 Scope of Public Policy

Public policy is all about solving the problems concerning the public in different walks of life. Public policy has a wider scope as it affects the lives of millions each day. Every one of us benefits from public policy directly, indirectly, and or collectively. Each of us gets benefitted from policies that enable us to get clean air, drinking water, sanitation, good public health, economic growth, and national defense. Often, public policy encompasses major areas like development policy, social justice, equality, national defense, and other national priorities.

> Every one of us benefits from public policy directly, indirectly, and or collectively.

In recent years, public policy is most commonly known for covering the areas like the provision of necessities like public health, housing, electricity, public transport, education, municipal facilities, environment, and other pressing social issues. In the words of the renowned political scientist, Yehezkel Dror, mega policies are those broad policies that reflect the national spirations like social justice, economic growth, and national defense (Yehezkel Dror, 1983).

Commenting on the broad scope of public policy, Michael Teitz (1968) observes that in the life cycle of modern man, a person is born in a public hospital, educated in a public school and public university, uses public transport, public telecommunications, public water, public parks, public library, public health systems, public safety from police, fire services, and utilizes various other public facilities. So, say, public policy and public systems have become all-pervasive in a man's daily life.

> The scope of public policy is generally determined by the type of governments that govern the society.

The scope of public policy is generally determined by the role assumed by the governments. In the last century, governments across the globe have assumed the role of 'welfare state'. Accordingly, the scope of the public policy has widened significantly in the area of economic and social welfare of the citizens. India, being a sovereign republic with a parliamentary form of government, offers huge scope for public policy-making from its constituents of the constitution such as the legislature, the executive, and the judiciary both at the national and state levels. In addition, nongovernmental organizations contribute to public policy-making. Hence, the scope of public policy in India is quite vast. People have high expectations from the governments in their service delivery. This has further widened the ambit of public policy.

The governments are not only providers of safety and security to their citizens and providing social welfare, but also principal innovators of technology, financiers of large-scale industries, and job creators. These trends have further expanded both the size and scope of public policy.

3. CHARACTERISTICS OF PUBLIC POLICY

Public policies portray the response of the governance system to the policy environment.

As we discussed in section 2.3, public policies are goal-oriented and are the outcomes of governmental actions. Public policies portray the response of the governance system to the policy environment. These policies display specific characteristics.

Let us list out the major characteristics of public policy for a quick understanding:

Dynamic: Public policy making is a dynamic process that requires continuous inputs of resources, feedback, and motivation.

Action-oriented: Public policies are not mere decisions, but result in actions. Public policies can be either positive (action-oriented) or negative (inaction).

Futuristic: Public policies are normally directed at the future.

Public interest: Public policies are mostly aimed at the public interest.

Goal-oriented: Public policies are deliberate, purposive, and goal-oriented. They are directed at accomplishing specific goals. Mostly these policies are implemented through government programs directed at attaining public welfare and national development

Government action: Public policies are the results of collective actions of the government/s. These policies are supported by the integrated efforts of all the governmental institutions

A good public policy is well-defined, well-targeted, well-planned, well-strategized, well-measured, and well-implemented to attain its goals.

In different forms: Public policies can be in various forms like laws, acts, ordinances, executive orders, notices, judicial pronouncements, etc. Mostly in India, the public policies are in written form.

Governmental priority: Public policies reflect the concerns and priorities of the government/s. Standup India program of the Government of India aims to support Scheduled caste and scheduled tribe and women entrepreneurs by providing bank financial assistance to the tune of 10 lakhs to 1 crore.

Powerful instrument: Public policies are the powerful instruments of the governments for pursuing governmental objectives for the socio-economic development of its citizens.

Well-targeted: Public policies are often designed to target certain sections of the societies in a particular geographical area for their development.

Political interest: Public policies are the results of the decisions of the political parties in the government/s. Hence, these policies are the outcomes of the political processes.

Enforcement: Public policies are enforceable by law and the governments have the authority to enforce their implementation. In simple terms, these policies are backed by the might of the government/s.

What is a good public policy and what are its characteristics?

A good public policy is well-defined, well-targeted, well-planned, well-strategized, well-measured, and well-implemented to attain its goals and objectives in a time-bound manner. Effective public policies tend to support the democratic processes and institutions and deliver the much-needed solutions to the problems of the public without creating any political rift or ruckus. Hence, a good public policy is effective both in its successful execution and measurable outcomes.

In India, the governmental policy actors include the legislature, the executive, the judiciary, and the administration.

Some of the characteristics of a good public policy are listed below:

A good narrative: A good policy has a sound narrative that is appealing to large sections of the population.

Scientific: A good public policy is often well-researched, knowledge-based, and evidence-based.

Inclusivity: A good public policy is inclusive in nature, and ensures the participation of the stakeholders.

Transparency: Openness and transparency are the hallmarks of a good policy. They are also democratic in nature.

Consistency: A good policy involves intra-policy and extra-policy coherence and is consistent with the law/s of the land.

Inbuilt mechanisms: A good policy is time-bound, self-terminating, and is inbuilt with effective mechanisms in addressing the implementation challenges.

Support of political leadership: A good policy is often coupled with the support of the political leadership and the executive machinery of the government.

3.1 The Players of Public Policy

Public policy making involves various key players like the Parliament, Vidhana Sabha, politicians, voters, media, interest groups, public opinion, public interest, the judiciary, bureaucrats, civil servants, administration, think tanks, experts, consultants, researchers, and academics.

Policy players, also called 'policy actors' include those constituents both within and outside the government in framing the public policy. Broadly, the governmental actors include the legislature, the executive, the judiciary, and the administration. The non-governmental actors include interest groups, think tanks, academics, the media, and more importantly, the general public.

4. TYPOLOGY OF PUBLIC POLICY

Public policy types are regulatory, distributive, redistributive, capitalization, and substantive.

As we discussed in section 2.4 that the scope of public policy is wide, the wider horizon of public policy domain gives scope for different types of public policy. Based on the purpose of the policy, the aims of the policy, the broad goals and objectives of the policy, and the types of states where they operate, we can classify public policies into different types. In this section, let us discuss some of the salient types of public policy.

Regulatory Policies:

These policies find their relevance as there is a need to regulate some sectors in the public interest. Regulatory policies can be in the area of the financial sector, economy, trade, business, safety, health, public utilities, use of national resources, etc. The governments usually set up regulatory authorities to govern and regulate those respective sectors. For example, the Reserve Bank of India (RBI) manages the economy, Insurance Regulatory and Development Authority (IRDA) regulates the insurance sector, the Securities and Exchange Board of India (SEBI) regulates the markets where securities are traded, and Pension Fund Regulatory & Development Authority (PFRDA) regulates the pensions, National Housing Bank (NHB) regulates the housing sector, Telecom Regulatory Authority of India (TRAI) regulates telecommunication, tariffs, and Cyber-Security, Bureau of Indian Standards (BIS) regulates standards and certification, and Atomic Energy Regulatory Board (AERB) regulates atomic energy and nuclear power. Hence, the policies made by these bodies in consultation with the government are generally termed regulatory policies. These policies are necessary for the smooth functioning and development of the respective sectors.

Distributive Policies:

A prudent allocation of scarce resources is necessary to improve the standards of the needy. Hence, distributive policies are targeted toward specific segments of society. These policies benefit the constituents of a particular region, class, section, or strata of society but the costs of the program are borne collectively. For example, distributive policies are vital in the sectors such as health, food, education, insurance, disaster relief, etc. Economic policies such as fiscal policy, monetary policy, and tax policy are distributive in nature. Thus, distributive policies are essentially concerned with the efficient allocation of resources leading to promoting equality and cohesion in society.

Redistributive Policies:

As the term 'redistribution' suggests, it is to reallocate or alter the existing distribution and spread to other areas. In simple terms, redistributive policies intend to relocate resources from one segment of the population to another. Primarily, redistributive policies are aimed at reforming the socio-economic sphere by way of re-arrangement of policies and shunning uneven distribution of income and wealth in the society. Redistributive policies help in realigning common goods and welfare services that are disproportionately distributed among the segments of the society resulting in the desired socio-economic change.

Redistributive policies are integral to the field of welfare economics, by alleviating inequality and fostering sustainable socio-economic and environmental development. Broadly, we can typify redistributive policies into two types: direct benefit transfers (money transfers) and educational scholarship transfers. While the former is directed at supporting adequate consumption, the latter is aimed at building human capital. Studies show that income redistribution policies help poverty reduction by minimizing inequality.

Efficient redistribution becomes necessary both for ethical and political considerations. Some of the examples of redistributive policies in India are land reform policies, progressive taxation policies, low-income housing policies, disproportionate assets confiscation policies, and others.

Capitalization policies as public public policies are unique, because of the absence of direct provision of public welfare in them.

Capitalization Policies:

Capitalization policies are a unique bunch of public policies which are largely made by the Union government in India for the state and local governments for providing financial subsidies for specific purposes. These purposes include infrastructure, socio-economic development, government businesses, and other major areas of governance. Capitalization policies are public policies, yet they are different from other types of public policies such as regulatory, distributive, redistributive, and substantive policies, because of the absence of direct provision of public welfare in these policies.

Substantive Policies:

The primary goal of the substantive policies is general public welfare leading to overall societal development. These policies do not aim at any specific segment of society, instead, their scope is large and encompasses large sections of society. These policies endeavor holistic development of society and operate in large areas. For example, policies related to education, employment, public health, law and order, anti-pollution, etc., are substantive in nature. These policies are formed in tune with moral standards in society and constitutional aspirations.

4.1 Levels of Public Policy

Public policy is framed at different levels of hierarchy. According to Edgar Norman Gladden, the levels of public policy can be at the political level, executive level, administrative level, and technical level (Gladden, 1966). In a sense, the levels of public policy are understood from the hierarchy of power that formulates the public policy.

In India, under the constitutional provisions, public policies are made at different levels of governance in their respective administrative domains.

In India, the levels of Public policy are based on the layers of hierarchy of power like national, state, district, municipality and panchayat.

TABLE 1.3 Public policies at different levels in India

	National	State	District	Municipality	Panchayat
Policy maker	Parliament	Legislative Assembly	Zilla Panchayat	Municipal Corporations/ Councils	Taluk/Village panchayats
Policy form	National Laws /Acts	State acts	Regulations	Rules	Resolutions
Policy form	Ordinance	Ordinance	Circular	Order	Order

5. THE PUBLIC POLICY LIFE-CYCLE

Every public policy has a life cycle involving different phases of policy.

Every policy has a life cycle which refers to distinct phases of the policy. Typically, the policy life-cycle involves stages like problem definition, policy formulation, and implementation. The public policy life-cycle has several stages operating dynamically. Howlett and Ramesh identify five stages of the policy cycle as (1) agenda setting, (2) policy formulation, (3) decision making, (4) implementation, and (5) evaluation (Howlett and Ramesh, 2003).

For a better understanding of the public policy life cycle, we identify nine stages: (1) problem identification, (2) information gathering, (3) discussion and debate, (4) political action including consideration and decision-making, (5) legislative proposal, (6) passing the law and regulation, (7) compliance and implementation, (8) evaluation, and (9) termination or renewal. Figure 1.1 illustrates the eight stages of the public policy life-cycle.

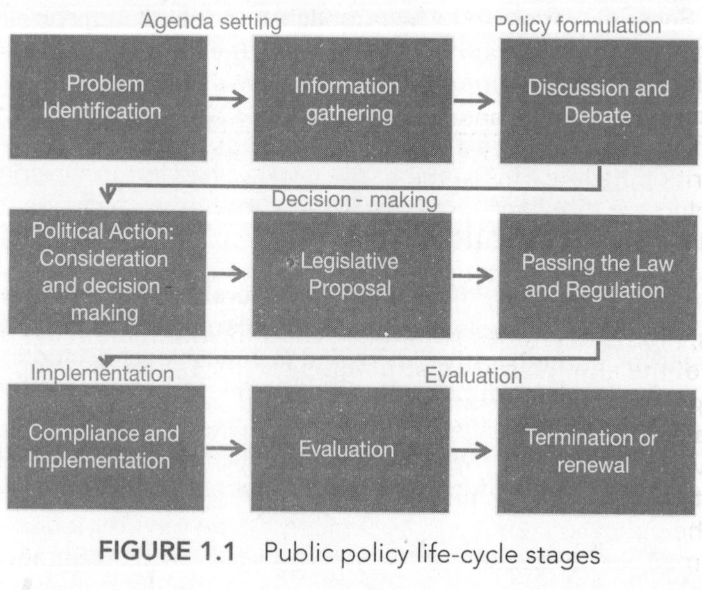

FIGURE 1.1 Public policy life-cycle stages

Agenda setting includes the stages of problem identification and information gathering. Policy formulation includes the stage of discussion and debate. Decision-making includes the stages of political action including consideration and decision-making, legislative proposal, and passing the law and regulation. Implementation includes the stage of compliance and implementation. Finally, the evaluation includes the stages of evaluation, and termination or renewal.

Agenda setting signifies a process wherein a problem is identified and relevant information is gathered. The problem is an issue concerning the public interest. This phase represents the formal identification of the public agenda (Cobb & Elder, 1972). In this phase, a public agenda is readied for discussion because the individuals and, or groups must have acknowledged that the situation is problematic, and relevant information has been gathered for a thorough discussion. In this phase, interest groups, think tanks, academics, the media, and more importantly, the general public help gather the much-needed information for setting the discussion agenda (McCool, 1995).

Policy formulation is the stage where the discussion and debate on the public agenda take place and a clear policy is formulated as an outcome. The draft policy as an outcome is reached only after all the possible solutions and policy options are deliberated and discussed thoroughly. Essentially this is the stage where different interpretations of both the problem and the possible solutions are made by the advocacy groups and interest groups to push their points of view on the problem. Finally, after long and systematic deliberations, the power relationships crystalize defining the direction of the intended policy proposal.

Decision-making is the stage where the policymakers arrive at the decisions and put the stamp on such decisions as laws are regulations. Pursuant to the policy proposal decided upon during the policy formulation stage, in this stage, the first political action on whether to consider the policy proposal for further process is decided upon by the political actors. Secondly, a legislative proposal for law-making is readied after due legislative consultations and discussion. Finally, the law is passed by the legislature for implementation as acts or regulations.

Implementation phase involves compliance with the newly passed law, act, or regulation and enforcing its proper implementation true to the spirit of the law. This stage of the policy cycle assumes significance as implementation strategies have a stronger bearing on the successful outcome of the policy. According to Sabatier and Mazmanian (1995), the eventual outcome of the policy relies on some vital factors like (i) the magnitude of the complexity of the problem, (ii) the policy targets, (iii)the resources committed for implementation, (iv) the availability of the administrative structures for the smooth implementation of the policy.

Evaluation phase of the policy life-cycle encompasses two stages viz., evaluation, and termination or renewal. During the evaluation stage, the outcomes are measured vis-à-vis the policy objectives. Quite often the policy evaluation is conducted by the government machinery and sometimes by consultants or academics (Howlett & Ramesh, 2003).

Based on the evaluation findings, the policy is determined for termination or renewal. Policies are decided for termination if the policy objectives are fully met or the policy was a disastrous failure. In case the policy objectives are yet to be achieved and the governmental actors decide to continue the policy, the policy is recommended for renewal.

For the sake of brevity, we present in Table 1.4 below the details of the actions that take place during the different stages of the policy life-cycle.

TABLE 1.4 Description of actions during the stages of the policy life-cycle.

No.	Phase	Stage	Description of actions
1	Agenda setting	Problem identification	• Identification of the problem • Documenting the gravity of the problem
2		Information gathering	• Identifying the pertinent data • Gathering evidence to further the cause of the problem • Exploring the possible solutions to the problem
3	Policy formulation	Discussion and debate	• Based on the information gathered, a public agenda is set • Different interpretations of the problem and solutions are made • Long and systematic deliberations are carried out • The draft of the public policy is developed
4	Decision-making	Political action: Consideration and decision making	• The draft policy document is provided for political action • The political actors decide on the draft policy as to consider or not
5		Legislative proposal	• Legal consultations are made • Further discussions to fine-tune the policy are made
6		Passing the law and regulation	• The final draft policy is passed to become a law or act or regulation
7	Implementation	Compliance and implementation	• Compliance mechanisms are designed • Implementation strategies are made • The policy is implemented through the pre-decided governance apparatus

(*Continued*)

TABLE 1.4 (Continued)

No.	Phase	Stage	Description of actions
8	Evaluation	Evaluation	• Government machinery, consultants, or academics evaluate the success of the policy. • Policy outcomes are measured vis-à-vis the policy objectives
9		Termination or renewal	• The policy is terminated if it has fully met the policy objectives • The policy is terminated if the policy was a disastrous failure • If the policy objectives are partially achieved and the governmental actors decide to continue the policy, the policy is renewed.

Conclusion

In this chapter, we have introduced the topic of public policy. The study of the public policy assumes greater significance as societies are changing fast and becoming increasingly complex due to technological changes, globalization, and various other global and domestic factors. To be precise, the public policy provides a mechanism to identify the socio-economic challenges and problems faced by society and find plausible solutions for attaining much-needed public welfare and economic prosperity.

Public policies can be described as a set of rules and regulations that are based on the values, principles, ideals, and cultural ethos of the society in which the governments make the decisions. The study of public policy has become multi-dimensional and interdisciplinary as it draws inputs from a wide range of social sciences. Public policy as a policy science has evolved around the nature and character of western philosophies. There is a need to bring Indianness to this policy science in its approaches.

Good public policies lead to better outcomes. As public policies are dependent on the environment, it is the responsibility of the government to interact with the environment and frame good policies for public welfare. Generally, good governments can provide good policies. Because good policies rest on the pillars of honesty, transparency, and democracy.

Based on the foregoing discussions, we can describe that "**public policy is based on the past, formulated in the present, and made for the future**."

Summary

- A policy is a statement of intent guided by a set of rules, principles, and regulations aimed at achieving specific goals.
- Policies guide our actions. They can be personal, organizational, and governmental. Policies assume significance because of their consistency, clarity, guidance, and accountability.
- A government policy is a guided action of the government. It is intended to bring positive outcomes to benefit society.
- A public policy goal is an anticipated situation or a state of affairs in a society or an organization.
- Public policy is for the public because it is formed out of the collective action of the governments, institutions, and concerned citizens of the society. Public policy is more bothered about public goods than private goods.
- Public policies are multi-dimensional and interdisciplinary with disciplines like political science, sociology, philosophy, public administration, and economics.
- As a policy science, public policy has evolved as a normative and value-oriented discipline.
- A public policy goal is an anticipated situation or a state of affairs in a society or an organization.
- The importance of public policy arises from its five elements viz., public interest, public sector, public finance, public property, and public law.
- The term 'public' largely refers to public ownership and, or public control for public purposes.
- What differentiates public policy from privacy policy are the factors like interest, power of policy making, consumption, investment, decision-making, provision of goods, ownership, and employment.
- Public policy has numerous definitions. The simplest of all is the one by Thomas Dye, who defines Public policy as anything a government chooses to do or not to do.
- It studies the intentions and actions of the government that affect the public. Kautilya's Arthashastra is one of the ancient treatises on public policy in India.
- Public policy has a wide scope. The scope of public policy is generally determined by the role assumed by the governments. Every one of us benefits from public policy directly, indirectly, and or collectively.
- Public policies portray the response of the governance system to the policy environment.
- A good public policy is well-defined, well-targeted, well-planned, well-strategized, well-measured, and well-implemented to attain its goals.
- In India, public policy players or policy actors include the Parliament, Vidhana Sabha, politicians, voters, media, interest groups, public opinion, public interest, the judiciary, bureaucrats, civil servants, administration, and think tanks, experts, consultants, researchers, and academics.
- The typology of public policy includes regulatory, distributive, redistributive, capitalization, and substantive policies.
- In India, the different levels of public policy are national, state, district, municipality, and panchayat.
- Every public policy has a life cycle involving different phases of policy. We identify nine stages: (1) problem identification, (2) information gathering, (3) discussion and debate, (4) political action including consideration and decision-making, (5) legislative proposal, (6) passing the law and regulation, (7) compliance and implementation, (8) evaluation, and (9) termination or renewal.

Key Words

Public policy	Personal policy	Organizational policy	Governmental policy
Problem definition	Policy goals	Policy instruments	Public good
Private good	Public interest	Public sector	Public finance
Public property	Public law	Public sector	Private sector
Policy environment	Policy players or actors	Regulatory Policies	Distributive Policies
Redistributive Policies	Capitalization Policies	Substantive Policies	Policy Life-Cycle

Questions

A. Quick Check

1) Discuss the statement: "Public policy as a discipline is fairly young."
2) Briefly discuss the functions of a policy.
3) Discuss the nature of a government policy vis-à-vis a personal policy.
4) Why is public policy so important?
5) Explain public policy as a policy science.
6) Explain the notion of 'public' in public policy.
7) What differentiates the public sector from the private sector?
8) Discuss and define public policy.
9) Discuss the scope of public policy.
10) Identify the characteristics of public policy.
11) Discuss the typology of public policy.
12) Describe the public policy life cycle.

B. Explore

1) "Public policy is based on the past, formulated in the present, and made for the future." Discuss this statement in detail.
2) Give an example of a popular public policy in India and discuss its elements.
3) List out major public policies in India since Independence.
4) "Public policy is all about solving the problems concerning the public." Analyze this statement.
5) What is good public policy? Identify its characteristics. Explain with an example in the Indian context.

References

Anderson, J.E. (1975). Public Policy Making. New York: Praeger.

Birkland A. Thomas (2001).An Introduction to the Policy Process – Theories, Concepts, and Models of Public Policy Making. 1st edition | Routledge (February 5, 2001) – Copyright © 2001

Clarke E. Cochran., Lawrence C. Mayer., T. R. Carr., N. Joseph Cayer., and Mark McKenzie. (2014). American Public Policy: An Introduction. 11th Edition | Cengage Learning (December 31, 2014)

Cobb, R. W., and Elder, C. D. (1972). Participation in American politics: The Dynamics of Agenda

Building. Boston, MA: Allyn and Bacon, Inc., @1972.

Daniel C. McCool (1994). Public Policy Theories, Models, and Concepts: An Anthology. Pearson (8 December 1994)

Dewey, John (1927). The Public and Its Problems. New York: Holt, Rinehart & Winston.

Douglass, B. (1980). The common good and the public interest. Political Theory, 8 (1), 103-117.

Dye, Thomas. R (1972). Understanding Public Policy. 15th edition | Pearson (July 14, 2021) – Copyright © 2017

Easton, David (1957). An Approach to the Analysis of Political Systems. *World Politics*, Vol. 9, Iss 3, pp. 383–400.

Edgar Norman Gladden (1966). The essentials of public administration: London Staple Press, 1966

Eyestone, Robert (1971). The Threads of Public Policy: A Study in Policy Leadership. Bobbs-Merrill Co (March 1, 1971)

Guy B. Peters (1999). American Public Policy: Promise and Performance. 5th edition | Chatham House Publishers Inc., U.S (March 31, 1999)

Heidenheimer, J, Arnold., Hugh Heclo., and Carolyn Teich Adams. (1990). Comparative public policy: the politics of social choice in America, Europe, and Japan. 3rd Edition | New York, NY: St. Martin's Press; Hounds mills, Basingstoke, Hampshire: Distributed by Macmillan Education Ltd., ©1990.

Henry, Nicholas (2012). Public Administration and Public Affairs. 12th Edition | Routledge (e-book: August 27, 2015)

Kevin B. Smith., and Christopher Larimer (2016). The Public Policy Theory Primer. 3rd Edition | Routledge (August 2, 2016) – Copyright @ 2017

Lineberry, Robert. L (1977). American Public Policy, What Government Does and What Differences It Makes. New York: Harper & Row.

McCool, C. Daniel (1995). Public policy theories, models, and concepts: An anthology. Englewood Cliffs, NJ: Prentice-Hall @1995.

Michael, Howlett., and Ramesh, M (2003). Studying public policy: policy cycles and policy subsystems. 2nd Edition | Toronto, Canada: Oxford University Press, 2003.

Parsons, W. (1995). Public Policy. Cheltenbam: Edward Elgar.

Sabatier P. A. & Mazmanian D. (1995). A conceptual framework of the implementation process. In Theodolou, S. Z. & Cahn, M. A. (Eds.), Public policy: The essential readings, (pp. 153-173). Upper Saddle River, NJ: Prentice-Hall.

Teitz, B. Michael (1968). Towards a Theory of Urban Public Facility Location. *Papers in Regional Science*. 21 (1), 35-51.

Further Readings

Diana DiNitto, and David H. Johnson (2016). Social Welfare: Politics and Public Policy. 8th Edition | Pearson @ 2016

Gautam Chikarmane (2018). 70 Policies that shaped India. Publisher: Observer Research Foundation. Available at https://www.orfonline.org

Paul Chaney (2011). Equality and Public Policy: Exploring the Impact of Devolution in the UK.

The University of Chicago Press.

Thomas R. Dye (2017). Understanding Public Policy. 15th Edition | Pearson @ 2017

William N. Dunn (2017). Public Policy Analysis. 6th New Edition | Routledge @ 2017

CHAPTER 2

Public Policy Process, Models, and Analysis

The purpose of this chapter is to provide an overview of the public policy process, models, and analysis. As we progress in this chapter, we will discuss first what a public policy process in general is. Then we discuss corporate political activities and how they affect public policy-making. In the third section, we will briefly explore the topic of Business political activities and their types like lobbying, political action committee contributions, policy advocacy, and coalition-building. In section 4, we discuss the nine public policy models viz., Process Model, Rationalist Model, Incremental Model, Group Model, Elite Model, Public Choice Model, Institutional Model, Polis Model, and Game Theory Model. Finally, in section 5, we provide an overview of public policy analysis.

Section 1: The Public Policy Process

Section 2: Corporate Political Activities

Section 3: Business Political Activities

Section 4: Public Policy Models

Section 5: Framework for Public Policy Analysis

Public policy has emerged as a policy science and an academic pursuit since the 1950s. Of late, this has become a full-fledged discipline encompassing several aspects of the public policy process and analysis. Public policy term has become ubiquitous. We find the role of public policy in every walk of our lives. In the previous chapter, you were introduced to the concept of public policy. After having been acquainted with the concept of public policy, in this chapter, we will discuss the public policy process.

> Public policymaking is an ongoing process. It is dynamic and continuous.

Public policymaking is an ongoing process. Public policies are driven by policy actors and implemented by institutions.

1. THE PUBLIC POLICY PROCESS

In a way, the public policy process is the study of how the state (government) uses its power or authority in public policy making. Essentially, it is about knowing how the governments initiate actions around public problems. For instance, the recent mass shootings in the US have revived the debate on gun control.

Many a time, public debates and discourses happen based on a single event or series of events. Sometimes, depending on the intensity of the impact of a single event, public policy debates are initiated. The Nirbhaya case in India that happened on December 16, 2012, is a classic case to understand how a single event can influence public policy. What happened on that day was a gruesome gang rape and brutal assault on a 23-year-old woman in Delhi. Massive protests broke out across India and more prominently in Delhi near the Parliament and Rashtrapati Bhavan as a result of an unprecedented uproar, demanding stricter laws against rape which led to the Nirbhaya Act (The Criminal Law (Amendment) Act, 2013) that came into force on April 3, 2013. On the other hand, a series of more than 100 cases of instant divorce in the form of triple talaq forced the government in the context of the Supreme Court judgment in August 2017 to make The Muslim Women (Protection of Rights on Marriage) Act, 2019 that made triple talaq illegal in India with effect from August 1, 2019.

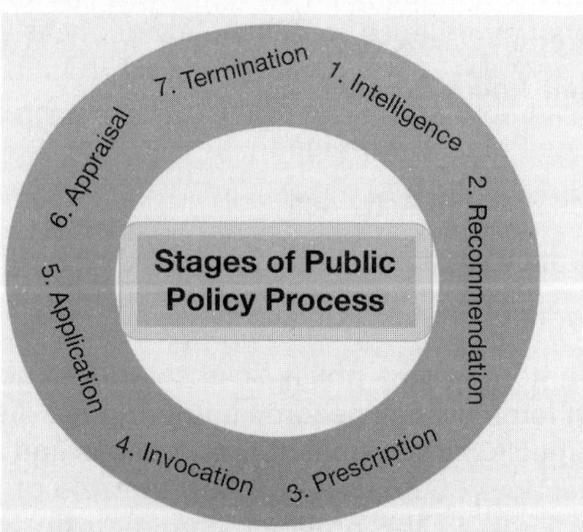

FIGURE 2.1 Policy-making process: Lasswell's conceptual map

Therefore, a single event of a massive impact or a series of events of intense public impact can lead to public policy making. Thus, we can understand that in the context of competing priorities or focused events, broadly four factors the political environment, the economic environment, the socio-cultural environment, and the administrative environment determine the public policy process.

From the theoretical perspective, the first to methodically broach the idea of the policy process was Harold Lasswell, a reputed political scientist considered the father of policy sciences during the 1950s (Lasswell, 1951). Pioneering the policy sciences, Lasswell was the first to explore the different stages of the public policy process as (1) intelligence, (2) recommendation, (3) prescription, (4) invocation, (5) application, (6) appraisal, and (7) termination. Figure 2.1 pictorially illustrates Lasswell's approach to the policy-making process.

Lasswell was the first to envisage the policy process as a sequence of steps in a life-cycle model. He approached the entire policy-making process in terms of 'stages' because they were considered a series of distinct successive steps in chronological order from the initial stage to that of termination (Lasswell, 1956). However, in the subsequent decades, several policy scientists including Anderson (1975), and Nakamura (1987) contributed to Lasswell's approach to develop stylized models eventually shaping it as what is today called the ***'textbook approach'***. Wayne Parsons characterizes the work of Lasswell as ***'policy orientation'*** that is multi-method and problem-focused. Parsons views the goals of the Lasswell approach as to map the policy process, options, and outcomes as an integrated knowledge in the form of an overarching discipline of public choices and decision making (Parsons, 1995).

Lasswell envisaged the policy process as a sequence of steps in a life-cycle model.

Generally, ***the public policy process is dynamic and continuous, in identifying and countering the public problems in an interacting approach with optimal solutions with new solutions or reforming the existing ones***. Lasswell's conceptual map of the policy-making process has seven stages. Different theorists have conceptualized the policy process into different stages.

According to Thomas Dye (2004), the policy process is categorized into six stages: (1) Problem Identification, (2) Agenda Setting, (3) Policy Formulation, (4) Policy Legitimation, (5) Policy Implementation, and (6) Policy Evaluation. However, Hogwood and Gunn (1984) identify nine major stages of the policy process: (1) deciding to decide, (2) deciding how to decide, (3) issue definition, (4) forecasting, (5) setting objectives and priorities, (6) options analysis, (7) policy implementation, (8) monitoring and control, evaluation and review, and (9) policy maintenance, succession, and termination. Interestingly, according to May and Wildavsky (1978) involves (1) agenda-setting, (2) issue analysis, (3) implementation, (4) evaluation, and (5) termination.

More popularly, according to Anderson (1984) and Michael Hill & Frederic Varone (2021), the ***public policy process is a multi-stage process that includes five major steps***: (1) Problem Identification, (2) Policy Formulation, (3) Policy adaption, (4) policy implementation, and (5) Policy Evaluation. We discuss below each of these steps in the policy process.

Public policy process is a five-step multi-stage process.

The Problem Identification stage involves agenda setting where the identified problems evolve as issues of public interest. Generally, a public problem is a situation where the public is dissatisfied with the present situation of improvements or continuation of an accepted situation. During this stage, the problems that exist will attract the attention of the individuals, interest groups, the media, political parties, and

Problem identification stage involves agenda setting where the identified problems evolve as issues of public interest.

social groups who articulate these issues as matters of public concern. Sometimes, elite opinion or influencers' comments trigger the issues of public interest to be identified as a public problem.

In identifying public problems, often the following criteria are followed:

a) Does the problem relate to a large population in society?
b) Does a large section of the population consider that situation as a problem of serious concern?
c) Are the people affected by the problem directly or even indirectly by the problem?
d) Is there a need for governmental intervention to make a policy to solve the problem?
e) Do the people seek and accept governmental intervention for effective resolution of the problem?

Policy formulation is the stage where the demands of the public are transformed into policies.

Policy Formulation is the second stage of the policy process when alternative strategies are formed to deal with the problems identified in the previous stage. These strategies should be effective in addressing the public problem and acceptable to the stakeholders. It is the stage when the demands of the public are transformed into policies. Mostly, acceptability is a course of action that needs political actors who wield considerable influence over policy making. Because of this, the political actors need to keep in mind the following aspects:

a) Technical soundness of the proposal
b) Suitability of the proposal in addressing the causes of the problem
c) The probable outcomes of the proposal if implemented
d) Economic feasibility in the proposal in terms of costs and benefits
e) Political acceptability of the proposal.

During this stage, both the sources inside and outside the government are involved. In the Indian context, the inside sources include the ministries, the bureaucracy, and agencies related to the government and the legislature. Mostly, the sources outside the government are policy networks, non-governmental organizations, research organizations, think tanks, civil society, academics, and various other organizations.

Essentially, this stage refers to the development of various policy options and narrowing down to specific policy choices by the government in addressing the problem. This stage involves intense debate and discussion as the interested parties try to force their favored policy choice.

Jones (1977) identifies three broad types of policy formulation based on the nature of decision-making: (1) Routine formulations, (2) Analogous formulations, and (3) Creative formulations.

Three broad types of Policy formulation are Routine formulations, Analogous formulations, and Creative formulations.

The ***routine formulation*** is a repetitive process where there is no major change. Because similar proposals of an issue are dealt with within the ambit of a policy agenda pursued by the government.

On the other hand, ***analogous formulation*** treats a new problem by searching for analogies based on experience. ***Creative formulation*** views any problem with a new perspective breaking from the past practice or precedence. Generally, we find more routine and analogous policy formulation approaches in vogue than the creative approach to policy formulation, even though the creative approach does happen.

Interestingly, in real-world scenarios, we find four types of combinations of plan and strategy. Many a time we come across good plans with imperfect strategies. Sometimes imperfect plans are associated with good strategy. Quite often we find an imperfect blend of both though it is important to have a perfect blend of both.

Policy adoption by the institutions of public authority legitimizes the policy effect.

The policy Adoption stage is when the government or the public institution accepts a particular policy and brings it to effect using its authority to do so. In simple terms, it is the stage of official authorization of the proposed policy decision which seems daunting. During this stage, the policy is decided, enacted, or legislated when a bill develops as a law. This policy legitimacy helps the people follow the directives of the policy. Several factors assume significance during this stage:

a) Societal preference for the policy
b) Relevance to the ruling party manifesto or agenda
c) Acceptability in the constituency
d) Public opinion about the policy
e) The extent of public interest served by the policy

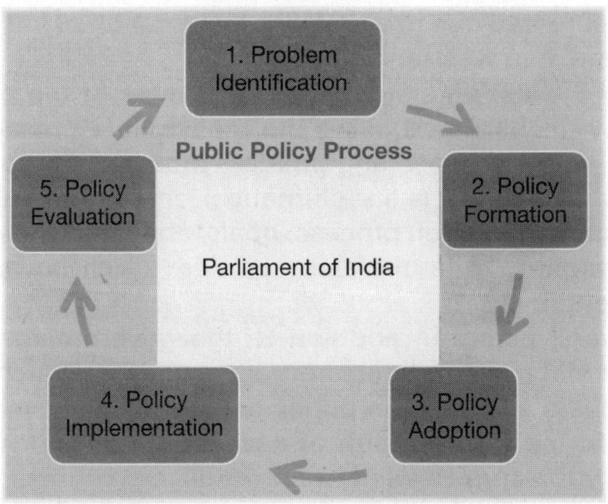

FIGURE 2.2 Public Policy Process

Policy adoption by the institutions of public authority legitimizes the policy effect. Policy adoption takes place when the lawmakers pass the proposal as legislation to make it a law or an act. For example, in the US, when congress passes the proposals, the policy is adopted as law, or in some cases where the US supreme court pronounces an important decision as a law.

Policy implementation involves bringing into effect the rules and regulations provided in the policy, or delivering the services, providing the necessities as per the respective policies.

Policy Implementation is the fourth stage of the policy process that happens after policy adoption. At this stage, the government's executive (the bureaucracy) implements the policy into action true to the spirit of the policy. The government officials make use of the public administration tools to put the policy into effect. This stage involves bringing into effect the rules and regulations provided in the policy, or delivering the services, providing the necessities as per the respective policies.

Successful policy implementation includes several actors like administrative agencies, lobbies or pressure groups, community organizations, judicial or sub-judicial bodies, review bodies, and task-forces reporting to legislative forums, etc.

An effective policy implementation stage according to Sabatier and Mazmanian (1979) involves (i) sound assumptions about the changes in target group behavior in line with the program goals and objectives, (ii) Clear policy structures and directives for maximizing the performance of the implementation process, (iii) People associated with the implementation process are well skilled both politically and managerially, (iv) Active support from institutions like the legislature, the executive and the judiciary, and (v) Continued prominence to the policy priorities.

In India, during this stage, policies are executed methodically through the various public agencies like administrative departments of the Union government, state governments, and local governments. An example of successful policy implementation is the implementation of the Goods and Services (GST) act across India. Sometimes policy implementation fails due to the following reasons, political disruptions, agitations, civil disobedience, communication challenges, misfit of the policy, etc. For instance, the three farm laws that were enacted by the Indian Parliament were not implemented due to agitations by a section of Indian farmers in Punjab, Haryana, and western Uttar Pradesh.

Policy evaluation is a systematic process of assessing the content, design, implementation process, goals, and policy outcomes.

The Policy Evaluation stage is the final stage of the policy process when the policy is assessed using the measurable outcomes in terms of its efficacy, equity, impact, and political practicability to know the realization of policy goals. It is a systematic process of assessing the content, design, implementation process, goals, and policy outcomes. Policy monitoring is done by the interested parties – both governmental and non-governmental.

Often, several actors in addition to the government agencies like non-governmental organizations, interest groups, researchers, academics, and the media evaluate the public policies. Policy evaluation, many a time, leads to the identification of new problems and triggers a new round of policy making (Howlett et al., 2009). Sometimes, policy evaluation faces challenges like assessing the accuracy of causality and its impact, diffusion in policy impact, difficulties in data collection, lack of cooperation and indifference by the stakeholders, and time constraints.

Factors like interest groups, nongovernmental organizations, lobbying, and corporate political activity tend to influence public policy making.

To sum up, in recent decades, the public policy process has evolved as a crucial activity in the area of the overall development of a nation. Every stage of the policy process is vital in developing an effective public policy. Knowing the process of policy making helps all the stakeholders in understanding their role and responsibilities toward public welfare. However, several factors like interest groups, non-governmental organizations, lobbying, and corporate political activity tend to influence public policy-making. A proper understanding of the policy process by the stakeholders not only influences the policy process positively but also in making the policy more effective in attaining its policy goals.

Before concluding this discussion, let us look at an example of the policy-making process. One of the recent policies of the Government of India that has gained the attention of public policy observers is the popularly referred FAME India Scheme under The National Electric Mobility Mission Plan (NEMMP) 2020. As part of the NEMMP 2020, the Department of Heavy Industry of the Government of India formulated the FAME (Faster Adoption and Manufacturing of (Hybrid &) Electric vehicles) policy was launched in 2015, and subsequently revised as the FAME II in 2019.

Policy identification was made by the government and other stakeholders like the electric vehicle (EV) manufacturers, dealers, and buyers. The agenda of clean mobility was placed in all the discussion for over a period of two years which created increased awareness among the public. Public comments and suggestions were invited on the proposed policy by the ministry. Further, an independent consultant was engaged for policy evaluation of Phase – I which was launched in 2015. The policy evaluation found that the overall outcomes of the policy were on expected lines as fuel saving and CO2 reduction were significant and were well below the FAME targets.

Based on the experience gained during Phase–I, the ministry conducted various rounds of discussion with industry associations and other stakeholders to seek their suggestions and feedback. Considering the feedback and the evaluation findings, a new policy was formulated with a proper incentive structure and submitted to the Cabinet for policy adoption. After the new policy of FAME was adopted, the implementation has been successful since 2019 with the active involvement of the stakeholders. Though the implementation has demonstrated a slow pace during the first phase, the second phase has gained momentum.

2. CORPORATE POLITICAL ACTIVITIES

The political environment affects not only the individuals in the society but the corporates also. Generally, when corporates face challenges to their performance whether it is related to taxation, licensing, subsidies, incentives, etc., corporates tend to engage in Corporate Political Activities (CPA). In the modern economies, after Kotler (1986) added a new "P" to denote "politics" to the "4Ps" of marketing, there have been numerous studies that have focused on how **corporate political activity (CPA)** has emerged as a firm's business strategy (Hillman, et al., 2004). Corporates in recent decades are found to increasingly tend to influence the policy-making activity to make favorable changes to the policy in terms of distribution of resources and regulation of the economy.

> Corporate political activity (CPA) is a corporate attempt to shape and influence the public policy as its corporate strategy to suit its objectives.

In a democratic system, the involvement of the corporates in the democratic decision-making processes takes place usually in the form of CPA. Several authors have defined CPA as *a non-market strategy of a corporate in attempting to shape and influence public policy to suit its objectives* (Hillman et al., 2004; Lawton et al., 2013). This domain of professional activity is also termed government relations. CPA enables the corporates in exerting systemic influence through public relations systems on the government decision processes to promote corporate economic interests. Corporate political activities can be in the form of lobbying, contributions to political parties, litigation, running election campaigns, appointing government members on their boards, etc. According to Hillman et al., (2004) corporate political activity of a firm is an attempt to manage political institutions and influence the political actors to make policies that are favorable to the firm's interests.

Policy science experts like Lawton, White, Rajwani, and others have keenly studied the corporates engaging with nonmarket political actors and their nexus in public policy making (Rajwani and Liedong, 2015; Mbalyohere and Lawton, 2018; White et al., 2018). ***Why do the firms resort to corporate political activity?*** Past studies inform that the firms involved in corporate political activity target political actors and capture advantages, besides avoiding institutional risks in the business environment. ***Do the firms gain from CPA?*** Evidence suggests that firms get benefitted from involving in corporate political activities. Dahan (2005) observes that by pursuing a corporate political activity, a firm gains political capital, a valuable resource that can combine with market-based strategies to boost the firm's competitive advantage.

Corporates using CPA benefit in terms of cost of borrowing, investment opportunities, obtaining licenses, production-linked incentives, export and import permissions, etc.

How does CPA help firm performance? Mellahi et al., (2016) state that the impact of corporate political activity and firm performance is elusive. However, McWilliams et al., (2002) state that corporate political activity benefits the firm by raising the costs to the rival firms. Hillman (2005) found that CPA benefits the firm performance in terms of a significant increase in its market capitalization. Also, evidence suggests that corporates using CPA benefit in terms of cost of borrowing, investment opportunities, obtaining licenses, production-linked incentives, export and import permissions, etc.

On the other hand, Puck et al., (2018) provide specific reasons that compel the firms to engage in corporate political activities as (1) Firms confront different laws at national and sub-national levels which make their business operations face challenges and higher costs, and (2) The regulatory measures in each market pose a substantial threat to their businesses and can negatively impact firm performance.

Can we equate lobbying to bribery? While the critics of lobbying equate it to ***'legalized bribery'***, lobbyists differ on the criticism because of the following reasons: (1) bribery is for circumventing an existing law, whereas lobbying is to influence the law itself. (2) Many countries like the US have legalized lobbying. (3) The lobbyists wield more power than a briber. (4) Evidence suggests that lobbying is more popular in the developed world, while lobbying is perceived as a part of corporate corruption in the developing world.

CPA influence public policy making in three stages: (1) Influencing public opinion, (2) Public policy formation, and (3) Post-adoption.

2.1 Role of Corporate Political Activities in Public Policy Making

Worldwide, there is an outcry that corporate involvement by the all-powerful mega corporations is adversely influencing public policy making. The concern is how their firms influence the democratic policy-making processes and in turn how these processes become downrightly dependent on corporate involvement (Nyberg, 2021).

Corporate political activities can influence public policy making broadly in three stages: ***(1) Influencing public opinion, (2) Public policy formation, and (3) Post-adoption.*** Table 2.1 lists the several types of activities undertaken by the firms under their corporate political activities to influence policy making. The firms influence public opinion with several strategies like, (i) Speaking out on socio-economic and political issues, (ii) Advocacy advertising, (iii) Image Advertising, and (iv) Influencing the economic knowledge of the public. During the policy formation stage, firms use strategies like (a) Business associations, (b) Industry and trade bodies, (c) Corporate lobbying, (d) Constituency building, and (e) Corporate political contributions. Firms attempt to influence policy-making during the policy adoption stage through (1) regulatory capture and (2) influencing judicial processes.

Political strategies under CPA are Reactive strategies, Proactive strategies, Defensive strategies, and Anticipatory strategies.

TABLE 2.1 Role of corporate political activities in influencing public policy making

I. Influencing Public Opinion	II. Public Policy Formation	III. Post-Adoption
• Speaking out on socio-economic and political issues • Advocacy advertising • Image Advertising • Influencing economic knowledge	• Business associations • Industry and trade bodies • Corporate lobbying • Constituency building • Corporate political contributions	• Regulatory capture • Influencing judicial processes

2.2 Political Strategies Under Corporate Political Activities

How do firms influence public policy making through corporate political activities? In the Political Science and Strategic Management parlance, firms adopt several strategies to influence policy making in their favor. Kristin Oliver and Ingo Holzinger (2008) state that such political strategies can be (1) Reactive strategies, (2) Proactive strategies, (3) Defensive strategies, and (4) Anticipatory strategies.

Reactive strategies are adopted by a firm when it is required to protect its strategic assets, hence it will be conscious in focusing on its efforts to align its internal processes following the requirements of the public policy. For instance, some firms in the highly regulated sectors such as pharmaceuticals, banking, finance, aerospace, etc., resort to reactive strategies to comply with the public policy.

Proactive strategies attempt to shape the very nature of public policy in the policy-making process. Firms using proactive strategies exploit the institutional environment with their ability to manipulate the processes. Such firms take an active lead in participating in professional associations, trade bodies, and media activities in influencing the policy proposal (Oliver and Holzinger, 2008).

Defensive strategies are used by the firms to prevent any undesirable change to the status quo of the policy that is in its favor. In case, they notice changes to the political environment that can lead to change in the policy, resort to vigorous measures to protect the future value of their assets. Generally, firms with limited management systems and structures and are unable to adopt rapid changes resort to these defensive strategies.

Anticipatory strategies are similar to reactive strategies in complying with public policies. However, contrary to the reactive strategies, they resort to a combination of internal and external resources to influence the policy environment.

To sum up, through corporate political activity (CPA) firms gain access to the public policy-making arena at the local level, subnational level, regional level, supranational level, and world level to pursue their interests. As a nonmarket strategy CPA has gained more prominence in the US and most of the developed world. Similarly, firms in the emerging markets and developing countries are pursuing CPA to gain access to the public policy domain. Corporate political activities and strategies mostly depend on the circumstances they conduct their operations. Often, firms are at crossroads in deciding where their strategies should act – regional, subnational, national, and supranational.

3. BUSINESS POLITICAL ACTIVITIES

Businesses involve in political activities largely due to two broad reasons: (i) competitive reasons, and (ii) economic reasons.

Worldwide, there is a growing momentum that businesses should be responsible for the ways they impact the planet, people, and the future. Yet, businesses are found to be actively involved in business political activities such as lobbying, political funding, and other forms of unholy nexus to undermine the regulations that benefit society. In democracies, the business-political nexus has often been seen as a mother of public concern. Surprisingly, even today, there are no effective structures for the public to monitor and scrutinize the scope and sway of business political activities because of which business political accountability remains elusive.

Businesses involve in political activities largely due to two broad reasons: (i) competitive reasons, and (ii) economic reasons. They engage in business political activities like (1) Lobbying, (2) Political contributions, (3) Public advocacy, and (4) Coalition building.

3.1 The Role of Lobbying in Public Policy Making

3.1.1 Lobbying

Business lobbying is a common phenomenon across countries. Lobbying is an activity carried out by businesses to influence governments and policymakers to make laws that are conducive to their businesses. ***Lobbying involves meetings with government policymakers who can influence policy-making activity.*** Business lobbying is made for different purposes like, protecting their business assets from policy shocks and benefiting from economic incentives like subsidies, tariffs, etc. At local levels, sometimes businesses resort to lobbying for favorable infrastructure to run their businesses, etc.

Lobbying involves meetings with government policymakers who can influence policy-making activity.

3.1.2 Types of Lobbying

Business lobbying can happen in various ways depending on the issues at hand and the prevailing political environment. According to Berry (1977), generally, there are three types of lobbying: (1) direct lobbying, (2) grassroots lobbying, and (3) electoral lobbying.

Lobbying types are direct lobbying, (2) grassroots lobbying, and (3) electoral lobbying.

Direct lobbying can be explained as a direct attempt to influence the policy-making process through a public official or his staff. It includes communications or interactions that are verbal or written, electronic, internet, social media channels, In-person meetings, and phone calls.

Grassroots lobbying is an activity of indirectly influencing a public authority in policy-making using some other person/s. This form of lobbying incurs costs like consulting services, sponsoring expenses, etc.

Electoral lobbying is an activity that is aimed at changing public policy by influencing election outcomes. It can be in the form of supporting a particular candidate or a political party to get them elected and later help in public policy making in favor of the business.

Lobbying is generally seen in a negative sense by society at large because it is more concerned about the firm's interest rather than the public interest. However, lobbyists argue that lobbying plays the role of communicating and expressing the firm's points of view and drawing the attention of the lawmakers for their desired purpose. Interestingly, no country in the world has banned lobbying though some countries like the US, Australia, Germany, and Canada have legitimized lobbying many countries are silent about legislating on this activity.

In the US, like any other interest group, major firms influence policymakers, regulators, and government officials to seek a favorable policy environment for their businesses. Often, firms hire influential lawyers, and former government officials as lobbyists who already know the functioning of the government as well as its structures to influence the policy-making process in favor of the firm.

3.1.3 Lobbying Spending Around the World

> The total lobbying expenditure in the US in 2020 was USD 3.53 billion.

> The pharmaceuticals industry in the US spent the highest amount of USD 306.23 million for lobbying in 2020.

> In the US, political lobbyist commands a median annual salary of around USD 1,16,800.

According to Statista©2022, the total lobbying expenditure by the firms in the US has steadily increased from a meager USD 1.45 million in 1998 to USD 3.73 billion in 2021. ***The total lobbying expenditure in 2020 was USD 3.53 billion.*** The pharmaceuticals industry in the US spent the highest amount of USD 306.23 million for lobbying in 2020, followed by electronic items manufacturers who spent USD 156.90 million. Google's federal lobbying expenditure in 2017 was about USD 18.04 million and increased to USD 21.21 million in 2018. However, its lobbying expenditure has declined to USD 9.5 million in 2021. One of the controversial aspects against lobbying was that in the US, the National Rifle Association (NRA) spent about USD 3.31 million for lobbying in 2021 as against its lobbying spending of USD 2.33 million in 1998.

In the US, political lobbyist commands handsome wages. According to Statista©2020, in 2021, the annual salaries ranged from USD 73,470 in the 10th percentile to USD 2,01,330 in the 90th percentile. The median annual salary was around USD 1,16,800. The number of active lobbyists in the US in 2021 was 12137. These lobbyists are mostly hired by the corporates and interest groups.

InfluenceMap, a think tank that analyses how businesses affect the climate crisis, in its Carbon Policy Footprint Report-2021, identifies that out of the 350 large companies in the globe, the top five companies that influenced most negatively were in order: ExxonMobil, Chevron, Toyota, Southern Company and Sempra, and the North American energy infrastructure company. The chart below shows the major firms wielding the powerful and most negative influence on global climate policy action.

3.1.4 Lobbying in India

> Lobbying in India is done by industry organizations.

In India, lobbying is perceived as unethical and the lobbyist an untouchable. Yet, the legal system in India has hesitated so far to bring a legal framework for lobbying like the developed world. This does not mean that lobbying does not exist in India. Industry organizations like the Federation of Indian Chambers of Commerce and Industry (FICCI), the Confederation of Indian Industry (CII), the Associated Chambers of Commerce in India (ASSOCHAM), and others are believed to have played active roles in influencing the governments in public policy making to suit the needs of the respective industry and thereby safeguard the industry interests. These bodies hold discussions with the government officials in the government offices to persuade policymakers for adopting favorable policies. Governments have justified these meetings stating that these meetings help them get an idea about the industry sentiments who form part of the stakeholders. However, these discussions are mostly opaque and not made known to the public.

India lacks a free and transparent policy structure in making lobbying unethical. Nonetheless, the recent corruption scandals involving lobbyists have mounted public pressure to legislate a law to regulate lobbying in India.

In India, there were efforts to legislate lobbying. A private member's bill was moved by Kalikesh Narayan Singh Deo, Member of Parliament in Lok Sabha to regulate lobbying which defined lobbying as "an act of communication with and payment to a public servant to influence" legislation or securing government contracts. However, the bill did not see the light of the day. William Dalrymple, author of "The Anarchy" states that the world's first lobbying scandal was that of the East India Company in 1693 in the UK (Dalrymple, 2019)

Several scandals and controversies have brought lobbying into the negative limelight in India. The most recent ones are the Niira Radia tapes and the Wal-Mart Lobbying in India. Niira Radia tape scandal rocked the corridors of power in 2010 when the Radia tapes recorded between 2007-2009 the conversations of lobbyist-cum entrepreneur Niira Radia involving leading businessmen, politicians, and journalists. The Wal-Mart lobbying scandal broke out in 2012 when Wal-Mart revealed to the US as a part of the routine disclosure that it spent a humongous for lobbying in India since 2008 to gain market access in India. Multinational lobbying drew intense emotions in the Indian public.

Being the world's largest democracy, India needs to have proper legislation for lobbying. It is incorrect to declare all forms of lobbying as immoral or unethical merely because of legislation. India needs to consider a proper form of legislation on lobbying in the public interest to make lobbying more transparent and principled.

3.1.5 The Role of PAC Contributions in Public Policy Making

Let us first understand what are these PACs. These are the Political Action Committees (PACs) whose purpose is to raise donations and distribute those funds to promote the political goals of their members. Political contributions are the most common sources of funds for political campaigning in the US. A contribution is defined as anything of value that is provided in any form to influence a federal election. What does a PAC do? In the US, a PAC is an organization that collects contributions from its members and donates such funds to political campaigns of the candidates in federal elections. PACs are of six types: (1) Connected PACs, (2) Non-connected PACs, (3) Leadership PACs, (4) Partnership PACs, (5) Super PACs, and (6) Hybrid PACs. We provide below a brief understanding of the different types of PACs:

> The purpose of PACs is to raise donations and distribute them to promote the political goals of its members.

TABLE 2.2 Types of Political Action Committees

No.	PAC Type	Description
1	Connected PACs	These political action committees collect donations from managers and shareholders of corporations and members of non-profit organizations, labor unions, interest groups, etc.
2	Non-connected PACs	These committees are not part of the party or the election candidate. However, these are authorized by the candidate or the party to make contributions.
3	Leadership PACs	Generally, a leadership PAC is a political committee that is directly established and controlled by the candidate/s running for federal office.
4	Partnership PACs	These are the PACs sponsored by partnerships. These PACs, besides making direct donations and contributions to the candidate, can also sponsor a nonconnected PAC.
5	Super PACs	These are political action committees (PACs) that collect unlimited contributions from individuals, corporations, labor unions, other PACs, and others to finance independent expenditures and political activity
6	Hybrid PACs	These political action committees raise unlimited funds through segregated bank accounts for independent expenditures, advertisements, and generic voter drives in federal elections in favor of candidates.

Credit: Federal Election Commission of the USA. Extracted from https://www.fec.gov/

Some examples of PACs are (1) CVS Caremark Employees PAC – Washington, D.C., (2) The Home Depot PAC – Washington, D.C., (3) International Council of Shopping Centers PAC (ICSC PAC) – Washington, D.C., (4) Target Citizens Political Forum – Minneapolis, MN., and (5) Wal-Mart Stores PAC For Responsible Government – Washington, D.C.

PAC Contributions in the US

Broadly, PAC contributions influence the legislators in two ways. First, they act like a spot market for political favors. Besides, they are believed to be exchanged for a cooperative equilibrium in the long run. Second, they tend to buy legislation through their access to the legislator. Figure 2.3 illustrates the contributions to PACS in the US from 2017-2018. The Corporate PACs made a contribution of USD 178.1 million during that period.

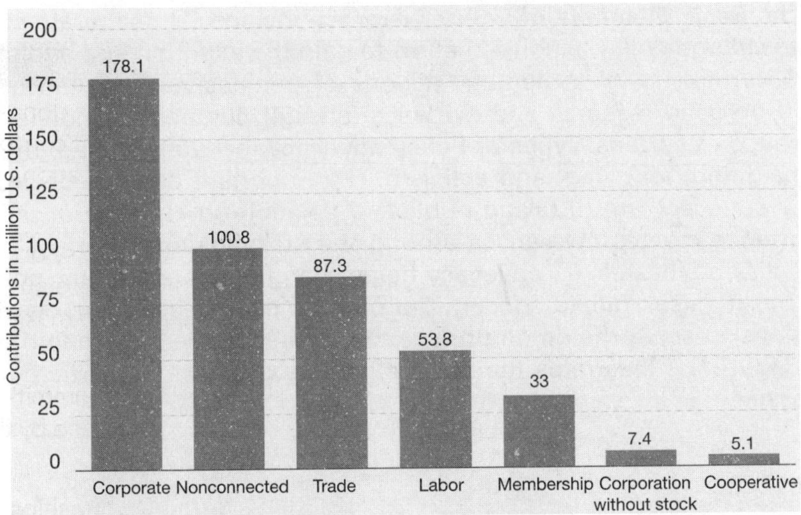

Credit: Data sourced from the Federal Election Commission, www.fec.gov, (c)Federal Govt. of USA, accessed Jan. 2023

FIGURE 2.3 Political Action Committees (PAC) contributions in the US from 2017 to 2018

3.1.6 Public Advocacy

Public advocacy involves deliberate activities of individuals, groups of individuals, or organizations aimed at influencing public attitudes and public policymakers to pursue their policy agenda. Advocacy encompasses all sorts of actions such as speaking, recommending, supporting, defending, arguing, or pleading on behalf of their policy agenda. On the other hand, ***People-centered advocacy includes all actions that are pursued to empower the people, more importantly, the marginalized sections***. Policy advocacy as a broad term comprises everything from an informal discussion, written report submissions, and filing Public Interest Litigations (PILs) to, creating and capacity building of civil society network of groups to influence the decision-makers of public policies. ***Policy advocacy can be in three ways: (i) self-advocacy, (ii) co-advocacy, and (iii) public advocacy.***

Policy advocacy is the action of the individuals or group of individuals, or network of organizations involving negotiations, mediations, litigations, dialogues, and communications that influence the decision-makers to act in favor of their policy preferences.

There are several definitions of policy advocacy. However, for a clear understanding, we define ***Policy advocacy as the actions of the individuals or group of individuals, or network of organizations involving negotiations, mediations, litigations, dialogues, and communications that influence the decision-makers to act in favor of their policy preferences***. Essentially, public policy advocacy involves a wide range of actions such as public education, capacity building of networks, litigation, lobbying, etc., to influence the policymakers. Some of the examples of public policy advocacy include public education, public information services, legal battles, commentary on regulations, and supporting individuals and organizations in getting the government benefits and services to which they are entitled to.

Policy advocacy types are self-advocacy, co-advocacy, and public advocacy.

The **Basic Elements of Policy Advocacy** include (1) deliberate strategy to change policy action, (2) effort to gain the attention and audience of policymakers, (3) systematic actions of persuasive communication based on solid research and evidence, and (4) pursued by individuals or groups of citizens. **Types of Policy advocacy** include advising, media campaigning, lobbying, and activism. The important benefits of public policy advocacy are (i) taking publicly a position on an issue of public importance creates awareness among the stakeholders to orient with the policy advocates, (ii) advocacy helps change or shape public policy, and (iv) it raises public concerns, promotes and presents sustainable solutions to serve the community, and (iv) it empowers the communities. Figure 2.4 illustrates the basic elements of effective public policy advocacy.

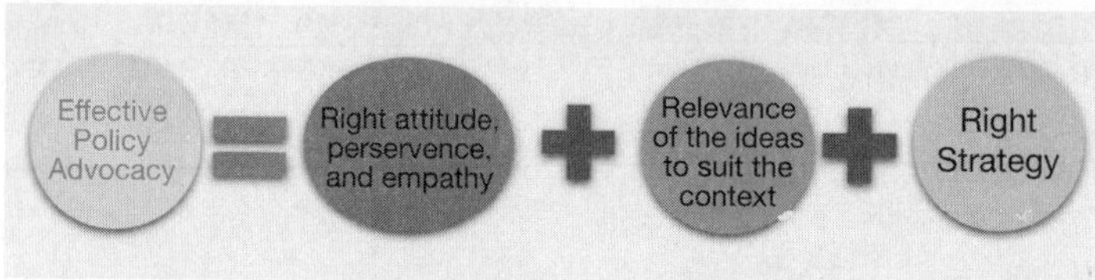

FIGURE 2.4 Elements of effective policy advocacy

Policy advocacy has often been seen with negative connotations in society. However, if pursued with genuine concerns with a concerted strategic, committed, forward-looking approach with the paramount public interest is seen with success, and communities getting greatly benefitted from it. Policy advocacy in India is still visibly not bright as there is a lack of credible civil society organizations and networks that are genuinely committed to the public cause.

Very few organizations did have the mass appeal as the Anna Hazare movement against corruption. However, such movements transformed into political parties making the people doubt the intentions of such mass movements. So, credibility matters in public advocacy to win the trust of the masses.

3.1.7 Coalition Building

Coalition-building is aimed at bringing together different groups of people to pursue and achieve a common goal.

Coalition-building is aimed at bringing together different groups of people to pursue and achieve a common goal. It is possible if the goals, values, and interests of different individuals and organizations are similar. Coalition-building helps in combining the resources for collective action to influence policymakers. Coalitions are greatly beneficial in creating awareness about the public cause, bringing the people together around a public cause, and generating sustainable solutions for societal problems. We can identify three main traits of a coalition (1) influencing or shaping public policy around a public cause, (2) influencing societal behavior on certain issues, and (3) being committed to building strong communities.

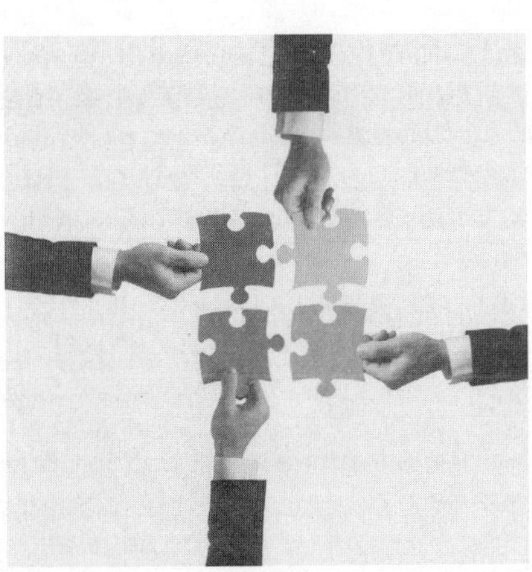

Coalitions are one of the effective strategies in public policy activities. As they pool the resources, talent, and strategy, for collective action, they foster an impactful campaign to influence the decision-makers. Some of the major features of coalitions are:

a) Specific common cause
b) Well-defined mission and vision
c) Broad-based stakeholders
d) Voluntary participation with commitment and trust.
e) Informal structures with a steadfast leadership
f) Consensus as cohesion
g) Committed financial and human resources
h) A common strategy to realize the vision

Coalitions wield more power and influence because of their collective strength and common focus which helps in impacting the decision-makers of public policy. Coalitions are found to be effective in influencing public policy and governance because they are effective in highlighting the public cause and pressuring the policymakers. They are immune to intimidation and harassment when an individual is in the pursuit of policy advocacy. According to CommGAP (2008), the success of effective coalition building depends on (1) problem identification and description, (2) Relationship building and stakeholder mapping, (3) Forming committed core membership, (4) Establishing credibility, (5) Expansion through credit networks, and (6) Sustainable transformation through collective action.

Always everything is not rosy with coalitions. Sometimes coalitions do fail due to some barriers to strong coalitions such as (i) turf issues, (ii) bad history, (iii) domination by "professionals" or some other elite, (iv) not rooted with the community, (v) minimal organizational strength, (vi) inadequate funding, (vii) lack of creative and steadfast leadership, and (viii) perceived costs outweigh the benefits to the coalition. Let us list out some of the advantages and disadvantages of coalition building.

Successful coalition-building depends on (1) problem identification and description, (2) Relationship building and stakeholder mapping, (3) Forming committed core membership, (4) Establishing credibility, (5) Expansion through credit networks, and (6) Sustainable transformation through collective action.

TABLE 2.3 Coalition building: Advantages and Disadvantages

No.	Advantages	Disadvantages
1	Widens the support base, networks, and connections.	Lack of credibility among the coalition members might cause public mistrust of the coalition.
2	Provides collective strength for advocacy efforts.	Disagreement on issues can lead to dissonance in the coalition instead of cohesion.
3	Protects the members from harassment and attacks.	Coalition building is not easy as it requires a long-time and perseverance.
4	Pooling of financial and human resources enables the delegation of tasks.	Turf tussles, power centers, and opacity in decision-making can cause fissures in the coalition
5	Avoids duplication of efforts and conserves resources.	Vulnerability to donor interference can lead to dilution of principles and values of the coalition.
6	Helps in enhancing the credibility and the power of collective advocacy for policy change.	The bad history of the coalition members can cause embarrassment to the coalition.
7	The peer support in the coalition encourages motivation which further leads to professional recognition.	Leadership issues can cripple the coalition's momentum.
8	Diversity in the coalition strengthens skills, experience sharing, materials, and methods, and reinforces collaborative spirit.	Interference by the elite and very few professionals in decision-making can delink the coalition from the masses.

Research shows that coalitions have been successful in addressing diverse issues because they offer appropriate mechanisms to bring together the individuals and the organizations in a dynamic collaboration for collective efforts aimed at policy change ranging from short-term to long-term policy solutions.

4. PUBLIC POLICY MODELS

Over the last three decades, several models of public policy formulation have evolved. A model is a concept with a well-defined construct. Knowing the public policy models helps us systematically understand the policy formulation process. Let us understand the following nine models of public policy making.

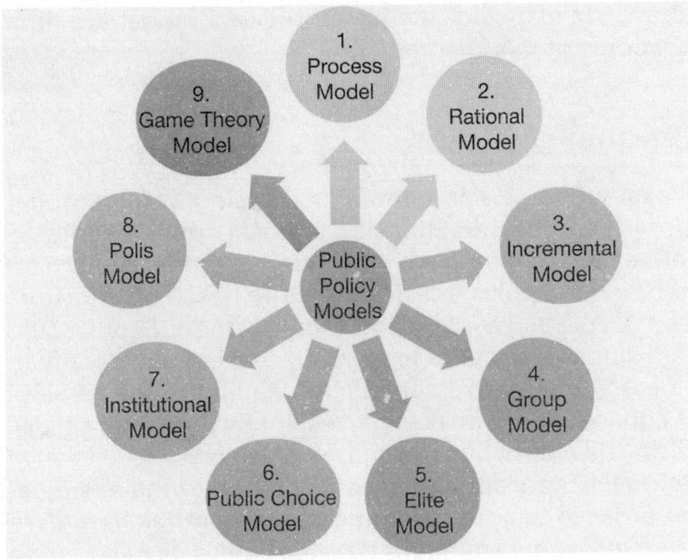

FIGURE 2.5 Models of Public Policy Formulation

4.1 Process Model

The process model is conceptualized as six sequential parts or stages of the policy process. It is also termed the 'textbook approach' to policy making (Jordan and Adelle, 2012). The six stages tend to link as a cycle, though they may not necessarily develop in a logical order. The six stages of the process model are illustrated in Figure 2.6.

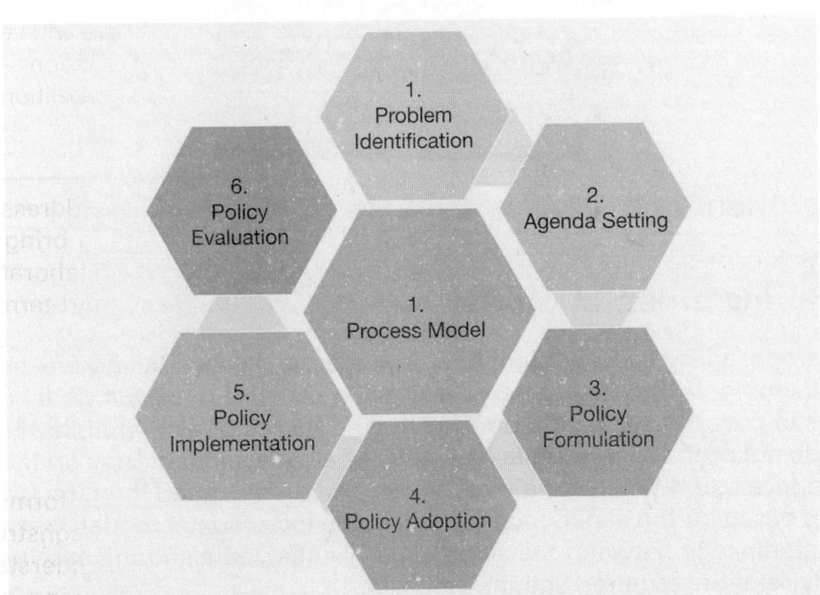

FIGURE 2.6 The Process Model of Public Policy Formulation

The above six stages of the policy process model are discussed in detail in section 1 of this chapter.

4.2 Rationalist Model

The two main characteristics of the rational model are goal specificity and formalization.

The rationalist model is also termed as Decision-Making Model. The rational approach emphasizes choosing the best option among all the policy alternatives based on logical thinking. This model is more concerned about organizing the policy-making structure based on undistorted information flow, accurate feedback, and value systems. Dror (1989) suggested five main steps be adhered to in policy making: (1) Identify the objectives, (2) Identify alternative approaches leading to the same objective, (3) Predict consequences of alternatives, (4) Evaluate the consequences, and (5) Select the alternative maximizes objectives.

The rationality concept underscores that policymakers must behave in a logical order in their decision-making. ***The rational model is identified with two main characteristics viz., goal specificity and formalization***. Several early theorists emphasized this model because of its rational perspective on rules, jurisdiction, constraints, performance, authority, directives, programs, and coordination of policymaking.

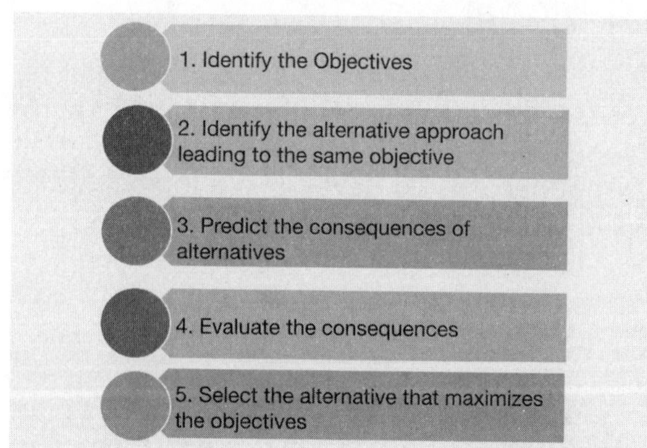

FIGURE 2.7 Rationalist Model of Public Policy Formulation

4.3 Incremental Model

As proposed by Charles Lindblom, in his book 'Policy-Making Process', the Incremental model has become popular because it reflects what happens in government (Lindblom, 1968). Lindblom argues that policymakers do not prefer to formulate new policies all of a sudden. They prefer to introduce a new policy on a small scale, and then expand them on large scale based on the experience gained. In the Incremental model, there is an interlinkage between the selection of values/goals and the empirical analysis of the required action.

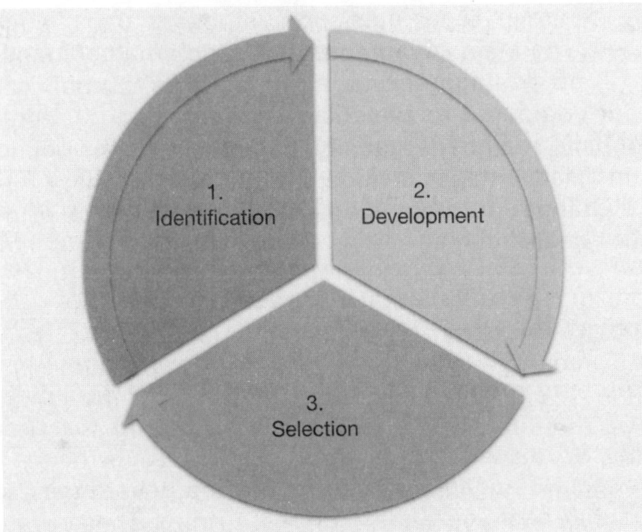

FIGURE 2.8 Incremental Model of Public Policy Formulation

Under the Incremental model, policies are extended slowly but steadily, after experiencing the functioning and practicability of the policy. The incremental model separates the policymaking process into minor steps. These steps are identification, development, and selection. The criticism against the Incremental model is that the policymakers are not rational as they consider limited alternatives in each step of the policy process. Incrementalism predicts that the legitimacy of previous policies will be accepted because the consequences of new programs cannot be predicted.

Policies are extended slowly but steadily, after experiencing the functioning and practicability of the policy in the Incremental model.

Credit: dedek / Shutterstock

INCREMENTALISM: TAKING SMALL STEPS TOWARD BIG GOALS. GETTY IMAGES

The Incremental Model is extensively used in democracies. However, Yehezkel Dror criticizes the Incremental model as a self-fulfilling prophecy as there is limited analysis. Some of the examples of the Incremental

The Incremental model is extensively used in democracies.

model are minimum age legislation, smoking bans, environmental standards, etc. The main advantages of the Incremental model are (1) its efficiency, (2) no wastage of time and resources, (3) politically expedient, (4) safer compared to sweeping changes, and (5) Incrementalism reduces conflicts, maintains stability, and preserves the political system. Some of the disadvantages include, and (a) beagle fallacy (failure to account for a change), (b) baby steps might face the risk of missing the overall policy goals

4.4 Group Model

According to the Group theory several groups are engaged in controlling the government to promote the policies that best serve their interest groups.

The Group theory model seeks to sustain societal equilibrium by balancing the welfare of several groups. ***According to the Group theory, public policy is an outcome of group tussle.*** Group theory states that several groups are engaged in controlling the government to promote the policies that best serve their interest groups. These groups can be political interest groups and can influence policymakers regarding societal demands. Most often, the policy will manifest the concern of the predominant group. Essentially, in the course of group struggle, the needs and pleas of the stronger pressure groups influence the public policy formulation.

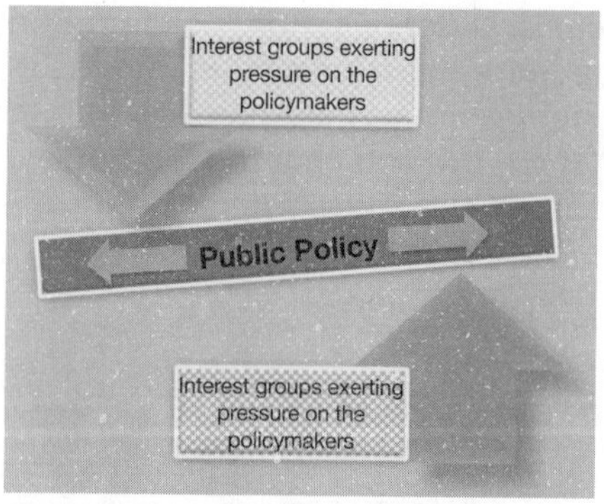

FIGURE 2.9 Group Theory Model of Public Policy Formulation

Group theory views that the task of the political system is to manage groups conflict by (a) determining rules of the game in group struggle, (b) managing compromises and balancing the varied interests, (c) endorsing compromises as public policy, and (d) implementing such compromises as public policy.

4.5 Elite Model

Public policy formation happens at the top echelons of society; hence it is top-down and not bottom-up.

Proposed by Italian political scientist, Gaetano Mosca, the Elite model of public policy states that ***elites formulate the public policies according to their preferences, ethics, and values.*** According to this theory, the ruling powerful elite (generally the political executive) makes the public policies. Public policy formation happens at the top echelons of society; hence it is top-down and not bottom-up. The Elite theory observes that the common masses are not heard due to their limited influence in the policymaking even though the policy is made for them. Because the powerful elite decides the policy formulation. The elite are a minuscule minority but an economically powerful section of the society wields greater power to decide the policies than the democratic power. Figure 2.10 shows the Elite model of public policy-making.

The major characteristics of the Elite model of public policy formulation are: (1) society is divided into a few who have power and many who do not have power, (2) the many who do not have power do not decide public policy, (3) elites influence masses more than masses influence elites, and (4) since the public policy reflects the values of the elite.

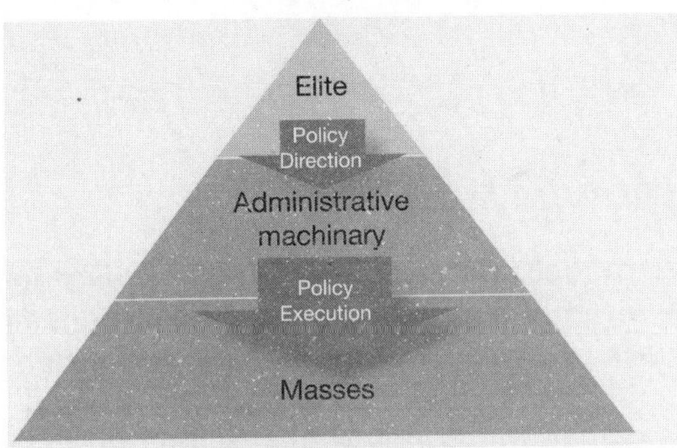

FIGURE 2.10 Elite Model of Public Policy Formulation

4.6 Public Choice Theory Model

The public choice theory model of public policy states that the perceived self-interest of the elected officials and government officials influence policymaking because of their official authority. Nobel laureate James M. Buchanan developed the public choice theory with Gordon Tullock. This model explains how public policy-making results from the actions of few elected individuals, or self-interested government policy actors. The main features of this model are (i) it is anti-bureaucratic, (ii) discourages bureaucratic administration, and (iii) promotes institutional pluralism. Some of the assumptions of the public choice model of public policy formulation are "***politics without romance***", public officials as self-interested actors, rent-seeking, and concentrated benefits, diffused costs.

The public choice theory model states that the perceived self-interest of the elected officials and government officials influence policymaking because of their official authority

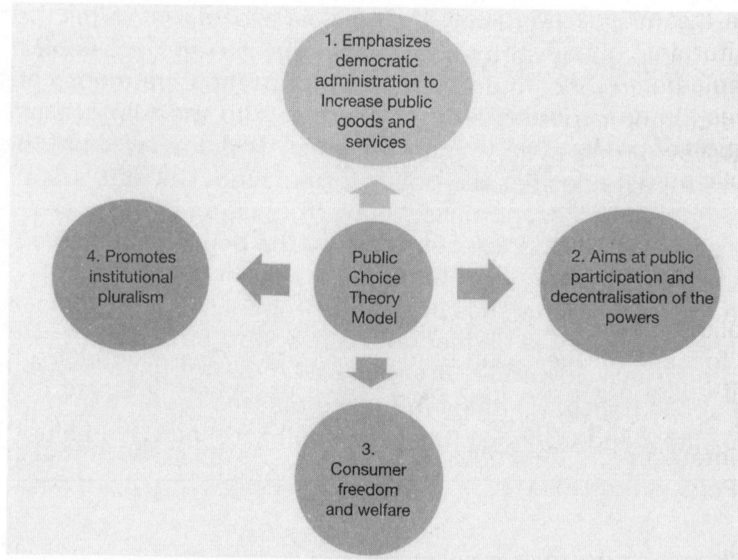

FIGURE 2.11 Public Choice Theory Model of Public Policy Formulation

4.7 Institutional Model

The institutional model contends that ***public policy formulation is an outcome of the internal agendas of the government institutions rather than the impact of external compulsions and influences***. According to this model, public policymaking is made by several individuals and groups like the Cabinet, the Prime Minister, the Members of Parliament, bureaucrats, and leaders of interest groups. The major characteristics of the Institutional model are (1) legitimacy: government imparts legal authority to policy, (2) shared values: the policy gets universal character, (3) enforcement: government can enforce legal penalties on policy violators, and (4) stability: institutional mechanisms provide stability to the policy, and (5) structure: the government provides a formal structure.

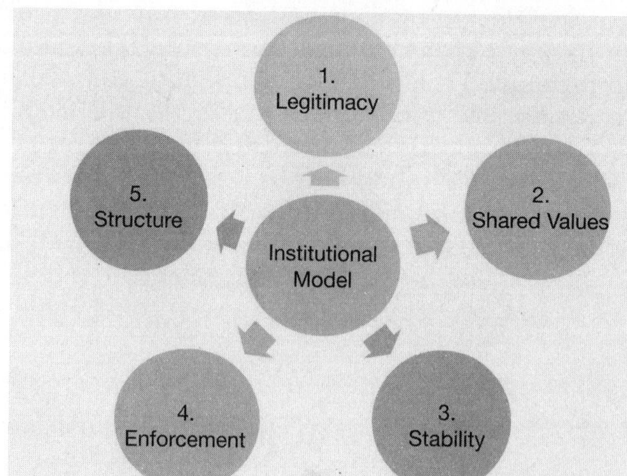

FIGURE 2.12 Institutional Model of Public Policy Formulation

The Institutional Model of Public Policy observes public policy as an institutional output. Because, public policy is decided, implemented, and implemented by the government institutions, the constitution establishes the fundamental institutional structure for policy making, and separation of powers, checks and balances, and federalism have effects on public policy.

According to the Institutional model, public policy as an institutional output.

4.8 Polis Model

The Polis model of public policy is a community-driven policy-making model focused on the common good. Deborah Stone defines a Polis as a small entity but large enough to have essential elements of politics (Stone, 2012, p.19). Groups and organizations are the building blocks of social interaction in the Polis model. A community is the unit of analysis in the Polis model. Examples of polis are a neighborhood, a small town, etc.

Polis model focuses on the community with concepts like altruism, self-interest, shared interests, loyalty, cooperation, and the common good. Polis model believes in the collective will, intention, and effort of the people in the communities. Altruism and self-interest are the motivations in the Polis model (Stone, 2012). Shared interests constitute the public interest in this model. ***Policies are made keeping in view the community's interests.*** Ideas and alliances; the quest for power, self and group welfare, and community interest are the main sources of change. The nature of social interaction in the Polis model is cooperation and competition. Influence from other individuals, groups, and society act as the source of ideas and preferences in this model. An important feature of this model is that laws of passion make things work.

Polis model believes in the collective will, intention, and effort of the people in the communities.

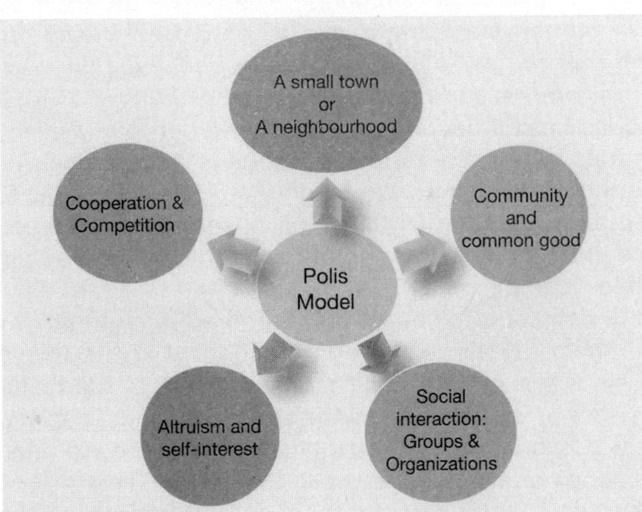

FIGURE 2.13 Polis Model of Public Policy Formulation

Polis model:
Ambiguity.
Non-decisions.
Hobson's choice.
Issue framing.
Labeling of alternatives.

The Polis model on the other hand is more focused on community and concepts such as shared interests, Altruism, self-interest, loyalty, co-operation, etc. It promotes cooperation and the good of the community as a whole. The criteria of decision-making in the Polis model are loyalty, family interest, and public interest. Some of the disadvantages of the Polis model are (1) There is ambiguity and incompleteness like information, (2) The main conflict is between self-interest vs. common interest, (3) The concept of public-interest differs from that self-interest, and (4) Difficult to change the behavior of the masses to shift from the individualist nature to community culture.

4.9 Game Theory Model

Public policymaking can be explained through the concept of social dilemmas.

Game theory is a method of contemplating strategic interactions between people. Game theory has gained importance in the fields of economics, political science, international relations, psychology, and various other disciplines that study the complexities of human interaction in decision-making. During the last decades, with the addition of more concepts and complex, real-life situations Game theory has evolved immensely.

It is interesting to know how game theory is used in public policy formulation. Public policymaking can be explained through the concept of social dilemmas. ***A social dilemma is a situation of collective action in which outcomes of the Nash equilibrium are below the Pareto optimality.*** According to Robyn Dawes two properties can be observed in the concept of social dilemmas: (i) every individual gets a better payoff for a socially-defective choice than for a socially-cooperative choice, irrespective of what the other individuals do, (ii) but all individuals will be better off if all of them cooperate than defecting (Dawes & Robyn, 1980).

In the field of public policymaking, the Game theory assumes that outcomes of human interactions can be explained based on the principles of rational choices by the players in policy-making like the people, the organizations, and the governments (Schelling, 2010). The game theory includes both independent and interdependent decision-making in organizations where the outcome depends on the decisions of two or more autonomous players. No single decision-maker has full control over other outcomes. Thomas Schelling observes game theory can explain how people tend to choose solutions in the absence of communication (Schelling, 2010).

Public policies are often made and enforced in multi-actor networks.

Public policies are often made and enforced in multi-actor networks. Since Game theory deals with the interaction of actors (players) helps in the analysis of the public policy process. Some of the features of the Game theory are (i) Game theory is the study of rational decisions in situations in which two or more participants have choices to make and the outcome depends on the choices made by each. (ii) The best outcome in game theory depends upon what others do. (iii) Decision-makers are involved in interdependent choices. (iv) Decision-makers must adjust their conduct to reflect their desires and also their expectations about what others will do. Thus, the Game theory model is useful as a rational choice in explaining the public policy process during competitive situations.

5. A FRAMEWORK FOR PUBLIC POLICY ANALYSIS

Policy analysis is a systematic investigation of available policy options based on evidence.

The term 'policy analysis' first coined by Charles Lindblom in 1958, has been in wide use since the evolution of the discipline of Public policy as a policy science. Policy analysis is a systematic investigation of available policy options based on evidence. It involves the evaluation of policy issues supported with evidence in the form of facts and statistics about the impact of the public policies. Put simply, ***the prime objective of policy analysis is to evaluate to what extent the public policies have met their goals.*** In its endeavor, policy analysis uses the methods and tools of social science in analyzing public policy efficacy. In doing so, policy analysts require skill sets of problem-solving, the ability to find alternate options, and carry out a scientific analysis.

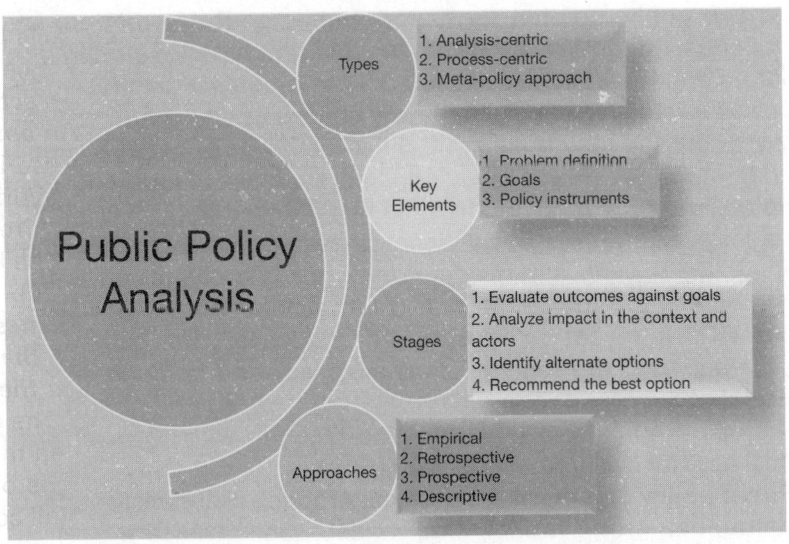

FIGURE 2.14 Public Policy Analysis Components

Three approaches to policy analysis are identified as (1) the analysis-centric, (2) the policy process, and (3) the meta-policy approach.

Policy analysis plays a crucial role in helping government officials understand how the socio-economic and political conditions have changed and know whether the policies are meeting the changing needs of society. The fundamental components of public policy analysis include (1) a problem definition, (2) goals to be achieved, and (3) the policy instruments required to solve the problem and accomplish the set goals. Three approaches to policy analysis are identified as (1) the analysis-centric, (2) the policy process, and (3) the meta-policy approach. From the theoretical perspective, some of the familiar approaches to policy analysis are elite theory, group theory, political systems theory and institutionalism, policy output analysis, incremental theory, and rational-choice theory. All these models are discussed in the previous section.

An example of policy analysis can be how the employment guarantee scheme has performed in India. For instance, the policy analysis of the Mahatma Gandhi National Rural Employment Guarantee Act by some agencies reveals that most applicants who apply to be enrolled for the guaranteed 100-day employment program did not get work and payment on time. This type of empirical policy analysis is based on facts and statistics.

6. CONCLUSION

This chapter has provided an overview of the public policy processes, models, and policy analysis. We discussed the different stages of the public policy process and how important it is to know the policy process. Corporate political activities have gained attention in recent decades because of the increasing role of corporates in public policy making. Corporate political activities influence public policy in different stages like public opinion formation, public policy formation, and the post-adoption stage. We discussed the different types of strategies under corporate political activities like Reactive strategies, Proactive strategies, Defensive strategies, and Anticipatory strategies.

We discussed how business political activities affect public policy as we understood the role of lobbying, different types of lobbying, lobbying spending, and how lobbying in India has affected public policy. Further, we understood the role of political action committees' contributions in public policy making and its different types like connected PACs, nonconnected PACs, leadership PACs, partnership PACs, super PACs, and Hybrid PACs. In recent decades, as policy advocacy has gained momentum, we analyzed the role of policy advocacy and its types in affecting public policy.

We also understood how coalition-building as a form of business political activity impacts policymaking.

Public policy models like the process model, rationalist model, incremental model, group model, elite model, public choice model, institutional model, polis model, and the game theory model. Finally, we could get an overview of public policy analysis.

Summary

- Public policymaking is an ongoing process. It is dynamic and continuous in identifying and countering the public problems in an interacting approach with optimal solutions with new solutions or reforming the existing ones.
- In the context of competing priorities or focused events, broadly four factors the political environment, the economic environment, the socio-cultural environment, and the administrative environment determine the public policy process
- Lasswell identified stages of the public policy process are (1) intelligence, (2) recommendation, (3) prescription, (4) invocation, (5) application, (6) appraisal, and (7) termination
- According to Thomas Dye, the policy process is categorized into six stages: (1) Problem Identification, (2) Agenda Setting, (3) Policy Formulation, (4) Policy Legitimation, (5) Policy Implementation, and (6) Policy Evaluation.
- Lasswell envisaged the policy process as a sequence of steps in a life-cycle model.
- The public policy process is a five-step multi-stage process.
- The problem identification stage involves agenda setting where the identified problems evolve as issues of public interest.
- Policy formulation is the stage where the demands of the public are transformed into policies
- Three broad types of Policy formulation are Routine formulations, Analogous formulations, and Creative formulations.
- Policy adoption by the institutions of public authority legitimizes the policy effect.
- Policy implementation involves bringing into effect the rules and regulations provided in the policy, or delivering the services, providing the necessities as per the respective policies.
- Policy evaluation is a systematic process of assessing the content, design, implementation process, goals, and policy outcomes.
- Factors like interest groups, non-governmental organizations, lobbying, and corporate political activity tend to influence public policy-making.
- Corporate political activity (CPA) is a corporate attempt to shape and influence public policy as its corporate strategy to suit its objectives.
- Corporates using CPA benefit in terms of cost of borrowing, investment opportunities, obtaining licenses, production-linked incentives, export, and import permissions, etc.
- CPA influences public policy making in three stages: (1) Influencing public opinion, (2) Public policy formation, and (3) Post-adoption.
- Political strategies under CPA are Reactive strategies, Proactive strategies, Defensive strategies, and Anticipatory strategies.
- Businesses involve in political activities largely due to two broad reasons: (i) competitive reasons, and (ii) economic reasons.
- Lobbying types are direct lobbying, (2) grassroots lobbying, and (3) electoral lobbying.
- Lobbying in India is done by industry organizations.
- The purpose of Political Action Committees (PACs) is to raise donations and distribute them to promote the political goals of its members.
- Policy advocacy is the action of the individuals or group of individuals, or network of organizations involving negotiations, mediations, litigations, dialogues, and communications that influence the decision-makers to act in favor of their policy preferences.
- Successful coalition-building depends on (1) problem identification and description, (2) Relationship building and stakeholder mapping, (3) Forming committed core membership, (4) Establishing credibility, (5) Expansion through credit networks, and (6) Sustainable transformation through collective action.
- Policy analysis is a systematic investigation of available policy options based on evidence.

Key Words

Public policy process	Legalized bribery	Political action committees (PAC)	Process model
Policy model	Public opinion	Connected PACs	Rational model
Policy orientation	Political strategy	Non-connected PACs	Incremental model
Problem identification	Reactive strategy	Leadership PACs	Group model
Policy formulation	Proactive strategy	Partnership PACs	Elite model
Policy adoption	Defensive strategy	Super PACs	Public choice model
Policy implementation	Anticipatory strategy	Hybrid PACs	Institutional model
Policy evaluation	Business political activities	Policy advocacy	Polis model
Routine formulation	Lobbying	Self-advocacy	Game theory model
Analogous formulation	Direct lobbying	Co-advocacy	Social dilemma
Creative formulation	Grassroots lobbying	Public advocacy	Policy elements
Policy structure	Electoral lobbying	Coalition-building	Policy instruments
Corporate Political Activities	Lobbyist	Public opinion	Policy analysis

Questions

A. Quick Check

1) Discuss the statement: "Public policymaking is an ongoing process."
2) Briefly discuss the Public Policy Process.
3) Discuss Lasswell's conceptual map of the policy-making process.
4) Why do the firms resort to corporate political activity?
5) Can we equate lobbying to bribery?.
6) Explain the role of corporate political activities in influencing public policy making.
7) Explain in brief the business political activities in the context of the public policy process.
8) Define and describe policy advocacy in the context of public policy.
9) Discuss the advantages and disadvantages of coalitions in the public policy process.
10) Briefly describe the framework of public policy analysis.

B. Explore

1) Consider a policy in the Indian context and analyze it using the popular five-stage process of public policy.
2) "India lacks a free and transparent policy structure in making lobbying unethical." Discuss this statement in detail.
3) Discuss in detail the types of political action committees (PACs).
4) Why do coalitions wield more power and influence in the public policy process?
5) Discuss and compare the different models of public policy. Which of the models is more suited to the Indian context?

References

Anderson, E James (1975). Public Policy-Making. London: Thomas Nelson & Sons Ltd., @ 1975

Anderson, J.E. (1984). Public Policy-Making. New York: CBS College Publishing. Rinehart and Winston, Inc. (3rd Edition).

Charles E. Lindblom (1968). The Policy-Making Process. New Jersey: Prentice Hall Inc.

CommGAP (2008). 'Coalition Building', Communication for Governance and Accountability Program (CommGAP), World Bank, Washington DC

Dalrymple, William (2019). The Anarchy: The East India Company, Corporate Violence, and the Pillage of an Empire. First Edition | Bloomsbury Publishing (September 10, 2019).

Dawes, R (1980). Social Dilemmas. Annual Review of Psychology, 31(1), 169-193.

Dror, Yehezkel (1989). Public Policymaking Reexamined. 1st Edition | Routledge, New York (October 25, 2017).

Dye, T.R. (2004). Understanding Public Policy. Englewood Cliffs: Prentice-Hall.

Hillman, A., G. Keim, and D. Schuler (2004). Corporate Political Activity: A Review and Research Agenda, *Journal of Management*, 30(6), 837-857.

Hogwood, W Brian., and Lewis, A Gunn (1984). Policy analysis for the real world. Oxford [Oxfordshire]; New York: Oxford University Press, 1984

Howlett, M. (2009). Policy analytical capacity and evidence-based policy-making: Lessons from Canada. *Canadian Public Administration*, 52 (2), 153-175.

IGNOU School of Law. CPI-102 Redressal of Consumer Grievances: Role of Various Stakeholders. Block 2: ROLE OF INDUSTRY BODIES AND VOLUNTARY CONSUMER ORGANISATIONS (VCOs). Accessed from https://egyankosh.ac.in on December 15, 2023.

Jones, C.O. (1977). An Introduction to the Study of Public Policy, 2nd Edition. North Scituate, Massachusetts: Duxbury Press.

Jordan, Andrew., and Camilla, Adelle. (2012). Environmental Policy in the EU Actors, institutions, and processes. 3rd Edition | Routledge, London (August 20, 2012).

Kotler, P. (1986). Mega marketing, *Harvard Business Review*, March-April, pp.117-124.

Lasswell, Harold D. (1951). "The Policy Orientation." In The Policy Sciences: *Recent Developments in Scope and Method*, eds. Daniel Lerner and Harold D. Lasswell. Stanford: Stanford University Press.

Lasswell, H.D (1956). The Decision Process: Seven Categories of Functional Analysis. College Park, Maryland: the University of Maryland, @ 1956

Lawton, T., McGuire, S., Rajwani, T., (2013). Corporate political activity: a literature review and research agenda. *International Journal of Management Reviews*, 15 (1), 86–105.

May, Judith V., and Aaron B Wildavsky (1978). The Policy cycle. 5th Edition | Beverly Hills: Sage Publications, ©1978.

Mellahi, K., Frynas, J. G., Sun, P., & Siegel, D. (2016). A Review of the Nonmarket Strategy Literature: Toward a Multi-Theoretical Integration. *Journal of Management*, 42(1), 143–173.

Michael, Hill., and Frederic, Varone. (2021). The Public Policy Process. 8th Edition | Routledge (March 31, 2021). Copyright Year 2021

Nakamura, T Robert (1987). The Textbook Policy Process And Implementation Research. *Review of Policy Research*, 7 (1), 142-154.

Nyberg, Daniel. (2021). Corporations, Politics, and Democracy: Corporate political activities as political corruption. *Organization Theory*, 2 (1), 1-24.

Oliver C., and Holzinger I. (2008). The Effectiveness of Strategic Political Management: A Dynamic Capabilities Framework. *Academy of Management Review*, 33 (2), 496-520.

Parsons, Wayne. (1995). Public Policy: An Introduction to the Theory and Practice of Policy Analysis. Cheltenham: Edward Elgar Publishing Ltd. @1995

Schelling, T.C (2010). Game theory: a practitioner's approach, *Economics, and Philosophy*, 26, 27–46.

Srivastava, D. (2021). All about lobbying in India with reference to other countries. iPleaders blogpost (January 12, 2021). Accessed from https://blog.ipleaders.in on December 12, 2023.

Stone Deborah (2012). Policy Paradox: The Art of Political Decision-Making. 3rd Edition | W. W. Norton & Company

Further Readings

Bardach, Eugene, and Eric M. Patashnik. 2015. Practical Guide for Policy Analysis: The Eightfold Path to More Effective Problem Solving. 5th ed. Washington, DC: CQ Press.

Birkland, Thomas A. 2016. An Introduction to the Policy Process: Theories, Concepts, and Models of Public Policy Making. 4th ed. New York: Routledge.

Dunn, William N., 2004, Public Policy Analysis: An Introduction, Upper Saddle, N.J.: Pearson

Lawrence D. Brown and Lawrence R. Jacobs (2008). The Private Abuse of the Public Interest: Market Myths and Policy Muddles | Chicago: University of Chicago Press

Paul Chaney (2011). Equality and Public Policy: Exploring the Impact of Devolution in the UK | Cardiff: University of Wales Press.

CHAPTER 3

Political Economy of Public Policy

The goal of this chapter is to provide an interesting overview of the political economy of public policy. As we proceed in this chapter, we will first discuss what is political economy. Thereafter, we will study the role of the state in public policy and particularly focus on the political and economic systems, the instruments of the state, and the changing role of the state. Understanding the different forms of government helps in appreciating their role in public policy. Accordingly, we discuss the presidential, parliamentary, unitary, federal, and confederation forms of government. It is interesting to know the nexus between the state and the markets. In this context, we discuss the conflictual and Unconflictual relationships, utilitarianism, and the relationship between the state and the economy. The most significant role of the state in policy making is in the area of economic development and welfare. Hence, we discuss the concept and relevance of a developmental state. In this regard, we will discuss the attributes of a developmental state, particularly the regulatory, administrative, technical, and extractive capacities of the developmental state. Continuing with the same theme, we discuss the economic rationale for state intervention in the economy in the context of market failure, public goods, externalities, asymmetric information, adverse selection, and moral hazard. We also study the functions of the state like minimal, intermediate, and activist functions. This section concludes with a narration of the evolution of the role of the state in India.

Section 1: The Political Economy

Section 2: The Role of The State

Section 3: Forms of Government

Section 4: The State and the Markets

Section 5: Developmental State

1. THE POLITICAL ECONOMY

The study of political economy has assumed far greater importance in recent times as it explores the interaction of political forces and economic activities in a society where the role of the state in the economy has grown in multitudes. It helps in understanding the relationships between society and the government in a holistic approach from a multi-disciplinary perspective as it investigates how economic systems are intertwined in both political systems and society. In a way, the study of political economy provides us with a clear understanding of why governments do what they do the society. The dynamic interactions between society and the political system have myriad implications on public policymaking which in turn affects the individuals and communities in the society. In this section, we find specific answers to the question - what is political economy? Besides, we will understand the components of political economy, political economy framework, and approach to political economy analysis.

1.1 What is Political Economy?

Political economy is the interrelationship between political policies and economic processes, and their influence on social institutions.

A straightforward answer is that political economy studies the interaction of politics and economics. Essentially, the political economy of a state or a nation implies how the political systems, legal systems, and economic systems dynamically interact and influence one another in achieving the economic wellbeing of the nation. Since economics is the study of the allocation of scarce resources in society, political economy explains how the confluence of political and economic factors impacts the lives of the people.

Defining political economy has been attempted by several political scientists. However, a simple dictionary definition of political economy states that ***it is the interrelationship between political policies and economic processes, and their influence on social institutions***. Regarded as the father of political economy, Adam Smith was the first to explore the topic of political economy in his most celebrated work, "***The Wealth of Nations***." Providing a comprehensive explanation of the market society, Smith states that the political economy looks at the market society as a decentralized, well-governed system where the prices coordinate the efficient allocation of resources in a competitive society. ***In the analysis of Adam Smith, what oeconomy is in a family, political economy is in a state or nation***. However, from the real-world perspective, Political Economy is inextricably intertwined with many other disciplines of Social Philosophy.

ADAM SMITH 1723-1790

The term political economy brings together into the limelight two critical disciplines, politics and economy. It is political as it involves the use of state power which is derived from politics. It is economics because it deals with the allocation of scarce resources to meet unlimited wants. Political economist Fran Stilwell defines political economy as a tool for understanding what shapes the material conditions in which we live and explains the factors shaping production, distribution, exchange, growth, and crises in capitalist economies (Stilwell, 2011)

According to Adam Smith, what oeconomy is in a family, and political economy is in a state or nation.

Simply put, political economy is the study of how political systems influence the economic systems and thereby the economic outcomes. The key concern of political economy is to explain the connection between governments and individuals, and in turn how public policy impacts society. ***Political economy is an interdisciplinary subject, that draws its contributions from the philosophies of politics, sociology, and economics.***

1.2 Components of Political Economy

In general, three types of political economy are well-known: (i) capitalism, (ii) socialism, and (iii) communism. Capitalism also termed *Market Economy* is an economic system in which production and prices are determined by unrestricted competition between privately owned businesses. Socialism also understood as *Command Economy* is a system where the government, rather than the free market, determines what goods should be produced, how much should be produced, and the price at which the goods are offered for sale. Capitalism often referred to as *Mixed Economy* is an economic system in which both the private enterprise and a degree of state monopoly (usually in public services, defense, infrastructure, and basic industries) coexist.

The three types of political economies are market economy, command economy, and mixed economy.

The political economy behavior is shaped by the interests (political interests), ideas (ideology), and the institutions (both informal and formal including the governments) in the society. To be more precise, the following represent the main components of political economy:

1. *Markets* – interaction between supply and demand that functions to allocate resources
2. *Property* – ownership of goods and services
3. *Public Goods* – goods provided and/or secured by the state
4. *Social Expenditures* – public expenditure for social welfare
5. *Taxation* – use of taxation policies for proper distribution of economic wealth of the nation
6. *Money, Inflation, and Unemployment* – use of money for controlling inflation and providing employment to the people
7. *Regulation* – rules or orders to set the boundaries of given procedures
8. *Trade* – access to goods and services from foreign states

The political economy analysis encompasses observing the dynamic interaction between structures, institutions, and actors

An important characteristic of political economy is the assumption that individuals are both self-seeking and rational in their behavior.

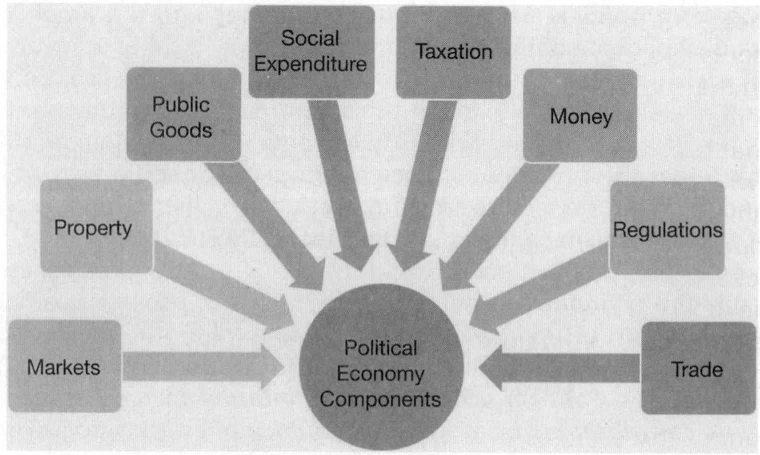

FIGURE 3.1 Political Economy Components

1.3 Political Economy Framework

Political economy assumes that resources are allocated not based on relative efficiency or merit but according to power. ***The political economy framework includes the political actors, the political actors' interests, and the political mechanisms and constraints.***

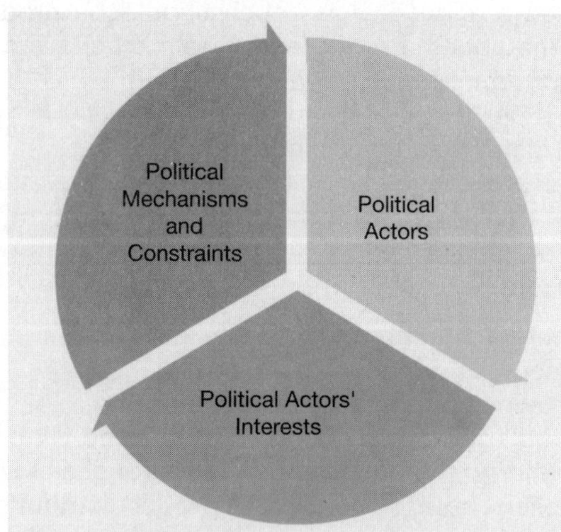

FIGURE 3.2 Political Economy Framework

Drazen identifies *four broad types of Political actors viz., Policymakers, Citizenry, Selectorate, and Coalitions.* Policymakers are the ones who make the policies using their power to do so. Citizenry represents the citizens who are impacted by the public policies even though they do not have a direct say in policymaking. Selectorate is the group that selects leaders or who controls the instruments of power that enable a leader to remain in office. The coalition represents the citizenry who come together to exert pressure on the policymakers to make favorable policies (Drazen 2008 p. 24). Essentially, policy actors strive for influencing the outcome of a policy process through either direct or indirect action.

The political actors' interests include the general societal welfare acquisition and/or retention of power. Political mechanisms include the systems and processes meant to select the political representation for policymaking, and the constraints include the formal rules that govern and control the systems and processes of political selections (Drazen, 2008)).

1.4 Political Economy Analysis

Political economy analysis studies power and money allocation among individuals and diverse groups in a society. It also gazes at the mechanisms that create, sustain, and change these interactions throughout time. The main goal of political economy analysis is to understand how politics and economics interact, in order to create better laws and programs. Political behavior is influenced by interests, ideologies, and institutions such as governments. This method is based on that idea discussed earlier.

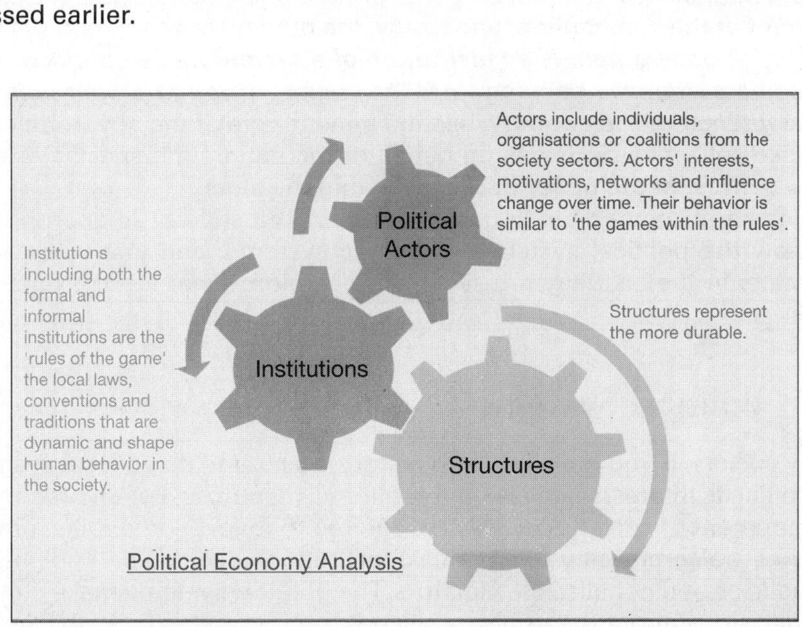

FIGURE 3.3 Political Economic Analysis

A political system is comprised of four major components like political institutions, political elites, masses, and the political culture.

The political economy analysis encompasses observing the dynamic interaction between structures, institutions, and actors (stakeholders). Structures represent the more durable specifics of the framework. Institutions including both the formal and informal institutions are the 'rules of the game', the local laws, conventions, and traditions that are dynamic and shape human behavior in society. Informal institutions too are just as important as formal institutions. Actors include individuals, organizations, or coalitions from the social sectors. Actors' interests, motivations, networks, and influence change over time. Their behavior is similar to 'the games within the rules'. The tools of political economy analysis help us to design and execute programs that have realistic and achievable objectives and probably achieve the expected outcomes (DFID, 2009). DFID identifies three levels of undertaking political economy analysis. They are at the Macro-level or country analysis, Sector-level analysis, and Problem-driven analysis.

2. THE ROLE OF THE STATE

Before beginning the discussion on the role of the state, let us first understand what a state and a government are. ***A state is a set of political organizations vested with ultimate powers to make collective decisions that are binding on the entire society and enforce them through the legitimate use of monopoly power.*** For instance, the parliament and its committees deliberate and decide on the policies, the government adopts the policies, the judiciary interprets the legality of the policies in the spirit of the constitution, and finally, the bureaucracy implements the policies. ***A government is an institution of a system made up of a group of people authorized people to run the country through proper policies in the interest of the nation.*** While the general role of the government is to make collective decisions on behalf of the nation, the specific role is to make most of the policy decisions within the state.

For an apt understanding of the role of the state, it is appropriate to know the political systems, economic systems, and instruments of the state. In the ensuing sub-section, we explore what are the political systems.

2.1 Political Systems

Every society, if you look back into history, has found its political system to protect its interests and allocate economic resources. For an organized development of society, people are required to follow some rules for the good of the community. The political institutions decide and implement the policies and penalize the violators. The political systems make collective decisions about the rights, privileges, duties, and responsibilities of the citizens for the systematic functioning of the state.

A political system is a set of recognized legitimate institutions that represent a "government" or a "state." A political system is comprised of four major components like political institutions, political elites, masses, and the political culture. According to Almond and Coleman (1960), the three key roles of a political system are: (1) to preserve and uphold the integrity of the society, (2) to reform and realign the main constituents of socio-economic, and socio-religious systems for realizing the collective goals of the society, and (3) to defend the honor and sovereignty of the nation from external and internal threats.

Broadly, three types of political systems exist: democracy, authoritarianism, and totalitarianism

On the other hand, Eisenstadt (1966) identifies three major functions of a political system legislative, decision-making, and administrative. David Easton (1953) views that a political system (a) allocates the resources to its citizen through policies, and (b) uses the authority to discipline the people. Broadly, we find three types of political systems that exist in the nations: democracy, authoritarianism, and totalitarianism. However, the classification of the political system can be simply made as democratic and nondemocratic. The democratic political systems are termed democracies. The non-democratic political systems include monarchies, authoritarian, and totalitarian regimes. To be specific, the nondemocratic political systems are monarchies, oligarchies, communism, and dictatorships.

2.1.1 Democracy

The term 'democracy' finds its origin in Greek, 'demos' for "people" and 'karatos' for "rule." The democratic political systems emphasize the 'rule by the consent of the governed.' A democratic political system is one where the citizens are sovereign and exercise control over the government. The people choose their representatives through the elections to form the governments. In a way, democracies empower the people to exercise their political control through elections and limit the powers of the head of the state while separating the powers between the political institutions based on the principles of equity, equality, civil liberty, human rights, and freedom. The well-known definition of democracy is credited to the former president of the US, Abraham Lincoln who stated in his famous 1863 Gettysburg address that "...***government of the people, by the people, for the people***..." Democratic systems tend to provide opportunities for all including the 'haves' and 'have-nots', poor and the downtrodden, rural and urban, educated and uneducated, etc.

Figure 3.4 lists the democratic principles like popular sovereignty, electoral system, public participation, separation of powers, human rights, and rule of law. Based on the operational systems, democracies are classified as direct democracies (pure democracy), representative democracies, participatory democracies, liberal democracies, parliamentary democracies, pluralist democracies, constitutional democracies, and socialist democracies (Jean-Paul, 2018). Figure 3.5 lists the types of democracies across the world.

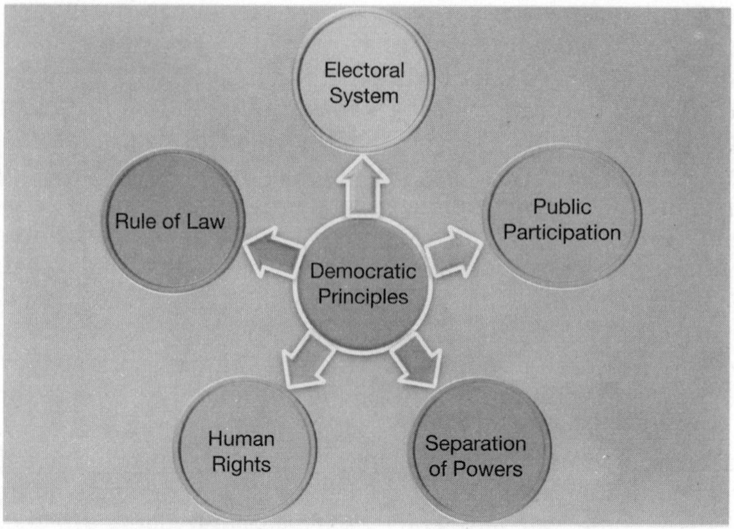

FIGURE 3.4 Principles of Democracy

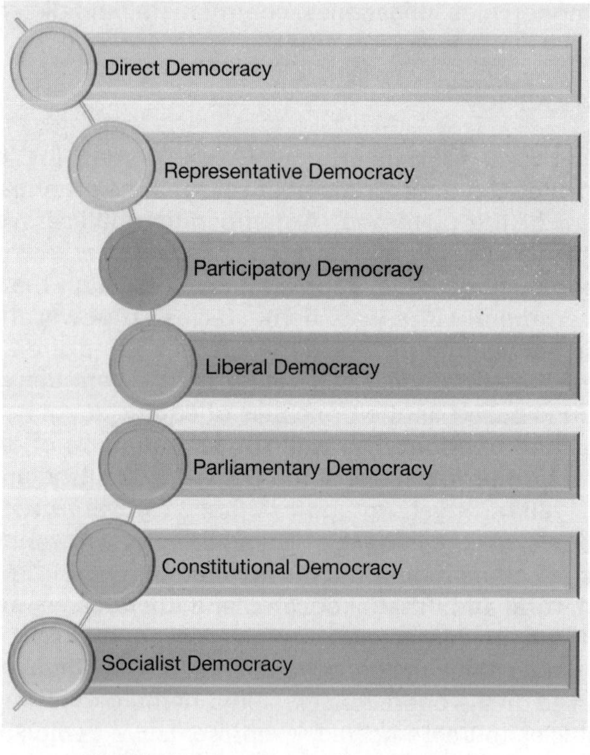

FIGURE 3.5 Types of Democracies

2.1.2 Authoritarianism

Authoritarianism implies that an individual or a group of individuals hold the entire power, and hence restricts or prohibits the popular people's participation in governance, and tends to repress any form of dissent. *Typically, authoritarian governments tend to possess a strong power center and limited political freedom. In these regimes, individual freedom is subordinate to the state and constitutional accountability is absent in the authoritarian regime.* For example, Venezuela under Hugo Chavez and Cuba under Fidel Castro exemplify authoritarian regimes.

The Vatican is an example of a theocratic monarchy where the political power is influenced by the religious principles of Christianity

FIGURE 3.6 Key Characteristics of Authoritarian Political Systems

Broadly, we can identify *four major characteristics of authoritarian regimes like limited political pluralism, emotional acceptance of the people as a necessary evil, minimal social mobilization, and vague executive powers.* Figure 3.6 shows the key characteristics of authoritarian political systems.

Authoritarian governments tend to possess a strong power center and limited political freedom

Monarchy

In monarchies, *total sovereignty is vested in one person as the head of state, called 'monarch', who holds the title and power until death or abdication.* Mostly, monarchs claim their position and power through the right of hereditary succession. Monarchies can be understood as constitutional monarchies and absolute monarchies. The Vatican is an example of a theocratic monarchy where the political power is influenced by the religious principles of Christianity.

Table 3.1 provides the list of some of the world's monarchies in 2022. Most of the constitutional monarchies are found in Europe and Asia.

TABLE 3.1 Some of the World's Monarchies in 2022

No.	Absolute Monarchies	Constitutional Monarchies	Constitutional Monarchies
1	Vatican city	Belgium	Japan
2	Saudi Arabia	Denmark	Jordan
3	Brunei	Netherlands	Malaysia
4	Oman	Norway	Thailand
5	United Arab Emirates	Spain	Bahrain
6	Eswatini	Sweden	Cambodia
7		United Kingdom	Kuwait
8		Bhutan	Qatar

The world's seven absolute monarchies are Vatican city ruled by the Pope, Saudi Arabia ruled by King Salman, Brunei (the Sultan of Brunei), Oman (Haitham binTariq Al Said of Busaid dynasty), United Arab Emirates (Mohammed bin Zayed Al Nahyan), and Eswatini (King Mswati III).

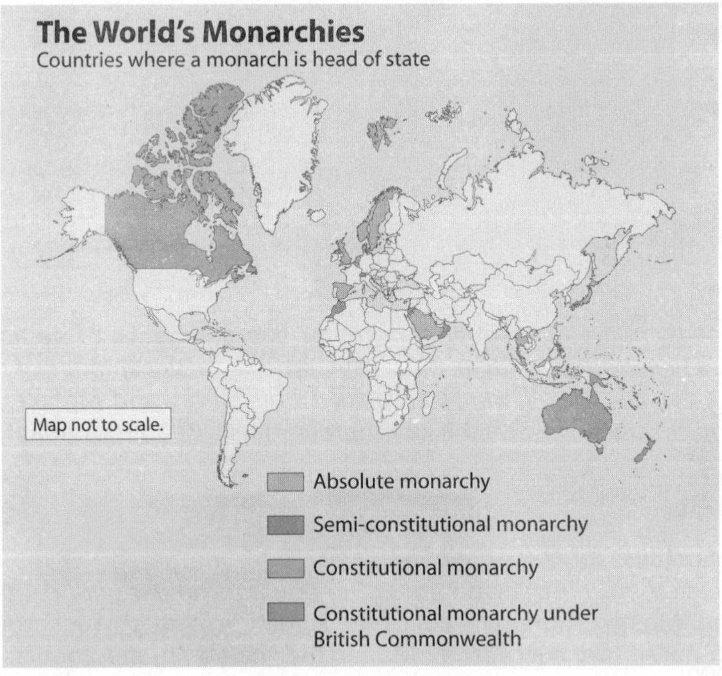

Oligarchy

An oligarchy is a power structure comprised of a few elite individuals or families who control political power in a country. Oligarchies go back to the 600s BCE when an elite group of educated aristocrats rules the Greek city-states of Sparta and Athens. Some examples of modern oligarchies are Russia, China, and Iran.

2.1.3 Totalitarianism

Totalitarian political regimes are inherently politically unstable owing to their leaders' lack of lawful power. Because of this concern of illegitimacy, authoritarian governments are vulnerable to upheaval and political instability. Totalitarianism, as defined by Carl Schmitt in 1927, is an extreme type of authoritarianism marked by excessive repression and total control over citizens' lives. People have little freedom in such institutions and face harsh sanctions even for minor criticism. One person or political party has complete control over all elements of human existence, with rival parties prohibited. Totalitarian regimes include those that are socialist, communist, theocratic, or dictatorial. Collectivism is implemented by total rule in communist systems. Communism is a sociopolitical philosophy that seeks to create a classless society in which all property and wealth are distributed equally.

The difference between communism and socialism is quite blurred and often confused

The difference between communism and socialism is quite blurred and often confused. Table 3.2 lists their differences.

TABLE 3.2 Difference between Communism and Socialism

Attribute	Communism	Socialism
Fundamental Philosophy	Economic contribution to the society from each according to his ability, distributed to each according to his needs.	Economic contribution to the society from each according to his ability, distributed to each according to his contribution.
Economy planned and monitored by	Central government	Central government
Ownership of Economic Resources	Individuals are not allowed hold personal property or assets.	Individuals are allowed to hold their personal property; however, all industrial and production capacity is government-owned, but managed by a democratically elected government.
Distribution of economic resources	Distribution of economic resources to the people is at no charge.	The distribution of economic resources to the people is according to individual ability and contribution.

(Continued)

TABLE 3.2 (Continued)

Attribute	Communism	Socialism
Class Differences	Class is abolished. No worker can earn more than others.	Classes exist but differences are diminished because some people can earn more than others.
Freedom of Religion	Religion is realistically banned or nonexistent publicly.	Freedom of religion is allowed

Dictatorship Regimes

Most historians believe that totalitarian regimes were formed in the frenzied aftermath of World War I. Some of the modern totalitarian leaders were Joseph Stalin of the Soviet Union, Adolf Hitler of Germany, Mao Zedong of China, Benito Mussolini of Italy, Kim Il-sung of North Korea, and Saddam Hussain of Iraq. The Taliban regime in Afghanistan can be considered an example of a totalitarian regime.

Some of the key characteristics of totalitarian political systems are (i) rule of a dictator, (ii) single ruling political party, (iii) Strict censorship of media, (iv) Constant pro-government propaganda, and (v) no public criticism of the government, (vi) unlimited police power, and (vii) ban on certain religious or political groups. While royal rule, is legitimized by blood descent, the socialist, communist, and theocratic regimes are endured because of their ideologies, and dictatorships are tolerated for their emotions.

Planetrulers.com reports that in 2022, there were 57 dictatorships in the world.

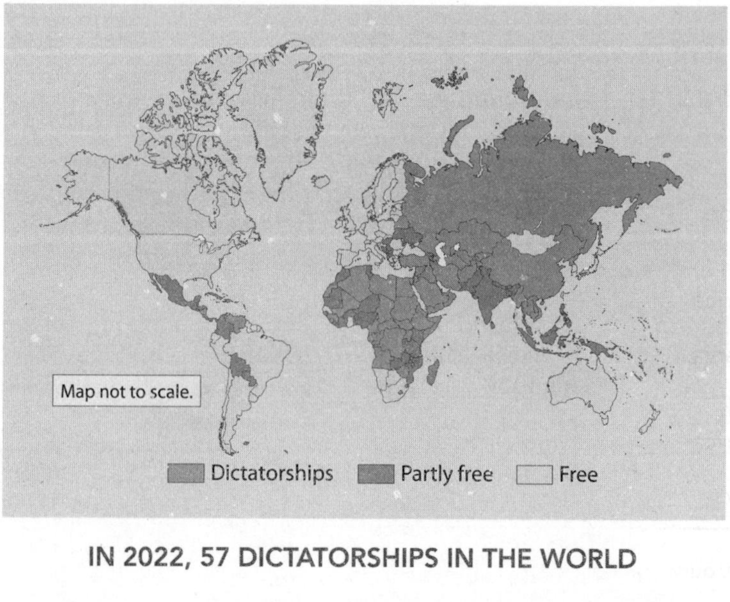

IN 2022, 57 DICTATORSHIPS IN THE WORLD

To sum up, democratic and authoritarian political systems are quite opposite in terms of legitimacy and political freedom. The key takeaways from this subsection are that political systems are broad of two types viz., democracies and authoritarian systems. While democracies respect the will of the people, authoritarian regimes suppress the political freedom of the citizen. In 2020, as per ourworldindata.org, there were 118 democratic and 53 non-democratic countries in the world. Further, worldpopulationreview.com states that in 2020 according to The Democracy Index compiled by the Economist Intelligence Unit racking 60 indicators, Norway is the top democracy with a score of 9.87, the United States scored 7.92, and India scored 6.61.

Figure 3.7 presents the spectrum of political systems observed in the world based on political freedom and legitimacy.

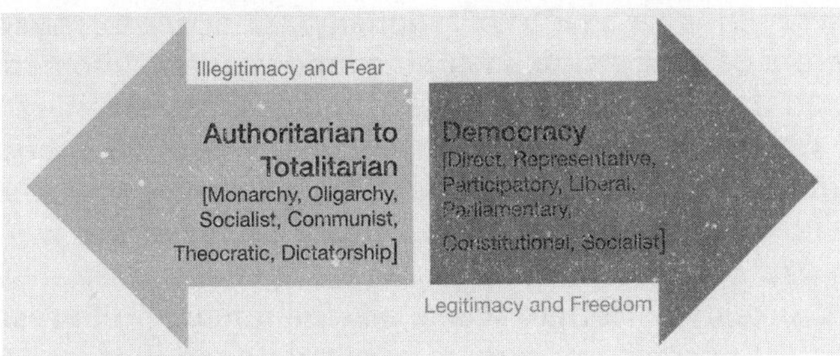

FIGURE 3.7 Spectrum of Political Systems

EXHIBIT 3.1 Number of Democracies and Non-democratic countries in the world

Entity	No. of Non-Democracies			No. of Democracies		
	1800	2020	Change (%)	1800	2020	Change (%)
Africa	1	33	3200	0	20	
Asia	9	33	267	0	13	
Europe	12	2	-83	0	43	
North America	0	4		1	19	1800
Oceania		2		1	12	1100
South America		1			11	
World	22	75	241	2	118	5800

Source: ourworldindata.org

Why are democratic political systems stable compared to the political instability of authoritarian or totalitarian regimes? There can't be a straightforward answer to this question. We need to appreciate the fact that China under an authoritarian communist regime for several decades has been able to provide both economic and political stability. However, many experiences the world over infer that authoritarian regimes have failed to provide stability. On the other hand, several democracies across the world have provided robust political stability.

2.2 Economic Systems

Economic systems regulate the factors of production, including land, capital, labor, and physical resources

An economic system is an approach in which societies organize and allocate available economic resources, services, and goods throughout a geographic region or a country. Essentially, the economic systems regulate the factors of production, including land, capital, labor, and physical resources. All the economies of the world face the problem of scarcity of resources, which limits production activities. *The three economic problems that the economic systems address are (1) what goods will be produced? (2) how will the goods be produced? (3) for whom will the goods be produced?*

What to produce? Human wants are unlimited, while resources are limited. The satisfaction of human wants requires the consumption of goods and services. Only finite amounts of a limited number of goods and services can be produced. The economy must choose its production plan carefully. Hence, what goods and services are to be produced in society and in what quantities? Scarcity of resources makes an economy face trade-offs as producing more of one commodity means producing less of another commodity.

How to produce? A particular quantity of a particular good or service can be produced in many different ways. The economy must choose a particular way of producing the specified amount of goods. A particular way of producing a particular good or service (or a set of goods and services) is called a technique of production. The question 'how to produce' is also known as the problem of choice of techniques.

For whom to produce? After the commodities have been produced, there remains the task of deciding how they will be distributed. Who will consume the produced commodities? "For whom to produce?" is also known as the problem of distribution.

Table 3.3 captures the major characteristics of the economic systems.

Economic systems matter in economic development. The economic systems are broadly organized into three types. Figure 3.8 shows the three well-known types of economic systems viz., Market Economy, Command Economy, and Mixed Economy. A market economy is an economic system in which production and prices are determined by unrestricted competition between privately owned businesses. A Command economy is a system where the government, rather than the free market, determines what goods should be produced, how much should be produced, and the price at which the goods are offered for sale. Finally, a Mixed economy is an economic system in which both the private enterprise and a degree of state monopoly (usually in public services, defense, infrastructure, and basic industries) coexist.

Knowing these economic systems is of great significance in the understanding of public policy. The understanding of economic systems enables us to know the economic systems interact with the public policy process. In the ensuing subsections, we will discuss the three economic systems in detail.

TABLE 3.3 Major Characteristics of Economic Systems

Economy	Market Economy	Command Economy	Mixed Economy
Property rights	Complete protection of property rights	Almost no property rights	Protection incomplete
Investment	Private investment domination	Public investment domination	Both coexist
Price determination	Markets	Government	Though markets determine the prices, the government can intervene
Resources	Private ownership & control	Complete government ownership and control	Both
Economic Freedom	Complete freedom	No economic freedom	Restricted by regulations

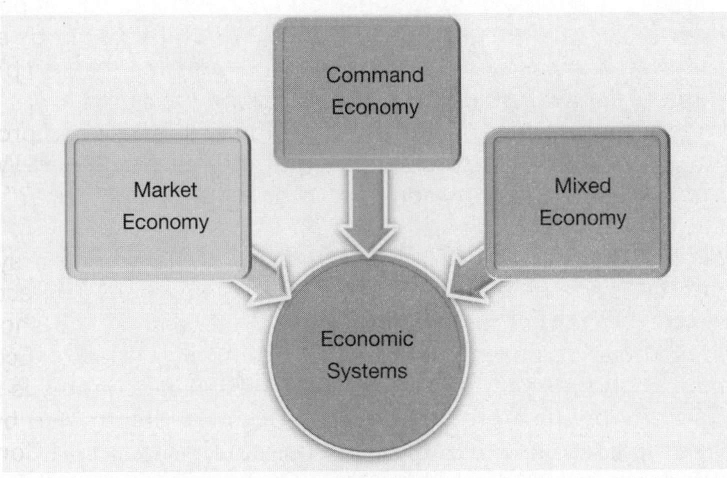

FIGURE 3.8 Types of Economic Systems

2.2.1 Market Economy

A pure market economy enjoys barrier-free economic exchange.

A market economy, also called a free-market economy is essentially governed by the forces of supply and demand with no governmental influence or intervention. However, in reality, all market economies are governed by some form of regulation. In simple terms, a market economy can be defined as one where goods and services are exchanged at will and by mutual agreement, without any force. A pure market economy enjoys barrier-free economic exchange. In reality, this form of a pure market economy is rare. In a market economy, all productive activities are privately owned whether it is what to produce or how to produce, or for whom to produce are all decided by the private sector. The governments generally play a more supportive role than an interventionist role.

The main characteristics of a market economy are: (a) private ownership of resources, (b) thriving financial markets, and (c) freedom to participate. **Private ownership of resources** signifies that the individuals, not the government, own or control the means of production, distribution, and exchange of goods, as well as the labor supply. **Thriving financial markets** refers to financial institutions such as banks and brokerages that exist to supply individuals with the capital to procure goods and services. These financial markets gain by charging interest, fees, and service charges on transactions. **Freedom to participate indicates** that the production and consumption of goods and services are purely voluntary, and the individuals are free to acquire, consume, or produce depending upon their own needs.

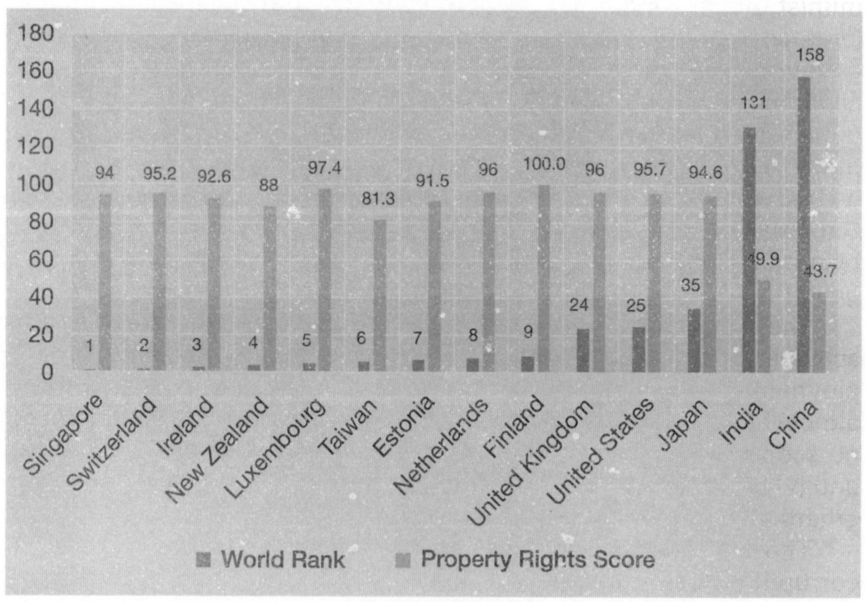

Credit: Data compiled by author from 2022 Index of Economic Freedom, https://www.heritage.org/index/about

FIGURE 3.9 Index of Economic Freedom-2022

Some examples of the market economy include the US, England, Switzerland, and Japan. The best example of a market economy is the US. Because the US has a free market where buyers and sellers decide the production and pricing of goods and services. According to the Heritage Foundation, the country ranking of economic freedom of countries reveals that in 2022, Singapore tops the list with Switzerland being second. Figure 3.9 shows the Index of Economic Freedom of selected countries in 2022. The UK, US, Japan, India, and China are ranked 24th, 25th, 35th, 131st, and 158th respectively.

2.2.2 Command Economy

Command economies are also called centrally planned economies as the central government of the nation controls all the economic activities of the nation. Rather than the free market forces of demand and supply, the government decides what will be produced and how will it be distributed. In a way, production levels, price levels, rationing of goods and services, and allocation of resources are decided by the government. In brief, in a command economy, all productive activities are publicly owned whether it is what to produce or how to produce, or for whom to produce are all decided by the public sector.

The idea of a command economy was outlined by **Karl Marx** in his Communist Manifesto as "***common ownership of the means of production.***" Hence, the command economy became a typical feature of communist regimes. Some of the command economy characteristics are (1) long-term central government's macroeconomic planning, (2) the central government allocates the country's resources like natural, human, and economic, and (3) Monopoly by the private sector is not allowed in any public utility sectors of the economy, hence all such sectors are owned by the government., (4) the government owns all the resources in the country and distributes them to its people, (4) limited property rights to the citizen, (5) the government regulates the wages and prices, (6) presence of black markets, (7) social equality, and (8) in some command economies, governments impose limits on the personal incomes of its citizen.

> Command economy is outlined as common ownership of the means of production.

The advantages of a command economy are: (i) the pace of economic activities can be faster as there is no politics or fear of law-suits, (ii) unemployment is always minimal and probabilities of mass unemployment are almost nil, (iii) no scope for private monopolies and abuse of markets, (iv) no scope for price gouging and deceptive advertising by private firms, and (v) basic services like education, health care, affordable housing, and others are typically made available free or at a minimal charge.

The command economies have some disadvantages like (a) rampant corruption by government officials, (b) lack of individual entrepreneurial innovations and initiations for economic development, and (c) inefficiencies, under-production, wastage, and leakages in government-owned production and distribution processes leading loss of resources, (d) lack of transparency lead to lack of trust and hence the citizen lives under the threat of law enforcement machinery, (e) stricter government regulations lead to black markets and illegal activities.

Countries like Cuba, Venezuela, North Korea, and the former Soviet Union are the major examples of command economies. Figure 3.3 shows the top command economy contributes in 2022 as per the Index of Economic Freedom provided by the Heritage Foundation. North Korea tops the list followed by Venezuela in the second rank and Cuba in the third rank.

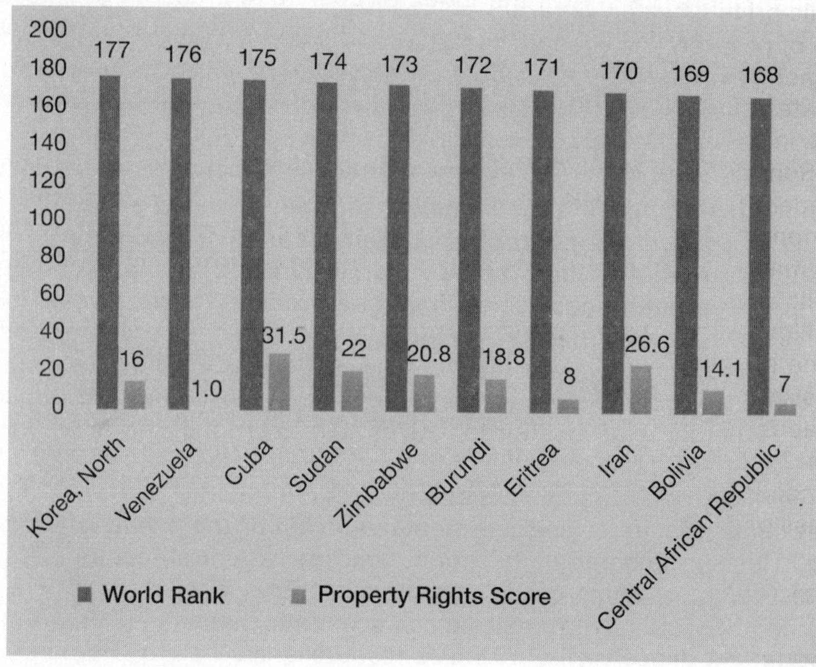

Credit: Data compiled by author from 2022 Index of Economic Freedom, https://www.heritage.org/index/about

FIGURE 3.10 Top Command Economies in 2022 based on Index of Economic Freedom

2.2.3 Mixed Economy

A mixed economy is an economic system in which both the private enterprise and a degree of state monopoly coexist. It combines both socialism and capitalism. A mixed economic system is a system that combines aspects of both capitalism and socialism. In a sense, a mixed economy protects private property and allows a certain level of economic freedom, but governments can interfere in any form of economic activity for the sake of a social cause.

According to Paul Krugman, there is no single definition for a mixed economy, which is a marriage of a profit-motivated, capitalist free market economy with the civic welfare concerned socialist economy. In simple terms, a mixed economy allows the coexistence of both the public and private sectors. The government sits in the driver's seat of the economy and makes the policies. While it encourages the private sector in some selected sectors it also regulates them rigorously. A mixed economy is an amalgam of all forms of economic systems mostly the market economy and the command economy where both the government and the individuals can exercise decision-making powers in their respective domains. That means a mixed economy allows private participation in the production and distribution of economic resources.

A typical mixed economy has the following characteristics: (1) mixed public-private sector, (2) a mix of private ownership and public ownership of property, (3) economic freedom, (4) central planning by the government, (5) demand and supply economy, (6) profit motives drive the private sector, and (7) social welfare drives the government interventions in the economy.

A mixed economy is a coexistence of both the private enterprise and a degree of state monopoly.

Some examples of mixed economies include the US, Iceland, Sweden, France, the UK, Russia, China, and India. The U.S. has a mixed economy where both capitalism and socialism coexist as it embraces the free market on one hand, and allows for government intervention for the public cause on the other.

Figure 3.4 shows the government spending as % of GDP in some of the selected mixed economies. The government role has not grown substantially during the period from 1991 to 2021. During these three decades, China has seen a positive increase of 3.22% followed by France with 2.65% and the UK with 2.63%. On the other hand, government spending has declined by 1.36%. India has experienced a negligible increase of 0.28%.

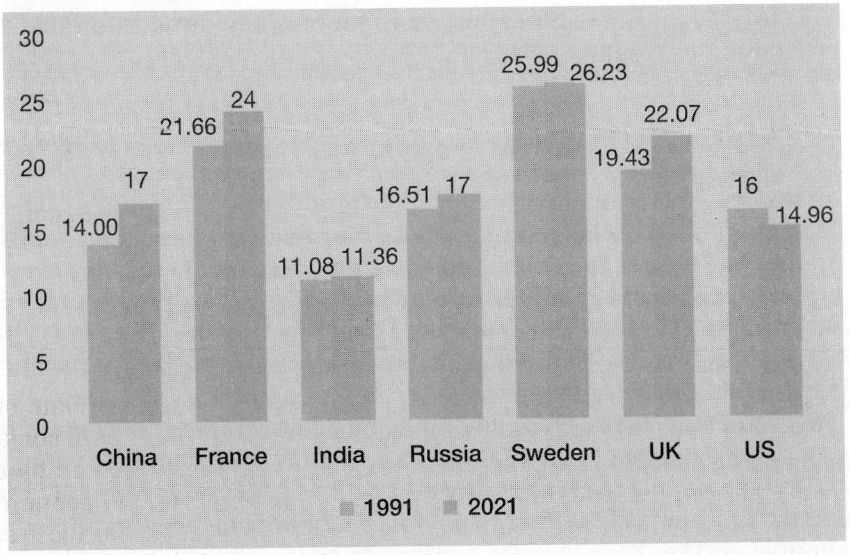

Credit: Data compiled by author from World Development Indicators of the World Bank Data

FIGURE 3.11 Government Spending as % of GDP

A mixed economy also has some advantages and disadvantages depending upon the types of governments in such countries. Some of the major advantages are (1) scope for improving the efficiency of the economy as the private firms tend to be more efficient than the government-owned, (2) limited government in economic activities allowing for the private enterprise to flourish, and (3) government regulations if used genuinely can avoid or reduce market failures. (4) effective government regulations can avoid monopoly power of private firms, (5) incentives and subsidies can promote positive externalities, (6) with the provision of proper 'safety nets', a degree of equality, social welfare, and reduced inequality can be established, (7) a good blend of performing private sector and efficient public sector can ably tackle poverty in the society and also encourage entrepreneurship, (8) with the efficient use of macroeconomic policies like the fiscal policy and monetary policy, macroeconomic stability can be maintained, (9) with systematic planning, the governments can lead the economic development in the country as per the national goals, and (10) consumer sovereignty is ensured because the goods and services are produced according to the consumer demand.

The disadvantages of a mixed economy are fewer compared to the advantages. Some of them are (i) Unhealthy competition between the public and private sector leads to some distortions in the economy, (ii) the private sector has no freedom, (iii) threat of nationalization of the private sector acts like hanging sword, (iv) inefficient public sector plagued with losses, leakages, and corruption causes wastage of taxpayers' money, and (v) government failures can cause unemployment and economic uncertainties.

To sum up, the success of a mixed economy largely depends on the role of the government. The main merit of a mixed economy is it has the power to prevent the exploitation by the monopoly firms as argued by Adam Smith in 'Wealth of Nations.

2.3 Role of the State

Humans are social beings; hence they tend to live in groups, which makes them need social institutions. As the societies grew, they needed formal organizations to protect the societies and provide for their socio-economic needs, the minimal role of the state was to provide for formal contracts as well. As societies became more and more complex, the roles of the state have also grown. In recent decades, the role of the state has been more of a welfare state.

In modern societies, the role of the state is to address the contemporary issues of its people. In doing so, it acts in unison with its sovereignty. A state according to Gerth and Mills (1948) is a human community that successfully claims its sovereign power to legitimately use for protecting its people and territory. A state comprises its legislature, executive, bureaucracy, institutions, security forces, law enforcement machinery, and defense forces.

The success of a mixed economy largely depends on the role of the government.

A state is guided by common ideologies of the people which bind them together in terms of their history, culture, race, civilization, religion, values, customs, geographical similarities, and various other aspects. Hence, the core purpose of the state according to Martin Wolf (2004) is to protect its people and the territory. In Wolf's view providing justice, protection, social safety, public goods, and correction of externalities are the genuine roles of the state.

Broadly, we can aggregate the roles of the state into ***(1) regulatory, (2) economic, and (3) administrative.*** A state assumes several roles in terms of its formal institution structure. The general role of the government in terms of economics, according to Musgrave (1959) is the allocation of resources. The state controls the allocation of resources including the production, distribution, and consumption of goods and services. In doing so, the state uses its legitimate macroeconomic policies to attain its stated policy goals. Institute for State Effectiveness lists ten major roles of a state: (1) governance, (2) security, (3) rule of law, (4) human capital, (5) infrastructure, (6) public finance, (7) engaging the markets, (8) citizen engagement, (9) resource or asset management, and (10) disaster resilience. Figure 3.12 shows the major roles of the state.

A state has three roles: regulatory, economic, and administrative.

A state's unique strengths are its powers to tax, prohibit, punish, and require participation. Good state intervention has helped many countries in East and South East Asia to grow and develop at unprecedented rates. On the other hand, bad state intervention has held back many more developing countries elsewhere in the world.

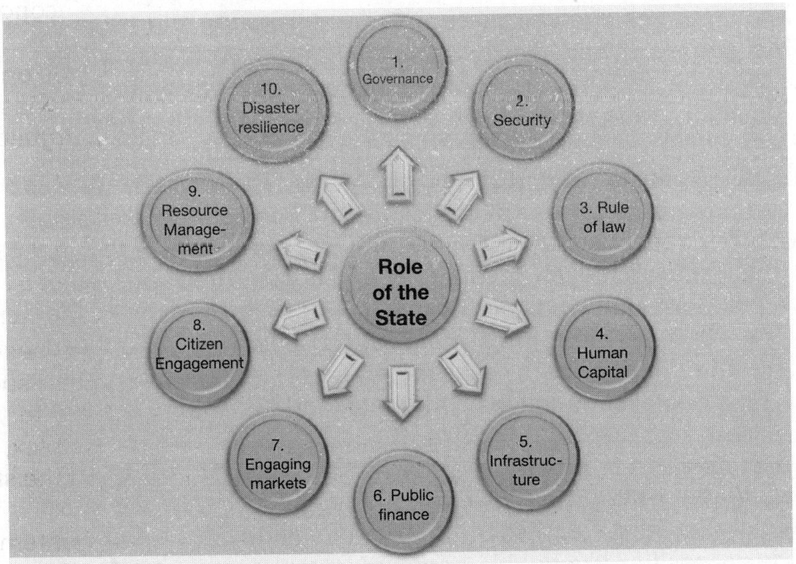

FIGURE 3.12 The Role of the State

2.4 Changing Role of State

Over a hundred years ago, a small farmer or a rural artisan in the countryside would never have felt the need for a state. Today it is entirely different. The state has grown and the world has shrunk. The same small farmers or the rural artisan's decedents use the state in their walks of life

The core purpose of the state is to protect its people and the territory.

in many ways, like sending their children to school, taking health care from hospitals and clinics, minimum support price from the government for their produce, production incentives in form of subsidies, interest subventions, etc., and many other services from the state.

Theoretically, several perspectives are professed about the ***origins of a "state".*** Of them, for a quick understanding of the origin of the state, ***four major theories are of interest: (1) the evolutionary theory, (2) force theory, (3) divine theory, and (4) social contract theory.***

According to the ***evolutionary theory***, the evolution of the state is historical and is the product of a long period of evolution into the complex structure of today's modern state. The proponents of the ***force theory*** of the origin of states like Hume, Oppenheim, Jenks-Bernhardy, and Trietschke argue that the state has originated as a result of force, i.e., based on the statement 'war begat the king.'

The ***divine theory*** of the origin of state claims that "the state was created by God and that rulers are agents of god." The earliest proponents of this theory were James-I, the first Stuart king of England, and Bousset in France. Interestingly, the theory of divine light was widely believed across Europe until the end of the eighteenth century. The ***social contract theory*** of the origin of state views that the state originated mainly due to the social contracts essentially between the individuals and the society.

The state has evolved through many forms like the tribal state, the oriental empire, the Greek city-state, the Roman world empire, the feudal state, and the national state. As the state transformed out of the chaos of feudalism to the recent form of a national state, they have taken different political systems like democracies, monarchies, oligarchies, communists, socialists, and dictatorship states. The process of evolution of state has passed through stages like (i) from simple to complex, (ii) growth of political consciousness, (iii) increase in arm and population, and (iv) balance between sovereignty and liberty. The evolution of a state into a "modern state" has not been a unilinear development. Cloete and Wissink (2000) observe three major approaches that influenced policy-making and shaped the role of the state: (1) A libertarian laissez-faire state, (2) a Socialist or collectivistic state, and (3) Welfare statism or neo-liberal state.

Today's state is mostly a welfare state. The concept of the welfare state appeared after 1890 in Europe and the US after the devastating impact of the Great Depression. The welfare state aims to provide its citizen the necessities like health, housing, education, and other public utilities. Figure 3.13 shows how some of the states like Brazil, China, France, India, Japan, Russia, South Africa, the UK, and the US have grown over the three decades from 1991 to 2021. Japan has experienced government spending growing from 13.60% to 21.63% of GDP, recording a positive change of 8.04% during the period. Chana has seen an increase in its government spending from 14% to 17.41% of GDP during the period. France has experienced a positive increase of 2.65%, moving from 21.66% to 24.30% of GDP.

From the economics perspective, ***the changing role of the state is particularly seen in the areas like public goods, natural monopolies,***

externalities, merit goods, built-in flexibility, stability and size of the public sector, cost-benefit analysis, and PPBS (Program Planning Budgeting System). The increasing role of the state in the welfare of citizens has gained prominence in recent decades, more particularly in democracies. The changing role of the state is gauged by the relative size of the state (public) and the private sectors.

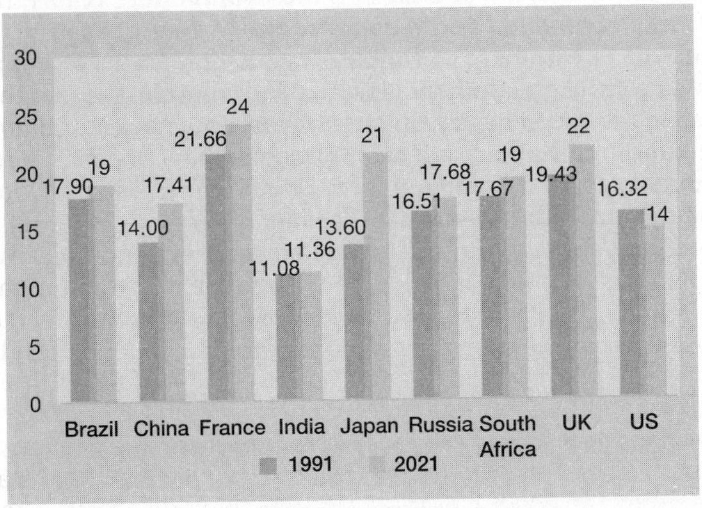

Credit: Data compiled by author from World Development Indicators of the World Bank Data

FIGURE 3.13 Changing Size of Government Spending as % of GDP

3. FORMS OF GOVERNMENT

A state exists because of a population in a particular territory with sovereignty represented by a government. ***A government by its very existence is an institution of the political process, through which the society formulates the policies and enforces them.*** Government is an important institution of the state through which a society makes and enforces its public policies.

Government is an important institution of the state through which a society makes and enforces its public policies.

Well-known ancient philosopher Aristotle was the first to study governments and classify them. Following Aristotle (384-322 B.C.) were Jean Bodin (16th century) and Montesquieu (18th century) in contributed to the study of governments. Further, Rousseau, Kant (18th century), and Mosca (19th century) made significant contributions toward classifying governments. In this subsection, we will understand what are the different forms of government and the driving philosophy behind every form of government. To make the classification of the different forms of government easy for the students to comprehend, Table 3.4 provides a glimpse of different forms of government.

First, let us look at the classification of governments based on their power structure. Broadly, ***four forms of government like Anarchy, Confederation, Unitary, and Federation*** are distinctly made. **Anarchy** is a form of government where there is 'no government', or even if a government exists it has no authority over the people. Different forms of anarchism include collectivist anarchism, anarcho-communism, philosophical anarchism, and egoist anarchism. A **Confederation** form of government can be described as a group of states joined together to accomplish certain common objectives. Nowadays, there are no such confederal states. The European Union is not a confederal state because it has characteristics of both confederal and federal forms. At best EU can be called a supranational government. A **Unitary** state is one where a single power generally a central government is ultimately supreme. Presently, most of the states in the world have a unitary form of government. China, Japan, Russia, France, and others are examples of unitary states. A Federation also popularly termed a **Federal** form of government is a union of partially self-governing small states in regions of a country. There is a clear division of powers between the federal government and the component states. The United States, India, Australia, the United Arab Emirates, the Islamic Republic of Pakistan, Switzerland, Malaysia, Venezuela, and the Federal Republic of Germany are some examples of federal governments.

TABLE 3.4 Forms of Government

No.	Power Structure	Source of Power	Ideology	Socio-Economic	Geographic
1	**Anarchy** 1. Collectivist anarchism. 2. Anarcho-communism. 3. Philosophical anarchism. 4. Egoist anarchism	**Autocracy** 1. Civilian 2. Military	**Monarchy** 1. Absolute 2. Constitutional 3. Elective	Colonialism	National government
2	Confederation	**Oligarchy** 1. Aristocracy 2. Meritocracy 3. Plutocracy	**Republic** 1. Democratic 2. Constitutional 3. Federal 4. Parliamentary 5. Presidential 6. Peoples	Capitalism	State
3	Unitary	**Democracy** 1. Direct 2. Liberal 3. Representative 4. Socialist 5. Pluralist 6. Presidential 7. Parliamentary	**Theocracy**	Communism	Provincial
4	Federation			Feudalism	Local
5				Socialism	City
6				Tribalism	Village

We classify the governments based on the source of power as Autocracy, Oligarchy, and Democracy. **An autocracy** is a form of government where the supreme power is concentrated in one person or polity. Examples of Autocracy are absolute monarchies like Saudi Arabia and The UAE, and the dictatorship of North Korea. **Autocracy** is classified into civilian and military autocracies. In the civilian form of autocracy, the autocrat is a civilian. Examples of **Civilian Autocarcies** are that of Adolf Hitler of Germany and Joseph Stalin of the Soviet Union. **Military Autocracies** are headed by military dictators like General Augusto Pinochet of Chile, and General Prayuth Chan-Ocha ofThailand.

An **Oligarchy** is a government by a few. A small group of elite rules the state and represses any apposition. Mostly Aristocracy, Meritocracy, and Plutocracy are the popular forms of oligarchies. In the past, Russia was considered an oligarchy. South Africa under apartheid, Colonial rulers of India, are also examples of oligarchy. An **Aristocracy** is a government by a few to govern the interest of all. According to Aristotle, the aristocrats were morally and intellectually superior and hence can rule others. A **Meritocracy** is a form of government where few people of political merit, knowledge, credentials, and ability to rule the society run the government. Nowadays, we do not find good examples of a meritocracy form of government. A **Plutocracy** is a form of government where there is rule by the rich. Wealthy people enter politics as elected representatives and control the government. Nowadays we do not find an exact example of plutocracy. However, the ancients of the government of the Roman Empire, Greece, Italy, and Japan were under plutocracy.

Democracy is a popular form of government. It is defined as government by the people, of the people, and for the people. People's will reigns supreme in democracies. People elect their representatives to govern the state. **Direct Democracy** is one where the citizens have greater power than those in a representative democracy. Switzerland is an example of direct democracy. **Liberal Democracy** emphasizes on separation of power in the government with an independent judiciary, a multi-party system with lots of checks and balances between the organs of the government. Some of the best examples of liberal democracies are India, the UK, the US, Japan, Brazil, and South Korea. **Representative Democracy** also called **Indirect Democracy** is one where the people elect their representatives to further choose the government. Such representatives are authorized to formulate, deliberate, and vote on the laws and policies. **Socialist Democracy** is where a softer version of socialism is well-aligned with liberal democratic principles. Democratic socialists do not subscribe to the ideas of Karl Marx or Lenin. Sweden is an example of socialist democracy. A **Pluralist Democracy** is a government where there is more than one power center. Essentially power is dispersed. Interest groups wield substantial influence on the government and its policy-making. Indian and the US are examples of highly pluralistic societies. A **Presidential Democracy** is one where the president of the country who heads the government is democratically elected by the people. A presidential form of government is also called a single executive government.

A **Parliamentary Democracy** is a form of government where the executive derives its power to govern from the parliament which is supreme and represents the will of the people. India is a good example of a parliamentary democracy form of government.

Another classification of governments into monarchy and republic is based on power ideology. A **Monarchy** is a government mostly by a family on behalf of a dynasty. A monarch embodies supreme power over the state and exercises sovereignty. Broadly, monarchies are classified into absolute, constitutional, and elective monarchies. An **Absolute Monarchy** is a government where a sovereign leader reigns supreme power without any limitations of constitution or law and is the head of the government. Countries like Vatican city, Saudi Arabia, Oman, Brunei, and Eswatini are some of the absolute monarchies. A **Constitutional Monarchy** form of government is where the monarch is only a constitutional and ceremonial head of the state but with no power. The constitution allocates power to the different organs of the state. Belgium, Bhutan, the UK, Cambodia, Thailand, Malaysia, Japan, Spain, Jordan, and Sweden are some examples of constitutional monarchies.

A **Republic** form of government is one where the country is considered a public matter. In a republic power is not inherited, instead, individuals elected by the public participate in forming the government. This is popularly observed in representative democracies. Widely known forms of a republic are Democratic, Constitutional, Federal, Parliamentary, Presidential, People's, and Islamic. The **Democratic Republic** is a government that is formed by the popular vote. Germany is an example of a democratic republic government. A **Constitutional Republic** form of government is one constitutional mandate that reigns supreme on the elected members and the other organs of the government. The US and India are examples of a constitutional republic form of government.

A **Federal Republic** government is a central government that includes the federation of states. However, the central law can encompass state laws. The US, India, Mexico, Switzerland, Australia, and Brazil are examples of federal republic governments. A **Parliamentary Republic** form of government is one where the head of the state is ceremonial, but the major powers of governance are vested with the parliament. The leader of the parliament usually the Prime Minister or Chancellor assumes more power being democratically elected by the people. Examples of the parliamentary republic are India, Israel Germany, and Singapore. A **Presidential Republic** government is one the head of the government is also the head of the legislature and is elected by the representatives of the people. Put simply, it can be described as an executive presidency separated from the elected legislature. Usually, the head of the government is called the president. Some of the examples of residential republic governments are the US, Mexico, Indonesia, and Brazil. A **People's Republic** is a government influenced by the people's revolutions. The Republic of China is a good example of this form of government. An

Islamic Republic government that is officially ruled by Islamic laws. Iran and Pakistan are examples of Islamic republics.

Theocratic governments are guided by ***Theocracy*** i.e., religious ideologies and a particular religious idealogy reigns supreme and is in a way exclusivist identity. There is no separation of the government from the religious power centers. ***Vatican city*** is an example of a theocratic state where the Christianity faith is supreme and there is no separation of power between the state and the church. The Pope is the head of the state. Formerly, Tibet was governed by the Dalai Lama who is the head of Buddhism in that region.

Another classification of governments is based on socio-economic conditions. They are Colonialism, Capitalism, Communism, Feudalism, Socialism, and Tribalism. A **Colonial** form of government is one where the politically weak natives are ruled by an external political power. India during the British rule was an example of colonial government. **Capitalism** is a form of government where free-market forces are allowed to pursue economic activities. The private enterprise is freely allowed to innovate, produce, and distribute economic goods. The US, Singapore, the UK, and Switzerland are some examples of capitalist countries. **The communist** form of government is one where the economic resources are owned by the government and a command economy is enforced. Cuba, Chile, China, and North Korea are examples of a communist governments. **Feudalism** is a medieval form of government mostly found historically in medieval Europe. In feudal societies, the ruler offers control of the land to warlords or fiefs for control in exchange for military service. Nowadays we do not find good examples of feudal government. **The Socialism** form of government is characterized by government ownership of all the means of production and is opposed to private ownership. Examples of socialist governments are Venezuela, the former Soviet Union, etc. **Tribalism** is a form of government based on tribes that are societies with a higher degree of centralization and led by a chief. The US has state or district-level tribal governments.

The governments are also classified based on the geographic coverage of their powers like **National government** at the country level, **State government** at the smaller geographies in a country, provincial government at the provinces, **local government** at the level of a district, or a taluka, or a block, or a Mandal, the **city government** also called municipal governments at city and town levels, and **village government** at the village level.

4. THE STATE AND THE MARKETS

Markets reduce transaction costs and create competition among the sellers.

The understanding of the Political economy in the West during the last two centuries has evolved around the role of the state in the economic activities of the society. However, in the Indian context, it was a Dharma, meaning a righteous duty. Since much of the study of Political economy has been influenced by Western thoughts let us briefly analyze the relationship between the state and the Markets. The central question in this discussion is what is the nature of the relationship between the states and the markets and how do they interact with each other.

As we discussed in the earlier sections, a "***state***" is a set of political institutions encompassing an explicitly well-defined geographic territory with a specific population, exercising sovereignty and legitimacy to use force to administer, control and protect the territory and its people. In simple terms, a state is also described as a human institution of the organized political community of a particular territory. On the other hand, a "***market***" is defined as the set of economic institutions in a modern economy that is influenced by an individual's self-interest. According to Adam Smith, conditioned by an "invisible hand" of market forces that balance the demand and supply of goods.

The state and market are two important institutions of a society, one is political and the other is economic, which have evolved to seek to intervene in each other's sphere. While the state has evolved to protect societal interests, the market has evolved to benefit from the economic activities of exchange of goods in the economy. Yet, the state has often intervened in the market depending on the type of government formed in that country. Across the globe, there is a tendency for the state to expand its overarching scope by formalizing institutions and their activities in the economy.

AN ILLUSTRATION OF A MARKET

A market in the modern context is a place or any arrangement where buyers and sellers come together to exchange some product or good at a mutually agreeable price. The exchange of goods takes place based on the contract either directly or through the agents of institutions between the buyers and the sellers. Markets reduce transaction costs and create competition among the sellers.

A complete market is one where all the components are available to deal with virtually any eventual circumstance. A market failure happens when the supply and demand of goods are imbalanced. That means more of a product is produced than its demand, or more of a product is demanded than its production.

From the perspective of the ***Consumer theory***, the role of the market is to maximize preference for the consumer with limited income or time. On the other hand, from the perspective of the ***Producer theory***, the market aims at maximizing the profit of the producer with limited capital. Markets can be broadly typified as product and factor markets. In the ***product market***, the buyers are the individuals and the sellers constitute the firms. Conversely, in the ***factor market***, the firms constitute the buyers and the individuals are the sellers.

Product and Factor Markets

Market	Buyers	Sellers
Product Market	Individuals	Firms
Factor Market	Firms	Individuals

4.1 Conflictual & Unconflictual Relationship

The relationship between the state and the market is broadly understood in two ways: (i) Conflictual relationship, and (ii) Unconflictual relationship.

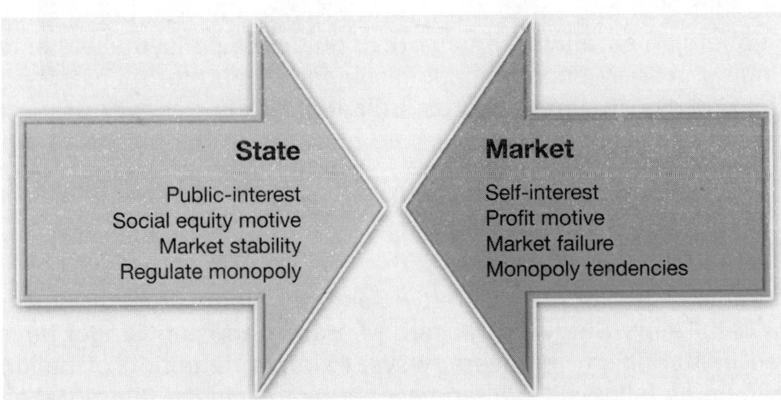

FIGURE 3.14 The State and the Market: Conflict of Interest

The conflictual relationship is something characterized by disagreement between the state and the market. Conflicts between the state and the market arise due to issues such as efficiency vs. fairness, freedom vs. equality, and self-interest vs. common interest. Generally, this kind of conflictual relationship arises in centrally planned economies. The state can resolve the conflicts that might arise in societal affairs: a market is one such societal affair. This kind of conflictual relationship is often noticed in a command economy and mixed economy

Generally, the state intervenes in a market to influence the level of production, set the standards for the production and distribution of goods, and regulate the prices of essential commodities. The state uses various instruments for market intervention that are not the same across time and space. Many a time, state intervention in developing markets is essential to control the market behavior and ensure proper distribution of goods for the needy and poor. For example, in India, the state intervenes in the agricultural produce market to procure the crops at a predicted price that is higher than the market price to protect the farmers who produce the crops. This kind of market intervention by the state helps in market stabilization. A state intervention assumes greater significance during times of market failure.

An Unconflictual relationship is characterized by agreement and unanimity between the state and market. In other words, we see an Unconflictual relationship between the state and the market when the state and market have similar goals and are driven by common interests, values, and ethics. In a free-market economy, the government and the markets enjoy an Unconflictual relationship.

4.2 Utilitarianism

Utilitarianism finds its relevance in the study of public policy because of its core idea that one must work for improving the well-being of everyone. It offers an excellent framework to guide the policymakers in terms of bringing in socio-economic, political, and legal reforms in the policy-making process. In simple words, utilitarianism is a theory of morality. It advocates for actions that promote pleasure or happiness as against those actions which result in harm or sorrow. Essentially, utilitarianism argues for the betterment of the entire society.

The Definition of Utilitarianism

Utilitarianism is a form of consequentialism according to which the most ethical choice is the one that produces the greatest good for a greater number of people.

Utilitarianism thinkers like Jeremy Bentham, John Stuart Mill, Harriet Taylor Mill, Henry Sidgwick, Richard M. Hare, and Peter Singer have described utilitarianism in several ways. I simple definition of utilitarianism can be as follows: "*Utilitariniasm aims to achieve the moral end to be sought as the greatest pleasure for the greatest number of persons.*" Utilitarianism emphasizes that morally everyone must encourage just total well-being. *Utilitarianism is a form of consequentialism according to which the most ethical choice is the one that produces the greatest good for a greater number of people.*

Utilitarianism is based on several viewpoints from related theories of ethics. Table 3.5 describes ***the four elements of utilitarianism: (i) Consequentialism, (ii) Welfarism, (iii) Impartiality, and (iv) Aggregationism.***

The two formulations of the utilitarian theory are the "principle of utility" and "greatest happiness".

TABLE 3.5 The Four Elements of Utilitarianism

No.	Element	Description
1	Consequentialism	Every human should morally promote just and good outcomes. Ultimately what matters in life from a moral perspective is to bring about good outcomes.
2	Welfarism	The well-being of individuals determines the value of an outcome. The three most predominant welfare theories are (i) hedonism, (ii) desire theories, and (iii) objective list theories.
3	Impartiality	Impartiality in utilitarianism builds on the principle of equal consideration of interests. Equal weight must be given to the interests of the individuals irrespective of the value of an outcome.
4	Aggregationism	The overall value in the world is the total well-being in it. In reality, many individuals and policy-makers endorse this view of aggregationism.

Features of Utilitarianism

Utilitarianism applies to real life as it argues that it is a virtue to strive for pleasure and happiness and avoid discomfort or unhappiness. Table 3.6 describes the main features of utilitarianism. The two formulations of the utilitarian theory are the "*principle of utility*" and "*greatest happiness*". Broadly, two types of utilitarianism include Act utilitarianism and Rule utilitarianism.

The main belief of utilitarianism is that "Nature has placed mankind under the governance of two sovereign masters; pain and pleasure."

TABLE 3.6 Features of Utilitarianism

Two Formulations of Utilitarian Theory		Two Types of Utilitarianism	
Principle of Utility	Greatest Happiness:	Act:	Rule:
The best action is that which produces the greatest happiness and/or reduces pain.	We ought to do that which produces the greatest happiness and least pain for the greatest number of people.	An Action is right if and only if it produces the greatest balance of pleasure over pain for the greatest number. (Jeremy Bentham)	An action is right if and only if it conforms to a set of rules the general acceptance of which would produce the greatest balance of pleasure over pain for the greatest number. (John Stuart Mill)

Principles of Utilitarianism

The main belief of utilitarianism is that "Nature has placed mankind under the governance of two sovereign masters; pain and pleasure." Three main principles of utilitarianism are notable: (1) pleasure (or happiness) is the only thing that truly has intrinsic value, (2) actions of humans are right in so far as they promote happiness, wrong in so far as they produce unhappiness, and (3) everyone's happiness counts equally. The principle of utilitarianism is more of consequentialism as it believes that the morality of an action is determined by its consequences.

The four theses of Utilitarianism are (i) Consequentialism: the correctness of actions is determined solely by their consequences, (ii) Hedonism: Utility produced by an act must be pleasure or happiness that we seek, (iii) Maximalism: a morally good action that produces the greatest pleasure, and (iv) Universalism: the consequences of the actions considered should be of everyone equally. The utilitarianism theory is an ethical theory that mostly determines the right actions from wrong actions by focusing on the outcomes of those actions, which is a form of consequentialism. Hence, the ethical choice should be the greatest good for the greatest number of people.

Types of Utilitarianism

There are many modern types of utilitarianism due to the contribution of many thinkers. However, broadly we classify eight types of utilitarianism for a better understanding of utilitarianism. Table 3.7 describes different types of utilitarianism.

TABLE 3.7 Types of Utilitarianism

No.	Utilitarianism	Description
1	Negative Utilitarianism	Negative utilitarianism was proposed by Karl Popper (1945). It emphasizes promoting the least amount of suffering for the greatest number of people.
2	Sentient Utilitarianism	Sentient utilitarianism emphasizes consideration of all "sentient beings" and not just humans in particular. Sentient beings are considered to be those who are conscious and feel pain.
3	Average Utilitarianism	Average utilitarianism proposes that a society must have an average utility of population that is measured by estimating the utility of all people and then dividing it by the number of people. Critics argue that it is simply an additive paradox.
4	Total Utilitarianism	Total utilitarianism suggests that it is best to measure utility by the total utility in society. It overcomes the criticism against the mere addition paradox of the average utilitarianism.

(*Continued*)

TABLE 3.7 (Continued)

No.	Utilitarianism	Description
5	Motive Utilitarianism	Motive utilitarianism integrates the motives people have for their actions, and accords weight to this while deciding if an action is morally right or wrong. It suggests that one must instill motives with practical value.
6	Rule Utilitarianism	Rule utilitarianism states that general moral rules should be followed during decision-making so that pleasure is maximized no matter how it is applied.
7	Act Utilitarianism or Case Utilitarianism	Act utilitarianism states that general rules that save time and money in the investigation must be followed to make utilitarianism more viable.
8	Two-Level Utilitarianism	Two-level utilitarianism states that both Rule-utilitarianism and Act utilitarianism must be used. Because, Rule utilitarianism is efficient in time and effect, while /act utilitarianism is more thoughtful and more critical in reflection.

The importance of utilitarianism in modern times is that it has major implications for our decision-making to lead an ethical life. As this theory emphasizes the equal well-being of everyone, it construes that we should imbibe helping others as a part of our life. Accordingly, public policy should imbibe the principles of utilitarianism in making the policies work for the greatest pleasure of a greater number of people. Further, utilitarianism can change people's lives in several ways leading to a growing movement of people committed to the well-being of the world.

The real-life applications of the theory of utilitarianism are as below. Let us assume that you help the drunken man to stand up and cross the street. If he crosses the street safely, your act was good, because the outcome of your actions resulted in happiness. On the contrary, in the same instance, if the drunken had slipped out of his hands and fallen on the street and met with injuries, your act was bad. Because the outcome of your actions resulted in pain or harm to that man.

The utilitarianism theory is also faced with criticism. One of the major criticisms is that utilitarianism ignores the rights of the individual in making the majority of people happy as an outcome of a moral decision. Another criticism is the failure of utilitarianism to differentiate between the well-being of known people and the unknown.

4.3 The State and the Economy

In public policy making, it is important to know the role of the state in the economy. We discuss here briefly how state intervention in the economy has several benefits and demerits. The state has several roles in the

The state has the legitimate power to tax its citizen and firms.

economy. Besides enforcing the rule of law, the state has to ensure the property rights of its citizen. It has to make macroeconomic policies and establish an effective regulatory mechanism to efficiently manage the economy. The major role of the state in an economy is to regulate the production, distribution, and consumption of goods and services to all the citizens of the state to achieve socio-economic equality and mitigate poverty.

The state has the legitimate power to tax its citizen and firms. State intervention in the economy should result in better outcomes. Good state intervention has greatly helped some countries like the ASEAN countries to grow faster with unprecedented economic growth rates. Sometimes, bad state intervention has hampered the economic growth of those countries.

Why the state intervenes in the economy? State intervention has several advantages: (1) achieving equality, (2) provision of public goods to the needy, (3) providing education, (4) environment protection, (5) limiting monopoly power in the economy, (6) price control through price ceilings and price floors, (7) providing subsidies and incentives to producers and consumers, and (8) providing proper infrastructure and policy environment for achieving the faster economic growth. However, there are some disadvantages of state intervention like (i) Government failure, (ii) Political pressure groups, (iii) Lack of incentives, (iv) nationalization of economic activities leading to fewer choices, and (v) effect on consumer behavior, and (vi) bureaucratic inefficiency.

5. DEVELOPMENTAL STATE

A developmental state aims at balancing economic growth with social development for the welfare of its people.

In the context of public policymaking, it is necessary to understand the developmental role of the state in the economy. A developmental state aims at balancing economic growth with social development for the welfare of its people. In this direction, the state uses its power and influence to bring in measures to tackle poverty through the expansion of economic opportunities and support schemes for the welfare of the deprived in society. Thus, the developmental state plays a significant role in shaping the structure and output of the economy.

5.1 Attributes of "Developmental" State

The term "***developmental state***" was first coined by Chalmers Johnson to describe states that follow a particular model of economic planning aimed at balanced socio-economic development of all sections of the society. Adrian Leftwich defines a development state as a "state whose politics have concentrated sufficient power, autonomy, and capacity at the center to shape, pursue and encourage the achievement of explicit developmental objectives (Leftwich, 1995).

Broadly, a developmental state is characterized by the following: (1) Active intervention in the markets and economy, (2) intimately involved in extensive macro- and micro-economic planning, and (3) effective regulation. ***The major attributes of a developmental state are (1) Regulatory capacity, (2) Administrative capacity, (3) Technical capacity, and (4) Extractive capacity.***

What are the major components that make a developmental state? The following constitute the important components:

- Determined developmental elite
- The core of developmentally determined senior politicians or bureaucrats, who have more influence over policy making than the political and legislative elites.
- These elites are not fixed and represent shifting coalitions of interests.
- Relative autonomy from special interests (class, regional and sectoral) means that these states can work in the 'national interest' (Jenkins, 1992).
- The economic bureaucracy in developmental states is very powerful and has the authority, technical competence, and insulation to make its strategies effective.

What differentiates a developmental state from good governance? Good governance at all stages is essential to economic growth. It is indeed a key factor for economic stability and political security. It is often observed that Good governance can result in enhanced economic benefits as it fast-tracks the economic transitions. Good governance depends on the political and institutional processes and their outcomes which are essential for achieving the development goals. Exhibit 3.2 Comparison of development state and good governance features

EXHIBIT 3.2 Comparison of development state and good governance features

Feature	Developmental State	Good Governance
Core aspect	Emphasis on state capacity and 'embedded autonomy'	Emphasis on transparency and accountability
Political regime	No normative commitment to any particular type of political regime, though many examples of 'successful' developmental states are authoritarian.	Normative commitment to democracy. Strengthening democratic rule is a key concern
State legitimacy	Derived from state achievements and performance	Derived from a democratic representation of the interests of the majority and the protection of the rights of the minority based on rules and procedures

(*Continued*)

EXHIBIT 3.2 (Continued)

Feature	Developmental State	Good Governance
Political will	Concern for national goals; commitment to core leadership is essential	Concern for effective constraints, normative orientation (legitimacy, human rights, democracy, macroeconomic balance)
Role of the state	The state should (actively) foster economic development but avoid capture by particular groups	No clear agreement among various proponents; the state should set a framework (rule of law) for markets/private actors

5.1.1 Regulatory Capacity

The regulatory capacity of the state indicates the ability of the state to establish and enforce rules throughout the society, including the traditional and religious realms. Fundamentally, regulatory capacity can be understood as the sum of all available resources (particularly, government departments, regulatory agencies, and courts) to the actors within the regulatory regimes to meet the objectives of regulations.

5.1.2 Administrative Capacity

The administrative capacity is one of the broad dimensions of state capacity. The administrative capacity is the ability of the state to manage the personnel and resources of the state and ensure accountability and efficiency in public goods and service delivery. Worldwide Governance Indicators is one of the measures of administrative capacity of the state.

5.1.3 Technical Capacity

The technical capacity of a state is the expertise and knowledge required to make and implement technical decisions as well as the policy tools and instruments necessary to implement those decisions effectively. In simple terms, technical capacity is the ability of a developmental state to transform broad policy objectives into programs and projects and to ensure their effective implementation.

5.1.4 Extractive Capacity

The extractive capacity of a developmental state is its ability to raise the revenues needed by the state to pay for the expenses of implementing state policies and goals, which include the revenue for hiring, paying, and providing public servants with the resources to work with. In brief, a developmental state's extractive capacity can be interpreted as the capacity for interaction between the state resources and the social resources.

Role of the State in Developing Countries

A developmental state is broadly understood as one that evinces a clear commitment to a national development agenda, that has a solid capacity and reach, and that seeks to provide growth as well as poverty reduction and the provision of public services. Thinking about the role of the state in development has differed over the past 50 years. State-led development was encouraged/supported in the 1950s and 1960s. The role of the state in development was re-evaluated based on the successful experiences of state-led development in "Asian Tigers" since the mid-1990s.

5.2 Economic Rationale for State Intervention

From the public policy perspective, it is required to know the economic rationale for state intervention. ***What is the rationale behind the state intervention in the economy?*** The rationale for the government intervention essentially emanates from four concerns: (1) allocative efficiency, (2) productive efficiency, and (3) dynamic efficiency in the economy. ***Generally, state intervention often finds its rationale as (i) to correct market failure, (ii) for macroeconomic factors, (iii) for socioeconomic factors, and (iv) to maximize social welfare.***

The rationale for the government intervention essentially emanates from four concerns: allocative efficiency, productive efficiency, and dynamic efficiency in the economy.

Allocative efficiency is important from the point of view of judicious and efficient use of scarce economic resources of a state and the social outcomes. Often there are situations when the market and the economy fail to ensure not only allocative efficiency but also productive efficiency. The poor functioning of the economy calls for state intervention. Figure 3.15 shows the situations of market failure and state intervention.

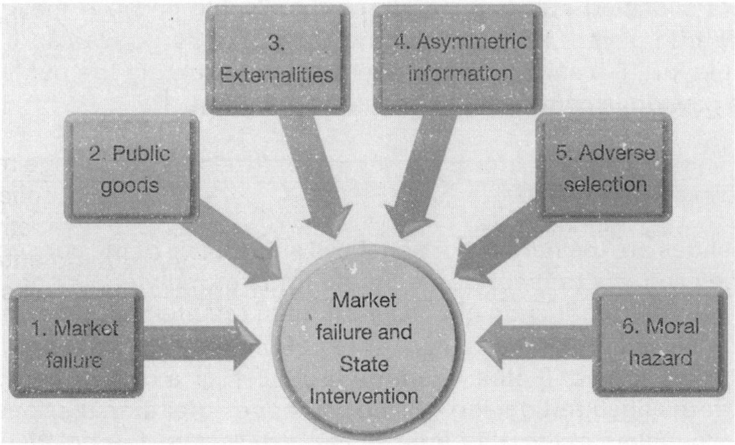

FIGURE 3.15 Market Failure and State Intervention

In the ensuing sub-sections, we will discuss some of the major situations which call for state intervention like (1) Market failure, (2) Public goods, (3) Externalities, (4) Asymmetric Information, (5) Adverse selection, and (6) Moral hazard.

5.2.1 Market Failure

Market failure is the inefficient distribution of goods and services in the free market

What causes market failure? A 'market failure' does not mean that a given market has stopped functioning. A market failure is a situation where efficient production or allocation of goods and services is not possible through market forces, thus leading to loss of economic and social welfare. Markets fail due to several reasons like Market inconsistency, lack of provision of public goods, presence of externalities, inequality of income and wealth distribution, monopoly power in the market, imperfect information, and facto mobility.

Market failure indicates the set of situations in which a market economy fails to efficiently allocate resources. Market failure is defined as the inefficient distribution of goods and services in the free market. A free market is characterized by the forces of supply and demand which determine the prices of goods and services. Any change in the forces of demand and supply will cause a price change. Market failure happens during the state of disequilibrium due to market distortion.

5.2.2 Public Goods

Public goods are those goods with characteristics of non-rivalry and non-excludability

Public goods are those goods with characteristics of non-rivalry and non-excludability, e.g., national defense, street lights, railways, roads, public parks, public libraries, etc. The problem with public goods is that they have a free rider problem. In simple terms, public goods are those which are consumed by many people in society. Their costs do not increase with the increase in consumers. Hence, they are non-rivalrous because they are allocated efficiently, and non-excludable because they cannot exclude non-payers from consuming them. Public goods can cause a market failure if a section of the population consuming the public good fails to pay while continuing to consume the good.

5.2.3 Externalities

Externalities are the harmful or beneficial side effects of the consumption of some products that are borne by the firms or individuals not directly involved in the production or consumption of the product. An externality can also be understood as a cost or benefit that arises from production and falls on someone other than the producer, or a cost or benefit that arises from consumption and falls on someone other than the consumer. While a negative externality imposes an external cost, a positive externality creates an external benefit. Positive externalities occur when spillover effects are beneficial to society. These are ***Uncompensated benefits***. Negative externalities occur when spillover effects are costly to society. These are ***Uncompensated costs***.

While a negative externality imposes Uncompensated costs, a positive externality creates Uncompensated benefits.

Production Externalities

Positive Production Externalities	Positive Consumption Externalities
Positive production externalities are less common than negative externalities.	Positive consumption externalities are also common.
For example, a beekeeper locates beehives in an orange growing area, the bees' primary purpose is to collect nectar to make honey, but they also assist in pollination to increase the productivity of orchards and vineyards. This increases production and profits for the farmers.	When you get a flu vaccination, everyone you come into contact with benefits.
Example: Training and Development of employees by firms	When the owner of a historic building restores it the value of nearby houses increases, so house prices and rents rise
	Example: Garden and beautification of one's home ads value to neighbor's home.

Consumption Externalities

Negative Production Externalities	Negative Consumption Externalities
Negative production externalities are common	Negative consumption externalities are a common part of everyday life.
Examples are noise from aircraft, logging and clearing of forests, and pollution	Smoking in a confined space poses a health risk to others; noisy parties or loud car stereos disturb others.
There is an incentive for firms to produce negative externalities, correcting externalities adds to costs and reduces profits	Example: Smoking in public places causes harmful effects on other non-smokers as well
Pollution lowers costs and increases profits.	
Example: Waste discharge by firms	

5.2.4 Asymmetric Information

In the study of public policy, it is important to know how markets fail and how public policy can provide the right solutions to the problems. Asymmetric information is experienced when one party in a transaction has more information or access to more information about the product and can exploit that information for his advantage putting the other party at disadvantage. To put it the other way, there is imperfect knowledge about the product between the two parties to the transaction. This kind of situation in the market will create an imbalance of power leading to market failures. ***Why is asymmetric information bad?*** Because it can lead to adverse selection and moral hazard.

There can be two approaches to asymmetric information

1. ***Signaling***, occurs when the better-informed party takes action to convey information to the less-informed informed party. For example, warranties, professional credentials, references from previous clients, etc.
2. ***Screening***, which occurs when the less-informed party takes actions intended to elicit private or hidden information from the better-informed party. For example, potential buyers may screen vehicles by having them inspected. Another example of screening is Education. Why do employers require a college degree for jobs that do not make use of any skill or knowledge that is learned in college? Much like the signaling hypothesis, requiring a college degree is a way for employers to identify those individuals who have more desirable attributes.

Implications of Asymmetric Information.

Hidden Characteristics: Whenever one side of a transaction knows something about itself that the other side does not know, we call them 'hidden characteristics.

Hidden actions: Whenever an economic relationship takes actions that the other side cannot observe is a situation of 'hidden cost'.

5.2.5 Adverse Selection

Adverse selection arises when one party to a transaction has more information than the other party about the good that is being exchanged

Adverse selection is when there is unequal information between the parties to the transaction i.e., buyers and sellers, which distracts the market and creates a situation that can lead to market failure. This is because one of the parties has more information than the other which creates a disadvantage for the other. Put simply, adverse selection arises when one party to a transaction has more information than the other party about the good that is being exchanged. As a consequence, the selection of goods available in the market becomes "adverse" to the interests of the less-informed party. Some examples can be used cars, employment relationships, and insurance.

5.2.6 Moral Hazard

Moral hazard involves the principal-agent problem

A moral hazard is a situation in which one party knowingly engages in risky behavior or fails to act in good faith because the consequence of such a risk will have to be borne by another party. In short, having been insured against risk, one party might behave inefficiently and transfer the risk to the other, otherwise, such a risk would not have been taken by that party. For example, a moral hazard occurs when governments bail out big companies.

Generally, moral hazard involves the principal-agent problem. If the principal is incapable of perfectly supervising the agent, the agent has an incentive to pursue their self-interest rather than the interest of the principal. In other words, people take hidden actions to take advantage of others' ignorance. A person who is poorly supervised has a propensity to involve in deceitful or otherwise adverse behavior. The principal-agent problem arises when agents (e.g., a firm's managers) pursue their own goals rather than the goals of principals (e.g., the firm's owners). A principal is an individual whom one or more agents to achieve an objective. An agent is an individual employed by a principal to achieve the principal's objective.

5.3 Functions of the State

Political thinkers from time to time have proposed several theories to outline the sphere of state and its functions. On the other hand, some idealists have regarded the state as an omnipotent entity and hence they entrust the state with every action relating to social life. From a holistic perspective, the key functions of the state are mostly classified as (1) economic, (2) political, (3) law enforcement, (4) humanitarian, (5) informational, (6) public health, and (7) defense.

We discussed in subsection 2.3 the various roles of the state, however in this discussion, according to the World Bank Report (1997), we broadly classify the functions of the state into three types: (i) minimal functions, (ii) intermediate functions, and (iii) activist functions.

5.3.1 Minimal Functions

The Minimal functions of the state are broadly understood as (i) Providing pure public goods, and (ii) Protecting the poor. Providing pure public goods includes defense of the state, enforcing law and order, protecting the property rights of the citizens, managing the macroeconomy of the state, and providing basic health care to the public. In the context of a welfare state or developmental state, protecting the poor is an important responsibility of the state and in this direction running anti-poverty programs has become a basic minimal function of the state. Further, in addressing the problems of the people during natural calamities and disasters, disaster relief has also been claimed as a minimal function of the state.

5.3.2 Intermediate Functions

The intermediate functions of the state are broadly classified as (i) addressing externalities, (ii) regulating monopoly, (iii) overcoming imperfect information, and (iv) providing social insurance. Addressing externalities involves providing basic education and protecting the environment. Regulating monopoly includes utility regulation, and ensuring antitrust (competition) policy. Overcoming imperfect information in insurance (health, life, pensions), financial regulation, and consumer protection. Providing social insurance comprises providing redistributive pensions, family allowances, unemployment allowance, and insurance to the poor.

5.3.3 Activist Functions

The activist functions of the state can be broadly understood as coordinating private activity, and asset redistribution. Coordinating private activity can be in the form of fostering markets, and cluster initiatives, coordinating public-private partnerships, and developing social capital.

5.4 The Evolution of the Role of the State in India

We have discussed earlier the role of the state, its political systems, economic systems, instruments of the state, the instruments of state policy, and changing role of the state in section 2 of this chapter. In this subsection, we will discuss the evolution of India as a developmental state. While appreciating the rise of the state in India, it is important to consider the special nature of the state-society relationship in the Indian context. As we know from the history taught to us, the idea of the Indian state grew during the national freedom movement. As India achieved political independence, the framers of the Indian constitution, have declared India as a sovereign, socialist, secular democratic, and republic. In its transformation as a developmental state, the Indian state has evolved over several phases.

In India, most of the political thinkers, leaders, and the public except for anarchists have always profoundly regarded the state as an important and inevitable institution. However, there have been disagreements over the role of the state in society. The orientation of the Indian state was set by the Indian National Congress party which led to the Indian freedom struggle. The founding elite of the Indian National Congress was not only influenced by the West but enamored of the Western philosophies though the ordinary people of the country were not even literate. The Congress party adopted the state-centered secular, socialist ideology which gave unprecedented accession to power. This led to the creation of a strong state in India.

For the ease of brief discussion from the developmental state perspective, we will look at the evolution of the role of the state according to World Development Report (1997) in the following phases:

1. The Nehruvian period, 1947-64
2. Garibi hatao period, 1966-77
3. The spending boom and rising fiscal deficits, 1977-91
4. The reform phase, 1991 to the present

The Nehruvian period (of India's first Prime Minister, Jawaharlal Nehru) promoted egalitarian ideals based on the principles of socialism which helped the ruling elite establish their influence over the society and economy. The creation of the Planning Commission (1950), the launching of Five-Year Plans (1951), formation of the National Development Council (1952) were notable steps in this direction (Chatterjee, 1997). Unlike the East Asian nations which focused on building strong market economies and supporting the rise of the private sector, India focused on building a powerful state. The philosophy of planned economy through the industrial policy was mostly centered around the public sector.

The Garibi hatao period spans around 1966-77. During this period, the then prime minister of India, Ms. Indira Gandhi, effected two major shifts in the role of the state in India. The first major shift was the activist role of the government in subsidizing agriculture through the provision of high-yielding variety seeds, agriculture credit, rural electrification, and the green revolution. The second major shift was the tightening of state control over almost every facet of the Indian economy through bank nationalization, insurance sector, price controls, etc., enlarged the stranglehold of the state on the entire economy. In a way, the entire economy was at the mercy of the state. Even with this command economy kind of scenario in the country, the economy did not grow beyond 3.5 percent per annum.

The period of spending boom and rising fiscal deficits, 1977-91 saw a major shift in the role of the state, where the government spending boom began to fund the antipoverty schemes which lead to the massive rise in fiscal deficits. Competitive politics further aggravated the fiscal situation, as the subsidies ruled the roost to please the electorate. The large deficit figure of 8.4 percent of GDP in 1985 contributed to the sudden spurt in the current account deficit. As 1991 approached, the country met with a situation of virtually no foreign exchange reserves leading to a Balance of Payments Crisis 1991.

The reform phase from 1991 onwards till the present saw sweeping reforms in the Indian economy. The reforms were essential as the state could not continue financing the large subsidies and heavy government spending. The need for private investment was essential, and hence privatization was pursued in the economy. The state adopted the policies of Liberalization, Privatization, and Globalization well-known as LPG reforms. Thus, the role of the state suddenly changed from principal investor to a facilitator of the private sector in the economy. Thus, the age-old Congress party's consensus on 'socialism' gave way to a new consensus on 'liberalization.'

To sum up, the Indian state has experienced massive reforms over the years. Today, the Indian state stands tall as a progressive developmental state with maximum economic liberalism.

Summary

- Political economy is an interdisciplinary subject, that draws its contributions from the philosophies of politics, sociology, and economics.
- The political economy framework includes the political actors, the political actors' interests, and the political mechanisms and constraints. The four broad types of Political actors are Policymakers, Citizenry, Selectorate, and Coalitions.
- A state is a set of political organizations vested with ultimate powers to make collective decisions that are binding on the entire society and enforce them through the legitimate use of monopoly power. A government is an institution of a system made up of a group of people authorized people to run the country through proper policies in the interest of the nation.
- According to Lincoln, democracy is a government of the people, by the people, for the people. democracies are classified as direct democracies (pure democracy), representative democracies, participatory democracies, liberal democracies, parliamentary democracies, pluralist democracies, constitutional democracies, and socialist democracies.
- Authoritarian governments tend to possess a strong power center and limited political freedom. Individual freedom is subordinate to the state and constitutional accountability is absent in the authoritarian regime. Four major characteristics of authoritarian regimes are limited political pluralism, emotional acceptance of the people as a necessary evil, minimal social mobilization, and vague executive powers.
- Monarchy is one where total sovereignty is vested in one person as the head of state, called 'monarch', who holds the title and power until death or abdication.
- Totalitarianism is considered an extreme form of authoritarianism where the rulers are extremely repressive and control their citizens' lives and destinies. Totalitarian regimes include Socialist, Communist, Theocratic, and Dictatorship regimes.
- The three economic problems are (1) what goods will be produced? (2) how will the goods be produced? (3) for whom will the goods be produced?
- A market economy is characterized by (a) private ownership of resources, (b) thriving financial markets, and (c) freedom to participate.
- Command economies are also called centrally planned economies as the central government of the nation controls all the economic activities. One of the main advantages of a command economy is no scope for private monopolies and abuse of markets. One major disadvantage of a command economy is rampant corruption by government officials.
- A mixed economy is an amalgam of all forms of economic systems mostly the market economy and the command economy where both the government and the individuals can exercise decision-making powers in their respective domains.
- A state is a human community that successfully claims its sovereign power to legitimately use for protecting its people and territory. It comprises legislature, executive, bureaucracy, institutions, security forces, law enforcement machinery, and defense forces.
- Origins of a "state" are explored by four major theories: (1) the evolutionary theory, (2) force theory, (3) divine theory, and (4) social contract theory.
- Broadly, three major approaches that influenced policymaking and shaped the role of the state are a libertarian laissez-faire state, a socialist or collectivistic state, and a welfare statism or neo-liberal state.
- A government by its very existence is an institution of the political process, through which the society formulates the policies and enforces them. Based on the power structure, the four forms of government are Anarchy, Confederation, Unitary, and Federation. Based on the source of power, three forms of government are Autocracy, Oligarchy, and Democracy. Based on power ideology three forms of government are Monarchy, Republic, and Theocracy.

Based on socio-economic conditions, the six forms of government are Colonialism, Capitalism, Communism, Feudalism, Socialism, and Tribalism. Based on the geographic coverage of their powers, the six forms of government are national government, state government, provincial government, local government, city government, and village government.

- A market in the modern context is a place or any arrangement where buyers and sellers come together to exchange some product or good at a mutually agreeable price.
- The relationship between the state and the market is of two types: (i) Conflictual relationship, and (ii) Unconflictual relationship.
- The four elements of utilitarianism are Consequentialism, Welfarism, Impartiality, and Aggregationism.
- The eight types of utilitarianism are Negative Utilitarianism, Sentient Utilitarianism, Average Utilitarianism, Total Utilitarianism, Motive Utilitarianism, Rule Utilitarianism, Act Utilitarianism or Case Utilitarianism, and Two-Level Utilitarianism.
- The major attributes of a developmental state are Regulatory capacity, Administrative capacity, Technical capacity, and Extractive capacity.
- The rationale for state intervention is to correct market failure, for macroeconomic factors, for socioeconomic factors, and to maximize social welfare.
- A market failure is a situation where efficient production or allocation of goods and services is not possible through market forces, thus leading to loss of economic and social welfare.
- Adverse selection is when there is unequal information between the parties to the transaction i.e., buyers and sellers, which distracts the market.
- A moral hazard is a situation in which one party knowingly engages in risky behavior or fails to act in good faith because the consequence of such a risk will have to be borne by another party.
- The three types of functions of the state are minimal functions, intermediate functions, and activist functions. The Minimal functions of the state are providing pure public goods and protecting the poor. The intermediate functions of the state are addressing externalities, regulating monopoly, overcoming imperfect information, and providing social insurance. The activist functions are coordinating private activity and asset redistribution.

Key Words

Political economy	Constitutional democracy	Federal	Unconflictual relationship
Oeconomy	Socialist democracy	Autocracy	Consequentialism
Citizenry	Monarchy	Aristocracy	Welfarism
Selectorate	Absolute monarchy	Meritocracy	Aggregationism
Political actors	Constitutional monarchy	Plutocracy	Market failure
Democracy	Oligarchy	Indirect Democracy	Public goods
Authoritarianism	Theocratic	Pluralist Democracy	Externalities
Totalitarianism	Dictatorship	Absolute Monarchy	Asymmetric Information
Direct democracy	Force theory	Constitutional Monarchy	Adverse selection
Representative democracy	Divine theory	Tribalism	Moral hazard
Participatory democracy	Anarchy	Product market	Signaling
Liberal democracy	Confederation	Factor market	Screening
Parliamentary decomcracy	Unitary	Conflictual relationship	liberalization

Questions

A. Quick Check

1) Why are democratic political systems stable compared to the political instability of authoritarian or totalitarian regimes?
2) What is a theocratic state? Explain with an example.
3) Why do monarchies exist even today?
4) What is the nature of the relationship between the states and the markets and how do they interact with each other
5) Why the state intervenes in the economy?
6) What differentiates a developmental state from good governance?
7) What are the major components that make a developmental state?
8) What differentiates a developmental state from good governance?
9) What is the rationale behind the state intervention in the economy?
10) What causes market failure?
11) What are public goods?
12) Why is asymmetric information bad?
13) Which are the two approaches to asymmetric information?

B. Explore

1) Why parliamentary democracy is well-suited to India than presidential democracy? Discuss from the public policy perspective.
2) Compare and contrast the federal and unitary forms of governments
3) The real-life applications of the theory of utilitarianism
4) Explain the evolution of the role of the state in India
5) Identify and explain at least five distinguishing features of the evolution of the state in India.
6) Discuss this statement – "The achievement of the Indian State is unparalleled given that it is a democratic poor society"

References

- Carl Schmitt (1927), "The Concept of the Political", Archiv für Sozialwissenschaft und Sozialpolitik, 58(1), pp. 1–33. Cf. George Schwab, 'Introduction', in Carl Schmitt, The Concept of the Political, University of Chicago Press, 2007, p. 5 n. 8.
- Chatterjee, Partha (1997). "Development Planning and the Indian State" in Partha Chatterjee (Ed.), State and Politics in India, OUP, Delhi.
- Cloete, Fanie., and Wissink, Henry (2000). Improving Public Policy. First Edition | Van Schaik, 2000.
- DFID (Department for International Development). 2009. "Political Economy Analysis How to Note." A DFID Practice Paper. London: DFID, July.
- Drazen, A (2008). Is there a different political economy for developing countries? Issues, perspectives, and methodology. *Journal of African Economies* 17(AERC Supplement 1) i23–i31.

- Easton, David (1953). The Political System: An Inquiry into the State of Political Science (p. 78). New York: Alfred A. Knopf.
- Gerth, Hans., and Mills, Wright (1948). From Max Weber: Essays in Sociology. 1st Edition | Routledge & Kegan Paul: London.
- Jean-Paul, Gagnon (2018). 2,234 Descriptions of Democracy: An Update to Democracy's Ontological Pluralism. *Democratic Theory*, 5 (1).
- Eisenstadt, S. N. (1966) Modernization: Protest and Change (Englewood Cliffs, NJ: Prentice-Hall).
- Gabriel A. Almond., and James S. Coleman (eds.) (1960). The Politics of the Developing Areas. Princeton, New Jersey, Princeton University Press, 1960, 591 p.
- Jenkins, Richard (1992). Pierre Bourdieu. London; New York: Routledge, 1992.
- Leftwich, Adrian (1995) Bringing politics back in: Towards a model of the developmental state, *The Journal of Development Studies*, 31 (3), 400-427.
- Martin Wolf (2004). The Role of the State in an Era of Globalization: The 2004 Sir Ronald Trotter Lecture. New Zealand Business Roundtable | (December 15, 2004).
- Musgrave, Richard A. (1959). The Theory of Public Finance: A Study in Public Economy. First Edition | McGraw-Hill, Inc. (January 1, 1959).
- Stilwell, Frank (2011). Political Economy: The Contest of Economic Ideas, 3rd Edition | Oxford University Press (15 December 2011)
- World Development Report (1997). Chapter 1: The Evolving Role of The State. P.24. Available at https://openknowledge.worldbank.org, accessed on 24-Mar-2021.

Further Readings

- Caporaso A James., and Levine P David. (1992). Theories of Political Economy. Cambridge University Press. Online publication date: June 2012.
- Mcloughlin, Claire (2009). Topic Guide on Political Economy Analysis. Updated Edition 2012. © Governance and Social Development Resource Centre (GSDRC), International Development Department, https://gsdrc.org/
- Miller, Raymond C. (2018). International political economy: Contrasting world views. 2nd Edition | Routledge (March 13, 2018).
- Murray N. Rothbard (2011). "Man, Economy, and State with Power and Market, Scholar's Edition." Joseph T. Salerno (Introduction), Paperback, 2nd edition, Ludwig von Mises Institute, May 4, 2011.
- Przeworski (1991). "Democracy and the Market." Studies in Rationality and Social Change, Cambridge University Press, July 26, 1991.
- Scott, Z., and Mcloughlin, C., (2014). Political Systems: Topic Guide, Birmingham: GSDRC, University of Birmingham, UK

CHAPTER 4

Public Policy – The Institutions and Collective Decision-Making

The purpose of this chapter is to present an interesting synopsis of the Role of Institutions in public policy decision-making. In this chapter, we will first study the theoretical foundations of the decision-making process, particularly group decision-making, and the advantages and disadvantages of group decision-making. In addition, we will discuss the classical or rational model and the administrative or bounded rationality model of group decision-making. Knowing the decision theory and its types will greatly enhance the understanding of the student about decision-making. Hence, we will discuss the six major theories like descriptive theory, normative theory, Condorcet's theory, Dewey's theory, prospect theory, and social choice theory. The public choice theory has greatly contributed to the field of public policy. We will know the major contributions of public choice theory and the Nirvana fallacy. Another major theoretical contribution to decision-making is the rational choice theory. We will study its assumptions, the logic of rational ignorance, and rational irrationality. It is necessary to know how political institutions make decisions on public policy. In this direction, we study the decision-making in legislative bodies with a particular focus on India. Finally, we conclude this chapter with a brief understanding of the democratic dilemma.

Section 1: Decision-making

Section 2: Decision Theory

Section 3: Public Choice Theory

Section 4: Rational Choice Theory

Section 5: Decision-making in Legislative Bodies

Section 6: Democratic Dilemma

1. THE DECISION-MAKING

Decision-making is a dynamic process.

In public policy, decision-making plays an important role all through the policy cycle. Decision-making by government administrators drives the public programs and policies which have a major impact on peoples' lives. It is crucial that at each stage of public administration, the government must take appropriate decisions to ensure smooth administration. In doing so, the government must adopt efficient decision-making processes, thereby the bureaucracy and the administrative staff of the government can easily follow those processes to arrive at proper public policy-related decisions. In this direction, as a student of public policy let us first understand what is a decision-making process.

1.1 Decision-Making Process

Decision-making is crucial in public policymaking. Decisions are choices of actions from among multiple feasible alternatives. Public institutions play a significant role in decision-making because they have a massive influence on policy outcomes. Their decisions based on good norms will benefit society in the public policy context. For example, a natural calamity occurs in some parts of the country. Then the government must take swift decisions to save life and property of the public. If the government fails to make decisions, there will be further agony in the life of the affected people. Generally, politics continues to be at the heart of all public policy deliberations. Good politics coupled with good policy can operate well to attain good outcomes.

Let us consider another example of a government decision regarding tackling the COVID-19 pandemic. The Indian government led by Prime Minister Narender Modi took swift decisions to save the lives of the people through creating awareness, providing medical care, and all related facilities to the public across the massive country. While doing this, the government took swift decisions involving the major stakeholders like the state governments, health experts, scientists, WHO experts, and others. With continued efforts, the government could successfully administer more than 2 billion doses of COVID vaccine in a widely spread country. Given this, we can understand that decision-making is vital for public policy.

Decision-making is defined as the process of choosing the best alternative option that can accomplish the desired change or advantage to a specific situation resulting in maximum benefits but least risk. Public policy decision-making implies the governmental actions to formulate, adopt, implement, evaluate, or modify the policies at different levels of the government. In simple terms, decision-making is an analytical activity where the best action is chosen among available alternatives. Essentially, in the context of public policy, decision-making is a dynamic process. According to Howlett et al., (2009) decision-making is the process of choosing the best from the available choices.

What is a good decision? To judge which is a good decision and which is a poor decision depends largely on the basic premise of the policy. There are two approaches to judging a decision as a good decision or a bad decision: (i) based on the outcome, and (ii) based on its alignment with the decision-maker's values and principles. In a way, the decision is the outcome of judging a given situation. Hence, Justice and Miller (2007) classify decision-making into judgmental and choice activities.

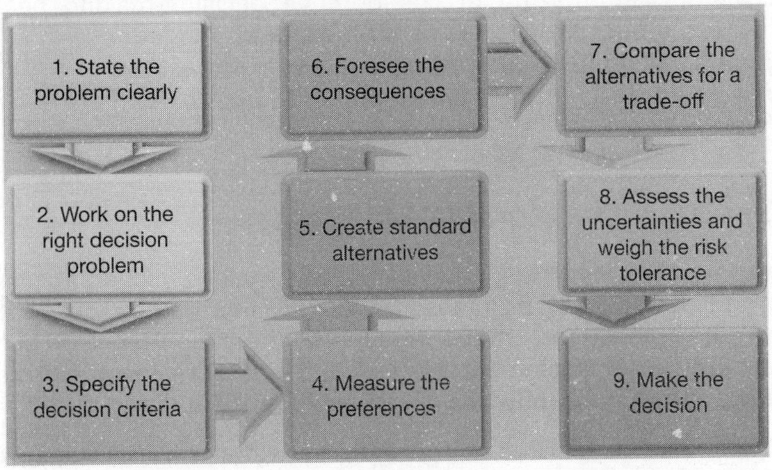

FIGURE 4.1 Nine Steps of Decision-making

Hammond et al., (2015) suggest nine general steps for a good decision-making approach. They are (i) state the problem, (ii) work on the right decision problem, (iii) specify the decision criteria, (iv) measure the preferences on the criteria, (v) create standard alternatives, and (vi) foresee the consequences, (vii) compare the alternatives for a trade-off, (viii) assess the uncertainties and weigh the risk tolerance, and (ix) make the decision. Figure 4.1 shows the nine steps of decision-making. However, according to Hitt et al., (2006), the decision-making process involves six stages: defining the problem, identifying criteria, gathering, and evaluating data, listing, and evaluating the alternatives, selecting the best alternative, and implementing and follow-up.

1.2 Group Decision-Making

In the public policy arena, most of the policy decisions are at the group level. In this context, understanding the nuances of group decision-making assumes importance. Group decision-making is regarded very highly by the public because it has the advantage of decisions drawn from the experiences and perspectives of several individuals. In the Indian context, even today in most of India, the informal panchayats decide on several issues of public policy at the local levels. The people accord more respect and adherence to such decisions. Essentially, group decision-making is ideal because it has the basis of ideas drawn from several

> Group decision-making is a collective or collaborative decision-making process where the individuals participate to decide jointly.

people not from a single individual. Moreover, due to its very nature, group decision-making is more creative, effective, and appealing to a large section of the people.

The state is made of the representatives of the people of the nation. ***A government decision is by nature a group decision and is often accepted by most people.*** Hence, the government is an institution that makes collective decisions for society. Group decision-making is also called collective decision-making or collaborative decision-making because the decision is not attributable to an individual. Accordingly, a simple definition of ***group decision-making*** is that ***it is a collective or collaborative decision-making process where the individuals participate to decide jointly.***

1.2.1 Group Decision-Making Process

The group decision-making process broadly includes seven stages: (1) identify the decision to be made, (2) analyze and gather related information, (3) establish the criteria, (4) identify the alternatives, (5) choose the best option, (6) implement the decision, and (7) review the decision. Figure 4.2 shows the group decision-making process.

Group decision-making is ideal because it has the basis of ideas drawn from several people not from a single individual.

Step 1. Identify the decision to be made:This is the very first stage where the group encounters the problem of what decision to be made. At this stage, the group must clearly define the problem and its significance.

Step 2. Analyze and gather related information: In this stage, based on the nature of the decision to be taken, the following questions need to be asked: What is causing this problem? For whom is this problem? What information is needed? What are those information sources? How accurate those sources of information are? All relevant information must be gathered.

Step 3. Establish the criteria: Criteria setting for determining the correct decision is an important stage of the group decision-making process. The set criteria based on the analysis of the gathered relevant information must be thoroughly ranked in order of importance. In a way, while establishing the criteria, the important question to be answered is: What criteria will help us choose the best decision to the satisfaction of many people.

Most of the policy decisions are at the group level.

Step 4. Identify the alternatives: The successful criteria setting will result in probable alternatives to choose. While doing so, two approaches are followed viz., thinking, and feeling. Thinking involves focusing on objective evaluation and methodical analysis. Feeling focuses on subjective evaluation and others' emotional reactions.

Step 5. Choose the best option: In this stage, the group must carefully evaluate the available alternatives based on agreed measures. In doing so, the group must weigh all the available evidence before choosing the best choice.

Step 6. Implement the decision: This stage involves knowing the means required to implement the decision and implement the decision. Precisely, in this stage, the following questions are answered to successfully implement the decision: what should be done with the decision? how it should be done? who should do it? when should it be done? What should it do? what is the order of implementing the decision?

Step 7. Review the decision: In this final step, it is time to know whether the decision was successful. Based on the feedback and review, new options can be generated or if the decision was found to be effective the same decision can be continued.

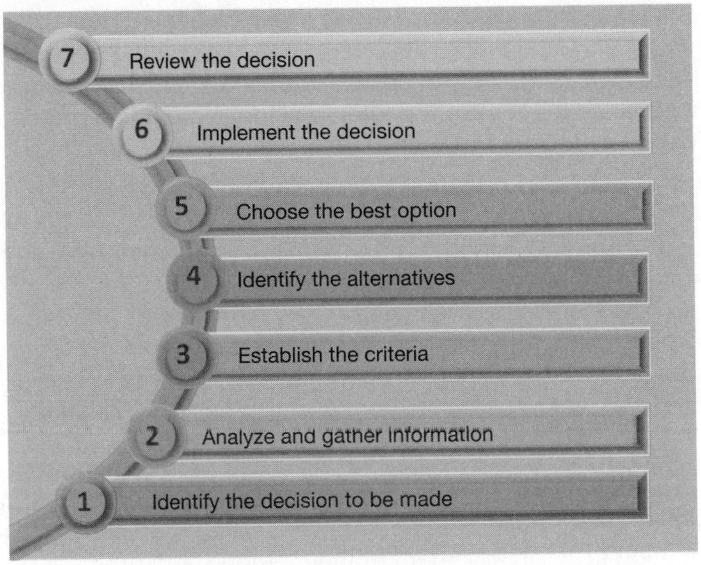

FIGURE 4.2 Group Decision-Making

The methods of group decision-making are (i) Ranking, (ii) Scoring, (iii) Voting, (iv) Multiple Votes and Voting Rounds, and (v) Delphi Method (Iterative convergence). The types of group decision-making include (1) Unanimous, (2) Consensus, (3) Majority Rule, (4) Expert decision, and (5) Executive decision.

1.2.2 Advantages of Group Decision-Making

In the context of public policy, undoubtedly, group decision-making is necessary and is of great significance as it helps in good public policy-making. First, let us know from the theoretical perspective, some of the major advantages of group decision-making which include: better information, diversity in opinions, democracy, greater acceptability, expert opinions, people's participation, and superior decisions. Table 4.1 briefly discusses the important advantages of group decision-making.

> The major advantages of group decision-making include better information, diversity in opinions, democracy, greater acceptability, expert opinions, people's participation, and superior decisions.

TABLE 4.1 Advantages of Group Decision-Making

No.	Advantages
1	As the general adage goes "*Two heads are better than one*", "*The more the merrier*", "*collective wisdom is always greater than individual wisdom*", and group decision-making is always better than individual decision-making.
2	*Better information*: A group is equipped with better and more vast information compared to an individual.
3	*Diversity in opinions*: The group members are several and have diverse backgrounds of knowledge and experience. Hence, they have unique and interesting ideas and viewpoints on the matter at hand. This provides a variety of approaches as well as wide coverage of areas around the topic of decision-making in providing better insights for group decision-making.
4	*Democratic and greater acceptability*: The decisions made by the group command more respect and acceptability than individual decisions, because the group is more democratic, while the individual decision can be perceived as autocratic.
5.	*Expert opinions*: The group can involve experts on the topic of discussion or call an expert to advise the group. Hence the availability of expert opinion is much more useful in decision-making.
6	*People's participation:* In a group, there is a scope for the individuals to present their ideas and opinions. The group dynamics help in creating active involvement of the members and promoting active participation of the members. Individuals' involvement in decisions leads to a higher level of acceptance and satisfaction.
7	*Superior decisions*: Groups are known to show superior prudence when assessing the available alternatives, particularly for complex problems.

1.2.3 Disadvantages of Group Decision-Making

Group decision-making is not free from demerits. As a student of public policy where group decision-making plays a key role, it is necessary to know about the disadvantages of group decision-making. Table 4.2 enlists the major disadvantages of group decision-making.

TABLE 4.2 Disadvantages of Group Decision-Making

No.	Disadvantages
1	*Time-consuming process*: As the group includes several individuals, organizing them, explaining the purpose of the meeting, and soliciting and receiving their views points, and opinions take considerable time. It is cumbersome to manage groups, particularly large groups. Thus, the time loss due to the group dynamics is substantial.
2	*Groupthink*: This is a situation where group members resort to seeking consensus by setting aside honest disagreements and debating alternate ideas. The group members avoid criticism of each other's ideas as well as prevent serious divisions within the group.
3	*Common information bias*: There is a possibility of overemphasizing the information held by the majority members in the group as the group opinion. This reduces the scope for seeking diverse views from other members.
4	*Risky Shift*: Groups tend to make risky decisions as every individual feels that it is a group decision, and if accusations are aired against the decision, they can be easily passed on as group responsibility. Whereas individuals tend not to take risky decisions.
5.	*Domination of decision leaders*: There can be situations where one or few individual members dominate the group in decision-making, sometimes out of self-interest or due to various other reasons. Quite often groups are dominated by one or two "decision leaders."
6	*Compromise decisions*: Quite often when the group cannot make a thorough decision, members resort to a compromise decision that is not in the right earnest. Social interactions might lead to hasty compromise. Such decisions are not whole-hearted, instead are made of different demands and social pressures.
7	*Group*: Informal groups within the group will distort the group decision-making process and will have a negative impact.

To sum up, group decision-making has better advantages than individual decision-making. Despite some inherent disadvantages of group decision-making, in the public policy domain, it is appropriate to go with the group decision-making process.

A government decision is by nature a group decision and is often acceptable to most people.

1.3 Models of Decision-Making

Literature provides different models of decision-making. However, in this discussion, we will limit our discussion to two fundamental models of decision-making that are significant in the context of public policy. These models are based on specific assumptions that act as a premise in decision-making.

1.3.1 The Classical or Rational Model of Decision Making

While making good decisions it is important to consistently look for better options to make better choices. In this direction, applying a classical or rational decision-making model is quite effective. We will now discuss how the rational decision-making model works and how we can understand this model from the perspective of policymaking.

The rational decision-making model maximizes the benefits and minimizes the costs of decision-making.

The main purpose of the rational decision-making model is to maximize the benefits and minimize the costs of decision-making. The main characteristic of the rational or classical decision-making model is its use of logical steps to choose the best option. It involves evaluating multiple possible alternatives to arrive at the best choice among the options. The main features of the rational model include: (i) clarity on problems, (ii) clear objectives, (iii) agreed criteria and weights, (iv) all possible alternatives are known to the group, and (v) the consequences are foreseen, (vi) the final decision is rational. Figure 4.3 shows the Rational or Classical model of decision-making.

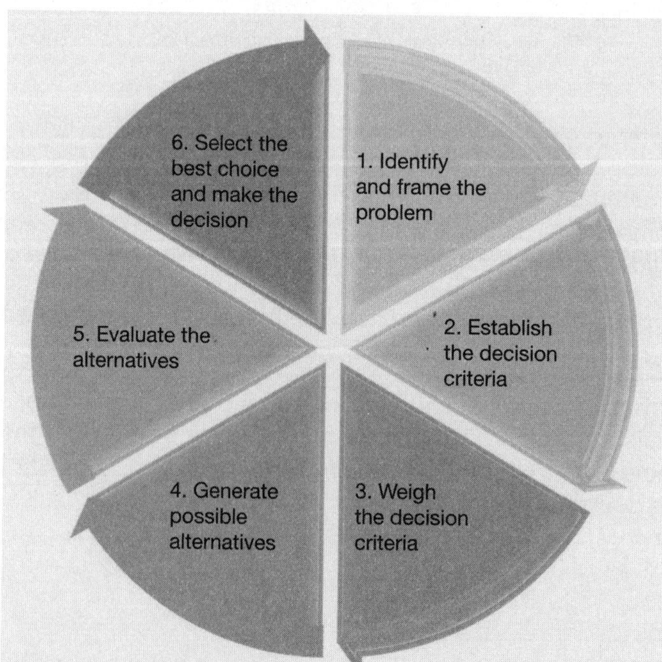

FIGURE 4.3 Rational or Classical model of Decision-Making

The first step in this model is ***defining the problem***. It begins by identifying the issue on hand and why a decision must be made and how important it is. Then by describing the problem the policymakers can foresee what is the desired outcome. Thus, a clear definition of the problem is made.

The second step is to ***establish the decision criteria***. In this step, elaborate efforts are made to gather the relevant information that is relevant to the issue, purpose, and goal. Undoubtedly, this step involves voluminous research and reflection.

The third step is ***weighing the decision criteria***. It is important to remember that the decision criteria must be measurable as possible, i.e., quantifiable without any judgment bias. These criteria should align with the core values and principles of public policy. It is also necessary to assess the criteria based on the budget, reliability, and safety aspects.

The fourth step is ***generating possible alternatives***. Based on the decision criteria that are weighed in, in this step potential options are decided. In doing so, evidence is provided for each of the possible solutions as to how it can attain the goal or overcome the challenge posed by the issue. Creative thinking and research skills of the group help in generating the best possible alternative.

The fifth step is ***evaluating the alternatives***. In this stage, the decision-making group must reflect on each of the alternatives to know why each of the possible alternatives is the best choice. After assessing the merits and demerits of each of the alternatives the final best choice must be made.

In the sixth step, the ***best choice must be made the final decision***. In this last stage, based on the careful evaluation of the multiple possible alternatives in the fifth step, the best choice is chosen as the solution. Essentially, the question: which choice is most appropriate and why? must be answered in this stage. Finally, the decision must be clear, without confusion or uncertainty associated with it.

The rational model is also typified as a normative model. Accordingly, some experts criticize this model as unrealistic because: (i) generating all the possible alternatives is next to impossible, and (ii) all decision-makers might not possess appropriate information-processing abilities involving rationality.

1.3.2 Administrative or Bounded Rationality Model of Decision-Making

The bounded rationality model of decision-making is also termed a human decision-making process because this model emphasizes satisficing rather than optimizing. That means a good decision is more important than the best possible decision. The heart of the bounded rationality model lies in its assumption that decision-makers often are okay with a good enough solution if not an ideal solution, because of the paucity of time, motivation, and other shortages. The notion of settling for an imperfect solution than an ideal solution is termed satisficing. The basic

> In the bounded rationality model, rationality is bounded because of the limited rationality of the decision-makers.

philosophy of satisficing is, finding a satisfactory solution rather than vying for the best one.

Proposed by **Herbert Simon**, this model is a Bounded Rationality Model, because of the limited rationality of the decision-makers. Simon calls a bounded rationality decision maker an *administrative man* than an *economic man*. The bounded rationality model assumes that humans as decision makers often make choices that are more satisfactory than perfect economic rationality. Because, satisfying the conditions of perfect rationality, requires more resources of time, energy, money, and organization.

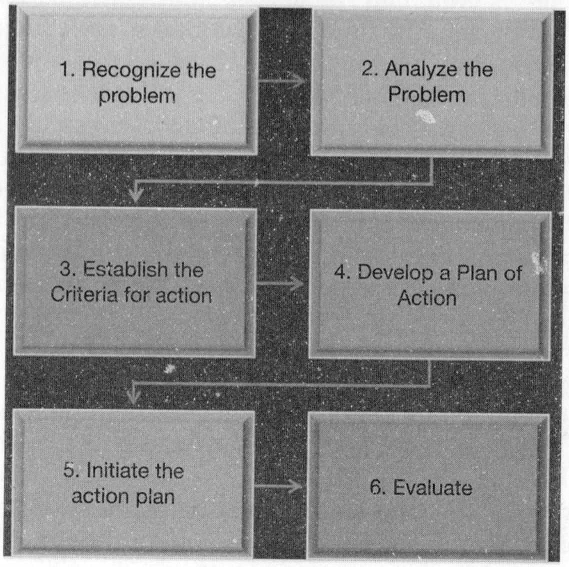

FIGURE 4.4 Administrative or Bounded Rationality Model of Decision-Making

Figure 4.4 shows the administrative or bounded rationality model of decision-making. Step 1 is the stage of recognizing the problem or the challenge that demands a solution. Step 2 is analyzing the problem by exploring the relevant data. Step 3 is establishing the criteria for achieving the expected outcomes that are satisfactory and sufficient though not the best. Step 4 is developing a plan of action by categorizing a set of alternatives, based on the probable consequences of each of the options. Step 5 is initiating the action plan. Finally, Step 6 is evaluating the decision as per the established criteria for a satisfactory solution.

Generally, government officials employ the bounded rationality model of decision-making while implementing and monitoring public policies. Because the government officials believe in satisficing because of the constraints faced by them. However, most of the policies are formulated employing the rational model of decision-making.

2. DECISION THEORY

The decision theory is all about the decisions to know how people make decisions. It evaluates how people make their choices while making decisions. It is a ***logical analysis of how decisions are arrived at while the decision-making environment is uncertain and the decision variables are unknown.*** In brief, the decision theory analyses the decision-making process. Decision theory is an interdisciplinary study of choice. In this subsection, we will succinctly study different decision theories viz., Descriptive theory, Normative theory, Condorcet theory, Dewey's theory, Prospect theory, and Social Choice theory. Figure 4.5 shows the Decision theories.

A decision theory evaluates how people make their choices while making decisions.

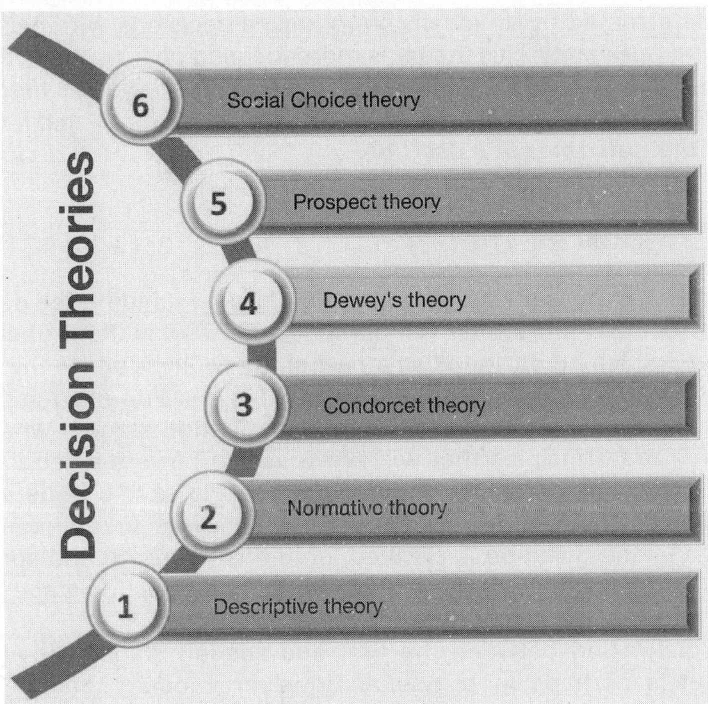

FIGURE 4.5 Decision Theories

Decision theory is an interdisciplinary study of choice.

2.1 Descriptive Theory

We will understand the importance of descriptive theory from the public policy perspective. However, first, we will look at descriptive theory from a theoretical perspective. ***A descriptive theory is about how people make decisions.*** The descriptive theory seeks to understand rationality by explaining and encapsulating the decisions in statistical terms. This theory looks at what constitutes the recapitulation of rational decision-making by the people. Descriptive decision theory characterizes and expounds on the regularities in people's choices while making decisions.

A descriptive theory looks at what constitutes the recapitulation of rational decision-making by the people.

Descriptive decision theory studies how irrational beings make their decisions. The descriptive theory framework broadly categorizes three types of decisions: (i) decisions under certainty, (ii) decisions under uncertainty, and (iii) decisions under conflict. In public policy, the decisions of the government officials can be explained using this descriptive theory as they face the above-mentioned three scenarios in their functioning.

2.2 Normative Theory

A normative theory is a prescriptive theory on how decisions should be made to maximize the value of the outcomes of a decision.

A normative theory is all about how decisions should be made. The normative theory contrasts with a descriptive theory which is about how decisions are made. It identifies optimal decisions where optimality is mostly determined by an idealist who makes decisions with perfect accuracy and rationality. This theory is more focused on how the most ideal decision must be made for a certain situation. ***A normative theory is a prescriptive theory on how decisions should be made to maximize the value of the outcomes of a decision.***

2.3 Condorcet Theory

Condorcet's theory is an insightful theory of understanding the decision-making process. Philosopher Condorcet (1743-1794) is the proponent of this theory which he designed as a part of the motivation for the French constitution in 1793. According to Condorcet, a decision-making process involves three stages: (i) discussion & examination stage – where one "discusses the principles that will serve as the basis for decision in a general issue; one examines the various aspects of this issue and the consequences of different ways to make the decision." (ii) opinion formation stage – "the question is clarified, opinions approach and combines to a small number of more general opinions." (iii) selection stage – "consists of the actual choice between these alternatives."

The distinction between the first and second stages provided by Condorcet is perhaps more useful. However, modern theories rarely make use of the contributions of Condorcet's theory.

2.4 Dewey's Theory

John Dewey dealt with the evolution of abstract thinking and explained what is relatively practical and direct. Dewey proposed five distinct types of common elements in the decision-making process. It is known as Dewey's five⊠stage decision process. According to Dewey, problem-solving consists of five consecutive stages:

(1) a felt difficulty,
(2) the definition of the character of that difficulty,
(3) suggestion of possible solutions,
(4) evaluation of the suggestion, and

(5) further observation and experiment leading to acceptance or rejection of the suggestion.

2.5 Prospect Theory

The Prospect theory of decision-making states that decision-making is all about choosing among the alternatives that are themselves based on judgments. This theory finds its origins in the contributions of Kahneman and Tversky on judgmental heuristics and the biases that can accompany assessments of frequency and probability. Prospect theory involves two phases: Phase 1. the Editing phase serves "to organize and reformulate the options to simplify subsequent evaluation and choice." Phase 2. is the Evaluation phase which evaluates the previous editing phase.

This theory finds its use in international relations in the realm of comparative politics. It was used to explain the rescue mission of the hostages in Iran and the Cuban missile crisis, and the nature of risk in economic restructuring in Latin American countries.

2.6 Social Choice Theory

Kenneth Arrow and Duncan Black popularized the social choice theory.

Social choice theory is the study of collective decision processes and procedures. Social choice theory is not a single theory, but a cluster of models aggregating the individual inputs into collective outputs. Social choice is a theoretical framework that analyses collectively the individual opinions, preferences, interests, or welfare to reach a collective decision or a kind of social welfare. ***This theory blends the elements of welfare economics and voting theory. It is methodologically individualistic but it aggregates the preferences and behaviors of individual members of society.***

The contributions of Kenneth Arrow and Duncan Black popularized the social choice theory during the 20th century. It has found its applications in welfare economics and social epistemology.

Social choice theory is methodologically individualistic but it aggregates the preferences and behaviors of individual members of society.

To sum up the discussion on Decision theories, we can opine that the application of the above theories is dependent on the situation and the stage of the policy process. From the public policy perspective, the institutions of the state i.e., the government bodies find the immense use of the above theoretical ideas in the public policy process. Hence, as a student of public policy, it is important to know the basics of these decision theories.

3. PUBLIC CHOICE THEORY

In this subsection, we discuss the Public Choice theory and its importance in the public policy arena. Public choice assumes greater significance in government decision-making because it is the result of the actions of individuals and policy actors. Knowing the applicability of the public choice theory is vital to the study of public policy.

3.1 Why Study Public Choice?

Public choice assumes greater significance in government decision-making because it is the result of the actions of individuals and policy actors.

Public Choice employs the tools of economics in the practice of politics and government in generating important insights into democratic decision-making.

The idea of public choice is the choice between the people and the social environment. From the behavioral economics perspective, people's demand, supply, and output of public goods are influenced by the political process of democratic decision-making. From the lens of political science, public choice endeavors to comprehend how public policies are derived and how are they influenced by political institutions.

Public Choice adopts the methods and tools of economics to study how politics and government work. This approach produces some surprising insights, and throws up a challenging question – how efficient, effective, and legitimate the political process is? The main assumptions of public choice are self-interest and rational actors; the main goal is to find an equilibrium with these assumptions. Both the assumptions: self-interest and rational actor can be moderated in certain situations. Even today it is observed that economists and many others propose ideas that would work only if the government were a benevolent despot.

The study of public choice helps in four ways: (i) to understand government behavior both in democracies and non-democracies, (ii) to comprehend the consequences of government behavior, and (iii) why do some countries fail to grow? (iv) to design getter constitutions, and (v) to avoid the Nirvana Fallacy.

3.2 Main Contributions of Public Choice Theory

The public choice theory has several contributions. The works of Kenneth Arrow, James Buchanan, William Niskanen, and Duncan Black have greatly contributed to the public choice theory. Among others, James Buchanan is well-known for his contributions to the "public choice theory" of economics, which revolutionized the way experts study economic and political decision-making. It has reformed the study of democratic decision-making processes. Mainly, Public Choice employs the tools of economics in the practice of politics and government in generating important insights into democratic decision-making. In simple words, ***the public choice theory is the application of economics to political science.*** It observes that politicians tend to make economic policies to be re-elected.

According to the "impossibility theorem", there is no mechanism for making collective choices, other than dictatorship.

The public choice theory has revealed that people economize as voters, and lobby groups aim to maximize the outcome for minimum effort following their expectations. This theory has used the tools of economics like profit, loss, price, and efficiency to analyze politics as well.

This theory highlights that collective decision-making is obligatory in some spheres. In the context of market failures and government failures, Butler (2012) observes that political decision-making is not an unprejudiced pursuit of public interest as it is always a struggle with friction between personal interest and group interest. According to the famed "***impossibility theorem***," of Kenneth Arrow, "***there is no mechanism for making collective choices, other than dictatorship***" because majoritarian democracy is inherently unstable as no electoral rule can show up unmanipulated results.

As a positivist theory, the public choice theory emphasizes the problem of combining individual preferences to maximize a social welfare function. Buchanan and Tullock in their famed book 'The Calculus of Consent' (1962), observe that ***public interest is a simple aggregation of private decision-makers.***

In the Indian context, for every issue, there are a billion viewpoints. Aggregating them to create collective decision-making is the focus of public choice theory. For example, many voices differ on the policy of reservations in promotions. However, in a democracy, the majority decision-making becomes the public policy despite several differing opinions on the issue.

3.3 Criticism Against Public Choice Theory

The postulations of public choice theory cannot be dismissed so lightly. James Buchanan one of the proponents of public choice theory was awarded the Nobel Prize for his work on public choice. Moreover, the public choice theory has gained increasing attention in the last 50 years in shaping public policy. However, the public choice theory is not devoid of criticism. Economist Steven Pressman argues that public choice theory fails to analyze the political behavior and the voting behavior of the public. Pressman (2004) identifies three issues with the public choice theory: (1) it fails to explain why people vote, change in their voting behavior, or the actual votes of people, (2) it fails to predict the behavior of the politicians, and (3) the evidence on the growth of governments contradicts the public choice propositions.

3.4 Nirvana Fallacy

The Nirvana fallacy is equating actual things with unrealistic, and perfect alternatives. It is a tendency to assume that there is a perfect solution to a particular problem. It is comparable to the concept of the "perfect solution fallacy." In a way, the Nirvana fallacy takes us to false dichotomies wherein we accept the presence of a 'perfect solution' that is incompatible with the 'current imperfect solution', or discard the 'current solution' assuming it as imperfect.

> The Nirvana fallacy is equating actual things with unrealistic, and perfect alternatives.

The Nirvana Fallacy is about ***rejecting a realistic solution because it does not meet the standard of an imaginary perfect solution.*** For example, economists often commit the Nirvana fallacy by comparing an 'imperfect market solution' to a 'perfectly working government solution'.

Public choice theory is a rebuttal to the Nirvana fallacy. We must compare a realistic market with a real government. Public choice is a theory of government failure to complement the theory of market failure. Thus, in the study of public policy, understanding the role of public choice theory in explaining the democratic decision-making process is quite useful.

4. RATIONAL CHOICE THEORY

Rational choice aims at maximizing the probability of reinforcement.

The rational choice theory has gained prominence in understanding the dynamics of public policy-making. Before discussing the rational choice theory, let us know what is a rational choice. Rational choice is the choice that aims at maximizing the probability of reinforcement. On the other hand, an irrational choice is sub-optimal i.e., with a lower probability of reinforcement. ***Rational choice means a knowingly tailored action to achieve an individual's objectives.*** The fundamental principle of rational choice theory is that the decisions made by individual actors will collectively produce aggregate social behavior. Because everyone decides based on his or her preferences and constraints.

4.1 Assumptions of Rational Choice Theory

Also called rational action theory, the rational choice theory is a framework for understanding the socio-economic behavior of the people. The disciplines of modern political science and sociology use this theory more often. Completeness and transitivity are the two key assumptions of the rational choice theory. ***Completeness*** means we can rank the actions as per the order of individuals' preferences. ***Transitivity*** is explained as if Action 1 is preferred to Action 2 and if Action 2 is preferred to Action 3, then Action 1 is preferred to Action 3. Some of the other assumptions of the rational choice theory are (i) humans are purposively goal-oriented, (ii) humans possess sets of hierarchically ordered preferences, (iii) humans make rational calculations, (iv) social structures, collective decisions, and collective behavior called as the emergent phenomena are the outcomes of rational choices made by utility-maximizing individuals, (v) emergent social phenomena comprise of a set of parameters for subsequent individual rational choices.

4.2 Theory of Rational Ignorance

It is interesting to know that sometimes some people make a deliberate choice of staying ignorant of an issue when the cost of informing oneself about the issue outweighs the potential benefits. This is what **Anthony Downs** called 'rational ignorance' in his famed book – An Economic Theory of Democracy. ***Why do people behave like this i.e., rationally ignorant?*** Because in such situations, people have no costs or lesser costs than the benefits by staying ignorant. In other words, the cost of acquiring information about the issue is much greater than the benefits that can be derived from that information. Hence, for them, it is rational to be ignorant.

For example, under rational ignorance, people do not bother to vote if the costs of becoming informed about the elections and the costs of voting are too high. Because, they feel that their vote is not a deciding factor, or even if they vote there is a negligible benefit. In democracies, voters tend to be rationally ignorant. In India, during most of the elections, in urban centers, the voting percentage is very low than in rural centers. The reason being even the educated and highly educated people in the urban centers tend not to vote but instead, go on a holiday trip on election day. Why is this behavior? When asked the urban educated voters say that there are no specific benefits for them even if they vote. Secondly, the polling centers are situated far away from their homes. To reach the polling centers, they will have to spend hundreds of rupees and then stand in the queue for voting and return to their homes. These costs associated with voting, make the educated voters in urban places prefer to take a holiday trip or simply rest at the home.

Rational ignorance occurs when the cost of acquiring information is greater than the benefits to be derived from the information.

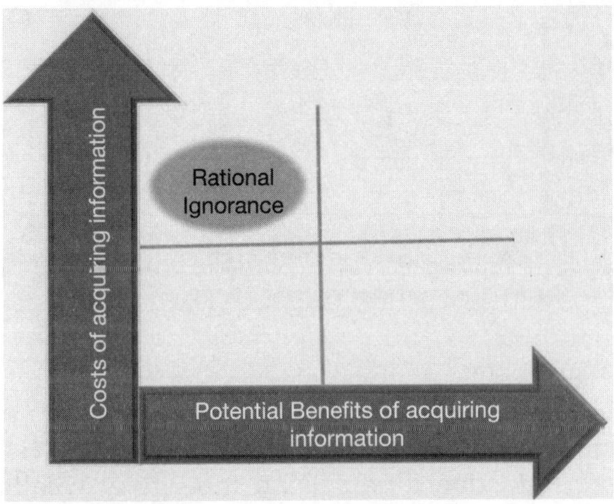

FIGURE 4.6 Rational Ignorance

Ignorance can lead to bad policies. This happens in elections as well. As the voter turnout is less in urban places, the people who voted are the ones who have mostly sold their votes or the die-hard supporters of the parties or the candidates. As a result, there is a possibility of not so good candidate winning the election. This can lead to not-so-good public policies. However, on the part of the voter, when the cost of acquiring information is greater than the benefits to be derived from the information, it is rational to be ignorant.

Irrationality is deciding without a proper reason.

4.3 Rational Irrationality

Rational irrationality is a situation wherein a person is instrumentally rational than epistemically irrational. According to Caplan that rational irrationality is like situations in which (i) some people have preferences

Rational irrationality is a reasoned decision founded on unreasonable evidence.

over belief, and (ii) for an individual, the marginal cost of having an irrational belief is low.

Simply put, *irrationality is deciding without a proper reason* i.e., the counterpart of rationality. However, when both the terms are conjoined as 'rational irrationality, it means that an ostensibly ***reasoned decision is founded on unreasonable evidence.*** In other words, rational irrationality is when a person assumes a belief as rational even though there is contrary evidence.

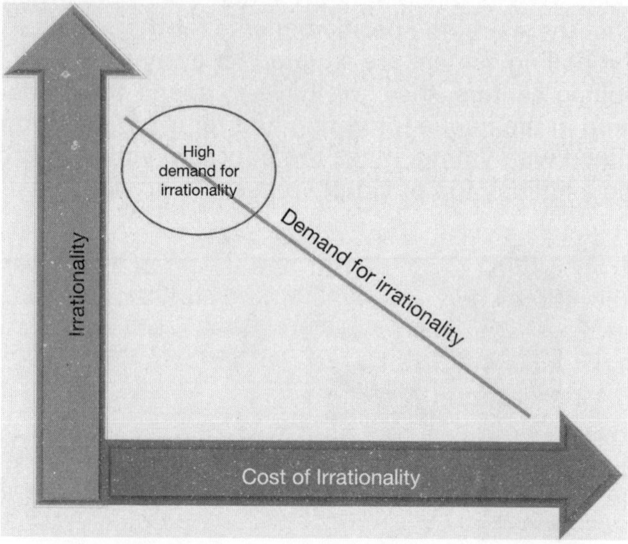

FIGURE 4.7 Caplan's Demand for Irrationality

According to Bryan Caplan, the rational irrationality framework emphasizes that an individual's perceiving the wrong wealth/irrationality budget constraint is indeed a challenge to rationality at the deepest level. Analyzing irrationality in a neoclassical economics framework, Caplan suggests that there is indeed a 'demand for irrationality' (Caplan, 2000). Figure 4.7 shows Caplan's Demand for Irrationality. Accordingly, a person's demand for irrationality is derived from the cost of irrationality. The demand curve of irrationality explains the amount of irrationality a person is willing to endure at any certain cost of irrationality. In line with the law of demand, the lower the cost of irrationality the higher the amount of irrationality demand.

5. DECISION-MAKING IN LEGISLATIVE BODIES

In a well-organized state, political institutions have well-laid responsibilities according to the constitution. Most of the governmental decision-making happens in these legislative bodies. ***A legislative body in a democratic state wields the legislative power and is often superior to the executive***

as it is the law-making body of the state. For example, in India, the law-making body of the Union government is the Parliament. The Indian Parliament, the ultimate supreme body of India is a bicameral body consisting of Lok Sabha and Rajya Sabha. Lok Sabha is the House of the people whose members are elected directly by the electorate during the Lok Sabha general elections held every five years. On the other hand, the state assemblies elect the Rajya Sabha members.

The legislature has five main functions (i) law-making including amending and repealing laws, (ii) ratifying treaties, (iii) supervising the executive, (iv) impeaching the members of the judiciary and executive, and (v) passing the budget and confirming the executive appointments. The legislative process in the Indian Parliament begins with the introduction of a bill. ***A bill is a rule in draft or a statute in the draft.*** If a minister introduces a bill, it is a government bill, on the other hand, if a member introduces a bill, it is a private member's bill. Thus, when a bill is passed by both the Houses of Parliament in India, the bill becomes law.

> A bill is a rule in draft or a statute in the draft.

It is widely known that all legislators are not experts on everything. Hence, the role of the committees is significant. ***In India, there are three types of committees, viz., standing committee, select committee, and joint committee.*** The decision-making by the legislators is confronted by several factors. Table 4.3 lists the major factors that influence the legislators' decision-making.

> In India, the three types of Parliamentary committees are the standing committee, select committee, and joint committee

TABLE 4.3 Factors Influencing the Decision-making of Legislators

No.	Major Factors
1	*Constituent Pressure*: The policy preferences of the electorate in their constituencies more often influence the legislators.
2	*Interest Group Politics*: Interest groups wield some influence on the legislators due to their ideological support, political contributions, etc.
3	*Political Complexity*: Some issues accompany political complexities that affect the legislators.
4	*Technical Complexity*: This arises when the legislators face situations of technical issues that are beyond their understanding knowledge.
5.	*Political Party Disputes*: Political party disputes often impact the decision-making of legislators.
6	*Public Involvement*: In some issues where there is the direct involvement of the public in the form of representations, agitations, blockades, etc.
7	*Jurisdictional Dilemmas*: Sometimes the legislators face jurisdictional issues during decision-making.

6. DEMOCRATIC DILEMMA

Democracy is a great principle, but not so great in its practice.

Many regard democracy as a better form of government compared with other forms of government because of the reasons like, promoting equality amongst citizens, enhancing the dignity of the individual, improving the quality of public policy decision-making, providing a system to resolve conflicts, and allowing scope to correct mistakes. Thus, ***democracy is a great principle, but not so great in its practice.*** This causes the democracy dilemma.

A proper understanding of the political economy of institutions helps in knowing how institutions affect the performance of political and economic systems. Democracies depend on the unrestricted exchange of ideas and information, nonetheless that freedom could be weaponized to wear away the very democratic debate. In a democracy, the government must echo the 'will of the people', yet at times, what the people need is not useful for them. Often it is observed that democracy disguises a structural conflict in the attempts of the people to take advantage of their powers and aspirations. Hence, the democratic dilemma is the choice between shrinking the over-government notwithstanding the widespread unhappiness of beneficiaries or sustaining it regardless of the alienation of taxpayers.

In recent years, the free flow of digital information and free speech through open forms of input and exchange have weaponized to inject falsehood, misinformation, intolerance, and hate leading to the debate on the democratic dilemma.

Summary

- Decision-making is the process of choosing the best alternative option that can accomplish the desired change or advantage to a specific situation resulting in maximum benefits but least risk.
- Group decision-making is ideal because it has the basis of ideas drawn from several people not from a single individual. The group decision-making process stages are identifying the decision to be made, analyzing, and gathering related information, establishing the criteria, identifying the alternatives, choosing the best option, implementing the decision, and reviewing the decision.
- The major advantages of group decision-making include better information, diversity in opinions, democracy, greater acceptability, expert opinions, people's participation, and superior decisions.
- The rational model of decision-making uses logical steps to choose the best option. The main features of the rational model are clarity on problems, clear objectives, agreed criteria and weights, all possible alternatives are known to the group, and the consequences are foreseen, the final decision is rational.
- The bounded rationality model assumes that humans as decision makers often make choices that are more satisfactory than perfect economic rationality. Government officials generally employ the bounded rationality model of decision-making in implementing and monitoring public policies.
- A decision theory is a logical analysis of how decisions are arrived at while the decision-making environment is uncertain and the decision variables are unknown. Major decision theories are Descriptive theory, Normative

theory, Condorcet theory, Dewey's theory, Prospect theory, and Social Choice theory.

- Public Choice adopts the methods and tools of economics to study how politics and government work. The main assumptions of public choice are self-interest and rational actors; the main goal is to find an equilibrium with these assumptions. The public choice theory is the application of economics to political science
- Nirvana fallacy is about accepting false dichotomies wherein the presence of a 'perfect solution' that is incompatible with the 'current imperfect solution' or discarding the 'current solution' is assumed as imperfect.
- The fundamental principle of rational choice theory is that the decisions made by individual actors will collectively produce aggregate social behavior. Completeness and transitivity are the two key assumptions of the rational choice theory.
- The theory of rational ignorance explains why are people rationally ignorant. It explains the relationship between the costs of acquiring information and the potential benefits of acquiring such information
- Rational irrationality is a situation wherein a person is instrumentally rational than epistemically irrational.
- A legislative body in a democratic state wields the legislative power and is often superior to the executive as it is the law-making body of the state. The legislature has five main functions (i) law-making including amending and repealing laws, (ii) ratifying treaties, (iii) supervising the executive, (iv) impeaching the members of the judiciary and executive, and (v) passing the budget and confirming the executive appointments.
- democracy is a great principle, but not so great in its practice. This causes the democracy dilemma.

Key Words

Decision-making	Rational decision-making model	Transitivity
Good decision-making	Decision criteria	Rational ignorance
Group decision-making	Bounded rationality model	Rational irrationality
Delphi method	Administrative man	Impeachment
Groupthink	Economic man	Jurisdictional Dilemmas
Common information bias	Perfect rationality	Democratic dilemma
Risky shift	Judgmental heuristics	
Decision leaders	Social choice	
Compromise decisions	Public choice	
Rationality	Nirvana fallacy	
Bounded rationality	Impossibility theorem	
Expert opinions	Rational choice	
Superior decisions	Completeness	

Questions

A. Quick Check

1. Describe decision-making. What are the major steps for good decision-making?
2. What is group decision-making? In the context of public policy, explain the group decision-making process.
3. Explain the merits and demerits of the group decision-making process.
4. Compare and contrast the classical or rational decision-making model with the administrative or bounded rationality decision-making model?
5. Explain Dewey's five‑stage decision process.
6. What is a social choice?
7. Why study public choice?
8. What is the Nirvana fallacy?
9. What is the logic of the famed "impossibility theorem" of Kenneth Arrow?
10. What is transitivity?
11. Why do people behave rationally ignorant?
12. What is a "Bill"?

B. Explore

1. "Two heads are better than one", "The more the merrier", and "Collective wisdom is always greater than individual wisdom". Discuss these adages in the context of group decision-making.
2. Herbert Simon calls a bounded rationality decision maker an administrative man than an economic man. Discuss in detail.
3. "Public interest is a simple aggregation of private decision-makers". Discuss this in the context of the public choice theory.
4. Why do we reject a realistic solution? Discuss.
5. Why do many urban voters not vote in the elections? Discuss.
6. Explain the decision-making process in the Indian context. What are the Factors Influencing the decision-making of legislators?

References

- Buchanan, James M., and Tullock, Gordon (1962). The Calculus of Consent: Logical Foundations of Constitutional Democracy. Ann Arbor, University of Michigan Press
- Butler, Eamonn (2012). Public Choice – A Primer. 1st Edition |The Institute of Economic Affairs, 2 Lord North Street, Westminster, London SWIP 3LB.
- Caplan, Bryan (2000). Rational Irrationality: A Framework for the Neoclassical-Behavioral Debate. Eastern Economic Journal, 26 (2), 191-211.
- Hammond, John S., Ralph L. Keeney, and Howard Raiffa. (2015). "Smart Choices: A Practical Guide to Making Better Decisions." Harvard Business Review Press, Boston, MA
- Hitt, Michael A., Chet, C Miller., Adrienne, Colella. (2006). Organizational behavior: a strategic approach. Hoboken, N.J.: Wiley, ©2006.

- Howlett, M., Ramesh, M. & Perl, A (2009). Studying Public Policy. Policy Cycles and Policy
- Subsystems (3rd ed). Oxford University Press Canada.
- Justice, Jonathan B., and Gerald J. Miller. (2007). Decision Making, Institutions, Elite Control, and Responsiveness in Public Administration History. In Handbook of Public Administration, 3rd Edition | Routledge.
- Pressman Steven (2004). What Is Wrong with Public Choice? Journal of Post Keynesian Economics, 27 (1), 3-18.

Further Readings

- Butler, Eamonn (2012). Public Choice – A Primer. 1st Edition |The Institute of Economic Affairs, 2 Lord North Street, Westminster, London SWIP 3LB.

CHAPTER 5

Principal-Agent Problems with Elected Representatives

The main goal of this chapter is to discuss the principal-agent problems with elected representatives and discuss the relevant theoretical foundations in understanding the topic. In this chapter, we will first outline the Principal-Agent problem and apply the concept to politics. In doing so, we will being with a discussion of the moral hazard in politics and analyze the political power and political actors. Inequality in political resources greatly affects society, hence we explore the topic of political inequality and discuss how the control of political resources gives an actor a political power base. Continuing the discussion on political resources, we will also understand the nexus between political resources and economic resources. In recent times, political money or political finance has gained much attention in the political economy of public policy. As such, we explore the topic of political money and other political resources. In our endeavor to understand how institutions play a major role in the socio-economic development of societies, we will study the three institutionalisms - historical institutionalism, rational choice institutionalism, and sociological institutionalism. Finally, we conclude this chapter with a brief discussion on the contributions of neo-functionalism in explaining the integration of societies, particularly in the case of Europe.

Section 1: The Principal-Agent Problem in Politics

Section 2: Political Resources

Section 3: Three Institutionalisms

Section 4: Neo-functionalism

1. THE PRINCIPAL-AGENT PROBLEM IN POLITICS

An inherent conflict of interest existing in any relationship leads to the principal-agent problem.

The principal-agent problem also called an agency problem or agency dilemma is usually found in businesses, law, politics, and other areas. The agency problem though seen as a sub-field of economics has profound implications in politics and public policymaking. An inherent conflict of interest existing in any relationship leads to the principal-agent problem. 167 democracies in the world elect their governments democratically. The people are the principal and the elected representatives who run the governments are the agents of the people that they represent. Conflict of interest occurs when the elected representatives' act in their self-interest against the interest of their principal i.e. public interest leads to the principal-agent problem in politics. In such situations, the main question that arises is "*Do such governments honestly represent their people?*" Some political thinkers say the word "representative" has turned out to be a questionable one in the real world, though apt in theory.

Why do situations of agency problems arise in politics?This is largely due to the problem of information asymmetry, where the people i.e, the voters are not perfectly informed about the political candidates. Because there always remains some degree of imperfectness and uncertainty about the traits, capabilities, and attributes of the political candidates. Moreover, during the election campaigns, mostly the candidates deceptively paint false pictures of themselves before their electorate by claiming integrity, honesty, excellence, ability, and loyalty to the voters. This happens of the political might or the money power of such dubious candidates using all sorts of things to impress the voters. On the other hand, honest candidates are forced out of the race as they do not want to pursue dirty politics.

The role of information asymmetry and the incentives to the elected representatives has resulted in the agency problem in politics. Originated from the economic analysis of insurance, the principal-agent problem has evolved greatly in political relationships. As more and more countries have embraced democracy over a period of years, the rising problem of agency dilemma has become a cause of concern in many democracies. In this chapter, we take an overview of what causes the principal-agent problem in politics, particularly in the case of elected representatives. In doing so, we will understand the concepts of adverse selection and moral hazard, information asymmetry, incentives, credible commitment, and know how the agency problem affects policy implementation and public policy-making.

1.1 Moral Hazard in Politics

The agency problem arises due to the issues of moral hazard and conflict of interest.

The principal-agent problem arises when an agent is allowed by his principal to make decisions on his behalf. ***An agent is a person or a group of persons who undertake actions on behalf of the persons or group of***

persons called the principal. In this relationship, it is to be noted that the principal makes decisions about the incentives of the agent. When the interests of the agent and the principal collide there arises a conflict of interest. The agent is concerned about his self-interest and knowingly well, the agent undertakes risky acts because the risk (loss) arising out of such acts are anyway borne by the principal. Thus, the agency problem arises due to the issues of moral hazard and conflict of interest. Accordingly, ***the principal-agent problem is the situation where the agent commits a moral hazard and acts in conflict of interest with the principal.*** In short, the problem arising when agents pursue their own goals or interests rather than the goals or interests of principals is called the agency problem.

Moral Hazard

An imperfectly monitored person tends to engage in dishonest or otherwise risky behavior that causes loss or damage to the principal.

Before discussing what is Moral hazard in politics, let us first know what is moral hazard. ***A moral hazard is defined as the propensity to undertake excessive risky acts wherein the costs or the losses are borne by the principal, not by the agent undertaking such risky acts.*** Simply put, the principal bears the risk that the agent is taking. A conflict of interest arises due to the principal-agent problem. Figure 5.1 Moral Hazard due to conflict of interest. ***Conflict of interest is defined as the divergence in the interests of the principal and the agent.*** A moral hazard is a reaction to incentives to increase the risk of a loss and is a consequence of asymmetric information. An imperfectly monitored person tends to engage in dishonest or otherwise risky behavior that causes loss or damage to the principal.

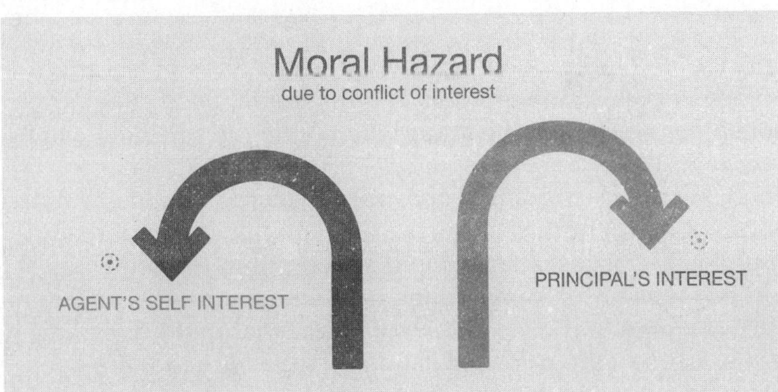

FIGURE 5.1 Moral Hazard due to conflict of Interest

Moral hazards and adverse selection occur due to information asymmetry.

Moral hazards and adverse selection occur due to information asymmetry. Figure 5.2 shows that Information asymmetry results in Moral hazard and Adverse selection. Hidden characteristics and hidden actions are the implications of information asymmetry. Whenever an agent or one side of a transaction knows something about itself that the other

Hidden characteristics and hidden actions are the implications of information asymmetry.

side does not know, it is called '***hidden characteristics***'. Hidden characteristics may be deficient in achieving efficient outcomes if everyone were to be fully informed. Whenever an agent or one side of an economic relationship takes actions that the other side cannot observe, it's called '***hidden actions***'. People resort to hidden actions to take advantage of others' ignorance. Because information is very limited due to information asymmetry, the agent resorts to hidden actions.

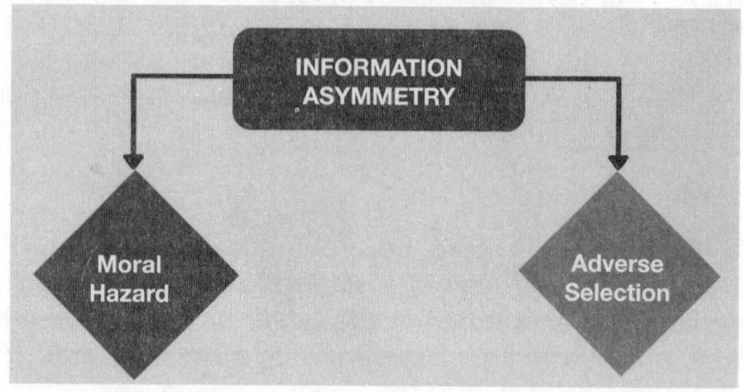

FIGURE 5.2 Information asymmetry results in Moral hazard and Adverse selection

Adverse selection concerns attributes of the agent that are not readily known to the principal

Adverse selection arises when one party to a transaction knows more about the attributes of the good being exchanged than the other party. As a result, the selection of goods available in the market may be "adverse" to the interests of the less-informed party. It includes a disproportionately large number with less desirable attributes. A moral hazard concerns the behavior of agents that is adverse to the interests of the principal. Adverse selection concerns attributes of the agent that are not readily known to the principal. For example, used cars, employment relationships, and insurance areas where adverse selection can be easily noticed.

Agency costs results due to the moral hazard.

Then, ***what are the effects of moral hazard?*** It leads to market failure because moral hazard alters the efficient allocation of resources. The agent typically possesses more information than the principal. This variance in possession of knowledge is called asymmetric information. As a result, the principal does not know what the agent does and how he performs. Further, the principal is unable to ensure that the agent acts in the principal's interest. Hence, there is an agency cost.

How can the agency problem be overcome? It is possible to some extent by realigning the incentives – although sometimes it is impossible.

The principal can monitor the agent rigorously

Can the principal overcome the moral hazard problem? The principal is aware of the outcome but not the actions of the agent. So the principal can monitor the agent rigorously. The effective monitoring of an agent's actions is possible only in theory because gathering complete information about the agent's actions is really too expensive and hence is difficult to implement.

Moral Hazard in Politics

In politics, the people (voters) are the principal and the elected representatives are the agents, because the elected representatives make decisions on behalf of the voters for the benefit of the entire nation. Generally, perfect agents work for the best interests of the principal. Similarly, good elected representatives work honestly for the best public interest without giving scope for conflict of interest. Because good agents do not resort to self-interest at the cost of the principal's interest. For example, in the case of India, former Prime Minister Lal Bahadur Shastri is known for his honesty and serving the cause of the public interest. However, the challenge in politics occurs when the elected representatives serve their vested interests ignoring the public interest. As the elected representatives assume power and take political control, self-interest reigns over public interest leading to moral hazard problems for the electorate.

Why do politicians ignore public interest? It is because, while exercising political power politicians are tempted to use their power and position to serve their ambitions ignoring the promises made to the electorate during the elections. Personal interests comprise benefiting their family and friends, and business partners contrary to the public interest. This kind of political behavior leads to rent-seeking and corruption in society. This behavior of the elected representatives is affected by three major factors: (i) the degree of power, (ii) the amount of extra profit, and (iii) the length of time spent in an office.

The rent seeking and corruption behavior of elected representatives is due to the degree of power, the amount of extra profit, and the length of time spent in office.

TABLE 5.1 Comparision of moral hazard at the politician and bureaucratic levels

No.	Moral Hazard At the Politicians' Level	Moral Hazard At the Bureaucratic Level
1	The public, or the individuals who vote, are the principals, while the politicians are their agents.	The public, or the individuals who vote, are the principals, while the bureaucrats are their agents in government.
2	Politicians are elected to represent their constituents, but they also tend to serve their interests.	The bureaucrats tend to be interested in maximizing their salaries, perks, public reputation, or power.
3	They give out as many favors as they can to political donors, without losing too many votes from their constituents to stay in office.	Since the bureau is a monopoly, dissatisfied customer is stuck contacting their political representative or going without the service.

Moral hazards in politics can be observed at two levels: (i) at the politician level, and (ii) at the bureaucratic level. Table 5.1 compares the moral hazard at the politician and bureaucratic levels. In recent times, we notice that ***representative democracy and bureaucracy create more problems than they are solving.***

India is ranked 85 according to the Transparency International's Corruption Perception Index 2021

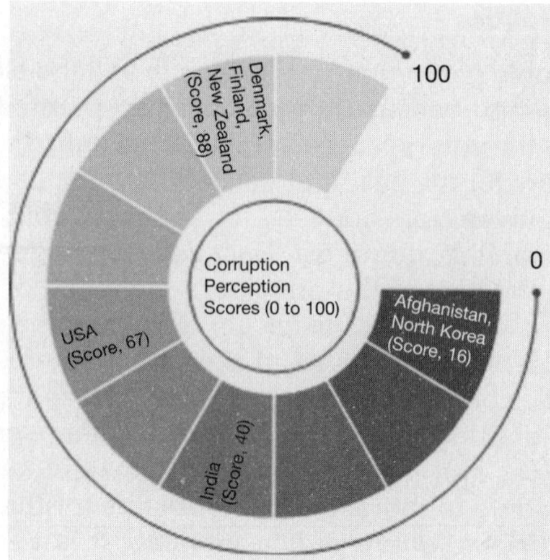

FIGURE 5.3 The Transparency International's 2021 Corruption Perception Scores

Influence is nothing but power in action.

Transparency International observes that corruption is becoming a driver of democratic decline across the world. Corruption has produced a vicious cycle in many countries, where corruption undermines the democratic institutions, in turn, the weakened institutions are unable to control corruption. Moreover, political corruption is much more dangerous than other forms of corruption, because it manipulates the policies, weakens the institutions, and influences the rules and regulations for private gain causing immense public loss. According to Transparency International's Corruption Perception Index 2021, Denmark, Finland, and New Sealand stand in the top ranks with very less corruption. Whereas the US considered a developed economy and the oldest democracy is ranked 27, India is ranked 85, Indonesia 96, the Philippines 117, and the worst performers are Afghanistan and North Korea with at 174th rank. Figure 5.3 shows Transparency International's 2021 Corruption Perception Scores.

1.2 Political Power and Political Actors

Politics is power in action

Power is control over others

Power allocates resources.

"Man is a political animal" – Aristotle. This statement takes into account the basic desire of every human to find fulfillment through a political community. Power is not an abstract afloat in the void, but it is indeed personified in humans. ***Influence is nothing but power in action.*** Power is a connection prevailing wherever a person can enforce his will on another person or other persons, causing the latter to obey whether they like it or not. ***Power is the ability to influence the conduct of others for the desired outcome.*** In simple words, *power is control over others.* Boulding (1989) defines power as the one that allows getting what we aspire to or desire. On the other hand, Wilson (1999) defines *power as one that allocates resources.* According to McClelland's Theory of Needs, power is a dominant motivator to achieve.

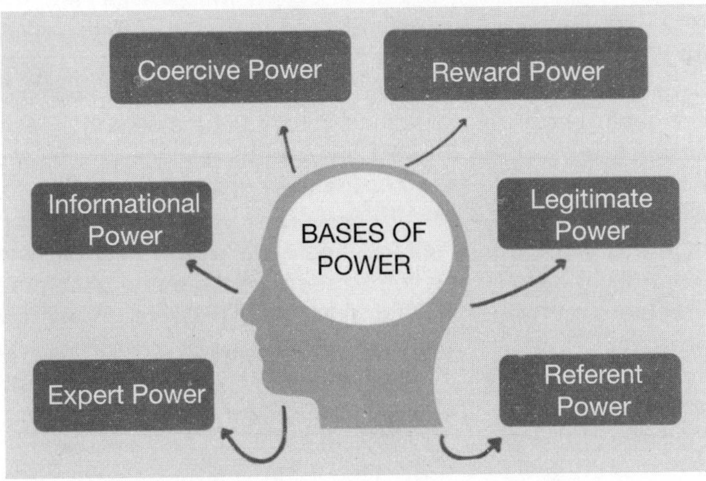

FIGURE 5.4 Types of Power

James French and Bertram Raven (1959) categorized power into five types: (i) coercive power, (ii) reward power, (iii) legitimate power, (iv) referent power, and (v) expert power. However, Raven (1993) added a sixth type of power informational power.

Figure 5.4 shows the six types of power. Coercive power is influencing others through fear and punishment i.e., a power based on fear. It is quite infamous as it is associated with the conventional definition of power. Reward power is exactly contrary to coercive power. It is compliance accomplished founded on the ability to give out rewards that are valuable to others. It influences by controlling resources and giving rewards when the target person values those potential rewards. Legitimate power arises out of one's position of authority a kind of hierarchical power. People with legitimate power can exercise both reward and coercive powers. Referent Power arises out of one's status in society. This works because the "followers" identify themselves with the leader and admire the leader. Expert power originates from the expertise or skill or knowledge of a leader. This power is associated with the qualification, credentials, and reputation of the leader. Informational power is founded on logic and information that could be used to influence the other's behavior. It is a power that originates from one's access to and control over information. Many a time information is more effective if it is "overheard" than presented directly.

There exists a nexus between ***dependency*** and power. Dependency is directly related to power i.e., the more that a person or group of persons are dependent on a person, the more power that person has. Dependency is created because of importance, scarcity, and nonsubstitutability.

TABLE 5.2 Understanding political power and political actors

Political Power	Political Actors
1. It is the capacity to affect significantly the political behavior of others and ultimately to shape and control important decisions on public policy. 2. Political power is based on control of political resources.	1. A political actor can be a person, a family, an interest group or its leadership elite, the leaders and sponsors of a political action committee, the leaders of a political party or one of its factions, a particular governmental institution, office or agency, or the entire government. 2. A Political actor possesses and exercises political power because of its control of certain things that are highly valued by large numbers of people within the society.

Power tends to corrupt, and absolute power corrupts absolutely

The British historian John Emerich Edward Dalberg said, "***Power tends to corrupt, and absolute power corrupts absolutely***". According to Dalberg, power is inherently evil and hence, political power and political actors should not be trusted. ***Politics is power in action.*** Political actors exercise their power. Political behavior is activity is an influence or an attempt to influence the distribution of resources. Table 5.2 illustrates the political power and political actors in a nutshell.

Control of political resources gives an actor a political power base.

Control of political resources gives an actor a political power base. The political actor can give away or withhold things that are highly valued in society. The political actor can allocate rewards to those who cooperate and behave politically in the desired manner and penalize those who do not. The political actor hence can impact significantly on the political behavior of other actors through the actual or promised use of rewards and penalties.

From the public policy perspective, it is essential to understand political power and its dynamics. Politicians are the ones who get elected in democracies and make policies and rules for the nation. Hence, the knowledge of power and politics is quite useful for a student of public policy.

2. POLITICAL RESOURCES

Political resources are the resources that are used in political decision-making that make claims toward a legislative or a decision-making body.

In the study of public policy, knowing about the political resources helps us in understanding the politics behind it and how these resources affect public policy-making. The control of particular things that are highly valued by most people in society creates political resources. Political resources are how one political actor can influence and control the political behavior of others using one or more forms of authoritative decision-making and governmental action. ***Political resources are the resources that are used in political decision-making that make claims toward a legislative or a decision-making body.***

Some of the major political resources are (1) Votes and other forms of political support, (2) Money, property, and other material possessions, (3) Information, knowledge, and skills, (4) Jobs, business contracts, business, and professional licenses, permission to extract minerals, timber, and other raw materials from government-owned land, and other means of making fortune, (5) Tax credits or reductions targeted to benefit particular groups and businesses firms or the economy as a whole, (6) authority to regulate and deregulate any economic sector, (7) economic security created out of social-welfare programs, (8) safety from illegitimate physical force, violence, and deprivation, (9) reputation and status in the society, (10) public policies supportive of one's ideology, and (11) and a countless variety of other values of political consideration.

2.1 Political Inequality

Every society is characterized by some other form of political inequality. In every society, different groups of people wield differing degrees of political power. The political power of these groups varies depending upon the level of political resources they possess. The political resources are not always evenly and equally distributed. ***The uneven and unequal distribution of political resources results in political inequality.*** In some societies, there is a higher concentration of power in a few elite groups and the rest is virtual with no power. Figure 5.5 illustrates political inequality. Accordingly, we can understand political inequality as the possession of unequal and exercise of unequal political power by the people in the society. Put simply, ***political inequality is the unequal influence over decision-making by political institutions and the resultant unequal outcomes.***

The political resources are not always evenly and equally distributed.

Political inequality exists because of the unequal distribution of political, social, and economic resources within the society. According to Dubrow (2014), political inequality hence reveals 'both unequal influence of political power and the unequal outcomes of political decisions, with the powerless in the political system being subjected to disadvantage.

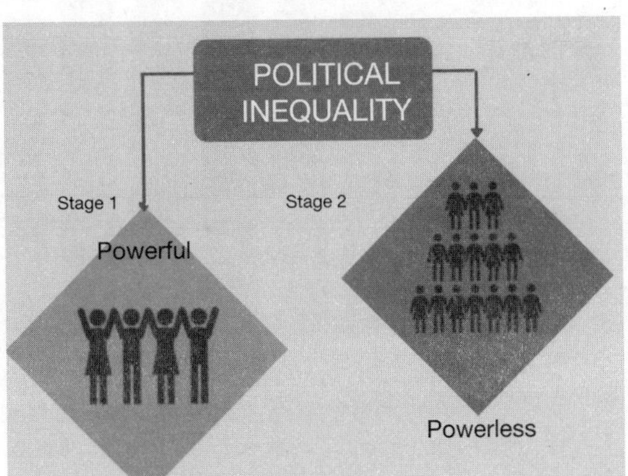

FIGURE 5.5 Illustration of Political Inequality

Why should we worry about political inequality? Because, political inequality threatens the integrity of democracy as it leads to the rigging of the political process in favor of the wealthy, uber-rich, the powerful, and the well-connected. Political inequality arises when few individuals or certain groups exercise bigger influence and control over the political decision-making and are entitled to benefit from unequal outcomes of such decisions, notwithstanding the (procedural) equality cherished in the democratic process. However, research shows that political inequality is closely connected with socioeconomic inequalities. ***Political inequality is a more complex, and multidimensional phenomenon, that is manifested in several spheres of society***. It is largely influenced by the resources, opportunity costs, beliefs, and power and influence.

Three major facts about political inequality are (i) political systems are more favorable to economic elites than the average citizen, (ii) political systems experience more participation from economic elites than the average citizen, and (iii) political systems are mostly represented by the economic elites than the average citizen.

According to the ***Political Inequality Index*** developed by Choi (2019) available at the Inter-university Consortium for Political and Social Research (Open ICPSR), the political inequality index is measured on a scale of 0 to 100; with 0 being near perfect equality, and 100 is near perfect inequality. In 2016, Germany showed the least political inequality with a 40.13 score, and Japan had the highest political inequality score of 67.07. India's political inequality score was 47.07. Appendix 5.1 shows the Political Inequality Index for the period from 1990 to 2016.

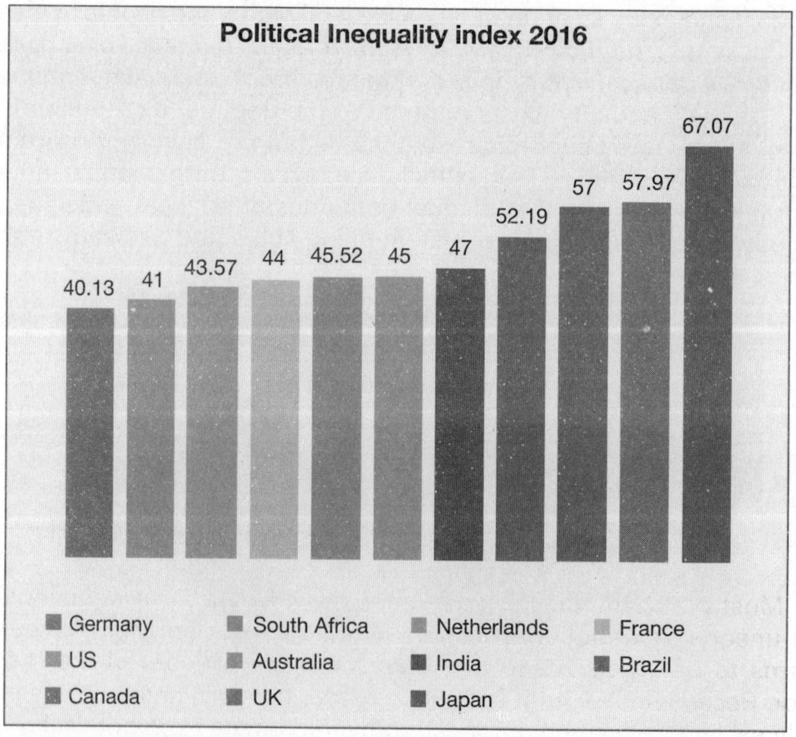

Credit: Graph made by author based on: Choi, Gwangeun. Political Inequality Index. Ann Arbor, MI: Inter-university Consortium for Political and Social Research [distributor], 2019-12-01. https://doi.org/10.3886/E101268V3, released under CCBY 4.0 International license

FIGURE 5.6 Political Inequality Index 2016.

2.2 Political Resources and Economic Resources

We know that political resources are the ones used in political decision-making that make claims toward a legislative or a decision-making body. On the other hand, economic resources such as money, property, and wealth constitute a prime source of political power. ***Economic resources are those resource items that can be used in the production of goods and services.*** Economic resources enable businesses to operate. Probably without them, production cannot happen. Broadly, economic resources are classified as natural resources, human resources, and capital resources. Natural resources include land, soil, fossil fuels, minerals, materials, flora, and fauna. Human resources include labor and human entrepreneurship. Capital resources are capital and technology. Sometimes, technology is implied as entrepreneurship.

Economic resources are those resource items that can be used in the production of goods and services.

In large societies, some persons and groups have greater amounts of disposable income and wealth which they can use for political purposes and gain significant political power for themselves. Those who make effective use of such political money possess and exercise greater political power than most members of society. In societies with private enterprise, a market economy, and a constitutional democratic system of government there is a wide distribution of economic and political resources due to varying talents and interests, and for the most part, have free play.

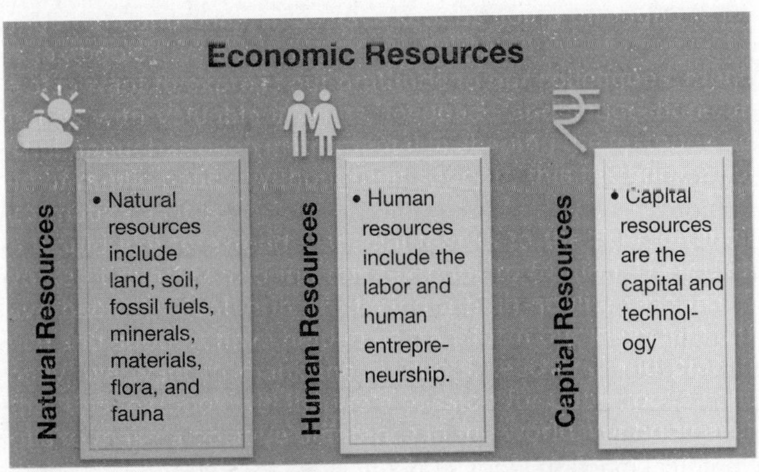

FIGURE 5.7 Types of Economic Resources

Mostly, *all democracies go through a level of political inequality.* With the unequal distribution of economic resources, democracy, therefore, seems to be impassive to the interests or preferences of the majority poor. Because those with economic resources dominate and systematically exclude those with poor economic resources from political power.

There is an unholy nexus between economic resources and political resources.

Because of the unholy nexus between economic resources and political resources, political inequality continues to thrive in most democracies and even threatens the very ideals of democracy. Those with comparatively greater social and economic resources have better influence

Political finance is the money collected and spent for political purposes.

over the political process, its decisions, and outcomes. This shows that possession of economic resources has access to political resources.

To illustrate this nexus between economic resources and political resources, let us consider the case of a person who owns a chain of educational institutional institutions. Every political party woos him to join their party and many a time he is made the minister. Why does he become a minister so easily irrespective of any party coming to power? How does he get political power? It is because the economic resources he has with him to the tune of thousands of crores attract the political parties to lure him to political power. This example shows how economic resources have an unholy nexus with political resources leading to political power.

2.3 Political Money and Other Political Resources

Political money also called political finance is the money collected and spent for political purposes. A narrow definition of political finance is that it is campaign and party funding. According to Vifredo Pareto (1935), three reasons motivate political finance: (i) ideological, (ii) social, and (iii) financial. The problems related to political finance are always at the heart of the debate on political corruption. In many countries, political donations are legal but have always been opaque. It is because the law gives scope for such loopholes to allow irregularity. For example, in 2001, Labor Party received a donation of GBR 125000 from billionaire Lakshmi Mittal which was alleged that it was in return for UK PM Tony Blair's help in the takeover of the Romanian Sidex steel plant. There are issues of concern around political finance or political money. Because political money hurts public policy.

A section of political scientists argues that a systematic arrangement for political funding is desired in democracies. Because in the absence of such funding, even the good candidates will resort to unethical means of fundraising leading to political corruption that will harm the public interest and public policy. In such situations, the interests and agendas of the government reflect biases in participation. Possession of or control over political money is essential; but it must be transparent, ethical, and legal. It is observed that political resource deficiencies lead to political silence. Hence, political inaction leads to political quiescence.

In India, all donations to the political parties above Rs. 20000 must be reported to the Election Commission of India by the political parties. However, Electoral bonds were introduced to cleanse the system of political funding. Electoral Bond is a bearer instrument in the form of a Promissory Note and an interest-free banking instrument. A citizen of India or a body incorporated in India can purchase the electoral bond. The purchaser of the electoral bond is allowed to buy an electoral bond only in compliance with the KYC norms and by making payment through a bank account. An eligible political party shall redeem the electoral bond only through a designated bank account. Association for Democratic Reforms (ADR) reports that a total of 18,299 Electoral Bonds worth Rs 9856.7246 crores were sold in twenty phases between March 2018 to April 2022 (ADR, 2022). Figure 5.8 reports the political finance collected through the electoral bonds in India from 2018 to 2021.

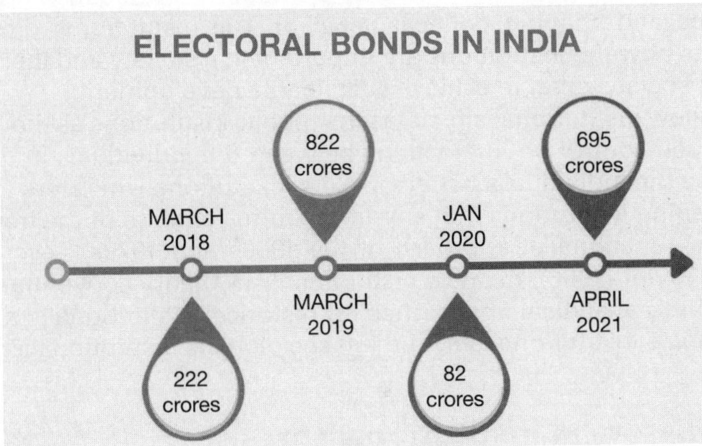

FIGURE 5.8 Political finance through electoral bonds in India

Source: Association for Democratic Reforms (ADR)

According to the Association for Democratic Reforms (ADR), the national parties in India received 3753 donations amounting to Rs. 593.748 crores during 2020-21. Some critics of the electoral bonds argue that even though on the face of it the electoral bonds are anonymous, the government can get to know the information of the donors from the government bank which issues the electoral bonds. This in turn can allow the government to harass those donors who have not donated to the ruling party or compel those donors to donate to the ruling party also.

3. THREE INSTITUTIONALISMS

Understanding how societies evolve and change due to various socio-political dynamics is of interest for a student of public policy. Knowing the role of social and political institutions is quite useful in understanding public policy. In this regard, the study of three institutionalisms is crucial. In the field of political science, institutionalism has gained increased attention due to the role political institutions play in shaping the social and political structures in society.

The ***Institution Principle*** acknowledges that political institutions offer incentives for political behavior, thereby influencing political structures. ***Why should we study institutionalism?*** As a student of public policy, one must know how political structures and political behavior are influenced by political institutions, which in turn impact public interest and public policy. In the study of institutionalism, the word "institution" encompasses customs, social behaviors, rules, way of living, and style of thinking.

According to the Institutional school of thought, economic life is mostly controlled by economic institutions and not by economic laws. From the political perspective, institutionalism includes a range of approaches that emphasize the role of institutions in influencing political outcomes and shaping political behavior. The institutional dimension discusses how the institutions are important in a society and their role in building social capital to achieve sustainable development.

The new institutionalism states that public institutions as the human-created self-control on interactions between the individuals in the society shape the individual's behavior. New institutionalism refers to a turn to privileging institutions that stemmed from a critique of the traditional structural-functionalist approach of the 1960s and 1970s. According to Hall and Taylor (1996), the new institutionalism theory conventionally involves three analytical approaches: (i) historical institutionalism, (ii) rational choice institutionalism, and (iii) sociological institutionalism.

3.1 Historical Institutionalism

Historical institutionalism uses institutions to find sequences of social, political, and economic behavior and change across time.

According to ***historical institutionalism***, the historical institutionalists' stance is between the two views: ***human beings are both norm-abiding rule followers and self-interested rational actors***. Historical institutionalists as scholars place special emphasis on the role institutions play in structuring human behavior. This approach to institutionalism focuses on the importance of institutions in explaining the behavior of individuals. Historical institutionalism is neither a particular theory nor a specific method. Historical institutionalism (HI) is a new institutionalist social science method that uses institutions to find sequences of social, political, and economic behavior and change across time (Steinmo, 2008). It is a comparative approach to the study of all aspects of human organizations and does so by relying heavily on case studies. It is best understood as an approach to studying politics.

A historical institutionalist disregards the belief that humans are simple rule followers or that they are simply strategic actors who use rules to maximize their interests. According to historical institutionalists, individual behavior, attitudes, and strategic choices form inside a particular social, political, economic, and cultural context. They argue that institutions persist because they provide an equilibrium. The actors will be worse off in the absence of institutions. Thus, historical institutionalism focuses on public policy and power groups.

3.2 Rational Choice Institutionalism

Rational institutionalists believe that people follow rules because humans are strategic actors in maximizing their gain.

Rational choice institutionalism is an analytical approach to institutionalism that states that the actors use the institutions to maximize their utility, and in turn, the institutions impact the rational behavior of the individuals. ***Rational institutionalists believe that people follow rules***

because humans are strategic actors in maximizing their gain. Farrell (2018) observes that for rational choice scholars, institutions are typically either *structures* or *equilibria*. Structures are the forces that make the actors choose one equilibrium or the other, and equilibria are the sets of strategies that offer no incentive for any actor to defect if other actor defects. Accordingly, institutions are generally considered as a set of rules. ***Rational choice institutionalism is considered the culmination of two discrete lines of inquiry i.e., social choice theory, and welfare economics.***

Rational choice institutionalism is considered the culmination of two discrete lines of inquiry i.e., social choice theory, and welfare economics.

Hall and Taylor (1996), four major features of rational choice institutionalism are (i) it employs a characteristic set of behavioral assumptions, (ii) it tends to look at politics as a series of collective action dilemmas where individuals seek to maximize preferences, (iii) it emphasizes the role of strategic interaction in the determination of political outcomes, and (iv) it employs a distinctive approach ranging from reductionist approach to intuitive approach to explain the origin of institutions. Thus, rational choice institutionalism focuses on public choice.

3.3 Sociological Institutionalism

Social institutionalism grew primarily as a subfield of organization theory. Sociological institutionalists claim that a "logic of appropriateness" influences the behavior of actors inside an institution. ***Social institutionalism envisages that the norms and formal rules of institutions shape the actions of those acting inside the institutions.*** Brunsson and Jacobsson (2000), March and Olsen (1989), Meyer and Rowan (1977), Meyer and Scott (1983), and Powell and DiMaggio (1991) have contributed immensely to the growth of sociological institutionalism. Farrell (2018) views that sociological institutionalism begins with the premise that institutions are organizing myths.

Social institutionalists define institutions broadly as symbolic systems, cognitive scripts, and moral templates.

Social institutionalists define institutions broadly as symbolic systems, cognitive scripts, and moral templates that provide the basis for interpretation, hence blurring the line differentiating the institution and culture that is underscored in political science. They view that institutions provide cognitive resources as well as norms that are adopted by the individuals. Actors adopt actions, not because of the instrumental value of those actions but because such actions augment their social legitimacy.

Hall and Taylor (1996) observe that sociological institutionalism has three specific features: (i) it defines the institutions more broadly than the political scientists in the sense that institutions are not merely a set of rules but include the symbols, signs, cognitive scripts, moral templates, rituals, and ceremonies, (ii) it follows a cultural approach to understand the relationship between the individual and the institution, (iii) it argues that the institutions develop not because of the means-end efficiency approach, but because it enhances the social legitimacy of the institution as well as the individual. Thus, sociological institutionalism focuses on organizational aspects.

4. NEO-FUNCTIONALISM

Neo-functionalism is a theory of regional integration that restrains globalization but restores territory as a unit of governance.

Before diving to understand neo-functionalism, let us first understand what is functionalism. ***What is functionalism?*** In social sciences, the theory of functionalism states that the premise of all societal aspects like institutions, roles, and norms serve a purpose and hence all are indispensable for societal growth and stability. Then ***what is neo-functionalism?*** In 1958, Ernst Haas, outlined Neo-functionalism, as what would seek to bring closer integration of societies without compelling the countries to integrate either too late or too rapidly. It ***is a theory of regional integration that restrains globalization but restores territory as a unit of governance.*** It is also considered to be the first European integration theory because it was a core part of an extensive deliberation among the supranational and intergovernmental perceptions on European integration.

Neo-functionalism seeks to explain the long-term change without micro-foundational theories of static preferences, bargaining, and institutional delegation. Neofunctionalism is more dynamic in nature. In its initial formulation, Neo-functionalism is parsimonious and predictive. This theory is more of a comprehensive synthesis instead of a single theory. From the anthropology perspective, Neo-functionalism emphasized the interactional modeling of the societal elements. This theory believes integration is a prospect rather than a fact and traces the process of social change.

According to Jeffrey C. Alexander Neo-functionalism tends to create a system of functionalism that is truly multidimensional comprising both micro and macro levels of analysis. Neo-functionalism believes in delegation meaning implicit trusteeship.

The logic of neo-functionalism is that when countries cooperate in a given sector, that cooperation would further incentivize them to cooperate in other related spheres. It holds the view that economic integration leads to increased interaction among the actors in the region of integration. Accordingly, sub-state actors and interest groups begin to cooperate at their levels for further integration. However, Neo-functionalism has been criticized for believing in an automatic integration process and lacking in accounting for growing protectionism.

APPENDIX 5.1 Political Inequality Index: 1990-1998

Country	Year	PII	Country	Year	PII	Country	Year	PII
Germany	1990	39.11	Germany	1991	42.94	Germany	1992	42.94
Australia	1990	53.96	India	1991	52.99	India	1992	53.41
India	1990	54.69	Australia	1991	54.19	Australia	1992	54.19
France	1990	56.84	France	1991	56.69	France	1992	55.83
Netherlands	1990	61	Netherlands	1991	61.40	Netherlands	1992	61.40
Japan	1990	62.41	Japan	1991	62.38	Japan	1992	62.38

(Continued)

APPENDIX 5.1 (Continued)

Country	Year	PII	Country	Year	PII	Country	Year	PII
United States	1990	64.89	United States	1991	65.50	United States	1992	62.43
United Kingdom	1990	66.53	United Kingdom	1991	66.53	Canada	1992	69.37
Canada	1990	69.90	Canada	1991	69.90	United Kingdom	1992	76
Brazil	1990	85	Brazil	1991	89.50	Brazil	1992	89.50
Germany	1993	42.94	Germany	1994	47.39	Germany	1995	46.47
Canada	1993	53.34	Canada	1994	55.77	Canada	1995	55.51
Australia	1993	59.91	Netherlands	1994	58.10	Netherlands	1995	56.26
France	1993	61.08	Australia	1994	59.42	South Africa	1995	57.81
United States	1993	61.40	United States	1994	62.45	Australia	1995	59.45
Netherlands	1993	61.40	France	1994	62.82	United States	1995	61
Japan	1993	71.28	South Africa	1994	63.42	France	1995	62.83
United Kingdom	1993	75.88	Japan	1994	71.17	Japan	1995	70.80
Brazil	1993	89.50	United Kingdom	1994	75.88	United Kingdom	1995	75.89
			Brazil	1994	82.75	Brazil	1995	82.85
Germany	1996	45	Germany	1997	44.72	Germany	1998	38
India	1996	52.33	South Africa	1997	51.22	South Africa	1998	47.12
South Africa	1996	53.60	India	1997	52.24	India	1998	50.66
Australia	1996	53.73	Canada	1997	52.50	Canada	1998	51.51
Canada	1996	55.10	Australia	1997	53.62	United Kingdom	1998	51.66
Netherlands	1996	57.46	United Kingdom	1997	53.97	France	1998	56
United States	1996	60	France	1997	57.76	Australia	1998	57.99
France	1996	62.41	Netherlands	1997	58.98	Netherlands	1998	58.23
Japan	1996	62	United States	1997	61.25	United States	1998	62.55
United Kingdom	1996	75.76	Japan	1997	62.36	Japan	1998	63
Brazil	1996	78.68	Brazil	1997	74.30	Brazil	1998	69.89

Credit: Table made by author based on: Choi, Gwangeun. Political Inequality Index. Ann Arbor, MI: Inter-university Consortium for Political and Social Research [distributor], 2019-12-01. https://doi.org/10.3886/E101268V3, released under CCBY 4.0 International license

APPENDIX 5.2 Political Inequality Index: 1999-2007

Country	Year	PII	Country	Year	PII	Country	Year	PII
Germany	1999	34.17	Germany	2000	33.67	Germany	2001	35.45
United Kingdom	1999	49	South Africa	2000	47.69	South Africa	2001	47
South Africa	1999	49.35	United Kingdom	2000	48.50	United Kingdom	2001	49.90
India	1999	50.28	India	2000	51.01	France	2001	50.56
Canada	1999	50.62	France	2000	51.86	India	2001	50.93
France	1999	52.19	Canada	2000	52.77	Australia	2001	52.82
Australia	1999	56.79	Australia	2000	56.45	Canada	2001	52.91
Netherlands	1999	59.72	Japan	2000	59.82	Netherlands	2001	59.84
Japan	1999	61.79	United States	2000	60.25	Japan	2001	60
United States	1999	62	Netherlands	2000	61.71	United States	2001	64.50
Brazil	1999	67.85	Brazil	2000	64.90	Brazil	2001	64.97
Germany	2002	37.27	Germany	2003	39.64	Germany	2004	41.77
South Africa	2002	46.84	South Africa	2003	44.40	South Africa	2004	42.79
India	2002	51	Australia	2003	51.13	Australia	2004	46
Australia	2002	51.20	India	2003	52.04	Canada	2004	49.95
United Kingdom	2002	52.28	Netherlands	2003	52.50	India	2004	50.63
Canada	2002	52.78	Canada	2003	52.65	Netherlands	2004	51.33
France	2002	52.91	United Kingdom	2003	54.50	France	2004	53.69
Netherlands	2002	59.55	France	2003	58.03	United Kingdom	2004	56.85
Japan	2002	61.54	Brazil	2003	61.74	Japan	2004	64
United States	2002	65.41	Japan	2003	63.83	Brazil	2004	68.45
Brazil	2002	65.96	United States	2003	67.57	United States	2004	70.04
Germany	2005	41.54	Germany	2006	41.36	Germany	2007	41.51
South Africa	2005	42	South Africa	2006	43.81	South Africa	2007	45.56
Australia	2005	45.78	Australia	2006	45.26	Australia	2007	47.40
Canada	2005	48.94	Netherlands	2006	49.88	Netherlands	2007	49.40
Netherlands	2005	49.65	Canada	2006	50.90	India	2007	51
India	2005	51.50	India	2006	51.30	Canada	2007	51.12
France	2005	60.16	United Kingdom	2006	60.89	France	2007	58.18
United Kingdom	2005	61	France	2006	61.11	United Kingdom	2007	60.92
Japan	2005	64.76	Brazil	2006	63.01	Brazil	2007	61.52
Brazil	2005	68.34	Japan	2006	64.81	Japan	2007	64.17
United States	2005	75.57	United States	2006	72.06	United States	2007	69.69

Credit: Table made by author based on: Choi, Gwangeun. Political Inequality Index. Ann Arbor, MI: Inter-university Consortium for Political and Social Research [distributor], 2019-12-01. https://doi.org/10.3886/E101268V3, released under CCBY 4.0 International license

APPENDIX 5.3 Political Inequality Index: 2008-2016

Country	Year	PII	Country	Year	PII	Country	Year	PII
Germany	2008	41.68	Australia	2009	43.53	Australia	2010	43.58
Australia	2008	44.65	Germany	2009	43.86	Germany	2010	44
South Africa	2008	47.45	Netherlands	2009	48.13	Netherlands	2010	48.70
Canada	2008	47.71	India	2009	49.67	India	2010	49.74
Netherlands	2008	48.96	South Africa	2009	49.74	France	2010	51.80
India	2008	50.93	France	2009	51.47	South Africa	2010	51.84
France	2008	51	Canada	2009	53.37	Canada	2010	53.75
Brazil	2008	60.54	United States	2009	58.72	United States	2010	56.65
Japan	2008	63.58	Brazil	2009	59.65	Brazil	2010	58.92
United States	2008	64.29	United Kingdom	2009	61.78	United Kingdom	2010	60.93
United Kingdom	2008	66.67	Japan	2009	62.22	Japan	2010	61.66
India	2011	44	Germany	2012	43.60	Germany	2013	41.55
Germany	2011	44.80	India	2012	44.71	India	2013	42
Australia	2011	47.93	France	2012	46.90	South Africa	2013	45.09
Netherlands	2011	49.09	South Africa	2012	46.99	Netherlands	2013	46.31
South Africa	2011	49.45	Netherlands	2012	47.09	France	2013	47.18
United States	2011	54.28	Australia	2012	47.30	Australia	2013	47.60
Brazil	2011	54.56	United States	2012	53.86	United States	2013	51
France	2011	54.80	Brazil	2012	53.92	Brazil	2013	52.60
Canada	2011	55	Canada	2012	57.12	Canada	2013	58.15
United Kingdom	2011	61.24	United Kingdom	2012	61.62	United Kingdom	2013	59.62
Japan	2011	62.55	Japan	2012	64.07	Japan	2013	63.86
Germany	2014	41.98	Germany	2015	40.86	Germany	2016	40
South Africa	2014	43.61	South Africa	2015	41.71	South Africa	2016	41.66
India	2014	45	Netherlands	2015	43.35	Netherlands	2016	43.57
Netherlands	2014	45.38	France	2015	46.23	France	2016	44.94
France	2014	46.72	India	2015	46.40	United States	2016	45.52
Australia	2014	46.77	Australia	2015	46.50	Australia	2016	45.64
United States	2014	49.80	United States	2015	48.73	India	2016	47
Brazil	2014	51.45	Brazil	2015	50.69	Brazil	2016	52.19
Canada	2014	59	United Kingdom	2015	58.88	Canada	2016	57.16
United Kingdom	2014	59.51	Canada	2015	59.36	United Kingdom	2016	57.97
Japan	2014	65.23	Japan	2015	66.10	Japan	2016	67.07

Credit: Table made by author based on: Choi, Gwangeun. Political Inequality Index. Ann Arbor, MI: Inter-university Consortium for Political and Social Research [distributor], 2019-12-01. https://doi.org/10.3886/E101268V3, released under CCBY 4.0 International license

Summary

- An agent is a person or a group of persons who undertake actions on behalf of the persons or group of persons called the principal. The principal-agent problem arises when the interests of the agent and the principal collide resulting in a conflict of interest that causes loss to the principal. The principal-agent problem is the situation where the agent commits a moral hazard and acts in conflict of interest with the principal
- Power is the ability to influence the conduct of others for the desired outcome. The five types of power are coercive power, reward power, legitimate power, referent power, and expert power.
- Political resources are the resources that are used in political decision-making that make claims toward a legislative or a decision-making body. major political resources are (i) Votes and other forms of political support, (ii) money, property, and other material possessions, (iii) Information, knowledge, and skills, (iv) Jobs, and businesses, and (v) Tax credits or reductions targeted to benefit particular groups and businesses firms or the economy as a whole, (vi) authority to regulate and deregulate any economic sector, (vii) economic security created out of social-welfare programs, (viii) safety from illegitimate physical force, violence, and deprivation, (ix) reputation and status in the society, (x) public policies supportive of one's ideology, and (xi) and a countless variety of other values of political consideration.
- The uneven and unequal distribution of political resources results in political inequality. Political inequality is a more complex, and multidimensional phenomenon, that is manifested in several spheres of society. All democracies go through a level of political inequality.
- The new institutionalism theory involves three analytical approaches: (i) historical institutionalism, (ii) rational choice institutionalism, and (iii) sociological institutionalism. In historical institutionalism, human beings are both norm-abiding rule followers and self-interested rational actors. Rational institutionalists believe that people follow rules because humans are strategic actors in maximizing their gain.
- Neo-functionalism is a theory of regional integration that restrains globalization but restores territory as a unit of governance.

Key Words

Principal-agent problem	Referent Power	Functionalism
Moral hazard	Expert power	Neo-functionalism
Conflict of interest	Informational power	Electoral bond
Information asymmetry	Political inequality	
Hidden characteristics	Political Inequality Index	
Hidden actions	Political resources	
Adverse selection	Economic resources	
Political power	Political money	
Political actor	Political finance	
Power	Historical Institutionalism	
Coercive power	Rational Choice Institutionalism	
Reward power	Sociological Institutionalism	
Legitimate power	Institution Principle	

Questions

A. Quick Check

1. Can the principal overcome the moral hazard problem?
2. What are the effects of moral hazard?
3. Why do politicians ignore public interest?
4. What is a Moral hazard in politics?
5. Why should we worry about political inequality?
6. What is neo-functionalism?
7. What is the logic of neo-functionalism?

B. Explore

1. Why do situations of agency problems arise in politics? Explain with an example.
2. Do you think representative democracy and bureaucracy create more problems than they are solving?
3. Analyze and compare 'Three Institutionalisms'
4. Do you think Electoral Bonds in India are a success in bringing transparency to political money? Justify your response.

References

- ADR (2022). Analysis of Donations Received by National Political Parties – FY 2020-21. Association for Democratic Reforms, Dated July 14, 2022.
- Brunsson, N. and Jacobsson, B. (eds) (2000) A World of Standards (Oxford, UK: Oxford University Press).
- Buchanan, James M., and Tullock, Gordon (1962). The Calculus of Consent: Logical Foundations of Constitutional Democracy. Ann Arbor, University of Michigan Press
- Choi, Gwangeun (2019). Political Inequality Index. Political Inequality Index3. zip. Ann Arbor, MI: Inter-university Consortium for Political and Social Research [distributor], 2019-12-01. https://doi.org/10.3886/E101268V3-78680 and http://doi.org/10.3886/E101268V3
- Dubrow J (ed) (2014) Political Inequality in an Age of Democracy: Cross-national Perspectives, Routledge.
- Farrell, H. (2018). The Shared Challenges of Institutional Theories: Rational Choice, Historical Institutionalism, and Sociological Institutionalism. In: Glückler, J., Suddaby, R., Lenz, R. (eds) Knowledge and Institutions. Knowledge and Space, vol 13. Springer, Cham. https://doi.org/10.1007/978-3-319-75328-7_2
- March, J.G. and Olsen, J.P. (1989) Rediscovering Institutions: The Organizational Basis of Politics (New York: Free Press).
- Meyer, J.W. and Rowan, B. (1977) Institutionalized organizations: formal structure as myth and ceremony, American Journal of Sociology, 83, pp. 340–363.
- Meyer, J.W. and Scott, W.R. (1983) Organizational Environments: Ritual and Rationality (Beverly Hills, CA: Sage).
- Peter A Hall and Rosemary C R Taylor (1996). Political Science and the Three institutionalisms. Political Studies, XLIV, 936-957.
- Powell, W.W., and DiMaggio, P.J. (eds) (1991) The New Institutionalism in Organizational Analysis (Chicago: University of Chicago Press).

- Steinmo, S. (2008). Historical institutionalism. In D. Della Porta & M. Keating (Eds.), Approaches and Methodologies in the Social Sciences: A Pluralist Perspective (pp. 118-138). Cambridge: Cambridge University Press. doi:10.1017/CBO9780511801938.008
- Vifredo Pareto (1935). The Mind and Society, Vol. 4 (London: Jonathan Cape, 1935).

Further Readings

- Butler, Eamonn (2012). Public Choice – A Primer. 1st Edition |The Institute of Economic Affairs, 2 Lord North Street, Westminster, London SWIP 3LB.

Module II

Public Policy Making

Module II: Public Policy Making

This module has four chapters:

Chapter 6 analyzes the concept of the parliamentary system and discusses the structure of political parties in India. It provides insights about the majority rule, median voter, and national interest and briefs on political actors and other influencers.

Chapter 7 provides an overview of India's government levels and the political executive. It discusses performance management in government in detail and the performance management system in the Indian government.

Chapter 8 discusses the role of the judiciary in public policymaking and covers the topics of the legitimate role of the state, judicial roles of the state, legislating from the bench, judicial activism, judicial restraint, the law of precedent, and the tradition of the judiciary in India.

Chapter 9 presents a synopsis of bureaucracy, Max Weber's bureaucratic form, main features, functions, dysfunctions, merits, and criticism of bureaucracy. In addition, this chapter describes Niskanen's model and highlights the role of bureaucracy in public policy.

CHAPTER 6

Public Policy Making–The Role of Political Parties and Parliamentary Democracy

The focus of this chapter is to know the role of political parties and parliamentary democracy in public policymaking. In doing so, we will first understand the parliamentary system and its different avatars: Westminster system, Consensus system, Unicameral system, and Bicameral system. In the second section, we familiarize ourselves with the different types of the party system and the classification of parties. To know about the political parties in India, we understand how the political parties are recognized and which are national and state-level political parties. In the third section, we discuss the majority rule in democracies and the different types of the majority, like the simple majority, an absolute majority, a special majority, and an effective majority. Another important aspect in democracies, particularly concerning voting, is the median voter concept. We discuss the median voter theorem in the fourth section. For every country, national interest is paramount. We briefly outline national interest, its components, classifications, and the methods to secure the national interest in the fifth section. Finally, in the sixth section, we explain how the political actors and influencers impact public policymaking. Overall, in this chapter, we understand how political parties play their role, particularly in parliamentary democracies in the public policymaking process.

Section 1: Parliamentary system

Section 2: Political parties in India

Section 3: Majority rule

Section 4: Median voter

Section 5: National interest

Section 6: Political actors and influencers

Public policymaking in the modern world is increasingly becoming complex. In democracies, the political parties play a crucial role in public policy-making. They invested public resources in the political parties to make effective public policies. However, the active participation of the citizen is gradually declining in the debates, consultations, feedback, and

Political parties are central to the idea of electoral democracies.

other public opinion-making processes. Hence, the role of political parties in public policies in these challenging times is immense in mobilizing public opinion for the proper policy-making process.

The very defining characteristic of the parliamentary system of democracy is the ultimate supremacy of the Parliament.

The parliamentary form of government is also called the ministerial or cabinet system of government.

Why do we need political parties in democracies? People prefer political parties because of two important reasons: (i) parties effectively reduce transaction costs, and (ii) overcome the dilemma of collective action. ***Political parties are central to the idea of electoral democracies*** as they represent the collective opinion of the people of the society. Hence, when they are in the government, they work as the agents of the public.

In a parliamentary system, political parties adopt inclusive models of policy development based on their party ideology, values, and principles. ***Democracies can thrive well, provided the political parties succeed in providing better policies for the good of the citizen over the long run.*** Good policy-making can happen when political parties select suitable candidates for the elections. Therefore, political parties have a greater influence on the participation of the citizen in the political process at local, subnational, and national levels.

1. PARLIAMENTARY SYSTEM

A ***Parliamentary System*** represents a form of government in which people directly elect their representatives to the legislature and the elected representatives, in turn, choose their leader who maintains the confidence of the house to be the chief executive of the government titled the ***Prime Minister*** or Chancellor. They vest the executive power of the government with the cabinet, which is headed by the Prime Minister, who is in turn responsible to the parliament (legislature).

The very defining characteristic of the parliamentary system of democracy is the ultimate supremacy of the Parliament (i.e., the legislative branch of democracy). The other two branches of a democratic form of government are the executive and the judiciary. Figure 6.2 illustrates the parliamentary form of democracy and its branches. While the judiciary is independent, the legislature and executive have a close association and share powers. The executive functions as the cabinet or council of ministers under the Prime Minister. If the Parliament has confidence in the Prime Minister, he holds his office. The parliamentary form of government is also called the ***ministerial*** or ***cabinet*** system of government.

The parliamentary system originated in Britain.

A parliamentary system is a democratic form of government in which the party or a coalition of parties with the greatest representation in the elected house of the parliament forms the government, and its leader becomes the prime minister or chancellor. The Prime Minister constitutes the executive drawing its members from the legislature. The parties with no majority in the house of the parliament serve as an opposition to the majority government and have the responsibility of challenging the government regularly. The elected legislature of the parliament can change the prime minister when he loses the confidence of the majority of the ruling party in the elected house of the parliament.

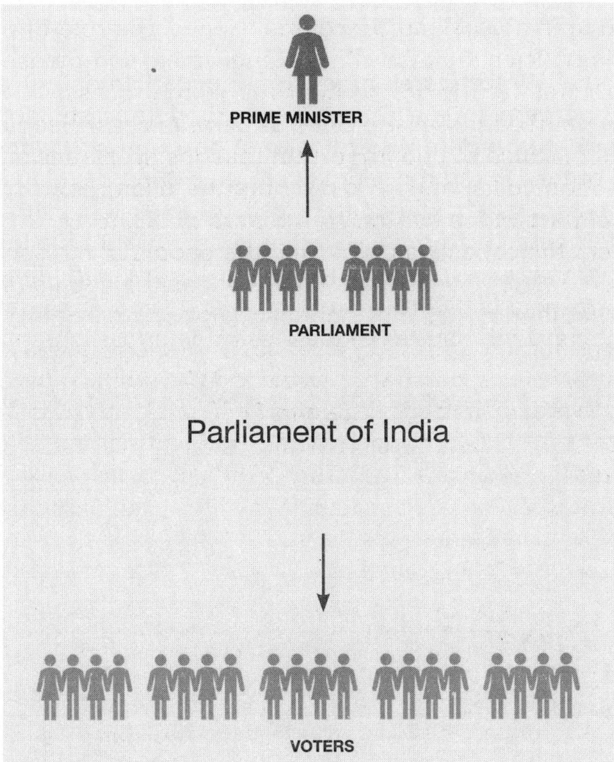

FIGURE 6.1 The Parliamentary System of Democracy

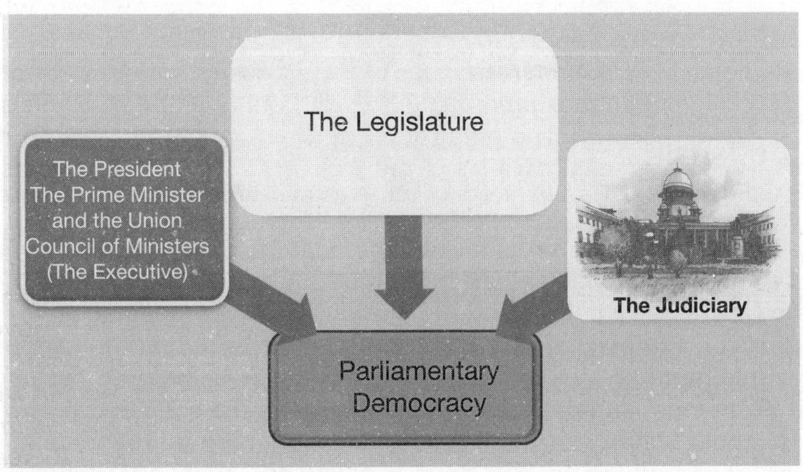

FIGURE 6.2 The Three Branches of Parliamentary Democracy

Primarily, ***the parliamentary system originated in Britain*** and later percolated to other parts of the world as the British ruled a large part of the world in the past. Let us now look at the different forms of the Parliamentary system.

1.1 Westminster System

Westminster model of the parliamentary system is common in the Commonwealth democratic countries.

Known as the ***Westminster model*** of the parliamentary system, this system is common in the Commonwealth democratic countries. This model gets its name from Westminster, a borough in London where the Parliament of the United Kingdom is situated. First developed in the UK, the Westminster System spread to British colonies. It has three key distinguishing elements: (i) an executive that is drawn from the legislature, (ii) the executive that is responsible to the legislature, and (iii) a ***ceremonial 'head of state'*** who is different from the real head of government. Figure 6.3 shows the salient features of the Westminster parliamentary system.

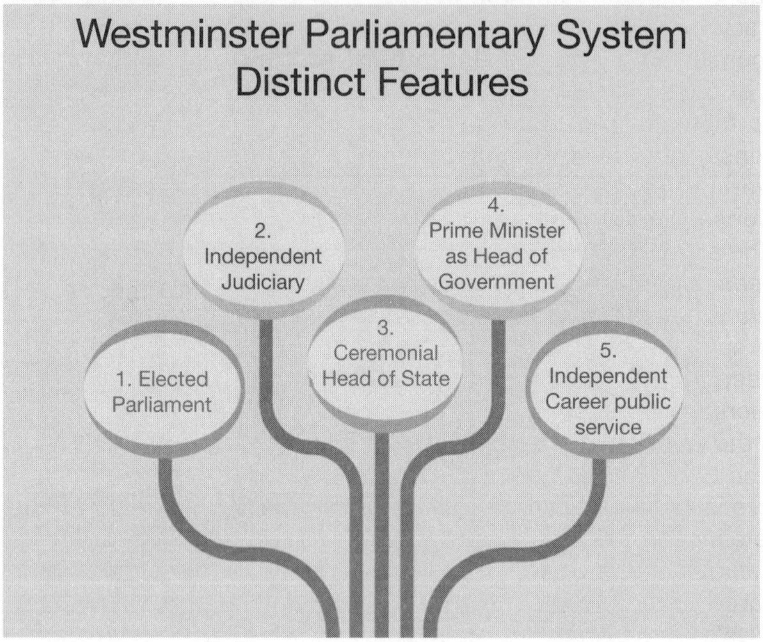

FIGURE 6.3 Salient Features of the Westminster Parliamentary System

The hallmarks of parliamentary democracy are the parliament, the executive, and an independent judiciary.

In a majoritarian democracy, "winner-takes-all".

The Westminster model follows the ***doctrine of separation of powers*** and accordingly, it has a clear division of powers among the branches of the parliamentary democracy: (1) the ***parliament*** is responsible for law-making, (2) the ***executive*** (a representative government) is responsible for implementing laws and government service delivery to the people, and (3) an independent ***judiciary*** that interprets the constitution and law.

Notable features of the Westminster model are (a) democratic elections, (b) a formal opposition, (c) rule of law, (d) Independent career public service, and (e) The speaker of the house runs the legislative business in the legislature, (f) the legislature has a particular term, (g) the executive or government has its tenure if it has the confidence of the legislature, and (h) it has two houses: House of Lords (or Senate) and a House of Commons also called Commons. The Westminster model is best suited for homogeneous societies.

About 36 countries have adopted the Westminster model of the parliamentary system with some variations, including India. Research confirms that in the Westminster model, parliament is powerful at the decision-making stage and has significant policy influence at successive stages of the policy process. According to Russel and Cowley (2016), the Westminster model's influence is both substantial and perhaps rising in terms of policy-making.

1.2 Consensus System

A consensus system of government has the cabinet appointed by the legislature without reference to political parties but as a part of a consensus or non-partisan democracy. People oppose this system of democracy because in this majoritarian democracy, "***winner-takes-all***". The consensus system of democracy, according to Lijphart (1999) is a form of government with institutional structures that allow power sharing to take place in politically heterogeneous or divided societies. The consensus democracy is called a non-partisan democracy. Countries like Switzerland, Belgium, Germany, Sweden, and Denmark have adopted the Consensus form of democracy.

The essence of the *Westminster model* is ***majority rule***, whereas the *consensus model* of government emphasizes the principle of "***as many people as possible***" and hence the consensus democracy model perfectly suits heterogeneous and deeply divided societies. The difference between majoritarian and consensus democracy is that the Consensus democracy is a response to the perceived risk of a tyranny of the majority in the Westminster model.

The essence of the Westminster model is majority rule, whereas the consensus model of government emphasizes the principle of "as many people as possible".

The two key characteristics of Consensus democracy are: (1) the executive is a grand coalition to allow all significant political forces to participate in governmental politics, and to share the political responsibility with all other forces, and (2) political behavior within the grand coalition is geared towards permanent negotiation and compromise.

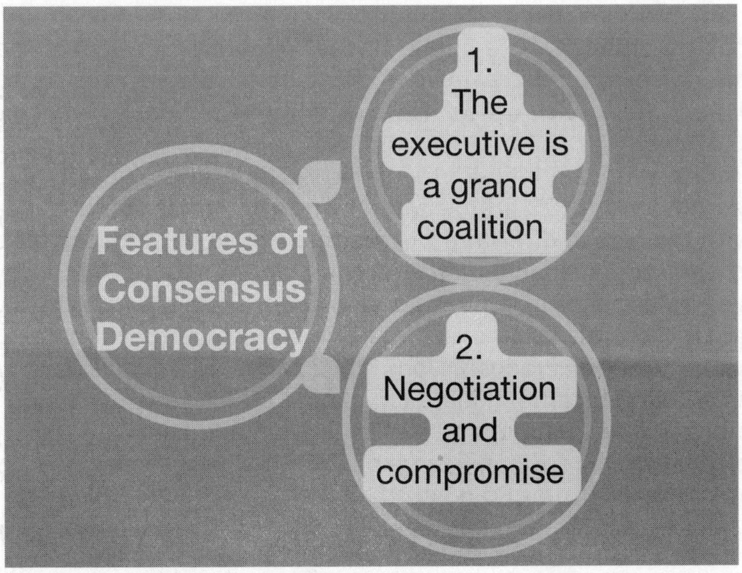

FIGURE 6.4 Key Features of Consensus Democracy

According to Lijphart, consensus democracies empower ethnic, religious, linguistic, and/or ideological minorities by bringing them into the governmental decision-making process and giving them leverage in the process of state policy formation.

1.3 Unicameral System

A unicameral parliamentary system means a single-house legislative system.

A unicameral parliamentary system is a government with only one legislative house or assembly. In Latin, *unicameral means a single-house legislative system*. Typically, small, and homogeneous countries adopt a unicameral form of parliament. Finland, Armenia, Bulgaria, Denmark, Dominica, Hungary, Luxembourg, Monaco, Malta, Ukraine, New Zealand, Serbia, Israel, Turkey, and Sweden have adopted the Unicameral parliamentary system. According to the Inter-Parliamentary Union (IPU), out of 190 parliaments across the world, 111 are unicameral.

In a unicameral parliamentary system, the process is faster and decision-making is easier.

The major advantages of a unicameral parliamentary system are (i) more efficient lawmaking, (ii) the legislative process is simpler, (iii) hardly any deadlock between the chambers, (iv) it reduces costs, and (v) faster and easy decision-making.

From the policy-making perspective, the unicameral system has several merits. The process is faster and decision-making is easier.

1.4 Bicameral System

A Bicameral parliamentary system comprises two separate houses or assemblies in law-making.

A Bicameral parliamentary system comprises two separate houses or assemblies in law-making. The main purpose of bicameral legislatures is to provide representation at the central or federal level of government for both the individual citizens of the country and the legislative bodies of the country's states. This bicameral system of legislature helps in distributing the power within two houses and provides an additional layer of checks and balances within the legislature instead of centralizing the law-making authority in a single house. According to James Madison, "***bicameralism would create two different bodies of men who might watch and check each other***." However, both the houses work together to make laws.

The Indian parliament is bicameral with the *Lok Sabha* and the *Rajya Sabha* involved in legislation.

According to the Inter-Parliamentary Union (IPU), out of 190 parliaments in the world, 79 are bicameral. The UK Parliament is a bicameral one with the House of Commons and the House of Lords. Similarly, *the Indian parliament is bicameral with the* ***Lok Sabha*** *and the* ***Rajya Sabha*** *involved in legislation.* Countries like France, Canada, and Italy have adopted bicameral systems. In India, even seven states, Karnataka, Bihar, Telangana, Andhra Pradesh, Jammu-Kashmir, Maharashtra, and Uttar Pradesh have a bicameral state legislative structure with the legislative assembly (Vidhan Sabha) and the legislative council (Vidhan Parishad). These are Karnataka, Bihar, Telangana, Andhra Pradesh, Jammu-Kashmir, Maharashtra, and Uttar Pradesh.

The ***major advantages*** of the bicameral system are (i) the second house or chamber with mostly equal powers to the first affords a more effective check and balance on government conduct, (ii) helps make better laws backed with thorough debates, and (iii) many times it is difficult for the ruling party of the government to dominate both the houses and pass the laws without effective scrutiny, (iv) provides for equal and adequate representation in a federal set up, (v) the second chamber checks the faulty legislation coming from the first house, (vi) works towards protecting the interests of minority groups, and public opinion, (vii) provides opportunities for the politically and administratively experienced people to be available in the art of law-making, and (viii) checks the excesses and cautions against the tyranny or dictatorship of one house or chamber.

The bicameral system has a rigorous policy-making process.

One can criticize the bicameral system for some of its disadvantages: (a) mostly, the second house or chamber has become the dumping ground for the electorally rejected politicians and for nominations, (b) duplication of functions, (c) substantial costs of law-making, (d) time-delays in law-making, (e) unnecessary rivalry between the two leading to a showing of the supremacy of each other, and (f) due to age factor, most of the members of the second house are dormant.

The bicameral system checks the excesses and cautions against the tyranny or dictatorship of one house or chamber.

From the policy-making perspective, the bicameral system has a rigorous policy-making process, nonetheless slower than the pace of law-making in unicameral systems.

TABLE 6.1 Distinguishing Features of Unicameral and Bicameral Parliamentary Systems

Feature	Unicameral	Bicameral
Number of legislating houses	One	Two
System of Government	Unitary	Federal
Members	Elected by the people	Elected by the people for one house and nominated for the other.
Sharing of Legislative Power	Concentrated in one house	Shared among the two houses
Decision-Making	Swift and efficient	Rigorous and time-consuming
Debates	Hasty deliberations	Thorough deliberations
The deadlock between the houses	Rarely	Often
Adopted in	111 countries	79 countries

1.5 Merits of a Parliamentary System

Public policy-making in a parliamentary system is more rigorous and effective with the active participation of the elected representatives.

The parliamentary system has several advantages in law-making. Because they derive the executive from the legislature, the law-making process is speedier than the presidential system, where the executive is independent. Compared to the presidential system where the president may belong to any one race or ethnicity or caste or ideology, in the case of the parliamentary system the elected representatives who represent the diverse sections of the society duly participate in the law-making process which is truly representative. The parliamentary system helps in reducing the bias in law-making because of the inherent nature of its functioning. The legislative power in the parliamentary system is much more divided compared to the presidential, where one person has the concentration of all powers. Further, a study by the World Bank suggests that they found parliamentary systems to be with less corruption compared with other forms of government.

Public policy-making in a parliamentary system is more rigorous and effective with the active participation of the elected representatives. It helps in serving the people with good public policies that the people will well accept because of the very nature of the parliamentary arrangement.

In the parliamentary system, as the ruling party enjoys the majority, it has a hold over the lawmaking process and hence it can pass the laws without much difficulty and enforce the policies and laws. It controls the executive and makes the executive accountable to the legislature for all its policies and actions. The coordination between the different ministries of the government is well-orchestrated as the ruling party has a direct hold over the government, whereas in the case of the presidential system the executive is independent of the legislature and hence the law-making process and control over the government is not so swifter.

The government in the parliamentary system is directly responsible for the parliament.

The government in the parliamentary system is directly responsible to the parliament (***responsible government***) as the legislature addresses all the issues of national importance and public concern. With an active opposition, they constantly put the ruling party government under public scrutiny and accountability on all its policies and actions and thus track the governmental operations.

The parliamentary system is better equipped to accommodate all sections of society than the presidential system.

Diverse people represent the parliament; gender, ethnicity, religion, race, region, and castes. Hence, the parliamentary system is better equipped to accommodate all sections of the society in the country and provide an ultimate platform for debating the issues of the entire country and making policies and laws as effective solutions. The parliamentary system offers flexibility to replace the government if the ruling party or the ruling coalition loses the confidence of the house and a new party or a new coalition can prove their majority in the house and replace the previous government. ***The parliamentary system provides for several checks and balances to control the ruling party from becoming all-powerful or dictatorial.***

1.6 Criticisms of a Parliamentary System

The parliamentary form of governance has some shortcomings when compared to the presidential system. One significant disadvantage is the government's inherent instability, since it can fall if it loses the confidence of the House. New factions in parliament could emerge due to this insecurity, seeking majority support for a new administration. Regrettably, this happens frequently and leads to lawmakers exchanging their support, which damages the nation's interests. Frequent no-confidence motions and political turbulence create uncertainty and delay decision-making and addressing public concerns. The legislative system struggles to make policy choices in coalition administrations because of conflicting interests. This inefficiency in decision-making has a negative impact.

The parliamentary system is unstable compared to the presidential system because the government can collapse at any time if it loses the confidence of the house.

In a parliamentary setup, there is often a loss of policy continuity as the governments keep changing and parties with different ideologies keep busy overturning or ignoring the previous government's decisions and policies. The parliamentary system suffers from the poor separation of the legislature and the executive because the legislature has a direct connection with the executive and hence the legislative cannot hold the executive accountable or put pressure on it.

To sum up, the parliamentary system over the decades has developed as an effective system of government in many countries because of its role in law-making, representation of people, coordination of the legislature and the executive, and control over governance. Despite legislative flip-flops and problems of coalitions, the parliamentary system continues to be the favorite model of government across the globe.

2. POLITICAL PARTIES IN INDIA

India is a parliamentary democracy and to know more about its government, in the previous section, we outlined the parliamentary system, its types, merits, and demerits. In a democratic setup, the political parties play a significant role in mobilizing public opinion and gaining representation for the people's aspirations in the governance of the country. Because of the importance of the political parties in a parliamentary setup, as students of public policy, we need to know about the political parties in India. However, before discussing the political parties of India, let us know about the types of parties and party systems in general, for a sound understanding of how political parties are effective in their role of representing the people.

A political party is a voluntary organization that mobilizes voters to promote shared interests.

The political parties are the unique features of a democratic form of government.

2.1 Types of Party System

Primarily, ***a political party is an organization that has mobilized a considerable number of people around a cause or an ideology, or specific goals***

and objectives, and vowed to serve the public interest. It espouses and articulates an ideology or a vision that is bolstered by people of common interests and goals. It helps in the process of opinion-formation and policy-making. ***A political party is a voluntary organization that mobilizes voters to promote shared interests***. It has a political agenda, a party constitution, and a hierarchy of political functionaries who guide its functioning. A political party has a distinct organizational structure.

The three main types of party systems are (i) One-party system, (ii) two-party system, and (iii) multi-party system.

Indeed, *political parties are the unique features of a democratic form of government.* Thus, the concept of a party system is an important aspect of a comparative study of political science. ***Why should we know about the party systems?*** Because knowing the political party systems helps understand the electoral system. The factors like the prevalent ideological pattern, balance of power, spheres of competition, and the nature of interactions form the principal institution of modern-day politics - a party system.

Across the world, one can observe different party systems. Broadly, we observe three main types of party systems: (i) ***One-party system***, (ii) ***two-party system***, and (iii) ***multi-party system***. In the ensuing subsections, we will understand these party systems exhaustively.

2.1.1 One-Party System

The 'one-party system' also called the 'single party system' or a 'mono-party system' means the existence of an only party in the polity.

The opposition in a single-party system is just unthinkable.

The single-party systems operate in situations in which they do not tolerate genuine political conflict.

The ***'one-party system'*** also called the ***'single party system'*** or a ***'mono-party system',*** means the existence of an only party in the polity. Such a system vetoes any presence of pluralism, both de jure and de facto. Hence, ***opposition in a single-party system is just unthinkable.***The critics argue why should we call a one-party system called a system. Because ***how can a single party create a system?*** However, within a party, there can be internal differences of opinion in the form of self-criticism and intra-party competition. However, one advantage of a single-party system is the consensus on issues leading to stable government and policy continuity. From the policymaking perspective, the single-party system has several advantages, but an important demerit is it does not accommodate different perspectives and diverse opinions or ideologies. We notice that single-party systems operate in situations in which they do not tolerate genuine political conflict.

In a single-party system, only one-party controls and runs the government and there is no competition. Only a single political party legally holds effective power in the country. The internal selection or election processes depend on only one of the two choices approach. The single-party system is common in Communist regimes like China, North Korea, Cuba, and Laos. Mostly, single-party states are dictatorships, police states, or authoritarian states and draw their ideological base from the political philosophies of Marxist-Leninist Communism and fascism. Therefore, mostly dictatorship and tyranny characterize a single-party system.

2.1.2 Two-Party System

Two major parties that dominate the political life of a country characterize a **'two-party system'** which is also called a **'Bi-party system'**. The American two-party system and the British two-party system are glaring examples of the two-party system. The interesting feature of the two-party system is that both parties dominate the electoral politics in such a way that more often both the parties come to power alternatively and gain command of the government. If one party loses in one election, it has every ability to win in the next election by defeating the opponent party. This two-party system gives the electorate an option to choose between the two.

Two major parties that dominate the political life of a country characterize a 'two-party system' which is also called a 'Bi-party system'.

What causes two major parties to dominate the political landscape? Economist Jeffrey Sachs observes that there is a link between the electoral system and the number of effective parties. The winner in such an electoral arrangement secures maximum votes, but not necessarily the majority votes. Exponents of this system consider that a two-party system prevents the dangers of fragmentation and helps run the government smoothly. Advantages to the two-party system include simplicity when citizens choose whom to vote for and lower chances of extremists gaining power.

Countries like the US (the Republicans and the Democrats), the UK (Conservative Party and Labor Party), Canada (Liberal Party and Conservative Party), Malta (The center-left Labor Party and the center-right Nationalist Party), South Korea (the liberals and the conservatives), Taiwan (the pro-unification Pan-Blue coalition and the pro-independence Total Pan-Green), Spain (the Spanish Socialist Workers' Party and the People's Party) have a two-party system.

2.1.3 Multi-Party System

A political system that allows for the functioning of two or more political parties across the political spectrum in running for all types of elections and gaining political power for policy-making is called a multi-party system. In such a system, two or more parties represent the electorate and control the public office. The multi-party system is the most common form of party system across the world. In this system, if one party fails to garner the majority, multiple parties can come together to form a coalition government. ***A multi-party system accommodates more diverse points of view in the policy-making process.*** Mostly, coalition governments formed by coming together of several parties are the characteristic feature of a multi-party system. The formation of a coalition government overcoming the ideological differences is because no single party gains a complete majority to form the government.

A multi-party system accommodates more diverse points of view in the policy-making process.

The multi-party system comprises liberal, conservative, and socialist parties and other groups from different ideologies and political narratives. In this system, several parties compete to gain political power, but often a coalition of two or more parties has a greater chance of gaining power. From the policy-making perspective, each party in the coalition competes to claim the success of a policy because of its contribution and attempts to brand its allies as responsible for the deficiencies and failures. Critics of this system point out that a multi-party system sometimes leads to political instability.

The ***major advantages*** of the multi-party system are (1) It accommodates diverse interests of different political interests and provides for a wide range of political representation, and (2) The electorate has a wide choice of choosing its representatives. In contrast, the demerits of the multi-party system are (i) mostly no single party can gain power alone, and (ii) it often leads to political instability as the competing interests of the coalition or alliance members lead to a disintegration of the ruling formation, and (iii) more often it appears to be chaotic.

Some examples of countries with a multi-party system are India, Brazil, South Africa, Indonesia, Philippines, Mexico, Germany, New Zealand, Israel, Denmark, Italy, Finland, and others. India, the largest democracy in the world, is a multi-party system democracy. ***Why multi-party system suits Indian polity?*** Because the social and geographical diversity in India demands multiple parties to represent the aspirations of the varied sections of the society and a single party cannot become a dictatorial party. However, for a significant period of Indian political history, the Congress party dominated the Indian political landscape.

2.2 Classification of Political Parties

The political parties are classified in several aspects. The political parties according to Maurice Duverger are classified based on the structure like the ***caucus, the branch, the cell, and the militia.*** The role of the political parties in public policy-making is quite significant in terms of ideological stances, organizational structures, and leadership. However, *from an ideological perspective, the popular classification includes conservative parties, liberal parties, and radical parties.* In this section, we briefly discuss these classifications.

2.2.1 Conservative Parties

The philosophy of conservatism emphasizes conforming to societal norms.

The philosophy of conservatism emphasizes conforming to societal norms. The conservatives reject the approach or behavior that does not go with the social belief system and well-accepted norms, heritage, culture, and societal interactions. Put simply, ***conservatism is a political belief that emphasizes the traditions of the society relying heavily on human dignity and the role of the individual in maintaining a society.*** The conservatives are also termed as traditionalists, orthodox, old-fashioned, and conventional. From the governance perspective, the conservatives believe in small governments i.e., minimal government. Essentially, they view that there should be minimal governmental interference in society and believe in the status-quo. They strongly believe that the government should espouse traditional morality. In modern-day political terminology, ***the conservatives are also called the right-wing***.

US congressperson Mike Johnson identifies seven core principles of conservatism. They are individual freedom, limited government, rule of law, peace through strength, fiscal responsibility, free markets, and human dignity. To be very brief, conservatives emphasize traditions and rely on the individual to preserve society.

From the policy-making perspective, ***the conservatives are known to advocate liberal economic policies, free markets, liberalism, privatization, deregulation, less governmental interference, and reduced government spending***. They view that secularism and moral relativism often threaten traditional social values and norms, and religious morals.

The conservatives are also called the "right-wing".

2.2.2 Liberal Parties

The liberals claim that they stand for freedom, adopt a progressive stance, are ready to make experiments, and do not conform to conventional views but reject the idea of a socialist panacea. The liberals promote a wide range of viewpoints like supporting individual liberty, democracy, secularism, rule of law, political freedom, freedom of speech, and freedom of religion. A clear definition of a liberal party is debatable because of the wider viewpoints that are drawn from multiple ideologies. The liberals believe in promoting a system that accepts all religions and does not encourage the dominance of a particular religion. However, in simple words, ***liberals can be defined as those who believe in a broad political spectrum derived from left-wing, right-wing, and centrist ideologies***. Mostly the liberals are termed the ***'center-left'***.

The conservatives are also called the "right-wing".

From the policy-making perspective, the liberals believe that the governments should intervene in the economy and reform the institutions to provide a wide range of public services for the well-being of society. However, they argue that the government should not regulate individual behavior.

The liberals are termed the "center-left".

2.2.3 Radical Parties

Radical parties aim at transforming the fundamental aspects of society or the political system. They argue for social change, structural change, revolution, and radical reforms in society, polity, and the economy. The radicals advocate for liberation from the privilege of landlords, and the nobles. They campaign for women's suffragette movements. Radical parties are active in Italy, Chile, and France. In India, the Radical Communist Party founded by M. N. Roy is an example of a radical party.

The radical parties believe in establishing a new order by overthrowing the existing institutions.

From the political economy perspective, the radical parties believe in establishing a new order by overthrowing the existing institutions.

2.3 Recognition of Parties in India

The Election of Commission of India (ECI) is an autonomous constitutional body that is responsible for administering the election processes in India.

In this subsection, we focus on the political parties in India and discuss the recognition of political parties. In India, the political parties are recognized as national parties and regional or state parties. The ***Election of Commission of India*** (***ECI***) is an autonomous constitutional body that is responsible for administering the election processes in India. Further, it registers and regulates the political parties.

2.3.1 National Political Party

According to the Election Commission of India (ECI), a political party is eligible for recognition as a national political party when any one of the following conditions is fulfilled:

(i) Which during the Lok Sabha or State Legislative Assembly Elections gets 6% of the total valid votes polled in at least four states and, apart from it, it gets 4 seats in Lok Sabha in one or more than one state.

or

(ii) Which gets 2% (11 seats out of a total 543) of the Lok Sabha in at least 3 states. For such a Political Party, it is not essential to get 6% of the total valid votes.

or

(iii) That political party must be recognized as a state-level political party in at least four states.

The importance of the National Party lies in its national presence.

The appeal of these parties is nationwide. Table 6.2 lists the national political parties in India.

TABLE 6.2 List of national political parties in India

No.	Party
1	Bhartiya Janta Party (BJP)
2	Indian National Congress (INC)
3	Bahujan Samaj Party (BSP)
4	Nationalist Congress Party (NCP)
5	Samaj wadi Party (SP)
6	Communist Party of India (CPI)
7	Communist Party of India (Marxist) (CPIM)

The importance of the National Party lies in its national presence. It aids in solving regional issues and strives for the upliftment of the entire population and the nation. It articulates policies for resolving major national issues. As an opposition party, it keeps a vigil over the ruling party at the national level.

2.3.2 State-Level Political Party

A political party, according to ECI, will be recognized as a State party in a State if any one of the following conditions is fulfilled:

(i) It gets 6% of the total valid votes of the Lok Sabha or states legislative assembly elections in a state, and apart from it, it gets 2 seats of the concerned state legislative assembly.

or

(ii) 3% share of the total seats of the state legislative assembly.

or

(iii) 3 seats of the legislative assembly, whichever is more,

or

(iv) One seat after 25 seats in the elections to the Lok Sabha in a state.

or

(v) 6% share of the total valid votes polled in all the Parliamentary areas of the Lok Sabha elections in the concerned state as well as it gets one seat in the Lok Sabha.

State political parties are those parties whose influence is limited to one or two states or a specific area. Table 6.3 lists some of the state-level political parties.

State political parties are those parties whose influence is limited to one or two states or a specific area.

TABLE 6.3 List of some state-level political parties in India

No.	State	Party
1	Delhi	Aam Aadmi Party (AAP)
2	Arunachal Pradesh	Arunachal Congress (AP)
3	Tamil Nadu	All India Anna Dravida Munnetra Kazhagam (AIADMK)
4	Tamil Nadu and Puducherry	Dravida Munnetra Kazhagam (DMK)
5	Assam	Asom Gana Parishad (AGP)
6	West Bengal	All India Trinamool Congress (AITC) All India Forward Bloc (AIFB)
7	Odisha	Biju Janata Dal (BJD)
8	Karnataka and Kerala	Janata Dal (Secular) (JDS)
9	Maharashtra	Shiv Sena (SS)
10	Telangana	Telangana Rashtra Samithi (TRS)

Source: Election Commission of India website

3. MAJORITY RULE

A "voting rule", generally, is a method for electing a winner from a set of candidates based on voters' informed preferences for those contenders.

Some of the voting rules are majority rule, plurality rule, rank-order voting, unanimity rule, and runoff voting.

The majority rule is a decision rule to select one from the alternatives that have a majority, meaning more than half the votes.

The term simple majority means more than half of the total.

The generally accepted axioms in the voting rule are Pareto property, anonymity, and neutrality.

In a democracy, the people's representatives are selected by a voting process. ***A voting rule, generally, is a method for electing a winner from a set of candidates based on voters' informed preferences for those contenders.*** The basic assumptions of a voting system are: (i) the voting system considers every voter equally, (ii) the voting system regards every candidate alike, and (ii) if there are only two candidates, the voting system chooses the majority preference. In a democracy, the rules are straightforward when two options are given. That is the majority way. But when there are more than two options, there arises a great deal of controversy around the majority rule. Some of the voting rules are *majority rule, plurality rule, rank-order voting, unanimity rule, runoff voting,* and others.

The majority rule is a decision rule to select one from the alternatives that have a majority, meaning more than half the votes. People often regard the majority rule procedure as a natural and optimal one for making social choices.

Generally, the theory of voting evaluates the voting rules analytically by probing which fundamental axioms they satisfy. The generally accepted axioms are *Pareto property, anonymity,* and *neutrality.* The first axiom, ***Pareto property,*** is the principle that if voters choose candidate x to candidate y, then y should not be chosen over x. The second axiom, ***anonymity,*** means one person one vote principle; and no voter should influence the outcome of the election process. The third axiom, ***neutrality*** means no candidate should get special treatment, i.e., no bias (Dasgupta and Maskin, 2008).

In the law-making arrangement, Indian legislative bodies follow four types of majority: (i) ***Simple majority, (ii) Absolute majority, (iii) Special majority, and (iv) Effective majority.*** Figure 6.5 illustrates the majority of types followed in India. In the ensuing subsections, we discuss each of these majority types.

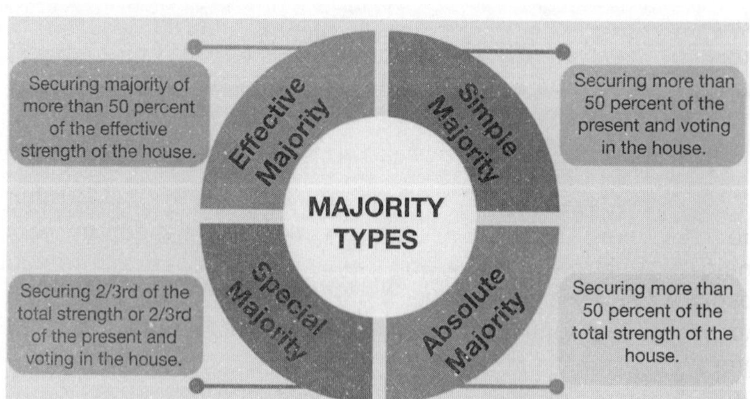

FIGURE 6.5 Majority Types

3.1 Simple Majority

The term simple majority means more than half of the total. Let us assume that you and your friends in your class are electing your class representative (CR). Your class strength is 40. But on the day of voting for choosing the CR, the attendance of the students was only 30. That means voting can take place without the attendance of all the students. If the 30 students who are voting on that day choose one of the candidates with 18 votes, it is a simple majority because 18 is more than 50 percent of the 30 who voted on that day.

A simple majority is also called a functional majority or a working majority.

In the Indian Parliament, a ***simple majority*** means ***more than 50 percent of the members present and voting***. A simple majority is also called a ***functional majority*** or ***a working majority***. A simple majority is more often used in Parliamentary business. The thumb rule is that wherever the majority is not defined then the simple majority is generally considered for voting.

Generally, in the Indian Parliament and state legislatures, a simple majority is followed in the following cases: (i) To pass an ordinary bill or money bill, or finance bill, (ii) To pass a no-confidence motion or adjournment motion or censure motion or confidence motion, (iii) To declare a financial emergency, (iv) To declare President's rule, and (v) To elect Speaker/Deputy Speaker of Lok Sabha and State legislatures.

3.2 Absolute Majority

An absolute majority means a majority of more than 50 percent of the total membership of the house. Presently, the Lok Sabha has a strength of 543 seats in 2022. In that case, the absolute majority refers to more than 50 percent of 543, i.e., 272. Essentially, an "***absolute majority***" means a majority of all electors, not just those who voted. We can term an absolute majority as the majority of the membership of the house. Generally, an ***absolute majority is not stipulated*** in the Indian Parliament for all purposes of law-making. However, for the formation of governments in the Union and the states, an absolute majority is required.

An "absolute majority" means a majority of all electors, not just those who voted.

3.3 Special Majority

As the term mentions special, a special majority is different from a simple majority. In simple words, any majority other than a simple majority, an absolute majority, and an effective majority are called a special majority. According to Article 249 of the Constitution of India, a special majority refers to a majority of 2/3 of members present and voting. This special majority is generally used for constitutional amendments.

A special majority refers to a majority of 2/3 of members present and voting.

We find four types of special majority in the Indian law-making process: (1) As per Article 249–which means a majority of 2/3rd members are present and voting. (2) As per Article 368–needs a majority of 2/3rd members are present and voting backed by more than 50 percent of the total strength of the house. (3) As per Article 61–requires the vote of 2/3rd members of the total strength of the house. (4) As per Article 368 plus state ratification by a simple majority.

3.4 Effective Majority

An effective majority means a majority of more than 50 percent of the effective strength of the house.

An effective majority means a majority of more than 50 percent of the effective strength of the house. The effective strength means the net of total strength after deducting the vacant seats. In the case of the Indian Constitution, wherever it mentions "*all the then members*", means it refers to the effective majority. In India, the effective majority principle is used for (i) removal of the vice-president, and (ii) removal of the speaker and deputy speaker of Lok Sabha and state legislative assembly.

4. MEDIAN VOTER

A Median Voter is one whose preference decides the outcome of majority voting.

In a majority voting model, the median voter plays a very important role in deciding the majority. Then, ***who is the Median Voter?*** Duncan Black (1948) was the first to state that the median voter's preferred candidate or policy is bound to win in a majority vote. Later in 1957, Anthony Downs provided a detailed explanation of the Median Voter in his book, "*An Economic Theory of Democracy*". Therefore, ***a Median Voter is one whose preference decides the outcome of majority voting.*** The median voter is usually in the middle of the ranking order of voters along the same dimension. Accordingly, Downs envisaged that politicians tend to converge towards the center because the median voter is at the center. If they move towards the extremes, there is a possibility of the opposition winning the voting. Hence, *this centripetal force of convergence of the politicians towards the center is called* ***Downsian competition.***

The centripetal force of convergence of the politicians towards the center is called Downsian competition.

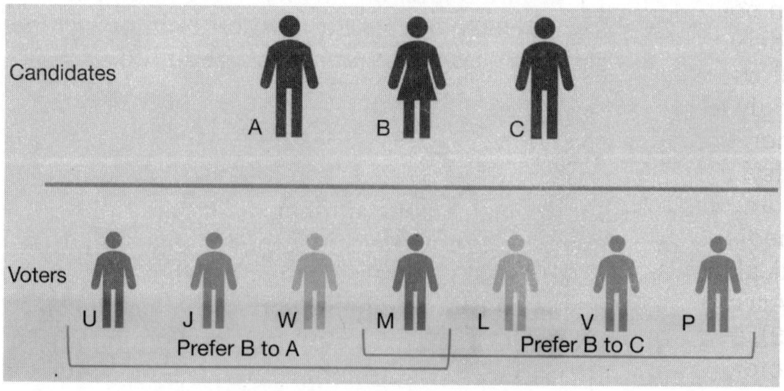

FIGURE 6.6 Median Voter

Figure 6.6 illustrates Median Voter. A, B, and C are the candidates in the voting process. Assume that there are 7 voters U, J, W, M, L, V, and P. The first four voters U, I, W, and M prefer B to A. The last four voters M, L, V, and P prefer B to C. According to the preferences, candidate B is closest to voter M who is in the middle of the order of a single dimension. Hence, M is called the Median Voter and his or her vote tends to decide the winner in the voting process. *The median voter is the voter whose vote is instrumental in determining the majority voting equilibrium.* The collective choice determined by majority voting is the preferred choice of the median voter.

The median voter is the voter whose vote is instrumental in determining the majority voting equilibrium.

The identity of the ***Median Voter*** can be as follows: (i) the median voter is like a dictator whose personal preferred choice determines the collective choice, and (ii) in a large population no one can be quite sure who the median voter is, (iii) the virtue of the median voter as dictator is also that the median voter, in general, does not know that he/she is the median voter.

4.1 Median Voter Theorem

The Median Voter theorem is mostly associated with public choice economics and statistical political science. ***The Median Voter theorem states that in a majority rule voting system, the candidate or party most preferred by the median voter will get elected.***

The Median Voter theorem states that in a majority rule voting system, the candidate or party most preferred by the median voter will get elected.

According to the theory, let us assume that a choice must be made from a set of alternatives that vary only in one dimension (for example, a left-right spectrum). In case all the voters are to exercise single-peaked preferences, then the option that is preferred by the median voter will win in a vote.

Median Voter Theorem says that majority voting will yield the outcome preferred by the median voter if preferences are single-peaked. The median voter is the one whose preferences are in the middle of the set of voters.

The Median Voter Theorem has widespread acceptance in the Political Economy literature.

In politics, few voters subscribe to extreme right ideology or extreme left ideology. But most of the voters are centrist i.e., those opposing political changes that would result in a significant shift of society either strongly to the left or the right. Because the median voter determines the winner, the winning of elections depends on how close a party's or candidate's manifesto is to the aspirations of the median voter, i.e., centrist. This implies that most of the parties attempt to include the aspirations of median voters in their manifesto. This results in the manifestos of all political parties looking more or less the same.

According to ***Harold Hotelling's Principle of Minimum Differentiation*** (1929), politicians generally gravitate toward the position near the median voter, or mostly toward the position preferred by the electoral system.

4.2 Median Voter's Choice and Optimal Solution

The Median Voter theorem is valuable for the light it sheds on the optimality (and the limits to the optimality) of certain voting systems. The median voter model lets the government policy be modeled like a simple application of the rational choice model in microeconomics.

> The policy implications of the Median Voter choice are found mostly in regulating public goods, direct benefit transfers to the elderly and the poor, national defense, etc.

The Median Voter choice policies tend to be relatively more stable than those based on an average voter choice. The features of median voter choice imply that public policies will be robust over a period, as voters are subject to the vicissitudes of life, technological change, and political surprises. ***The Median Voter Theorem has widespread acceptance in the Political Economy literature.*** Because it is quite suitable to derive some interesting testable inferences about the connection between the voting population and the policy outcome.

The policy implications of the ***Median Voter choice*** are found mostly in regulating public goods, direct benefit transfers to the elderly and the poor, national defense, etc. Models based on the Median Voter choice provide useful qualitative forecasts of public policy, particularly in a well-functioning democracy.

5. NATIONAL INTEREST

'***National Interest***' is a key concept in public policy. According to Morgenthau, "the meaning of national interest is survival—the protection of physical, political and cultural identity against encroachments by other nation-states". In simple terms, the *national interest*, a key concept of international relations, encompasses the political interests, security interests, economic interests, cultural interests, and all other interests of a country. To be precise, ***we define National Interest as the claims, objectives, goals, demands, and interests that a nation always tries to preserve, protect, defend, and secure in relations with other nations.*** We also describe national interest as the values, desires, and interests that nations seek to protect or achieve concerning each other".

5.1 Components of National Interest

> The necessary components of national interest are physical identity, political identity, and cultural identity.

National interest has broadly two components: (1) ***necessary or vital components***, and (2) ***variable or non-vital components.*** Table 6.4 lists the components of national interest and their features. According to Morgenthau, the necessary or vital components of national interest are vital for survival or national identity. The necessary components of national interest are subdivided into three parts: ***physical identity, political identity, and cultural identity.*** To achieve this necessary or vital component of "survival", a state can go to any extent, even a war.

The second component of national interest is variable or non-vital components. These are dependent on situations and circumstances. The factors such as decision-makers, public opinion, party politics, sectional, or group interests, and political or moral factors determine the variable or non-vital components of national interest. These are the objectives the nations want to fulfill but need not be at the cost of war.

TABLE 6.4 The Components of National Interest.

Necessary or Vital Components:	Non-Vital or Variable Components of National Interest:
1. *Physical identity*: It includes territorial identity. 2. *Political identity*: It means politico-economic system. 3. *Cultural identity*: It stands for historical values that are upheld by a nation as part of its cultural heritage.	1. The non-vital components are those parts of national interest that are determined either by circumstances or by the necessity of securing the vital components. 2. A host of factors determines these—the decision-makers, public opinion, party politics, sectional or group interests, and political and moral folkways.

5.2 Classification of National Interest

The national interest is classified as primary interests, secondary interests, permanent interests, variable interests, general interests, and specific interests.

We perceive national interest in several ways. However, Robinson (1967) classifies national interest into six types (i) ***primary interests (ii) secondary interests, (iii) permanent interests, (iv) variable interests, (v) general interests, and (vi) specific interests***. However, international interests are added as the seventh. Figure 6.7 illustrates the seven classifications of national interest.

The ***Primary Interests*** are the interests non-negotiable for a state and the state will go to any extent to secure these interests like physical identity, political identity, and cultural identity. Secondary interests include those that are next to the primary interests, like protecting the citizens abroad, ensuring immunities of diplomatic staff, etc. The ***Permanent Interests*** include the long-term interests of the nation. The ***Variable Interests*** are dependent upon the situation. These interests can bypass the primary and permanent interests. The ***General Interests*** are international peace, food security, and environmental protection apply to most nations. The ***Specific Interests*** are specific to nations. ***International Interests are*** further classified into (i) *identical interests*, (ii) *complementary interests*, and (iii) *conflicting interests*. Identical interests are common in many countries. The complementary interests complement to specific interests of a nation. The conflicting interests include those which are neither complementary nor identical.

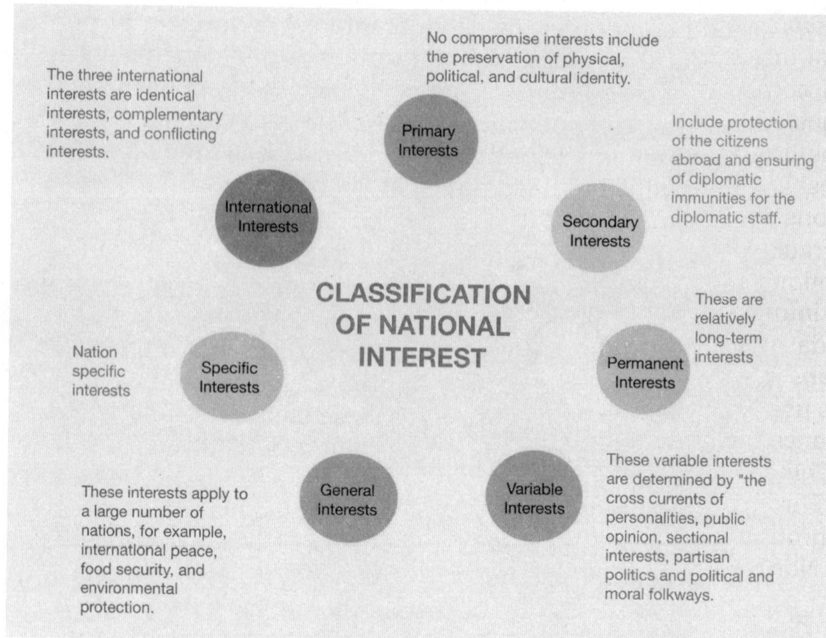

FIGURE 6.7 Classification of National Interest

5.3 Methods for the Securing National Interest

The five methods of securing national interest are Diplomacy, Propaganda, Economic means, Alliances and treaties, and Coercive means.

We so far discussed the national interest and its classifications. It is important to know how sovereign nations secure their national interests. Research shows that nations adopt different methods to secure their national interests. In Figure 6.8 we broadly identify five methods of securing national interest: *(1) Diplomacy, (2) Propaganda, (3) Economic means, (4) Alliances and treaties, and (5) Coercive means.*

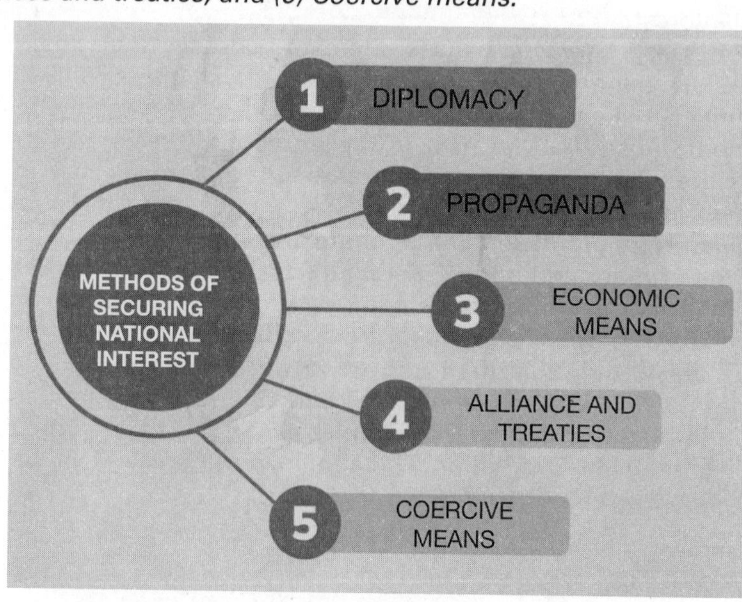

FIGURE 6.8 Methods of Securing National Interest

Diplomacy is one of the effective persuasive measures to secure national interests. In the process of diplomacy, countries negotiate, bargain, compromise, and coordinate to achieve their desired ends and outcomes. More often, we use this method as an effective means of conflict resolution. The second method, ***Propaganda,*** is indeed an art of salesmanship of a country. It is all about impressing and convincing other nations about the goals, stances, and objectives of the nation. According to Frankel, "Propaganda is a systematic attempt to affect the minds, emotions, and actions of a given group for a specific public purpose." The information technology revolution has greatly supported this propaganda method of nations to secure their national interests. ***Economic Means*** is a method in which the economically rich and developed countries use their economic might in the form of economic aid and loans to advance their interests in the international arena. An example of this can be China's Belt and Road Initiative (BRI).

Through ***Alliances and treaties,*** two or more countries come together through legal binding to secure their national interest. For example, the North Atlantic Treaty Organization (NATO) of the US and its allies form a military alliance to secure their national interests. The nations use ***Coercive Measures*** as a method to secure their national interests through interventions, embargoes, boycotts, retaliations, sanctions, severance of relations, etc.

6. POLICY ACTORS & INFLUENCERS

Policy actors are those who influence public policy-making either directly or indirectly or informally. They include both institutional actors and non-institutional actors. Some of the notable policy actors are non-governmental organizations, civil society fora, community organizations, industry unions, labor unions, and other notable organizations. Public policy research shows that public opinion, political parties, interest groups, opinion makers, media, and others greatly influence public policy making.

> Notable policy actors are non-governmental organizations, civil society fora, community organizations, industry unions, labor unions, and other notable organizations.

6.1 Interest Groups

Interest groups are organized groups that have like-minded individuals as members with common objectives to carry out programs and activities to influence government institutions, government officials, and policymakers. These include business confederations, chambers of commerce, trade bodies, professional organizations, labor unions, advocacy groups, citizen groups, and lobbies. Interest groups organize various types of programs and activities including promotional activities, and educational activities to pursue their cause. These groups actively campaign for public policies that are in their interest. For example, environmental interest groups work for legislation or policies toward reducing carbon emissions and other related activities.

> Interest groups are organized groups that have like-minded individuals as members with common objectives to carry out programs and activities to influence government institutions, government officials, and policymakers.

The interest groups are classified as economic interest groups, professional interest groups, and public interest groups.

The communication media includes news media, social media, and web media,

Though interest groups actively work for influencing policymaking, however, their disproportionate and opaque influence might lead to administrative corruption, undue influence, and state capture, favoring particular interest groups at the cost of public interest.

Based on their motivation, interest groups are classified as (i) ***economic interest groups*** including individual corporations and business organizations; (ii) ***professional interest groups*** such as trade unions and farmers; (iii) ***public interest groups*** including human rights groups, environmental groups, among others (Chari et al., 2010).

The interest groups, though play a very important role in public policy-making, there are advantages and disadvantages. Table 6.5 lists the pros and cons of interest groups.

TABLE 6.5 The Pros and Cons of Interest Groups

Pros: Potential Benefits	Cons: Undue Influence
1. Interest groups can enrich policy-making by providing valuable knowledge and insights on specific issues. 2. Interest groups help in bringing to the public focus the burning issues of policy making and organize public debates. 3. Interest groups actively work for anti-corruption drives and hold government officials accountable.	1. Interest groups can cause undue influence, which is more subtle and not necessarily illegal. 2. The opaque and disproportionate influence of some pernicious interest groups can result in an adverse impact on policy making.

6.2 Public Opinion

As public opinion provides clear evidence of public perception, the policymakers find it difficult to ignore.

In public policy making, particularly in democracies, public opinion has a greater impact. *What is public opinion?* ***Public opinion is an aggregate of the individual viewpoints, attitudes, philosophies, and beliefs about a particular issue or topic expressed by a substantial population of a community.*** It wields a powerful influence on politics by way of its "latent" aspects. More often, it restrains the policymakers and government officials from making undesirable and unpopular policies or laws.

Public opinion is crucial in democracies because it influences public policy, impacts government actions, provides feedback to the political actors of policymaking, and, more so, it facilitates self-rule in democracies. It is considered very powerful in democracies because lawmakers, politicians, and others use public opinion as their weapon to pursue their agenda. As public opinion provides clear evidence of public perception, the policymakers find it difficult to ignore. ***How can we measure public opinion?*** The election results, opinion polls, media reports, etc., can measure public opinion. Public opinion motivates politicians to make laws that are required for society and the economy.

6.3 Communication Media

In the era of globalization, communication media has a powerful influence on our lives, particularly in democracies. All three types of communication media, such as ***news media, social media***, and ***web media,*** exert tremendous influence on society. ***It can influence individual behavior, beliefs, and attitudes***. It can change society either positively or negatively by its ability to manipulate, inspire, persuade, and compel individuals, organizations, governments, and even the world at large.

The communication media can influence individual behavior, beliefs, and attitudes.

In the public policymaking area, media can contribute to setting the agenda for the public, and policymakers by way of prominently emphasizing which issues are important at a certain time. The media can shape the public agenda that addresses the societal issues in the country that need governmental attention. It determines what public matters and what the people will think and be concerned about. It keeps a close watch on the government and others in power and exposes their wrongdoings. A responsible media serves a greater role in public policymaking by determining the issues for the public agenda. *Because of its powerful impact on society and governments, media has emerged as the fourth pillar of democracy* in addition to the legislature, the executive, and the judiciary (Sigrid Koch-Baumgarten and Katrin Voltmer. 2010).

Because of its powerful impact on society and governments, media has emerged as the fourth pillar of democracy.

Across the world, the media has, over a period, progressively intertwined with the fabric of democracy. Its role in molding public opinion and thereby the voter opinion. The 24x7 news media is bombarding the public with opinionated views and news. Through the opinion polls, focus group discussions, media surveys, studio debates, etc., media exerts a strong impact on the public and thereby on public policymaking.

6.4 Policy Communities

Policy communities *are a specialized grouping of groups of pressure groups, media, activists, academics, and others who pursue a particular agenda in the public policy arena and endeavor to influence the policymakers.* Policy communities represent the building blocks of policy studies in most developed democracies. Most policy theories put them at the heart of the policymaking process.

Policy communities function at certain levels of the government and are usually not prominently visible to the public.

According to Leslie Pal (2014), policy communities are "the actors in a policy network, presumably those who share at least some common language and conceptual reference points but who may be opponents on the issue."

Most public policy is processed mainly through small expert policy communities that analyze the issues. These *policy communities function at certain levels of the government and are usually not prominently visible to the public.*

Summary

- Political parties are central to the idea of electoral democracies. Democracies can thrive well, provided the political parties succeed in providing better policies for the good of the citizen over the long run.
- A Parliamentary System represents a form of government in which people directly elect their representatives to the legislature and the elected representatives, in turn, choose their leader who maintains the confidence of the house to be the chief executive of the government titled the Prime Minister or Chancellor.
- The Westminster model of the parliamentary system has three key distinguishing elements: (i) an executive that is drawn from the legislature, (ii) the executive that is responsible to the legislature, and (iii) a ceremonial 'head of state' who is different from the real head of government. A consensus system of government has the cabinet appointed by the legislature without reference to political parties, but as a part of a consensus or non-partisan democracy. People oppose this system of democracy because in this majoritarian democracy, "winner-takes-all". A unicameral parliamentary system is a government with only one legislative house or assembly. A Bicameral parliamentary system comprises two separate houses or assemblies in law-making.
- A political party is a voluntary organization that mobilizes voters to promote shared interests. The three main types of party systems are (i) One-party system, (ii) two-party system, and (iii) multi-party system. From an ideological perspective, the popular classification includes conservative parties, liberal parties, and radical parties. In India, there are national parties and state parties. The Election of Commission of India (ECI) is an autonomous constitutional body that is responsible for administering the election processes.
- A voting rule, generally, is a method for electing a winner from a set of candidates based on voters' informed preferences for those contenders. The majority rule is a decision rule to select one from the alternatives that have a majority, meaning more than half the votes. The four types of majority are (i) Simple majority, (ii) Absolute majority, (iii) Special majority, and (iv) Effective majority.
- A Median Voter is one whose preference decides the outcome of majority voting. The Median Voter theorem states that in a majority rule voting system, the candidate or party most preferred by the median voter will get elected. The Median Voter Theorem has widespread acceptance in the Political Economy literature.
- 'National Interest' is a key concept in public policy. National Interest is defined as the claims, objectives, goals, demands, and interests that a nation always tries to preserve, protect, defend, and secure in relations with other nations. The necessary components of national interest are subdivided into three parts: physical identity, political identity, and cultural identity. The national interest is classified into six types: (i) primary interests (ii) secondary interests, (iii) permanent interests, (iv) variable interests, (v) general interests, and (vi) specific interests. The five methods of securing national interest: (1) Diplomacy, (2) Propaganda, (3) Economic means, (4) Alliances, and treaties, and (5) Coercive means.
- Policy actors are those who influence public policy-making, either directly or indirectly, or informally. We classify the interest groups as economic interest groups, professional interest groups, and public interest groups. Policy communities represent the building blocks of policy studies in most developed democracies.

Key Words

Parliamentary system	Simple majority	Communication media
Westminster system	Absolute majority	Policy communities
Consensus system	Special majority	Policy actors
Unicameral system	Effective majority	Mono-party system
Bicameral system	Voting rule	Bi-party system
Cabinet	Pareto property	Multi-party system
Majority rule	Median voter	Coalition government
Multi-party system	Downsian competition	
Conservatives	National interest	
Liberals	Diplomacy	
Radicals	Propaganda	
National parties	Interest groups	
State parties	Public opinion	

Questions

A. Quick Check

1. Why do we need political parties in democracies?
2. What do you mean by the doctrine of separation of powers?
3. What does "winner-takes-all" mean?
4. Why should we know about the party systems?
5. What causes two major parties to dominate the political landscape?
6. Why multi-party system suits Indian polity?
7. Explain the national and state parties in the Indian context.
8. What is a majority rule? Explain the different types of majority in the Indian context.
9. Who is a median voter? Explain the median voter theorem.
10. Explain national interest and its classification.
11. How can we measure public opinion?
12. Explain the role of communication media in public policymaking.

B. Explore

1. Why did India choose the Westminster system of Parliamentary democracy? Discuss.
2. Do you agree the Bicameral parliamentary system has served the interests of India appropriately? Discuss.
3. "During coalition government regimes, the parliamentary system is unable to make quick policy-making because of the internal competing interests in the coalition." – Discuss in the Indian context.

4. Analyzetheroleofcommunicationmediaintheindiandemocracy.
5. Comment on national interest in the context of India.

References

- Chari, R., Hogan, J., and Murphy, G. (2010). Regulating Lobbying: A Global Comparison. Manchester University Press, Manchester 196 pp.
- Dasgupta, Partha., and Eric Maskin (2008). On The Robustness of Majority Rule, Journal of the European Economic Association, 6 (5), 949–973.
- Downs, Anthony (1957). An Economic Theory of Political Action in a Democracy. *Journal of Political Economy*. 65 (2), 135–150.
- Duncan, Black (1948). On the Rationale of Group Decision-making. *Journal of Political Economy*, 56 (1), 23–34.
- Leslie Pal (2014), Beyond Policy Analysis – Public Issue Management in TurbulentTimes, Fifth Edition, Nelson Education,Toronto.
- Lijphart, Arend (1999). Patterns of Democracy (1999). New Haven: Yale University Press.
- Robinson, Thomas W. (1967). A National Interest Analysis of Sino-Soviet Relations. *International Studies Quarterly*, 11 (2), 135-175.
- Russell, M. and Cowley, P. (2016). The Policy Power of the Westminster Parliament: The "Parliamentary State" and the Empirical Evidence. *Governance*, 29 (1), 121-137.
- Sigrid Koch-Baumgarten, and Katrin Voltmer. (2010). Public Policy and the Mass Media: The Interplay of Mass Communication and Political Decision Making. 1st Edition, Routledge.

Further Readings

Congleton, Roger (2003). "The Median Voter Model" (PDF). In Rowley, C. K.; Schneider, F. (eds.). *The Encyclopedia of Public Choice*. Kluwer Academic Press. ISBN 978-0-7923-8607-0.

CHAPTER 7

Public Policy Making–The Role of The Executive

This chapter focuses on the role of the executive in public policy making and implementation. We first discuss the levels of government like the Union Government, State Government, and Local Government in India. Thereon we provide a detailed illustration of the executive in India, which includes the parts of the executive like the political and permanent executive, the functions of the executive, and the types of the executive. The effective functioning of the executive is crucial for successful policymaking and policy implementation. In this context, we will discuss performance management in government in detail. In doing so, we first discuss the power of performance management and then present a taxonomy of performance evaluation approaches in the government. To gain from the international experiences, we present a brief discussion about the prevailing international models of performance management in government. In the final section, we discuss the performance management system in India. Wherefore, we briefly discuss the institutional setup for performance management and the critical issues challenging performance management in government.

Section 1: Levels of Governments in India

Section 2: The Executive

Section 3: Performance Management

Section 4: Performance Management System in the Indian Government

1. LEVELS OF GOVERNMENT IN INDIA

In the modern world, governments have assumed greater significance due to their ever-increasing roles in society. The governments not only protect societies, but they also carry out a wide range of activities in the areas of social protection and economic development. Under social protection, the governments provide a legal and social framework for the citizens with rights and responsibilities. Under the economic development responsibilities, the governments provide the public goods,

The governments not only protect societies, but they also carry out a wide range of activities in the areas of social protection and economic development.

redistribute income, regulate the markets, correct the externalities, synchronize the external trade, encourage competition, and ensure efficient allocation of resources to achieve economic growth, and economic well-being, and higher standards of living. In the last century, the role of the government has grown as a welfare state and hence the governments have grown in size.

India is a federal parliamentary constitutional democratic republic.

The Union government is the executive of the Republic of India.

In India, the constitution provides for three levels of government in line with its vast geography and diversity, and culture. At the national level is the Union government or the Government of India. At the state levels are the State governments, and at the local levels like at district, taluka, and village levels are the Local governments. Figure 7.1 illustrates the hierarchy of the levels of government in India.

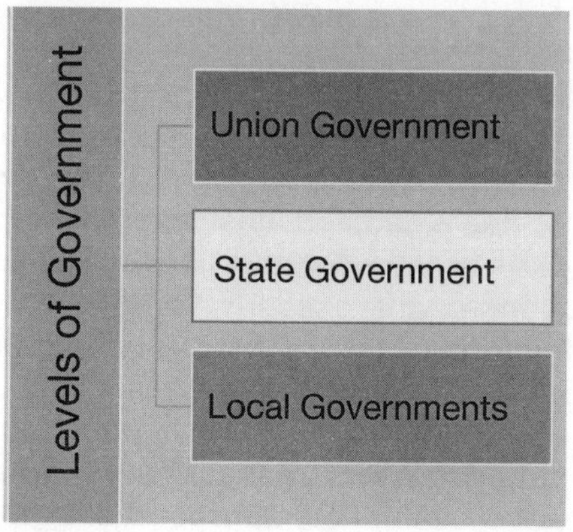

FIGURE 7.1 Levels of Government in India

India is a federal parliamentary constitutional democratic republic; the people in a democratic setup elect all three levels of government. The Election Commission of India holds the elections for these governments to form as per the constitutional provisions and the mandate. According to their spheres of authority, the governments at their levels engage in public policymaking and administration activities.

1.1 The Government of India

The Prime Minister heads the Union Council of Ministers under whose advice the President acts.

The Union government or the Government of India is the executive of the Republic of India. In constitutional terminology, it is also called the federal executive. ***The president holds the highest position of executive authority and acts as the head of state.*** However, in a parliamentary system, the Prime Minister is the chief executive with powers conferred to run the government, as he is an elected representative appointed by the parliament. The Prime Minister heads the Union Council of Ministers under whose advice the President acts on various matters. The Government of India is based in the capital of India, New Delhi.

For a student of Public Policy, it is also essential to know the structure of government to have a proper understanding of law-making. According to the Constitution of India, the Government in India or the Central or the Union government is divided into three main sections namely the executive, the legislature, and the judiciary. Figure 7.2 depicts the structure of the Union Government of India, which shows the responsibility of each section of the government.

The Constitution has divided Government in India into three main sections, namely the executive, legislature, and the judiciary.

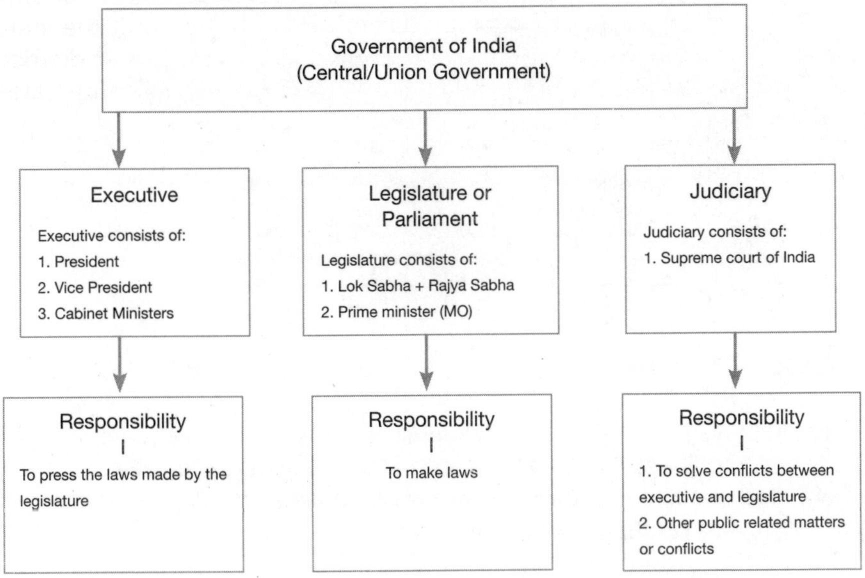

FIGURE 7.2 The Structure of the Union Government of India

1.1.1 Law-Making Process in the Government of India

In India, the government plays a vital role in law-making. Figure 7.3 illustrates the law-making process at the level of the Government of India. The fundamental function of the Parliament is law-making. The executive headed by the Prime Minister with its Union Council of Ministers prepares the legislative proposals that are to be brought before the Parliament as bills. At his stage of law-making, the executive decides about the various policies and introduces the bills to the Parliament. The bills are debated and deliberated in both the houses of the Parliament i.e., the Lok Sabha and the Rajya Sabha. After the debate, they put the bills to vote, and if passed by both the Houses of the Parliament, they will present them before the President of India for his assent and approval. When the President signs the bills approved by the Parliament, they become the Acts or Laws. When the bills become Laws, the respective departments of the government put them into administration for public use.

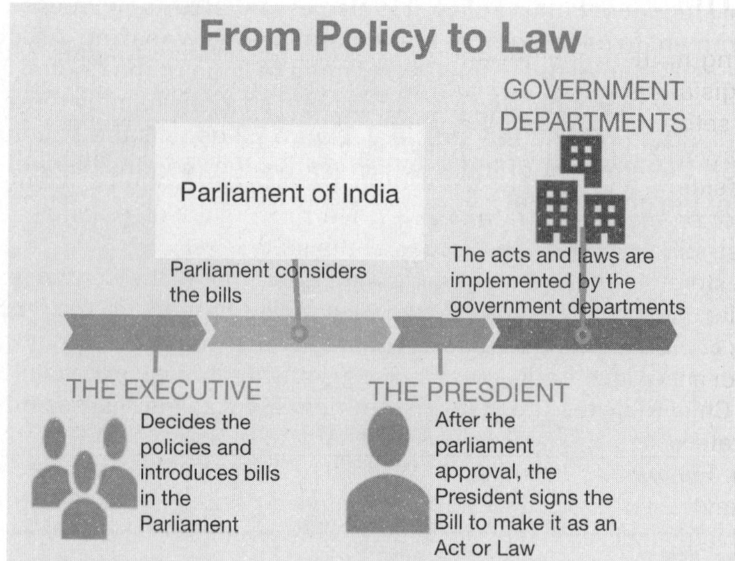

FIGURE 7.3 The Role of the Government of India in Policymaking

When the President signs the bills approved by the Parliament, they become the Acts or Laws.

The President administers the Union territories through a Lieutenant Governor or an administrator.

These laws have the highest legal sanctity and are enforceable in the courts of law. These laws, before coming into existence, pass through certain stages such as the ***Pre-drafting stage, Drafting Stage, parliamentary stage, and post-Parliamentary stage.***

At the Pre-Drafting stage, the proposal from the concerned ministry department goes through five sub-stages: (i) Formulation of Legislative Proposal, (ii) Pre-Legislative Consultation Policy, (iii) Consultation with the Ministry of Law & Justice, (iv) Approval of the cabinet, and (v) Sending memorandum to the Ministry of Law & Justice.

At the Drafting Stage, the Ministry of Law & Justice will prepare the draft bill within 30 days of receipt of the proposal and, after completing all the administrative formalities at this stage, they send the draft bill to Parliament. At the stage of Parliamentary procedure, the bill undergoes 3 readings. In the first reading, they set the legislative process in motion with the introduction of the bill in the House of Parliament. In the second reading stage there can be a general discussion of the bill or in addition to the general discussion the house can refer the bill either to the Joint committee, Select Committee, or for the opinion of the public. At the stage of the third reading, they move the bill before the house of Parliament to pass the bill. The passing of an ordinary bill requires a simple majority to be present and vote. In the post-Parliamentary procedure, when a bill is passed by both houses, the government presents the bill for the assent of the President. The bill becomes the Act or Law only after the assent of the president, and finally, it is published in the Official Gazette of the Government of India for public information.

1.2 The State Government

According to the Constitution of India, the State Governments with the state legislatures make laws at the state level under their authority. In a federal setup, the state governments have certain privileges and powers of law-making. In India, there are 28 states and 8 Union territories. The President administers the Union territories through a Lieutenant Governor or an administrator. State governments are responsible for the administration of needs and issues at the state level.

The Governor acts with the advice of the State Council of Ministers headed by the elected Chief Minister.

The structure of the state government is like that of the Central government with some changes. ***The Governor, who is appointed by the President of India, constitutionally presides over the state government.*** However, the Governor acts with the advice of the State Council of Ministers headed by the elected Chief Minister. The state government handles internal security and other state issues. Figure 7.4 shows the structure of the State Government in India. Every state in India has a legislative assembly. However, some states have bicameral legislature (legislative assembly: Vidhan Sabha and legislative council: Vidhan Parishad), and the majority of the states have a unicameral legislature (legislative assembly: Vidhan Sabha).

Every state in India has a legislative assembly (Vidhan Sabha) i.e., a unicameral legislature.

Some states in India have a bicameral legislature (legislative assembly: Vidhan Sabha and legislative council: Vidhan Parishad).

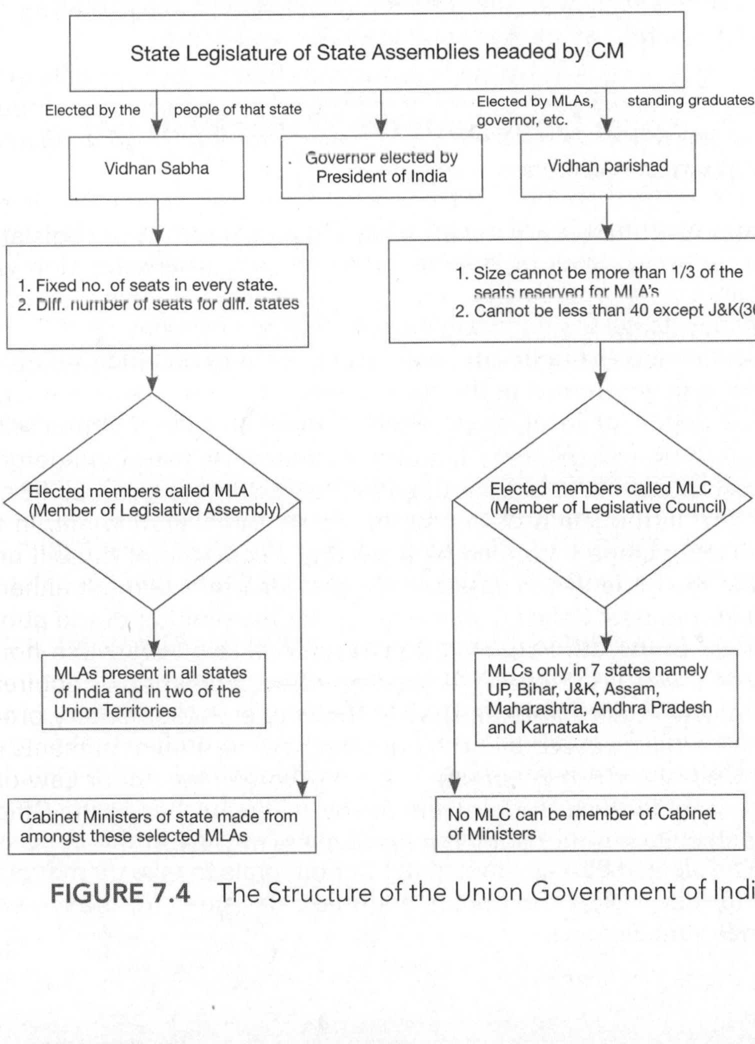

FIGURE 7.4 The Structure of the Union Government of India

1.2.1 Law-Making Process in State Government

Law & Order is a state subject.

The bills at the state legislature are of two types: ordinary bills and money bills.

The money bill must be first introduced in the legislative assembly.

The President issues ordinances at the center and the Governor at the state in times of necessity when the respective legislatures are not in session.

The Constitution of India authorizes the State Legislature to make laws on the subjects mentioned in the State List and the Concurrent List of powers between the state and union governments. The primary function of the state legislature is to make laws. In the law-making process, the states have jurisdiction over state subjects like education, agriculture, public health, sanitation, hospitals and dispensaries, and several other departments. More significantly, ***law & order is a state subject and hence the state governments are responsible for maintaining the internal security, law, and order in the state.***

Generally, ***the bills at the state legislature are of two types: ordinary bills and money bills.*** While the money bill must be first introduced in the legislative assembly (Vidhan Sabha), the ordinary bills can be introduced in either of the two houses (Vidhan Sabha or Vidhan Parishad). When the bills are passed after the debate in the state legislature, a regular bill becomes law after the assent of the Governor. Occasionally, like the President at the national level, the Governor at the state can also issue ordinances in times of necessity when the state legislature is not in session. The ordinances have the force of law; however, they must be ratified within a period of six weeks by the state legislature.

1.3 The Local Governments: Panchayati Raj in India

In India, the Local Governments are the third tier.

The Panchayati Raj structure comprises Zilla panchayat at the district level, Taluka panchayat at the taluka or block level, and Gram panchayat at the village level.

The Local Governments are the third tier of governments in India that are founded on the concept of local self-government for administering the local affairs by the local bodies like city corporations, municipal councils, Zilla panchayats, taluka panchayats, and the gram panchayats. While the municipalities are at the urban level local governments, the panchayats are the local governments in the rural areas.

The structure of local government bodies in India comprises two broad categories: (1) Municipal Corporations for urban areas, and (2) Panchayati Raj institutions for rural administration. Figure 7.5 illustrates the Panchayati Raj structure as a basic unit of administration in India. It comprises three levels: ***(1) Zilla panchayat at the district level, (2) Taluka panchayat at the taluka or block level, and (3) Gram panchayat at the village level.***

The 73rd Constitutional Amendment, 1992, gave Panchayati Raj institutions the constitutional status to encourage democracy at the grassroots level and the self-participation of the people in the matters of local administration. The local governments are elected bodies that function like the state governments. Local people choose their representatives to be on these bodies. The Constitution provides for the reservation of seats for women and other weaker sections of society in the panchayat bodies. The elected bodies meet at regular intervals to take up matters of concern for discussion and debate and make decisions for implementation in their jurisdictions.

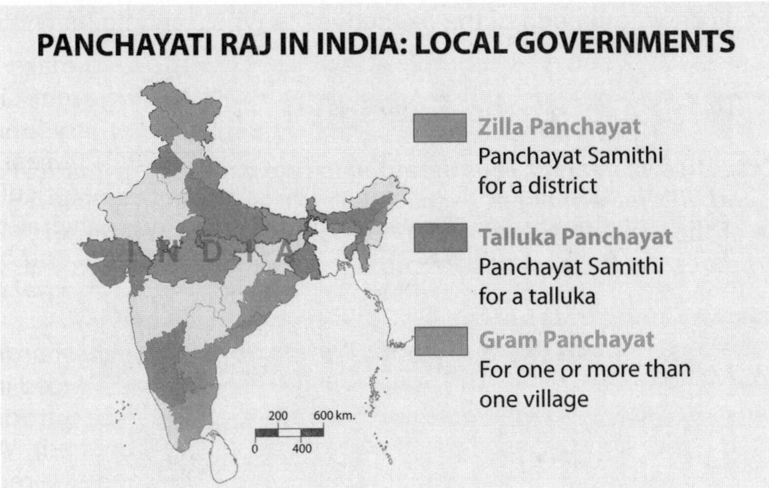

FIGURE 7.5 Panchayati Raj: Basic unit of Administration

The following are some of the powers and responsibilities of Gram Panchayats. They identify the beneficiaries of various developmental schemes of the Union and State governments. Gram panchayats support the implementation of welfare schemes of the higher governments like mass education, family welfare (Ayushman Yojana), sanitation (Swachh Baharat Abhiyan), and drinking water provision (Har Ghar Jal), farmers' welfare (PM Kisan Samman Nidhi Yojana) and others. They also decide on the local taxes like property tax, rents, and fees in their jurisdictions.

After the legislature, the Executive is the most powerful organ of the government.

2. THE EXECUTIVE

The Executive is the second most powerful organ of the government after the legislature. It implements the laws passed by the legislature and the policies of the government. As we discussed in previous chapters, the rise of the welfare state has vastly enlarged the functions of the state and the executive. Often, in common usage, people tend to identify the executive with the government, which is not. ***In modern times, as the state expands, the power and the role of the executive have grown in multitude.***

We can look at the term 'Executive' in two dimensions: a broad form and a narrow form. In its broader form, it includes the functionaries, political power-holders (the Political Executive), and permanent civil servants (the Permanent Executive). The permanent executive undertakes the implementation of laws and policies and performs the administrative roles of the state. The Executive in its narrow form often means only the executive heads (i.e., the Political Executive). The ministers head the government ministries and departments, formulate the policies, and supervise the implementation of the laws and policies of the government.

Let us know the parts of the executive, its types, and its functions.

2.1 Two Parts of the Executive

We understand the executive in two parts: the political executive and the permanent executive.

The Executive, in general, is understood in two parts: (i) the Political executive, and (ii) the Permanent executive. This classification is based on the nature of the executive in terms of the political angle and tenure. Figure 7.6 compares the Political and Permanent Executives of government.

The Prime Minister heads the political executive at the national level and the Chief Minister heads the political executive at the state level.

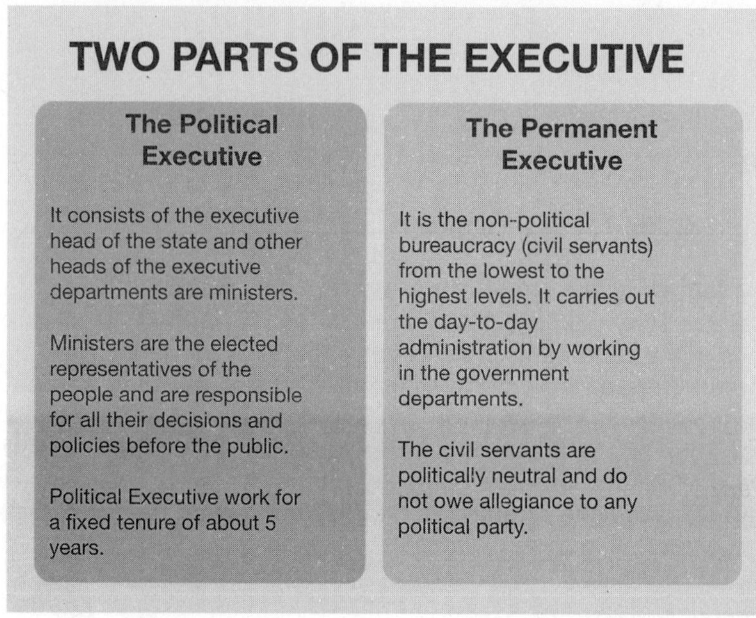

FIGURE 7.6 The Political and Permanent Executives of Government

2.1.1 The Political Executive

The Political Executive is more powerful.

According to the Indian Constitution, the Political Executive at the Union level consists of the President, the Vice-President, and the Council of Ministers with the Prime Minister as the head to aid and advise the President (Source: India Book 2020 - A Reference Annual). At the state level, the Political Executive comprises the Governor and the State Council of Ministers, headed by the Chief Minister to aid and advise the Governor. Figure 7.7 shows the Executive in India. ***In the hierarchy of the executive, the President is the highest authority in India, followed by the Government of India, State governments, District administration, and local governments in the rural areas.***

The Permanent Executive is apolitical

The ***Political Executive*** is more powerful because the people elect it, and hence are responsible for the people. It comprises mostly of the ministers and other elected representatives who work for fixed tenure generally for five years. The political executive remains in power if it enjoys the confidence of the legislature. It is accountable to the people for the consequences of the decisions and their implementation.

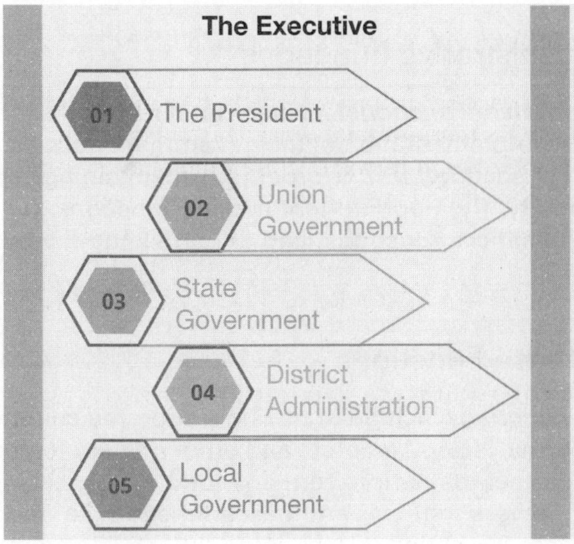

FIGURE 7.7 The Executive in India

2.1.2 The Permanent Executive

The ***Permanent Executive*** is a non-political structure of bureaucracy that is neutral to political affiliations. ***It comprises the civil servants right from the lowest to the highest levels. It carries out the day-to-day administration of the government departments.*** The government appoints the bureaucracy on a salary for a long tenure till their age of retirement and hence they are permanent in the executive. The civil servants in India include those in the Indian Administrative Service (IAS), Indian Police Service (IPS), Indian Foreign Service (IFS), Indian Revenue Service (IRS), etc. The permanent executive remains in power, irrespective of the change of the political executive. It is not answerable to the people as we do not elect them representatives. The permanent executive assists the political executive in taking their decisions and implementing them. The cabinet secretary is the highest-level civil servant in India.

2.2 Functions of the Executive

We can understand the functions of the executive under three areas: ***(i) Policymaking, (ii) Administrative functions, and (iii) Defense functions.***

> Policymaking, administrative functions, and defense are the three main functions of the executive.

2.2.1 Policymaking Functions

The main ***policymaking functions*** include economic policies, social policies, foreign policymaking, and the conduct of foreign relations, treaty-making functions, defense policies, and various developmental policies.

2.2.2 Administrative Functions

The Administrative Functions include (i) directing, supervising, and monitoring the implementation of the government policies, (ii) maintaining the internal security, law & order, (iii) maintaining, and protecting the state property, (iv) appointment-making functions, (v) semi-judicial functions, (vi) financial functions, and (iv) providing the public goods to the citizens.

2.2.3 Defense Functions

The Defense Functions include (i) having a supreme command and control over the Army, Navy, Air Force, and other military forces, (ii) defense functions to protect the nation from any form of aggression and attacks from foreign powers, (iii) war and peace functions to declare war if required to protect the nation, (iv) to carry out activities to protect the national resources and borders.The political executive at the Union level is empowered to declare martial law during times of emergencies.

2.3 Types of the Executive

The executive in general is classified into four broad types (i) Nominal /Titular and Real Executives, (ii) Hereditary and Elected Executives, (iii) Single and Plural Executives, and (iv) Parliamentary and Presidential Executives.

2.3.1 Nominal / Titular and Real Executives

> In India, the head of the state is a Nominal Executive.

In this type of executive, the head of the state is a ***Nominal Executive,*** like the President in a Parliamentary democracy or the monarch in a democracy. The ***Real Executive*** is the one who commands a wide range of power in the government like the Prime Minister in a Parliamentary democracy.

2.3.2 Hereditary and Elected Executives

> The elected representatives gain power in a democracy.

The ***Hereditary Executives*** are those who assume executive powers because of their hereditary or genetic lineage or by birth. For example, in monarchies, a member of the monarchy will assume the executive position. On the other hand, the ***Elected Executives*** are the elected representatives of the people in a democratic system. For example, the Prime Minister in a Parliamentary system is an elected executive.

2.3.3 Single and Plural Executives

A ***Single Executive*** refers to a single person who does not share powers with others as in the case of the President of the United States of America. On the other hand, ***Plural Executive*** refers to an arrangement where more than one person shares the powers of the executive.

The United States of America has a single executive, i.e., the President.

2.3.4 Parliamentary and Presidential Executives

A ***Parliamentary Executive*** is an arrangement where the elected representative in a Parliamentary system is chosen to exercise the powers of the executive. For example, In India, the prime minister heads the executive of the Government of India, even though the President is the ceremonial head of the state. The prime minister heads the cabinet, which is the executive of the government in a parliamentary system. A ***Presidential Executive*** is a system where the president is the executive head of the government. For example, the President of the US.

3. PERFORMANCE MANAGEMENT

From the public policy perspective, the performance of the executive matters immensely. Because the inefficient performance of an executive will retard the economy and create more hardship for the citizens. Therefore, the performance of the executive assumes greater importance. Then let us first understand '***what is performance?***'. According to the **Report of the Committee on Performance Management in Government**, '***Performance***' refers to the ability of the government to acquire resources and put them to efficient (input-output relationship) and effective (output-outcome relationship) uses to achieve the desired outcomes. The committee report defines '***performance management***' as a broad system of defining and measuring performance, besides developing incentives for individuals and organizations. Performance management covers the processes of planning, implementing, reviewing, evaluating, and reporting to gauge the impact of policies and programs. Further, it promotes growth and learning and recognizes that capacity building and improvement in individual performance lead to better achievement of organizational goals.

In a democracy, the performance measurement of the executive is important.

3.1 The Power of Performance Measurement

The performance measurement of the executive in a democracy is crucial as it enables the government to know how is its performance and how is the citizen feedback about the functioning of the executive in carrying out the policies and laws enacted by the legislature. Measurement is very essential because, as the saying goes, "***what gets measured gets done***". If we do not measure the results, we cannot uncover success from failure. The governments need to inform the public about their success. If the government cannot find success in the performance of the executive,

The performance management approach mainly aims at knowing the effectiveness of policy delivery.

it cannot reward the functionaries and motivate them further. If the government cannot find success, it should recognize the failure. By recognizing failure, it can then learn from the mistakes that caused the failure and work towards improving the government machinery in public service delivery. Thus, the constant cycle of improvements helps in improving public delivery. Hence, measurement is necessary to demonstrate the results and win public support.

3.2 A Taxonomy of Performance Evaluation Approaches

Governments conduct a performance evaluation of public policy delivery using several approaches: ***Managerial Approaches***, ***Systems Approach***, ***Formative Approach***, ***Performance Measurement Approach***, and ***monitoring and Control Compliance approach.*** They designed these approaches according to the different evaluation criteria. Figure 7.8 briefly presents a taxonomy of performance evaluation approaches.

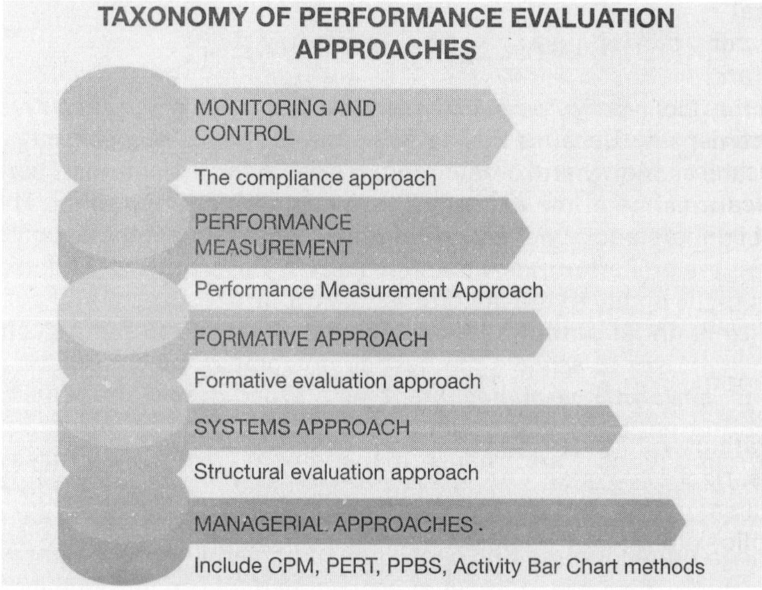

FIGURE 7.8 A Taxonomy of Performance Evaluation Approaches

3.2.1 Managerial Approaches

These include the Critical Path Method (CPM), Program Evaluation and Review Technique (PERT), Planning-Programming-Budgeting System (PPBS), and Activity Bar Chart.

CPM and PERT have wide recognition in performance evaluation not only in the private sector but also in the public sector. These approaches are more suitable for massive public policy program evaluation. The CPM and PERT approach aim at controlling the network of activities and outcomes during the policy implementation stage.

The CPM technique seeks to identify the activities that are crucial to successful policy implementation. This technique provides a clear path right from the beginning stage to the end stage of the program implementation and the overall estimated time required to complete each of the critical activities of the program implementation.

The PERT Method graphically estimates the time and resources required for policy implementation. In this method, three types of uncertainty duration estimation approaches are involved: (i) the most probable duration, (ii) the shortest forecast, and (iii) the longest forecast. The PERT technique is mostly used in large-scale policy programs of rural development involving a high level of uncertainty around the accomplishment of a policy program.

The PPBS Approach sets clear goals, outcomes, and valuations to create a proper analytical approach to review the cost-benefit analysis of the program over a period of years. Derived from the classical rational approach, the PPBS approach reviews the goals, objectives, needs, and challenges, and provides proper tools for monitoring, review, and feedback. However, there are opinions that the PPBS technique has not been effective in its utility.

Activity Bar Chart methods are used for measuring and monitoring the technical performance of a public policy by providing plans for each technical activity of the policy and its deliverables. This method is quite useful in implementing low-cost housing schemes for the poor.

3.2.2 Systems Approach

This approach looks at performance management as a review of a system of activities. It emphasizes monitoring the efficient use of inputs in generating the highest quality outputs in accordance with the policy outcomes. Hence, a systems analyst is more focused on evaluating how the overall sequence of program activities consumes the inputs to produce the policy outputs for successful policy implementation.

3.2.3 Formative Approach

The formative approach emphasizes formative evaluation, which begins in the implementation stage by monitoring how the program is managed and provides timely feedback to help improve the policy implementation process. To effectively monitor the program implementation, relevant data at the right time at the right intervals is necessary. In this direction, Management Information Systems (MIS) helps in routinizing the data collection process. With the advent of information technology, they enable the government departments with sophisticated data management systems that greatly aid the performance management of public policies.

3.2.4 Performance Measurement Approach

The performance management approach largely aims at knowing the effectiveness of policy delivery. The uniqueness of this approach is monitoring the program implementation using the *performance indicators* (PI). This is one of the effective performance management approaches as they determine the progress of program implementation in moving towards the program goals, identify the problem areas; and contribute to improving personnel management overall as well. Hence, ***the PIs greatly help in improving the capacity of the bureaucracy to control organizations and personnel for better program implementation.***

3.2.5 Monitoring and Control Compliance

This compliance approach relies on the philosophy that a good policy must have an effective means of enforcement. Successful policy implementation requires a mix of enforcement models. For effective enforcement, Boulding suggests a strategy mix of threat, exchange, and love.

3.3 Approaches to Performance Management in Government: International Models

The world over, several approaches to performance management in government are adopted in accordance with their needs, suitability, and affordability. We briefly discuss here some of the important models of performance management in selected countries.

3.3.1 Public Service Agreements (United Kingdom)

The UK uses public service agreements (PSAs) for performance evaluation.

The public service agreements (PSAs) specifically outline the objectives of the program implementation for the field department entrusted with the responsibility of program implementation. The Prime Minister's Delivery Unit and the respective government department enter into an agreement in this regard. The PSAs set out the time-bound targets for achieving the strategic objectives in a time-bound manner say within a period of three years.

3.3.2 Strategic Plans (The United States of America and South Africa)

The United States of America and South Africa use Strategic Plans.

The United States and South Africa use Strategic Plans as approaches to performance management in their governments. South Africa captures the department objectives in 3-year strategic plans which are later converted into operational work plans and performance agreements. The

United States uses Strategi Plans designed for five years, outlining the policy and operational objectives.

3.3.3 Pluri-Annual Planning Program (Brazil)

Brazil follows a Puri-Annual Planning Program, which divides all the governmental schemes into about 400 programs. Each of the programs has a dedicated program manager at the level of a senior civil servant who is held accountable for achieving program outcomes. The program targets are the performance management agreement terms for the civil servant.

New Zealand & Australia use Balanced Score Cards.

3.3.4 Balanced Score Card (New Zealand & Australia)

New Zealand and Australia follow a Balanced Score Card approach for performance management. A Balanced Score Card is an approach with a set of measures that are directly linked to the organization's strategy. The program managers evaluate the financial performance, process, feedback, and success rate using the score cards.

3.3.5 Performance Contracts (Kenya)

Kenya uses performance contracts to measure the performance of program implementation. The performance contracts are akin to PSAs in the UK. These are the agreements between the government and the department or the government agency with clear service standards and targets. The performance contracts provide incentives for achieving the set targets.

Kenya uses performance contracts.

4. PERFORMANCE MANAGEMENT SYSTEM IN THE INDIAN GOVERNMENT

As the technological revolution has provided many tools for data collection and monitoring, several effective tools for performance management systems have evolved over the years. *The Government of India has introduced '**New Public Management**' in public administration, stressing 'results' or 'performance' to improve the efficiency and the effectiveness of public service delivery.* The government has put in place a well-planned institutional framework for performance management in public program implementation. In addition, it has stipulated a robust performance appraisal mechanism for its civil servants through a well-designed system of 'performance management. ***The Second Administrative Reforms Commission's Tenth Report, 2008*** has detailed the performance management system in India. Figure 7.9 diagrammatically illustrates a template of the performance management system in government.

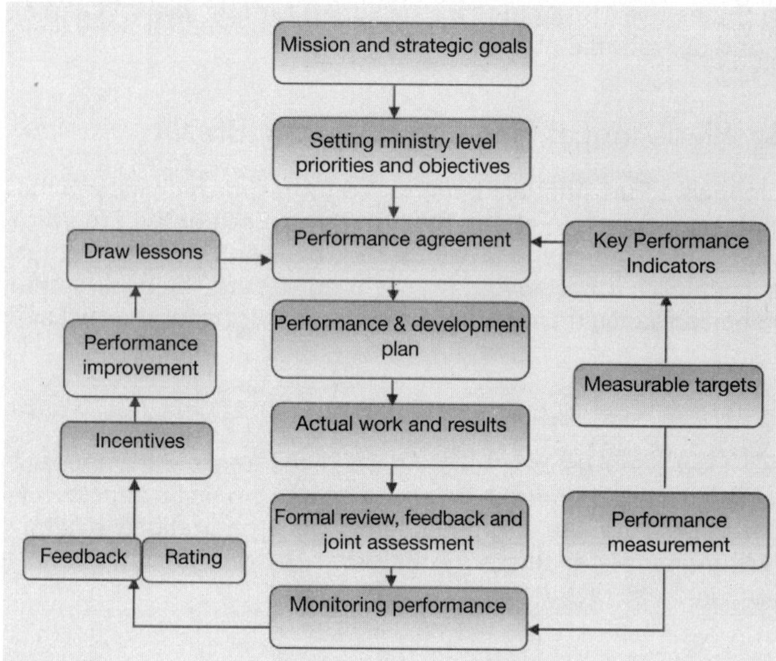

Credit: Adapted from Second Administrative Reforms Commission's Tenth Report, 2008

FIGURE 7.9 A Template for Performance Management System in Government

4.1 Institutional Setup for Performance Management of Programs and Projects

The institutions like NITI Ayog, the Ministry of Statistics & Program Implementation (MoSPI), and the Department of Audit and Accounts help in performance management.

India is a federal parliamentary constitutional republic and has its unique institutional setup for performance management of programs and projects comprising the institutions like NITI Ayog, the Ministry of Statistics & Program Implementation (MoSPI), and the Department of Audit and Accounts.

Results-Framework Document (RFD) helps in performance management process.

According to the Proceedings of the Global Roundtable on Government Performance Management, the Government has established a ***Performance Management Division*** (PMD) in the Cabinet Secretariat in January 2009 to infuse effective performance culture in the government. The PMD is the designated oversight agency responsible for designing effective mechanisms for performance monitoring and evaluation in government departments regularly. The PMD has developed a ***Results-Framework Document*** (RFD) which the government departments can use for highlighting the departmental objectives and priorities for each financial year as well as reporting achievements of the department vis-à-vis the pre-specified targets indicated in their RFD. Figure 7.11 shows the performance management grid to illustrate how the Results-Based Management Framework functions as a combination of ex-ante performance and managerial performance.

On the other hand, in cell # 4, we find the combination of agency performance with ex-post performance resulting in the need for conducting impact studies.

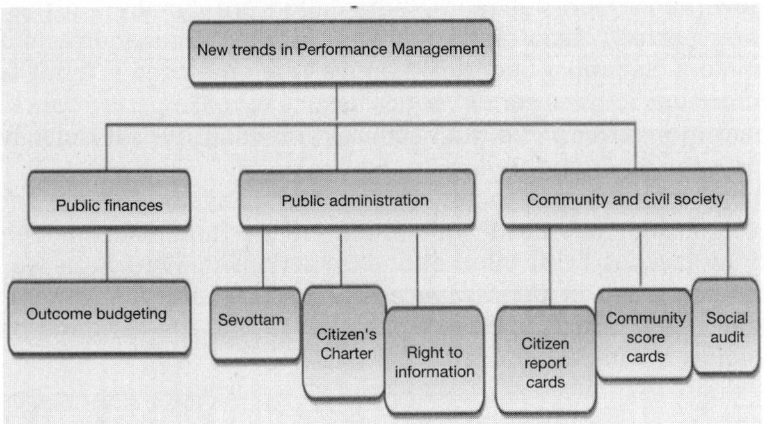

Credit: Report of the Committee on Performance Management in Government

FIGURE 7.10 A suggested Model of Performance Management in Government

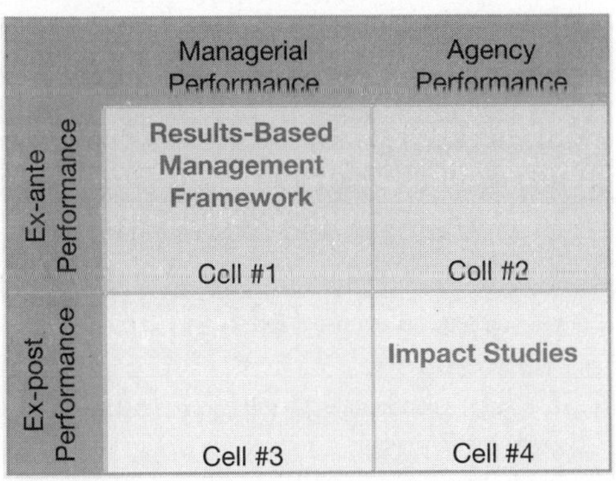

FIGURE 7.11 Performance Management Grid

The Proceedings of Global Roundtable on Government Performance Management reports that the ***RFD comprises Six Sections: (1) Ministry's Vision, Mission, Objectives, and Functions, (2) Inter se Priorities among key objectives, success indicators, and targets, (3) Trend values of the success indicators, (4) Description and definition of success indicators and proposed measurement methodology, (5) Specific performance requirements from other departments that are critical for delivering agreed results, and (6) Outcome/Impact of activities of Department/Ministry.***

The Report of the Committee on Performance Management in Government has suggested new performance management in line with the new trends.

4.2 Critical Issues in Performance Management in Government

There is a need to benchmark the existing systems in consonance with the strong theoretical foundations of performance management.

The governance and policy implementation are dynamic in this ever-changing society. Accordingly, the performance management of the government also must undergo changes when the need is felt. The government must address certain critical issues to make performance management more dynamic and effective in meeting the set objectives in tune with the emerging trends.

There is a need to benchmark the existing systems in consonance with the strong theoretical foundations of performance management and draw lessons from international experiences. We source some of the critical issues in performance management in government from the Report of the Committee on Performance Management and present them below in Table 7.1.

TABLE 7.1 Critical Issues in Performance Management in Government

Individual	1. Absence of quantification of targets and evaluation against the achievement of targets 2. Unclear performance standards 3. Neglect of job fit-in appointments, and frequent transfers 4. Lack of mechanism to motivate for good performance 5. Absence of appropriate punishment/reward mechanisms 6. Absence of clear linkages between the individual, organizational, and program performance
Ministry or Department	1. Funds granted to ministries are never linked with the progress of work or the targets set out in the performance budget 2. Lack of clarity regarding purpose and objectives of Action Plans 3. Inability to measure performance in the absence of appropriate indicators
Public enterprise	1. Most PSEs rated excellent or good despite declining performance 2. The tendency of public sector enterprises (PSEs) to show profits in the short-run by sacrificing long-term interests 3. Lack of scope for true negotiation 4. No mechanisms to enable the movement of accountability to lower levels
Issues at program/ project	1. Focus on inputs and process compliance neglects the outcomes and impacts 2. Lack of measurable indicators 3. The dichotomy between plans and budgets

Credit: "Report of the Committee on Performance Management in Government. https://darpg.gov.in/sites/default/files/Performance_Management.pdf"

Overall, there is a strong need to reform the performance management in government for effective policy implementation. As the government is ever growing, the programs are also increasing. A paradigm shift in our approaches to performance management like accountability, service agreements, social audit, etc., at different levels of government functionaries is necessary to fine-tune the performance management system in the government. Effective policy implementation is the key to the success of the program objectives and attaining the broader objectives of economic growth and higher standards of living with peace and harmony.

Effective policy implementation is the key to the success of the program objectives.

Summary

- In India, the constitution provides for three levels of government in line with its vast geography and diversity, and culture. At the national level is the Union government or the Government of India. At the state levels are the State governments, and at the local levels like at district, taluka, and village levels are the Local governments. The Government of India is the executive of the Republic of India. The Governor, who is appointed by the President of India, constitutionally presides over the state government. However, the Governor acts with the advice of the State Council of Ministers headed by the elected Chief Minister.
- The Panchayati Raj structure in India comprises (1) Zilla panchayat at the district level, (2) Taluka panchayat at the taluka or block level, and (3) Gram panchayat at the village level. The 73rd Constitutional Amendment, 1992, gave Panchayati Raj institutions the constitutional status to encourage democracy at the grassroots level and the self-participation of the people in the matters of local administration.
- After the legislature, the Executive is the most powerful organ of the government. The Executive, in general, is understood in two parts: (i) the Political executive, and (ii) The Permanent executive. In the hierarchy of the executive, the President is the highest authority in India, followed by the Government of India, State governments, District administration, and local governments in the rural areas. The Political Executive is more powerful because the people elect it, and hence are responsible for the people. The Permanent Executive is a non-political structure of bureaucracy.
- Policymaking, administrative functions, and defense are some of the functions performed by the executive. The four broad types: Nominal / Titular and Real Executives, Hereditary and Elected Executives, Single and Plural Executives, and Parliamentary and Presidential Executives.
- From the public policy perspective, the performance of the executive matters immensely. Governments conduct a performance evaluation of public policy delivery using several approaches like Managerial Approaches, Systems Approach, Formative Approach, Performance Measurement Approach, and Monitoring and Control Compliance approach.
- Some of the international models of performance management are Public Service Agreements, Strategic Plans, Pluri-Annual Planning Program, Balanced Score Card, and Performance Contracts.
- The Government of India has introduced 'New Public Management' in public administration, stressing results or performance to improve the efficiency and the effectiveness of public service delivery. The Second Administrative Reforms Commission's Tenth Report, 2008 has detailed the performance management system in India.
- Results-Framework Document (RFD) comprises Six Sections: (1) Ministry's Vision, Mission, Objectives, and Functions, (2) Inter se Priorities among key objectives, success indicators, and targets, (3) Trend values of the success indicators, (4) Description and definition of success

indicators and proposed measurement methodology, (5) Specific performance requirements from other departments that are critical for delivering agreed results, and (6) Outcome/Impact of activities of Department/Ministry.

- Overall, there is a strong need to reform the performance management in government for effective policy implementation.

Key Words

Ordinary Bills	Titular Executive	Program Evaluation and Review Technique (PERT)
Money Bills	Hereditary Executive	Planning-Programming-Budgeting System (PPBS)
Local Government	Single Executive	Activity Bar Chart
Panchayati Raj	Plural Executive	Public Service Agreements (PSAs)
Zilla Panchayat	Parliamentary Executive	Strategic Plans
Taluka Panchayat	Presidential Executive	Puri-Annual Planning Program
Gram panchayat	Systems Approach	Balanced Score Card
Political Executive	Formative Approach	Performance Contracts
Permanent Executive	Critical Path Method (CPM)	Results-Framework Document (RFD)

Questions

A. Quick Check

1. Who holds the highest position of executive authority and acts as the head of state? Explain.
2. Explain the structure of the Government of India with your comments.
3. Briefly explain the law-making process in the Government of India
4. Constitutionally who presides over the state government? Explain.
5. Discuss Panchayati Raj in India.
6. Discuss the two parts of the executive.
7. Explain the hierarchy of the executive in India.
8. Why is the political executive more powerful?
9. What are the four types of the executive?
10. Briefly explain the international models of performance management.

B. Explore

1. India is a federal parliamentary constitutional democratic republic. Discuss this statement in the context of the Executive.
2. Discuss the functions of the executive in detail.

3. Discuss the taxonomy of performance evaluation approaches.
4. Critically analyze the performance management system in India.

References

- Boulding, K., 1990, Three Facts of Power, Sage, London
- Proceedings of Global Roundtable on Government Performance Management held at New Delhi, India, December 11-12, 2013. http://tgpg-isb.org
- Report of the Committee on Performance Management in Government Available at https://darpg.gov.in/sites/default/files/Performance_Management.pdf
- The Second Administrative Reforms Commission's Tenth Report, 2008. https://darpg.gov.in/sites/default/files/personnel_administration10.pdf
- The Government of India website

Further Readings

- Palumbo, D.J., 1987, The Politics of Program Evaluation, Sage, Newbury Park, California.

CHAPTER 8

Public Policy Making: The Role of Judiciary

The goal of this chapter is to offer a brief overview of the legitimate role of the state and, more particularly, the role of the judiciary in public policymaking. In this chapter, we will first take a broad outlook of the legitimate role of the state in a democracy and then we focus more on the judicial roles of the state like administration of justice, interpretation, and application of laws, protection of rights, guardian of the constitution, law enforcement, conducting judicial inquiries, advisory functions, arbiter role in a federal system, judicial review, role in law-making, and role of the judiciary in policy-making. The role of the judiciary is more prominent in its legislating from the bench. We will understand how judges legitimately legislate in a democracy and what are its limitations. In recent decades, judicial activism has gained prominence. We discuss judicial activism and its costs to the economy. The contrast to judicial activism is judicial restraint. We discuss the principles of stare decisis, which provide the basis for judicial restraint. In Common Law, the law of precedent is well known. We discuss the doctrine of precedent, its elements, types of precedents, and the merits of using the precedents. In the last section, we present a brief on the tradition of the judiciary in India comprising, Common Law Tradition, and checks on the judiciary.

Section 1: Legitimate Role of The State

Section 2: Judicial Roles of The State

Section 3: Legislating from the Bench

Section 4: Judicial Activism

Section 5: Judicial Restraint

Section 6: Law of Precedent

Section 7: Tradition of Judiciary in India

> A state is "a community of people exercising a sovereign power over a particular territory."

What is the state? The State is fundamental to our knowledge of the interaction between politics and modern societies. It is axiomatic to say that the 'state' performs a central role in the working of modern societies. To begin with, let us know that the term 'State' is from the Latin word 'status' which means "condition of a country". However, ***a state is***

A state should possess (i) a permanent population, (ii) a defined territory, (iii) government, and (iv) power and authority to undertake pacts, treaties, and relations with other states.

A state has the following essential minimal functions: war making, state making, protection, extraction, adjudication, distribution, and production.

"a community of people exercising a sovereign power over a particular territory." In other words, a state is a sovereign institution vested with powers of law-making and law enforcement.

From the international law perspective, they adopted the definition of a state at the Montevideo Convention on the Rights and Duties of States, held in Montevideo, Uruguay, on December 26, 1933. Accordingly, **a state should possess *(i) a permanent population, (ii) a defined territory, (iii) government, and (iv) power and authority to undertake pacts, treaties, and relations with other states.*** Put simply, a state is a physical territory with its permanent population and institutions. On the other hand, ***a sovereign state is a state with a government that has the sovereign power and authority to make treaties and agreements with other states.***

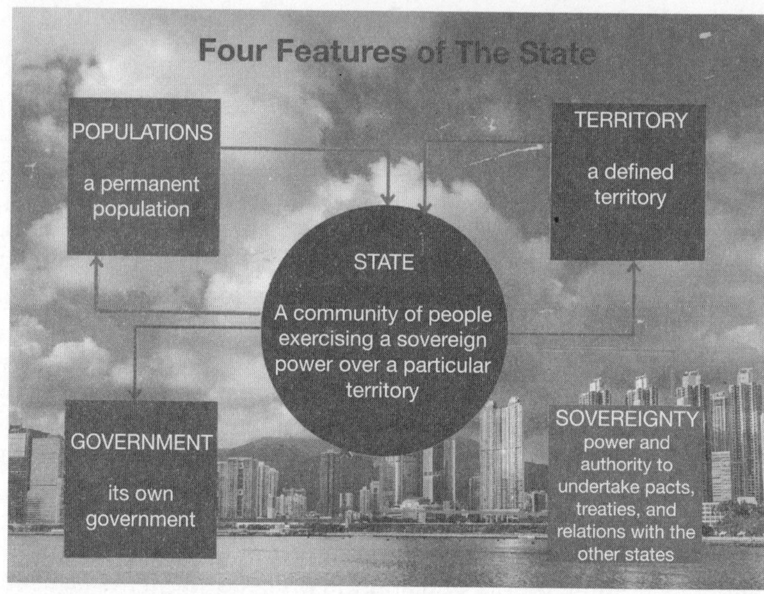

Credit: Lee Yiu Tung. Shutterstock

FIGURE 8.1 Four Features of The State

According to Charles Tilly, an American sociologist, and political scientist, a state has the following essential minimal functions: (1) ***War making***–eliminating or neutralizing its rivals, (2) ***State making***–exterminating or eradicating the rival entities inside its territory, (3) ***Protection***–liquidating or knocking off the enemies of their patrons, (4) ***Extraction***–annexing and claiming the means of carrying out war-making, state-making, and protection, (5) ***Adjudication***–magisterial and legitimate settlement of disputes among its population, (6) ***Distribution***–ensuring efficient allocation of goods and services among its population, and (7) ***Production***–controlling and regulating the production and transformation of goods and services produced by its population (Tilly, 1985).

From the theoretical perspective, the literature defines 'state' from different viewpoints based on their disciplines depending on the origin, sphere, function, nature, and features. Some of the important theories of state are the ***Liberal*** (where the state gives the individuals the opportunity of a civilized living in a society and the state acts neutrally), the ***Marxist*** (they view the state as a dynamic institution constrained by social forces, and class structure), the ***Welfare*** (a welfare state appears to be less of a charity but more of an entitlement), the ***Liberal-Egalitarian*** (a state should intervene for establishing the principles of justice and equality in the society), the ***Libertarian-Minimal*** (a state must not do anything more than providing services, because by doing so it violates people's rights and hence cannot be morally legitimate), and the ***Post-modernist*** *view* (a state is a meta-narrative that is an important ingredient of the totalizing converse of modernity).

Prominent theories of state are Liberal, Marxist, Welfare, Liberal-Egalitarian, Libertarian-Minimal, and the Post-modernist view.

Country, State, and Nation

These terms are often used interchangeably. Let us know them with their distinguishing features. A ***Sovereign State*** *is a state with its legitimate institutions and a permanent population living on an ongoing basis, a territory with universally accepted boundaries, and a government with authority and power to make treaties and accords with other states.* It has the power to issue a legal tender that is acknowledged across boundaries. ***Non-sovereign states*** are those that have features of sovereign states but are officially considered non-sovereign. Some of the examples are Bermuda, England, Greenland, Hong Kong, Northern Ireland, Puerto Rico, and Scotland.

A Sovereign State is a state with its legitimate institutions and a permanent population living on an ongoing basis, a territory with universally accepted boundaries, and a government with authority and power to make treaties and accords with other states.

A **Nation** is a *substantially large culturally homogeneous population that inhabits a specific territory and inherits common history, culture, and legacy.* A **Nation-State** *Is a nation of people that has a sovereign state of its own.* In nation-states, a large majority of people share the same ancestry and culture. Iceland and Japan are the best examples of nation-states. We use the term country in a less-political manner to mean a state, a sovereign state, or a nation-state. They view the states and sovereign states as political entities. However, the nations and countries are not necessarily viewed so.

LEGITIMATE ROLES OF THE STATE

Public policymaking is a complex process with the involvement of different organs of the state. In this context, let us first understand the legitimate roles of the state. The '***legitimacy***' which is a central feature of power relations, implies the acceptance of authority and power among both political elites and citizens. It lies at the heart of state-citizen relationships. ***State legitimacy*** *in state-society relations is vital.* ***Legitimacy is a litmus test for a state***. Every state requires some degree of legitimacy to govern effectively. In the absence of legitimacy, there can be chaos, conflicts, and disorder in society. The states become legitimate when the citizens confer on them the required authority to rule over them. The

A Nation is a substantially large culturally homogeneous population that inhabits a specific territory and inherits common history, culture, and legacy.

State legitimacy in state-society relations is vital.

feasibility of the development of the state largely depends on the depth and durability of the state's legitimacy. A range of sources, like the effectiveness of public institutions, service delivery, effective taxation, social protection measures, and the degree of representation and accountability, give rise to State Legitimacy.

The Dimensions of Legitimacy

The five features of multidimensionality of legitimacy are predictability, justifiability, equity, accessibility, and respectfulness.

The dimensions of legitimacy according to Beetham include (i) **legal validity** – conformity to rules, (ii) **justifiability** in terms of shared beliefs, and (iii) **expressed consent** to legitimation (Beetham, 1991). On the other hand, Robert Lamb conceptualizes the multidimensionality of legitimacy into five features: ***(i) predictability, (ii) justifiability, (iii) equity, (iv) accessibility, and (v) respectfulness*** (Lamb, 2014).

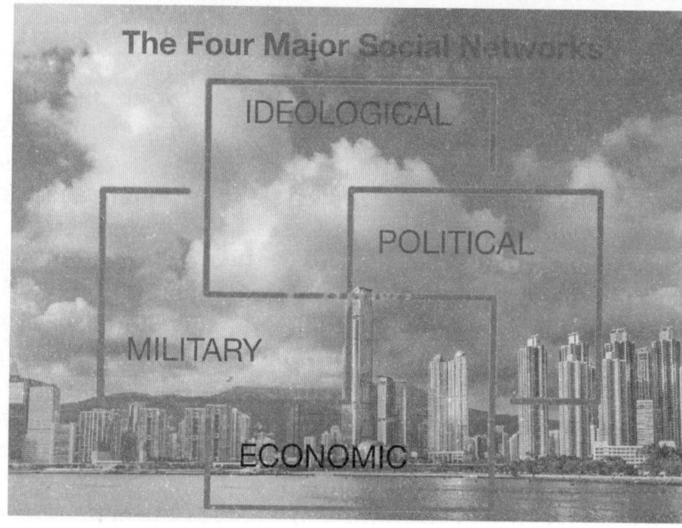

Credit: Lee Yiu Tung. Shutterstock

FIGURE 8.2 Mann's Overlapping and Intersecting Socio-spatial Networks of Power

The societies are characterized by imperfect interactive systems of "Overlapping and intersecting Socio-spatial networks of power" like ideological, economic, military, and political.

Explaining the role of the state, Michael Mann claims that societies are characterized by imperfect interactive systems of "**Overlapping and intersecting Socio-spatial networks of power**". The four major social networks — **(i) *ideological,* (ii) *economic,* (iii) *military,* and (iv) *political***—are granted immense autonomy, which are the power sources (Mann, 1986). Accordingly, the role of the state is a "space" that controls the overall behavior of the different social networks. On the other hand, William Domhoff claims that the "*state is an autonomous space laying down rules and adjudicating disputes in specific territories*" (Domhoff, 1996).

1. THE LEGITIMATE ROLES OF THE STATE

The state, with its state legitimacy, has several roles toward its citizens. Figure 8.3 lists the legitimate roles of the state.

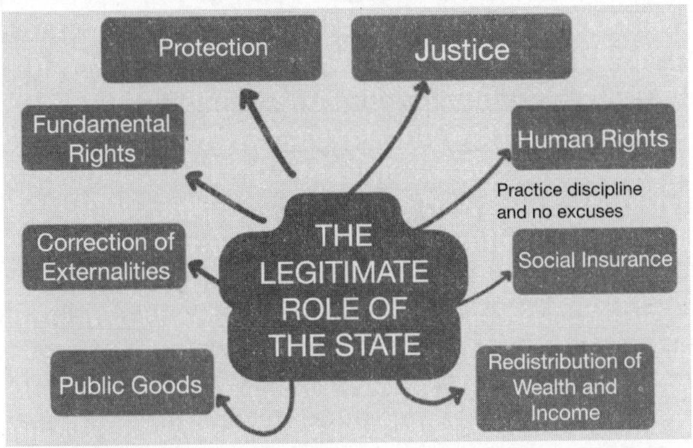

FIGURE 8.3 The Legitimate Roles of The State

1.1 Protection: The state should protect the citizens from internal and external aggression.

1.2 Justice: It must ensure the provision of justice to all sections of the society without any discrimination.

1.3 Protecting Fundamental Rights: One important role of the state is protecting the fundamental rights of its citizens.

1.4 Securing Human Rights: Recent theorists argue that the state should secure the human rights of its citizens.

1.5 Correction of Externalities: The state must correct the externalities in the economy and benefit its citizens in their economic activities.

1.6 Social Insurance: Providing social insurance is another important role of the state toward its citizen as most of the poor sections of the society do not have the economic power to insure themselves against possible risks.

1.7 Provision of Public Goods: One of the major economic roles of the state is ensuring the provision of public goods and services to all its citizens without any discrimination.

1.8 Redistribution of Wealth and Income: It is the responsibility of the state to ensure that it redistributes the wealth and income of the state among its citizens based on the principles of equity and equality.

2. JUDICIAL ROLES OF THE STATE

The primary role of the judiciary in a state is to guard the rule of law and defend the supremacy of law.

The judiciary plays an important role in a democracy. ***Through its power of judicial decisions, it significantly influences society***. *The primary role of the judiciary in a state is to guard the rule of law and defend the supremacy of law.* It protects the rights of the citizen, resolves disputes following the law, and ensures the features of democracy in a state without giving way to any form of dictatorship. The judiciary has a vital role

Judiciary has a special role as an arbiter in a federal system.

The judiciary makes the rules and enforces them for the systematic and effective administration of justice.

In a democracy, the judiciary is the guardian of the Constitution.

in public policymaking that affects society in the economic and social aspects.

We discuss below some of the major judicial roles of the state like (1) Administration of Justice, (2) Interpretation and Application of Laws, (3) Protection of Rights, (4) Guardian of the Constitution, (5) Law Enforcement, (6) Conducting Judicial Inquiries, (7) Advisory Functions, (8) Arbiter Role in a Federal System, (9) Judicial Review, (10) Role in Law-making, and (11) Role of Judiciary in Policy-making.

2.1 Administration of Justice

In a democracy, the primary role of the judiciary is the administration of justice to the people. Whenever a citizen approaches the judiciary, it becomes the responsibility of the judiciary to administer justice as per the law of the land. In the process, the judiciary has the superior powers to impose penalties on those found guilty of violating the laws of the land or the rights of other citizens. All citizens have the right to approach the judiciary for seeking redressal and compensation when they fear any harm to their rights or after they suffer any loss or damage. The judiciary can decide all cases of its citizens concerning the grant of compensation.

Besides, the judiciary is not a department of the government. Being an independent organization, it administers its nature, set-up, functioning, and delivery of justice through its rules. These rules govern the selection, recruitment, and functioning of judges and other judicial officers and personnel of the judiciary. The judiciary makes the rules and enforces them for the systematic and effective administration of justice.

The judiciary interprets and guides the executive in applying the laws of the land.

An independent judiciary means the executive and the legislature do not influence and interfere with the functioning of the judiciary.

2.2 Interpretation and Application of Laws

An important role of the judiciary is to interpret and guide the executive in applying the laws of the land following the Constitution. Generally, the judiciary interprets the laws before deciding the disputes and then orders for proper application of the laws of the land. As per the constitutional provisions, the judiciary can interpret every law made by the legislature. If the law is in contravention of the constitutional principles, the judiciary can cancel such laws enacted by the legislature.

In general, the five sources that guide the interpretation of the Constitution are (i) the text and structure of the Constitution, (ii) the intentions of the founders of the Constitution, (iii) prior judicial precedents, (iv) the social, political, and economic consequences of alternative interpretations, and (v) principles of natural justice.

2.3 Protection of Rights

The Constitution has entrusted the judiciary with the supreme responsibility of protecting the rights of citizens. The citizen can approach the judiciary whenever his rights are infringed by the state or other non-state actors and seek restoration of the rights. The decisions of the judiciary are binding on all sections of society.

2.4 Guardian of the Constitution

In a democracy, the Constitution is the supreme law of the land. The judiciary, as a watchdog of democracy, acts like the guardian of the Constitution. An unbiased, effective, and independent judiciary greatly helps in the effective functioning of the democracy. An independent judiciary means the executive and the legislature do not influence and interfere with the functioning of the judiciary and the judges function without any fear or favor.

2.5 Law Enforcement

The judiciary not only delivers justice but also has the power to enforce the law and its decisions. It has the authority to direct the executive to enforce its decisions. The judiciary can summon anyone who is required to know the truth.

2.6 Conducting Judicial Inquiries

The executive very often seeks the judiciary to help conduct enquire some serious incidents. The judges head the inquiry commissions to investigate the alleged errors and omissions on the part of the alleged culprits. The government appoints commissions of inquiry to investigate complicated matters and problems.

> Commissions of inquiry are appointed by the governments to investigate complicated matters and problems.

2.7 Advisory Functions

The executive quite often requests the judiciary to provide advisory opinions on legal aspects. For example, according to the Indian Constitution, the President has the power to refer a matter to the Supreme Court of India for clarification on a question of law or fact that is of immense public importance. However, it should be known that the Supreme Court is not bound to give advice, and the President is also not bound to oblige the advice of the Supreme Court. The utility of such advisory functions is that the legal opinion given by the judiciary is useful in avoiding unwanted litigations later by suitably changing the legislation.

> The legal opinion given by the judiciary is useful in avoiding unwanted litigations later.

2.8 Arbiter Role in a Federal System

Judiciary has a special role as an arbiter in a federal system. Any disputes that arise between the central government and the state governments must be arbitered by the judiciary. As an autonomous body, the judiciary acts like an umpire between the central government and the

> The judiciary must decide all legal disputes between the center-state disputes.

state governments. The judiciary must decide all legal disputes between the center-state disputes.

2.9 Judicial Review

Prima facie, if any law passed by the legislature is inconsistent with the constitutional principles, the judiciary can undertake a judicial review of such a law. If such a law is in contravention of the constitution, the judiciary can declare such law unconstitutional and inapplicable. Even though the term judicial review is not mentioned in the constitution, the judiciary has the power to strike down any law that goes against the spirit of the constitution.

The judiciary has the power to review the legislation if they violate the fundamental rights or the constitutional provisions. This judicial review power extends to the state legislature as well. The power of judicial review, as exercised by the judiciary, has recognized that the basic structure of the Constitution is unalterable.

2.10 Role in Law-Making

The judiciary has a crucial role in law-making. Its decisions determine the meaning, nature, scope, and extent of the laws made by the legislature. Judicial decisions often constitute a major source of law-making. The judge-made laws also influence law-making by the state. Often, the interpretation of laws by the judiciary qualifies as law-making because these interpretations define the laws.

2.11 Role of Judiciary in Policy-Making

The Supreme Court in India has significantly contributed to public policymaking.

Through judicial decisions and judicial reviews, the judiciary significantly influences public policy-making. On many socio-economic issues, the judiciary has actively contributed to policy-making related to social welfare, economic upliftment, gender equality, ownership of property, and equal protection under the law. The judiciary also examines whether the public policies adhere to constitutional principles. The Supreme Court in India has significantly contributed to public policymaking. Therefore, the judiciary has a major role in policy-making.

3. LEGISLATING FROM THE BENCH

Law-making is the domain of the legislature.

Can judges legitimately legislate? If they can, what are its implications and limitations? Is judicial legislation desirable? The classical positivist jurisprudence states that law-making is the responsibility of the legislature. The 19th-century jurists like Bentham, and Austin, and the 20th-century jurists Hart, Kelsen, and others are of the strict opinion that law-making is the domain of the legislature.

Legislating from the bench in a representative democracy can be a substitute for the failure of other branches of government and a contribution to good governance. But it can also be a threat to the core of democracy where the law-making is in the domain of the elected representatives. Even though legislating from the bench can be a substitute for the failure of the legislature, it remains a grave threat to the electorate, the ultimate stakeholders of democracy.

In India, the Supreme Court has repeatedly turned to judicial legislation using its powers under Article 141, claiming that it was meant to fill the void formed by the alleged legislative vacuum. Since the early eighties, the scope of judicial legislation has broadened due to the locus stand in the public interest litigation matters.

The process of legislating from the bench is restricted by its very nature.

The judiciary has found interesting tools for its penchant for law-making, like the doctrine of precedent, construction of statutes, bringing the omission of the legislature, or filling the gaps by using discretion. The process of legislating from the bench is restricted by its very nature and hence cannot be a perfect parallel to the legislative process.

The judicial pronouncements have a strong influence on the current and future laws, policies, and rules that the legislature and the executive will make. The judiciary exercises its power under the doctrine of judicial review, where the actions of the legislature and the executive are subject to judicial review.

The limitations of the judge-made laws are that the policy choices the judiciary makes are based on interpretations of existing law. The judicial decisions are dependent on what the judge would prefer to do and can be tampered with by their perceptions, ideologies, whims, and fancies. The basic limitation is that judge-made law does not fit well with the concept of democracy where the electorate is the supreme law-makers.

The basic limitation is that judge-made law does not fit well with the concept of democracy.

4. JUDICIAL ACTIVISM

Judicial activism began in the United Kingdom. The unwritten constitution of the UK gave scope for judicial review and, therefore, gave birth to judicial activism. The terms such as "***judicial activism***," "***judicial supremacy***," "***judicial absolutism***," and "***judicial anarchy***" are used interchangeably. However, "judicial activism" is based on their ideologies, opinions, values, and interests. "Judicial activism" as a concept contrasts with "***judicial restraint***." ***Judicial activism is an approach by the judiciary to decide constitutional issues invalidating the legislative or executive actions in a democracy.*** A judge becomes a ***judicial activist*** when he/she strays away from the precedent, makes policy with rulings, and decides contrary to the spirit of constitutional coordination of respect among the three pillars of democracy: the legislature, the executive, and the judiciary.

Judicial activism" as a concept contrasts with "judicial restraint.

The scope of judicial activism is so wide that no exact definition exists. There is no statutory definition for judicial activism and the constitution has no specific mention of it. However, supporters of judicial activism assert it as a proper form of judicial review. According to them, the

The theories of Judicial Activism are The Theory of Vacuum Filling and The Theory of Social Want.

judiciary must use its powers to correct injustice, particularly when the other organs of government have failed to act. The supporters of judicial activism argue that the judiciary must play an active role in policymaking.

4.1 Theories of Judicial Activism

The **Theory of Vacuum Filling** and the **Theory of Social Want** argue that the following reasons give way to judicial activism: (i) near collapse of responsible government, (ii) pressure on the judiciary to step in, (iii) judicial enthusiasm to participate in social reform and change, (iv) legislative vacuum left open, (v) the constitutional scheme, (vi) authority to make a final declaration as to the validity of a law, (viii) role of the judiciary as guardian of fundamental rights, (ix) public confidence in the judiciary, (x) enthusiasm of individual players.

Judicial activism is a dynamic process of judicial outlook.

In a transforming society, judicial activism is a dynamic process of judicial outlook. We understand judicial activism in recent times as an approach followed by some judges within the limits of the constitution to correct the deficiencies and flaws of the executive. Through judicial activism, the judges act as individual policymakers and independent trustees on behalf of the citizens of the country. However, nowhere it is mentioned in the constitution that in a democracy a single person can make laws, however good that law is.

Judicial activism draws criticism from the fact that a single or few judges together make rulings based on their considerations rather than directing the legislature to correct the laws. If a single person makes the laws, then it can also be considered autocratic. On the other hand, the judiciary could advise the legislature to pass laws instead of a judge making the laws in a democracy. Hence, many learned people view that judicial activism does not go with the spirit of democracy. **Judicial activism is seen as a tussle to show the supremacy or power of the judiciary over the other organs of the state**, i.e., the legislature and the executive. Further, judicial activism leads to creating strains on the democratic principle of respecting each organ of the state.

Judicial activism is seen as a tussle to show the supremacy or power of the judiciary over the other organs of the state.

What are the costs of judicial activism? Every law has pros and cons. When a single judge makes the law, what are the costs associated?

Firstly, a single judge does not know to analyze and evaluate thoroughly the social and economic costs of the policy.

Secondly, a single judge does not make the social cost-benefit analysis and does not comply with the economic ramifications of the judge-made policy.

Thirdly, there are several economic spillovers of judge-made law, in that case, who pays the bill? Often, judicial activism has resulted in distributionally regressive and socially costly decisions.

Judicial activism has resulted in distributionally regressive and socially costly decisions.

5. JUDICIAL RESTRAINT

***Judicial Restraint** is a concept of judicial interpretation that urges judges to limit the exercise of their power.* According to judicial restraint, judges must hesitate to strike down laws made by the legislature unless they are brazenly unconstitutional. *Judicial restraint makes the judiciary follow the doctrine of **"Stare decisis"** which means that a judiciary must follow the precedent set by previous judicial pronouncements under similar circumstances.* This helps in ensuring continuity and uniformity in the administration of law.

Judicial restraint makes the judiciary follow the doctrine of "Stare decisis" which means that a judiciary must follow the precedent set by previous judicial pronouncements under similar circumstances.

Judiciary must decide the issues based on:

(i) the original intent of those who wrote the constitution,
(ii) Precedent–past decisions in earlier cases,
(iii) the judiciary should leave policymaking to the legislature
(iv) Judiciary should "restrain" from establishing new policies with their decisions.

Among the three organs of the state, the judiciary has the power to define the limits of all three. Therefore, the judiciary must exercise utmost restraint in the exercise of its powers with utmost humility and self-restraint. For example, in the In S.R. Bommai v Union of India case, the judges stated that there are certain situations where the political element dominates and no judicial review is possible.

6. LAW OF PRECEDENT

The *Law of Precedent* or the *Doctrine of Precedent* originally grew in England in a dearth of codified laws. The benefit of the law of precedent is to provide certainty, stability, predictability, and uniformity to the administration of justice. ***Stare decisis** is the legal term that refers to the law of precedent.* It is recognized in common law that previous judicial decisions guide the court rulings. The meaning of the Latin term *stare decisis* is *"to stand by things decided"* or *"let the decision stand."* ***The law of precedent is defined as the legal principle to determine the points in litigation as per the precedent.*** A precedent is a previous example or a case that provides an exemplar or a rule for subsequent behavior, and a pattern upon which succeeding behavior is based (Dias, 1964). Put simply, a precedent is a notion or a law or a rule that was laid down during a previous legal case. Quite often, the judiciary must decide on similar cases with similar facts accordingly.

Stare decisis is the legal term that refers to the law of precedent.

What are the elements of a precedent? Generally, we find two elements: (i) a **concrete decision**—obligatory upon disputing parties of a case, and (ii) an **abstract principle**—obligatory on a subsequent judge. According to John William Salmond (1862-1924), ***a 'Precedent' is law-making by the judiciary themselves in the administration of justice*** (Salmond, 1907).

The law of precedent is defined as the legal principle to determine the points in litigation as per the precedent.

6.1 Types of Precedents

The two broad types of Precedents are Authoritative precedents and Persuasive precedents.

Salmond classifies legal precedents as (1) ***Authoritative precedents***: There are considered legal sources of law, that a subsequent judge is bound to follow, and (2) ***Persuasive precedents***: These are historical sources of law, where judgments of foreign courts, judicia dicta, and decisions of the Privy Council. The Constitution of India considers the precedents as sources of law.

In India, the decisions of the Supreme Court of India are 'authoritative precedents' binding on all other subordinate courts. Similarly, the decisions of the High Courts in India are 'authoritative precedents' binding on subordinate courts within its jurisdiction, however, they are 'persuasive precedents' not binding on the courts outside its jurisdiction.

The law of precedent gives certainty to the law-making process.

What are the merits of using the precedents? The doctrine of precedents serves as a reminder and as a foundation to build on cases. The precedents are founded on customs and hence reflect public opinion. They give certainty to the law-making process. They guide judges to think practically and more sensibly without any prejudice.

7. TRADITION OF JUDICIARY IN INDIA

In the commonwealth countries, the Common Law Tradition is more profound and vivid. As soon as the colonies became independent from Great Britain, instead of establishing a new legal system, they continued the British Legal System with minor modifications. Thus continued the tradition of English law, which is known as the Common Law Tradition.

The Common Law Tradition is more profound in the Commonwealth countries.

The evolution of Common Law found its origins in Great Britain, as there was no written constitution. Judge-made laws became legal precedents. ***The foundation of the Common Law is in the doctrine of stare decisis.*** Stare decisis as defined earlier means to depend or base on the previously decided cases. That construes that when a legal situation arises, if a similar situation was decided earlier, then the previous decision is binding on the current situation as well. The major advantages of the Common Law Tradition are efficiency and stability.

The foundation of the Common Law is in the doctrine of stare decisis.

What checks our courts? The judiciary is powerful and does not tolerate any criticism. Often it is said that it shows its superiority over the other organs of the democracy by undermining the doctrine of separation of powers. In such a situation, who checks the judiciary? We notice *four broad types of checks on the judiciary: (1) The Legislature checks, (2) The Executive checks, (3) Judicial Traditions and Doctrines, and (4) Public opinion.*

The four broad types of checks on the judiciary are The Legislature checks, The Executive checks, Judicial Traditions and doctrines, and public opinion.

Legislative Checks: The legislature can go for impeaching and removing such judges who cross the defined lines. The legislature has the power to amend laws and revalidate the laws that are declared ultra vires by the judiciary.

Executive Checks: The Executive can control with its power to appoint the judges and the Chief Justice.

Judicial Traditions and Doctrines: The Judiciary is bound by the procedure established by law, as well as judicial traditions and well-established doctrines in the delivery of justice.

Public Opinion: Public opinion supported by strong, vigilant media and civil society organizations plays a useful role in bringing checks on the judiciary at times when it is found crossing the thin lines of the doctrine of separation of powers stipulated in the Constitution.

To sum up, the judiciary plays a significant role in public policymaking through its power of judicial review. The judges like policy-makers, consciously or insentiently, cause changes in society while delivering judgments that are powerful in their impact. Using the power of judicial review, we often find the judiciary to be an activist in shaping public policy by modifying the policies framed by the legislature. In India, there are several instances where the Supreme Court (also called the Apex Court) has actively played an important role in public policymaking related to socio-economic issues.

Summary

- A Sovereign State is a state with its legitimate institutions and a permanent population living on an ongoing basis, a territory with universally accepted boundaries, and a government with authority and power to make treaties and accords with other states. The legitimate roles of the state are protection, justice, protecting fundamental rights, securing human rights, correction of externalities, social insurance, provision of public goods, and redistribution of wealth and income.
- The major judicial roles of the state are the administration of justice, interpretation, and application of laws, protection of rights, guardian of the constitution, law enforcement, conducting judicial inquiries, advisory functions, arbiter role in a federal system, judicial review, role in law-making, and role of the judiciary in policy-making.
- Legislating from the bench in a representative democracy can be a substitute for the failure of other branches of government and a contribution to good governance. The limitations of the judge-made laws are that the policy choices the judiciary makes are based on interpretations of existing law. The judicial decisions are dependent on what the judge would prefer to do and can be tampered with by their perceptions, ideologies, whims, and fancies.
- Judicial activism is an approach by the judiciary to decide constitutional issues invalidating the legislative or executive actions in a democracy. The scope of judicial activism is so wide that no exact definition exists. There is no statutory definition for judicial activism and the constitution has no specific mention of it.
- Judicial Restraint is a concept of judicial interpretation that urges judges to limit the exercise of their power. Judicial restraint makes the judiciary follow the doctrine of "Stare decisis" which means that a judiciary must follow the precedent set by previous judicial pronouncements under similar circumstances. This helps in ensuring continuity and uniformity in the administration of law.
- A precedent is a previous example or a case that provides an exemplar or a rule for subsequent behavior, and a pattern upon which succeeding behavior is based. The law of precedent is defined as the legal principle to determine the points in litigation as per the precedent. Salmond classifies legal precedents

as Authoritative precedents, Persuasive precedents.

- The evolution of Common Law found its origins in Great Britain, as there was no written constitution. The foundation of the Common Law is in the doctrine of stare decisis.
- What checks our courts? Four broad types of checks on the judiciary are the legislature checks, the executive checks, judicial traditions and doctrines, and public opinion.

Key Words			
Legitimacy	Jurisprudence	Judicial Anarchy	Doctrine of Precedent
State legitimacy	Judicial Activism	Judicial Restraint	Authoritative Precedents
Judicial inquiry	Judicial Supremacy	Judicial Activist	Persuasive Precedents
Arbiter	Judicial Absolutism	Stare decisis	Common Law
Judicial Review			

Questions

A. Quick Check

1. What is the state?
2. What are the differences between a country, state, and nation?
3. What is State legitimacy in state-society relations?
4. Can judges legitimately legislate? Explain.
5. Explain the demerits of judicial activism.
6. What is Stare decisis?

B. Explore

1. Compare the conceptions of the welfare State and the minimal State and offer your comments
2. Bring out the importance of the role of the Judiciary in public policymaking
3. "Judicial activism is seen as a tussle to show the supremacy or power of the judiciary over the other organs of the state" - Discuss
4. What are the merits of using the precedents? Explain the use of authoritative precedents and persuasive precedents in the Indian context

References

- Beetham, D. (1991).The Legitimation of Power. NewYork: Palgrave Macmillan.
- Dias, RWM (1964). Jurisprudence. London Butterworth 1964 (2nd Ed) 1970 (3rd Ed) 1976 (4th Ed) 1985 (5th Ed.
- Domhoff, G. W. (1996). State autonomy or class dominance? Case studies on policy making in America. Hawthorne, NY: Aldine de Gruyter.
- Lamb, Robert D. (2014). Rethinking legitimacy and illegitimacy – a new approach to assessing support and opposition across disciplines. A Report of

the CSIS Program on Crisis, Conflict, and Cooperation. Center for Strategic and International Studies, Rowman & Littlefield, New York, US.

- Mann, M. (1986). The Sources of Social Power. New York: Cambridge University Press.
- Salmond, John William (1907). Jurisprudence or The Theory of The Law, 1-2 (2nd ed. 1907.
- Tilly, Charles (1985). "War Making and State Making as Organized Crime". In Peter). Evans; Dietrich Rueschemeyer; Theda Skocpol (eds.). Bringing the State Back In. Cambridge: Cambridge University Press. pp. 169–191.

CHAPTER 9

Public Policy Making: The Role of Bureaucracy

This chapter intends to present an understanding of the role of bureaucracy in public policymaking. In this chapter, we will first discuss bureaucracy in detail and know what bureaucracy is, bureaucrat, bureaucratic elitism, and the major characteristics of bureaucracy. To provide a theoretical perspective on bureaucracy, we will then discuss Max Weber's Bureaucratic Form and the six major principles: authority hierarchy, formalized rules, specialization, impersonality, formal selection, and career orientation. We will then identify the major features of bureaucracy and the public perceptions of bureaucracy. Subsequently, we distinguish the functions and dysfunctions of bureaucracy. In the next section, we briefly describe the important merits of bureaucracy, such as division of labor, efficiency of work, ease of administration, rules, and regulations, and consistency and continuity. In addition, we distinguish the main criticisms of bureaucracy as red tape, rigidity, routine conduct, nepotism, bureaucratic delays, and corruption. Later, we explain that Niskanen's model of bureaucratic behavior demonstrates why bureaucrats tend to maximize their budgets. Finally, we present a discussion on the role of bureaucracy in public policymaking, policy implementation, policy monitoring, and policy analysis.

Section 1: Bureaucracy

Section 2: Max Weber's Bureaucratic Form

Section 3: Main Features of Bureaucracy

Section 4: Functions of Bureaucracy

Section 5: Dysfunctions of Bureaucracy

Section 6: Merits of Bureaucracy

Section 7: Criticism of Bureaucracy

Section 8: Niskanen's Model

Section 9: Bureaucracy and Public Policy

1. BUREAUCRACY

The permanent executive or the bureaucracy plays a critical role in the policy cycle.

As we discussed in the previous chapters, *public policymaking involves several actors*. Principally, it is the political executive and the legislature that frame the policies and play an authoritative role. But the permanent executive or the bureaucracy plays a critical role in the policy cycle. Because the bureaucracy is the repository of inputs (including information, facts, figures, etc.) for public policymaking. Moreover, the bureaucracy makes numerous rules using its power and authority for executing and implementing the policies made by the legislature. In addition, the bureaucracy decides by addressing the individual cases using its magisterial powers. Thus, ***bureaucracy as a permanent executive in the organizational set of the government has an immense influence on public policy***.

The bureaucracy makes numerous rules using its power and authority for executing and implementing the policies made by the legislature.

The bureaucracy uses its discretion during policy implementation.

The role of bureaucracy is enormous at all stages in a policy cycle, like agenda setting, policy formulation, decision making, implementation, and evaluation. More particularly, the role of the higher bureaucracy in public policy has grown exponentially over the decades. It is because, on one hand, the political executive is overburdened with their political responsibilities and on the other, the legislature is fully hard-pressed to legislate timely on matters of public interest. This has created huge scope for the ever-growing administrative discretion, favoring the higher involvement of bureaucracy in public policymaking. Interestingly, although the bureaucrats are expected to execute the policies on the dictates of the political executive, there are umpteen instances where the bureaucracy uses its discretion during policy implementation.

1.1 What is Bureaucracy?

In common parlance, bureaucracy means a set of non-elected government officials with a hierarchy of authority characterized by specialized functions of public responsibilities. More often, the term bureaucracy is used in a negative tone because of the red tape, officialdom, and intemperance. Max Weber (1864-1920) was the first to use the term – *'bureaucracy'* in his book, The Theory of Social and Economic Organization, to describe a form of organization that can be adopted for both private and public organizations.

Several definitions explain bureaucracy. For example, according to one definition, "*bureaucracy is a professional corps of unelected officials organized in a pyramid hierarchy, working under formal uniform rules and procedures*." Another definition is that "*bureaucracy is an administrative mechanism of the government that has compartmentalized workflows with specialized departments of nonelected officials*."

More often, the term bureaucracy is used in a negative tone because of the red tape, officialdom, and intemperance.

FIGURE 9.1 Hierarchy of Bureaucracy

A bureaucrat is a person who works in a bureaucracy or is part of a bureaucracy.

1.1.1 Bureaucracy, Bureaucrat, and Administration

Bureaucracy is a large complex structure that handles the everyday business of an administration. *A **bureaucrat** is a person who works in a bureaucracy or is part of a bureaucracy.* The administration comprises the large established offices and administrators of the government. The offices have specific missions and objectives. Based on their merit, skill sets, knowledge, and experience, the bureaucrats are responsible for specific assignments.

The term ***bureaucracy*** is derived from the word "***bureau***" in French for small desks, referring to the king's traveling businesspeople who established small desks in town squares. They meant "*rule by desks*", "*government by clerks*", etc. Therefore, often bureaucracy is meant for the "*government of small desks*". Bureaucrats are also called "***civil servants***" who are permanent employees of the government hired based on competitive examination and merit.

Bureaucracy in democracy is considered the permanent executive. The terms '*Bureaucracy*' and '*Civil Service*' are interchangeably used as synonyms.

In a narrow sense, the term '*Bureaucracy*' is used to mean those superior and high-ranking public servants who occupy top-level positions in the hierarchy of government administration. On the other hand, in its broader sense, '*Bureaucracy*' means the entire gamut of government administration encompassing employees at all levels in the hierarchy.

Bureaucrats are also called "civil servants" who are permanent employees of the government.

The administrative cadre in the (civil services) bureaucracy asserts itself as a distinct subsystem with pronounced autonomy of bureaucracy.

'Bureaucratic Elite' is a special political group with a distinct exclusive materialistic, intellectual, and moral dominance over those they administer.

1.2 Bureaucratic Elitism

Who is an elite? Put simply, an 'elite' is composed of a small band of individuals enjoying superior status in the political system, 'carry out all political roles, monopolizes power, and appropriates the benefits that power brings with it. '***Bureaucratic Elite'*** *is a special political group with a distinct exclusive materialistic, intellectual, and moral dominance over those they administer.* It is mostly termed as a governing class that rules the organizational working of the state with a hierarchy of legal and logical order. For example, the administrative cadre in the (civil services) bureaucracy asserts itself as a distinct subsystem with pronounced autonomy of bureaucracy.

A member of bureaucracy is a bureaucrat.

The bureaucratic elite effectively shields itself from other functional groups and commands close rapport with the political executive. Its members occupy key positions in the governmental hierarchy and wield enormous power and authority over policymaking. The bureaucratic elite has manifested an extraordinary strength and influence even during varying socio-political situations to assert its 'supreme' status in state and society. The prestige, political influence, social esteem, power, authority, and perpetuity of tenure for the bureaucratic elite provide further stimulus for elitism to remain and breed forever.

According to Gaetano Mosca, Vilfredo Pareto, and Max Weber, the origin of the *'bureaucratic elite'* was in the political elites that formed the administrative systems. The thriving persistence of bureaucratic elitism in South Asia has been one of the most disliked legacies of British colonial rule.

1.3 Who are "Bureaucrats"?

The bureaucrats implement government policies made by the legislature and the political executive.

A member of bureaucracy is a bureaucrat. A bureaucrat can be a government official or a person of governmental authority, or the head of a public sector organization with enormous power and authority. General administrators, revenue authorities, tax collectors, government accountants, police officers, and military officials are some examples of classical bureaucrats.

The bureaucrats enforce laws; they have agency powers of the government, which include demanding reports, auditing books, monitoring contracts, tracking company obligations, and regulating citizens' actions. The bureaucrats implement government policies made by the legislature and the political executive. They train these bureaucrats in putting the public policies into practice. They have a specific career path.

In India, bureaucracy is an extremely complex system consisting of Indian civil services, state services, employees of the local governments, and technical and managerial staff running public sector undertakings. **Charles Cornwallis introduced bureaucracy in India and is known as *'the father of civil service in India'*.** The framers of the Indian Constitution gave importance to an impartial and non-partisan, professional bureaucracy selected purely based on merit. The Cabinet Secretary of India is perhaps the most powerful bureaucrat with enormous power to influence policy-making in India as a coordinating bureaucrat of the Union Cabinet.

1.4 Bureaucracy – Characteristics

The major characteristics of bureaucracy are (i) it is a system of rules and regulations that are enforced in an organization, (ii) used to control and regulate people's behavior, and (iii) it is often associated with red-tape, complicated procedures for a simple job, (iv) prolonged decision-making and indifferent approach to solve people's problems, (v) too rigid and highly inflexible toward citizens' concerns, (vi) perceived by almost all as inefficient, lethargic, indifferent, and egoistic, (vii) characterized by too much of hierarchy and rule of law that is insensitive to the common public, (viii) confined to standardized procedures, methods, and practice, (ix) characterized by division of labor and compartmentalization of departments, and (x) it has the rule-making authority.

> Weber defines "bureaucracy as a highly structured, formalized, and impersonal organization."

2. MAX WEBER'S BUREAUCRATIC FORM

Max Weber, a German sociologist, and political economist was the first to propose the Theory of Bureaucracy. According to Weber, all business tasks must be divided among the employees based on task specialization and competencies and stated that an organization must have a defined hierarchical structure and clear rules, regulations, and lines of authority which govern it. Weber defines "***bureaucracy as a highly structured, formalized, and impersonal organization***."

Max Weber's bureaucracy ideally has the following three authorities: traditional authority, charismatic authority, and rational-legal authority.

1. **Traditional authority**: where acceptance of those in authority arises from custom and tradition
2. **Charismatic authority**: where acceptance of authority arises from the qualities of the ruler.
3. **Rational legal authority**: where acceptance arises out of the office, the position of the person in authority is bounded by the rules and procedures of the organization.

2.1 The Six Major Principles

Max Weber's Bureaucratic Form is based on six major principles: *(1) authority hierarchy, (2) formalized rules, (3) specialization, (4) impersonality, (5) formal selection, and (6) career orientation.*

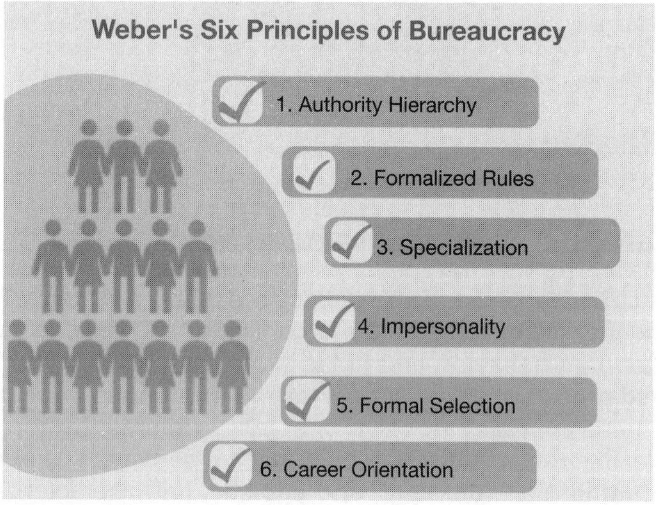

FIGURE 9.2 The Six Major Principles of Bureaucracy

2.1.1 Authority Hierarchy

A bureaucratic organization has two essential components, viz., chains of command, and positional roles or functions in an organization.

Bureaucracies are based on a pyramid structure with a chain of command running from top to bottom. A hierarchy lets you know who works for whom: who is the boss, and where you fit on the chain of command. This hierarchy is a simplified diagram of how a business chain of command works. In a bureaucratic establishment, each level controls the level below it. A formal hierarchy is the basis of central planning and centralized decision-making. A bureaucratic organization has two essential components: (i) chains of command, and (ii) positional roles or functions in an organization. These two components together form the *Authority Hierarchy.*

The Authority Hierarchy is important because it provides formalized rules for who must give orders to whom within an organization. This leads to power dynamics with ones at the higher level of the hierarchy, giving commands to those lower down the hierarchy through formalized channels.

2.1.2 Formalized Rules

A bureaucratic organization applies rules to exert control. Therefore, the higher levels can easily make the lower levels seamlessly execute the decisions. The bureaucracy does its work according to a set of established regulations and procedures.

In an ideal bureaucracy, the formal rules and regulations guide the execution of tasks. The manuals contain the documentation of such rules and regulations. In addition, directives, circulars, instructions, policy communications, and handbooks also help guide the efficient functioning of the bureaucratic organization by providing clarity on the tasks and procedures.

> An ideal bureaucracy is guided by formal rules and regulations guide the execution of tasks.

2.1.3 Specialization

In a bureaucratic organization, there exists a division of labor and the specialists handle the tasks with knowledge of those tasks. Hence, the organization classifies its workforce based on their competencies and skills to perform the work. Every bureaucrat has certain defined duties and responsibilities. That is, every job is classified with specific knowledge skills, and abilities and filled by someone who knows how to do that job.

Adam Smith was the first to theorize about the division of labor. However, according to Weber, a well-functioning bureaucracy with specialization of work or division of labor will be more productive than one without specialization of labor. Specialization or division of labor improves the quality of work and helps bring down the costs. On the other hand, an organization without division of labor might end up with unskilled labor handling tasks, resulting in less efficient output with higher costs.

> Specialization or division of labor improves the quality of work and helps bring down the costs.

2.1.4 Impersonality

According to the principle of impersonality, in a bureaucratic organization, all the employees are treated impartially, which means without bias and not allowing individual differences to influence the working relationships.

Weber argued that an ideal bureaucracy must be autonomous, impartial, and impersonal to achieve the objectives of bureaucracy. He emphasized that employee relationships must be professional rather than

> Weber's bureaucracy emphasizes that employee relationships must be professional rather than personal.

personal. Because an impersonal bureaucratic environment can foster better decision-making, purely based on evidence and critical thinking. In the process, rules are well-defined, clear, and applied without any bias to everyone across the board. This approach helps in avoiding favoritism, nepotism, and outside interference.

2.1.5 Formal Selection

Bureaucracy relies on technical qualifications and skills for both formal selection and promotion of its workforce.

An ideal bureaucracy relies on technical qualifications and skills for both formal selection and promotion of its workforce. This concept provides an incentive for the workers to develop their competencies to perform more efficiently, thus saving the costs to the organization. In addition, this approach helps the workers in ensuring their job security and performance-related rewards.

2.1.6 Career Orientation

In an ideal bureaucratic organization, the employer must provide a clear career orientation for the workers. According to the principle of career orientation, there should be a perfect match between the skills of the workers and their jobs for harnessing the best outcomes. This principle emphasizes that the organization should provide a clear career path for all its employees to motivate them and achieve higher levels of productivity. Thus, everybody wins! This way!

3. MAIN FEATURES OF BUREAUCRACY

Specialization – delegation of authority and division of work is one of the main features of bureaucracy.

Bureaucracy has numerous features that distinguish it from other types of administration. They are (i) Permanent character, (ii) Hierarchical organization – a clear chain of command, (iii) Non-partisan character, (iv) Professionalism - professional, trained, and expert class, (v) Structured rules and regulations, (vi) Class consciousness, (vii) Public service spirit as the ideal, (viii) Bound by a code of conduct, (ix) Administration, (x) Specialization – delegation of authority and division of work, (xi) Competency of jurisdiction, (xii) Formal relationships, (xiii) Record keeping, (xiv) Fixed salaries, (xv) Formal communication means, and (xvi) Achievement-oriented career.

3.1 Public Perceptions About Bureaucracy

Bureaucratic delays cost the taxpayers in terms of both time and money.

Many do not like bureaucracy across South Asia. Despite its several merits, it has been a structure of dislike for the citizen because of many reasons. First, South Asia inherited bureaucracy from the British, who ruled with an iron fist and harassed the public like animals. Second, bureaucracy is impersonal and dehumanizing with no respect and sentiment towards the citizen. Numerous formalities beyond the comprehension of the common public make bureaucracy disliked by many. People feel that it is rule-bound and does not heed the genuine grievances of the public.

Third, the 'red tape and rampant corruption in the bureaucracy make it the worst form of administration, particularly for the poor common citizen. Particularly, corruption at the top levels of the hierarchy of bureaucracy has been very dangerous and ruining the economy. Fifth, it does not encourage effectiveness and innovation because of its indifferent attitude. Sixth, the mountains of paper and too many rules only slow down the speed of government work. Seventh, bureaucratic delays cost the taxpayers in terms of both time and money.

The public feels that the bureaucracy has only served themselves and the politicians and not the society.

Eighth, more than anything else, the bureaucrats are infamous for their arrogance, non-responsiveness, elitism, apathy, unkind approach, high living disproportionate to their requirement with official vehicles, bungalows, palatial residences, unlimited allowances, excessive benefits, and many free assistants, orderlies, and security not only for them but also for their families and extended families. Ninth, the public feels that the bureaucracy has only served themselves and the politicians and not the society.

Tenth, there is no rigorous system of performance appraisal and evaluation for the bureaucracy, yet no accountability, but there is always a job guarantee with a lifelong pension and other facilities, even for their family. Overall, the bureaucracy has disappointed the public.

Bureaucracy is infamous for red tape.

4. FUNCTIONS OF BUREAUCRACY

Broadly, the functions of bureaucracy are (i) Implementation of governmental policies and laws, (ii) Role in policy formulation, (iii) Running of administration, (iv) Advisory function, (v) Role in legislative work, (vi) Semi-judicial work, (vii) Collection of taxes and disbursement of financial benefits, (viii) Record keeping, and (ix) Role in public relations.

Implementation of governmental policies and laws is one of the main functions of bureaucracy.

5. DYSFUNCTIONS OF BUREAUCRACY

Bureaucracies do have some unintended dysfunctions or limitations too. We discuss below some of the dysfunctions of a bureaucratic structure like Bureaucratic Delay, Disproportionate Paperwork, Impersonality, compartmentalization, and the Empire Building.

The feature of impersonality in bureaucracy, emphasizes the primacy of contractual responsibilities than human relationships.

5.1 Bureaucratic Delay

Bureaucracy is infamous for red tape, meaning too much time delay in executing the tasks. The procedures are too many, rigid, and tame-taking. Moreover, the bureaucrats are known for shifting responsibility and blame games. Rules were originally designed to serve organizational efficiency, however; they tend to become all-important.

Bureaucracy fosters the preservation of redundant jobs.

5.2 Disproportionate Paperwork

Bureaucracy by nature resorts to too-much paperwork as every decision and action must be put in writing. Maintenance of documents is all important for the bureaucracy. Hence, the bureaucracy loses its focus on achieving the objective and ends up with only paperwork, leading to an inordinate wastage of time, space, and stationery.

5.3 Impersonality

Bureaucrats want to increase the number of subordinates reporting to him to demonstrate that as his or her symbol of status, power, and prestige leading to empire building.

The nature of impersonality results in a lack of human touch in the work. In the process, a bureaucratic organization does the job more mechanically than purposively. Organizational procedures, rules, and regulations are prioritized over an individual's concerns, needs, and emotions. The official positions are given prominence more than the persons. The primacy is on contractual responsibilities than human relationships. Relationships in the bureaucracy are based on the rights and duties of each role, so they are depersonalized and this led to rigid behavior. Decision-making tends to be programmed and hence discourages the search for further alternatives.

5.4 Compartmentalization

Bureaucracies are known for compartmentalization of work and employees. As the works are classified into watertight compartments, it restricts the flow of the work. It creates a long chain of workflow which can get affected adversely if even a single worker does not complete the job. Besides, bureaucracy fosters the preservation of redundant jobs. Moreover, because of jurisdictional issues, bureaucrats end up doing nothing but the public is at a loss.

5.5 Empire Building

It is a commonly observed fact that bureaucrats tend to use their positions to perpetuate self-interests or of their sub-units at the cost of the public interest. Quite often, a senior bureaucrat wants to increase the number of subordinates reporting to him to demonstrate that as his or her symbol of status, power, and prestige. Bureaucracy has become more powerful and it is hard to mitigate the problems and misery caused by the bureaucracy.

6. MERITS OF BUREAUCRACY

Despite several dysfunctions, bureaucracy has some advantages. We discuss below some major advantages like division of labor, efficiency of work, ease of administration, rules, and regulations, and consistency and continuity.

6.1 Division of Labor

Division of labor makes the work easier and steers to specialization.

6.2 Efficiency of Work

Bureaucracy encourages competency, leading to an increase in the work efficiency of the employees. It helps in managing the hierarchy of the bureaucratic structure.

Bureaucracy renders administration easier.

6.3 Ease of Administration

Bureaucracy renders administration easier. In a bureaucratic arrangement, keeping control of the administration, and effecting essential adjustments as soon as required, is possible at convenience. In addition, introducing new rules, procedures, and guidelines as per needs from time to time is easier despite the organization is large.

Bureaucracy fosters perpetual succession.

6.4 Rules and Regulations

Bureaucratic rules and regulations are usually clearly stated and cultivate a sense of obedience to the subordinate employees. Thus, it reduces or avoids the possibility of disobedience or non-adherence to the organizational rules, procedures, and protocols.

6.5 Consistency and Continuity

Bureaucracy is called the permanent executive in the government and hence it represents consistency and continuity. Bureaucracy fosters perpetual succession. It is not person dependent but on the position. A considerable consistency is noticeable in bureaucratic organizations because the rules and procedures are pre-decided for every task. The clearly defined duties and responsibilities for each of the jobs help to ensure no ambiguity and uncertainty, thereby no conflict of duties arises.

The bureaucratic structure is shaped by determining the duties and responsibilities. In addition, bureaucracy stipulates systematic relationships among personnel. The inflexible structure helps the easy functioning of the system.

7. CRITICISM OF BUREAUCRACY

Bureaucracy is not the favor of many. They criticize it for its numerous demerits or limitations. We briefly discuss below some of the major demerits like red tape, rigidity, routine conduct, nepotism, bureaucratic delays, and corruption.

Bureaucracy stipulates systematic relationships among personnel.

7.1 Red Tape

Bureaucracy is full of paperwork, red tape, and slow decision-making, which does not serve the interests of the public.

By its very nature, bureaucracy goes by a specific set of rules and regulations. This causes inflexibility and often leads to inefficiency. Too much paperwork and red tape cause more problems for the public. Red tape also affects decision-making with inordinate delays because they make each decision after several discussions at different levels of positions after recording them in numerous documents. A lot of paperwork is required even for very simple work. Thus, bureaucracy is full of paperwork, red tape, and slow decision-making, which does not serve the interests of the public. Too many rigid procedures, numerous policies with no flexibility for special circumstances, too various forms to fill out, and lines to wait.

7.2 Rigidity

In the bureaucracy, rules and regulations are rigid and obstinate. This rigidity does not foster initiatives and creativity in the organizations. In addition, the bureaucrats are also not interested in change and resist change in the systems and processes. They resist change like the introduction of new technology also because they are adjusted to the existing system.

7.3 Routine Conduct

Bureaucracy is too big to handle.

Bureaucracy does not encourage initiatives and innovations. The staff is looked upon as a machine and not like individuals who have emotions. Hence, they do not have the feeling of belongingness toward the system or the organization. Bureaucracy is so complicated and agencies are performing similar or sometimes the same functions. In addition, federalism makes this more complicated—many services are provided at both the state and national levels. Bureaucracy is too big to handle.

7.4 Nepotism

It is difficult to fire an incompetent bureaucrat and even more difficult to change/close a bad bureaucracy.

Bureaucracy is often associated with the problem of nepotism. The superiors at the higher levels of the hierarchy favor their people and their quick rise in the system over those worthy candidates. Lack of incentive to be productive results in inefficiency. Bureaucracy is lawmaker because the regulations end up affecting the law. The duty of implementing laws often allows bureaucrats to interpret those laws. It is difficult to fire an incompetent bureaucrat and even more difficult to change/close a bad bureaucracy.

8. NISKANEN'S MODEL

William Niskanen developed the **Niskanen's Budget Maximizing Model** or **Niskanen Model of Bureaucratic Behavior** in the 1970s. He argued that rational bureaucrats are motivated to seek to proliferate their budgets to enhance their power and authority, and thereby potentially reduce social efficiency. Put simply, ***Niskanen's model hypothesizes that a bureaucrat heading a public administration department or a unit will always try to maximize his department's budget so that his salary, benefits, status, power, and privilege are also enhanced.***

Niskanen's model states that a bureaucrat heading a public administration department or a unit will always try to maximize his department's budget.

If we look at Niskanen's model through the lens of public policy, we can notice that the more services the department delivers, the greater will its budget be. In this case, the bureaucrat's objective is to maximize the services subject to the social welfare break-even point. However, it is the responsibility of the executive to decide the allocation of the budget to the department of the bureaucrat.

Niskanen's Budget Maximizing Model of budgetary behavior has proved to be popular in the public choice circles.

Why do bureaucrats tend to maximize their budgets? The theory of bureaucracy by William Niskanen states that bureaucrats want more for their agencies and programs. Because, Niskanen (1971) argues that bureaucrats tend to focus on maximizing perquisites of public office, public reputation, power, etc., because opportunities for monetary gains are minimal.

Niskanen formally founded the economic analysis of government bureaucracy in 1968 (book: "Bureaucracy and Representative Government"). Niskanen's bureaucracy theory is based on a relatively simple output: the bureaucracy usually produces a level of public goods equal to double the social optimum. ***The bureaucracy demands a budget that will satisfy not only the production and cost functions reflecting the supply of the public goods, but also their utility functions.*** This model of budgetary behavior proved popular in the public choice circles.

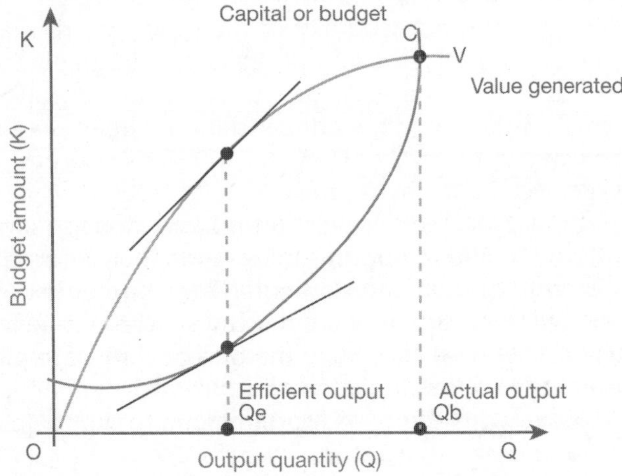

FIGURE 9.3 Graphical illustration of Niskanen's budget maximizing model

The actual output is higher than the efficient output. Because the bureaucrat has the critical information that is more advantageous for the successful implementation of the program than the other sponsors.

Figure 9.3 is a graphical illustration of Niskanen's budget maximizing model. Suppose a bureaucrat demands a higher budget and C is the budget line. V represents the value generated out of the budget spent on the programs. The efficient output is at Qe, where both the slopes of C and Q are the same. However, as Niskanen proposed that the bureaucrats have incentives to expand their budgets, in this case, the bureaucrat aspires to build a bureaucratic empire and enhance his status by maximizing the budget. Then, with the maximized budget, his departmental budget spending, and the value generated, is the same at Qb which is the actual output. The actual output is higher than the efficient output. *Why does this happen? Because the bureaucrat has the critical information that is more advantageous for the successful implementation of the program than the other sponsors.* The bureaucrat proposes Qb because it maximizes the size of the bureau. Of course, the constraint of C is not higher than V.

9. BUREAUCRACY AND PUBLIC POLICY

The political executive is largely dependent on the bureaucracy in the process of the policy cycle.

The role of bureaucracy in public policy formulation is enormous. Bureaucracy plays an all-important role in the entire policy cycle. Bureaucrats provide the data to the political executive for policy formulation and provide feedback on the merits and demerits of the proposed policy. Based on the feedback of the bureaucracy, alternate policies are formulated if required. Overall, the political executive is largely dependent on the bureaucracy in the process of the policy cycle.

The public policy process has been multi-actor-centric, because the legislature, the executive, and the bureaucracy collaborate closely. However, in practice, the administrative processes have transgressed and transcended the demarcated roles. It is because the legislature makes the laws and policies in the form of constitutional and legal enactment formats. It is the bureaucracy of the government that plays an active role in the entire policymaking process, to a large extent.

The top bureaucracy exercises greater influence on the public policy cycle.

In Parliamentary democracies like India, the public policy formulation and implementation are largely dependent on the bureaucrats at the higher echelons of the hierarchy. They work in close coordination with the political executive in achieving the policy objectives. This makes the role of the bureaucracy even more important and thus calls for trust between the political executive and the bureaucracy. Accordingly, politics is a sine qua non for bureaucracy. Particularly, the top bureaucracy exercises greater influence on the public policy cycle. The public policy functions, especially at the top echelons of the bureaucracy, are manifold.

The bureaucrats play multifaceted roles like policy innovators, policy formulators, policy designers, policy advisors, policy implementors, policy analysts, and policy evaluators. Therefore, bureaucracy has an inevitably vital role in the whole public policy process.

9.1 Role of Bureaucracy in Public Policy Formulation

It is said, "***Policy formulation, on paper, is the craftsmanship of the legislature.***" However, in practice, as the policymaking process involves problem identification and agenda setting, bureaucracy is profoundly engaged in the proper formulation and modeling of public policies. The bureaucrats in their day-to-day functioning bring new alignment to the rules and regulations in the conduct of governmental affairs and contribute much to the policymaking process by providing much-needed information, suggestions, and analytical inputs (Beteille, 2000). Thus, the bureaucrats perform input functions in the policymaking process.

The bureaucrats perform input functions in the policymaking process.

The higher-level bureaucracy being in proximity and working in tandem with the political executive, it becomes expediency for the bureaucracy to assess the policy problems, ideas, and proposals in terms of economic and social viability. In addition, they also ascertain the administrative capacity in terms of the availability of the required personnel for policy implementation, monitoring, and evaluation. The expertise of the bureaucracy coordinated with the judiciousness of the political executive greatly serves the cause.

What factors favor bureaucracy in policy formulation? Broadly, five factors like (i) Information base, (ii) Knowledge, (iii) Experience, (iv) Continuity, and (v) Advisory expertise put the bureaucracy at an important role in the policy formulation stage.

9.1.1 Information Base

The higher bureaucracy derives its prominence from the constitution as it has a constitutional responsibility to assist the government in policymaking within the larger framework of the constitution. The superior bureaucrats advise the political executive about the scope of the proposed policy, its constitutionality, its economic feasibility, and its implementability. The bureaucracy is the prime source of required information for the policymaking process. It provides the preparatory material, discussion notes, problem analysis notes, data analysis, and others for the policy-making process.

The bureaucracy is the prime source of required information for the policymaking process.

9.1.2 Knowledge

The top bureaucracy often works like a think tank of the government. It is meritorious and educationally qualified, with adequately equipped with theoretical knowledge. This vast knowledge of the bureaucracy is quite useful while analyzing the policy proposals in terms of administrative hurdles, the possible repercussions, and methodological options. Bureaucracy collects a range of data for policy decisions and helps in analyzing the underlying problem and choosing the right policy alternative that influences policy making.

This vast knowledge of the bureaucracy is quite useful while analyzing the policy proposals.

9.1.3 Experience

The top bureaucracy has rich experience during which it has gained a reservoir of knowledge about public policies and their implementation. Experience matters. Accordingly, the bureaucracy is well equipped to provide useful inputs out of their vast experience in policy formulation.

> The bureaucracy is well equipped to provide useful inputs out of their vast experience in policy formulation.

9.1.4 Continuity

In a Parliamentary democracy, the political executive can keep changing. However, the bureaucracy continues permanently, because the government usually appoints them for the public service career. Hence, the bureaucracy is also called the permanent executive. The permanence of the service of the bureaucrats further strengthens their position to assist the government in the policy formulation process. This permanency of service enables the bureaucracy to gain enormous knowledge, particularly in the field of public service, which in turn helps the bureaucrat to initiate policy suggestions, ideas, and concerns to the political bosses for possible policy formulations.

9.1.5 Advisory Expertise

> The bureaucracy offers factual advice to the political executive on the policy options.

Bureaucracy, with its superior knowledge, experience, and continuity, is replete with adequate expertise to advise the political executive on policy formulation. The bureaucracy must offer factual advice to the political executive on the policy options. In a way, this implies that the bureaucrats dominate the fact-checking, scrutiny, and recommendation side of policy formulation.

Bureaucrats in their policy advising functions have an indirect impact because it is dependent on the political executive as to how the bureaucratic advice is received and put into policy mode. In general, bureaucracy tailors its advice to fit into the policy scheme of the executive.

> In their role of policy implementation, the bureaucracy performs an output function.

9.2 Role of Bureaucracy in Public Policy Implementation

> Bureaucracy tailors its advice to fit into the policy scheme of the executive.

The policy implementation true to the spirit of the policy plays a vital role in the policy cycle. In a governmental setup, bureaucrats are the agents and the government the principal. As the agency of the government, the bureaucracy must implement the policies of the government enacted as and when. Proper implementation of policy helps enhance the credibility of the political executive as well as boost the image of the bureaucracy.

In their role of policy implementation, the bureaucracy performs an output function. The bureaucrats perform functions like (i) executing the policies and rules of the government, (ii) sprucing up the entire administrative machinery for effective implementation of policies and programs, and (iii) providing advice to the political executive about the strategies for effective program implementation. For effective program implementation, the bureaucracy addresses the challenges like the problems and issues during the implementation, resources required for policy execution, the nature of the workflow for smooth implementation, etc.

An interesting side of policy implementation by the bureaucracy is that a bureaucrat implements public policy in a political environment. Because of this, the bureaucratic decisions are often a mix of political and administrative factors. At the same time, the bureaucrats cannot dissociate themselves from the ideology of the government.

Policy execution is, of course, a complex process, where the bureaucrats must take some decisions themselves. By the very nature of their positions, it empowered bureaucrats to take certain decisions during the policy implementation process. While exercising such discretion, the bureaucrats can influence the policy process. As the bureaucracy is solely responsible for policy implementation, the public, as well as the political executive, will blame the bureaucracy for any delays or lacuna in policy implementation.

> The bureaucracy is solely responsible for policy implementation.

9.3 Role of Bureaucracy in Public Policy Monitoring

The primary goal of policy monitoring is to gather policy-relevant information that will allow the bureaucrat to advise the political executive on policy outcomes for adapting the prevailing policy or devising new policy options. In the process of policy monitoring, the bureaucracy must act like the 'eyes and ears' of the government in collecting policy feedback.

The policy monitoring stage expects the bureaucracy to determine whether the policy implementation process is in coherence with the policy objectives. More often, public policies must be implemented in a time-bound manner. In doing so, targets must be achieved and reported to the political executive. When the political executive conducts policy monitoring and review meetings, it is the responsibility of the bureaucracy to provide feedback. *The bureaucracy employs several approaches to policy monitoring, such as Front-end Analysis, Process evaluation Approach, Availability Assessment, and Evaluation Synthesis approach.*

> The bureaucracy to determine whether the policy implementation process is in coherence with the policy objectives.

Depending upon the nature of policies being implemented, the monitoring approach is fine-tuned as a piece-meal approach, ongoing approach, annual or biannual basis, etc. If policies are embedded with targets for implementation, then monitoring becomes easy, as the bureaucrat must determine how the targets are achieved. If the policy implementation is made into quantifiable terms, the more tangible and quantitative the policy goals, the more effective would be the policy monitoring process.

> The policy analysis activity is a highly demanding function.

9.4 Role of Bureaucracy in Public Policy Analysis

As we understood in the initial chapters, policy analysis comprises not only scrutinizing and giving policy improvements, but also evaluating the policy outcomes and policy choices. The policy analysis activity is a highly demanding function. The bureaucrats are often hard-pressed in their daily routines and under the burden of an overload of work. This makes it difficult to expect detailed policy analysis reports from the bureaucrats. In this regard, it is desirable to train some of the senior bureaucrats with the such bent of mind to excel in policy analysis and oversee the process.

For effective policy analysis by the bureaucracy, the bureaucrats must view the policies from the prism of the political executive so that proper analysis is possible. Of late, policy analysis has become turned out to be a problematic aspect due to the overload of the bureaucracy, which calls for involving academics, researchers, and professional policy analysts.

Overall, to sum up, we could understand that bureaucracy is omnipresent in a democratic setup, particularly in public policy. The bureaucracy wears many hats: policy innovators, policy designers, policy drafting experts, policy formulators, policy implementers, policy advisers, policy monitors, and policy analysts.

Summary

- 'Bureaucracy' means the entire gamut of government administration encompassing employees at all levels in the hierarchy. Weber defines "bureaucracy as a highly structured, formalized, and impersonal organization." It has three authorities: Traditional authority, charismatic authority, and Rational legal authority. A bureaucrat is a person who works in a bureaucracy or is part of a bureaucracy.
- Max Weber's Bureaucratic Theory is based on six major principles: authority hierarchy, formalized rules, specialization, impersonality, formal selection, and career orientation.
- The main features of bureaucracy are permanent character, hierarchical organization, non-partisan character, professionalism, structured rules and regulations, class consciousness, public service spirit as the ideal, bound by a code of conduct, administration, specialization, competency of jurisdiction, formal relationships, record keeping, fixed salaries, formal communication means, and achievement-oriented career.
- The main functions of bureaucracy are Implementation of governmental policies and laws, role in policy formulation, running of administration, advisory function, role in legislative work, semi-judicial work, collection of taxes and disbursement of financial benefits, record keeping, and role in public relations.
- The major dysfunctions of bureaucratic structure include bureaucratic delay, disproportionate paperwork, impersonality, compartmentalization, and empire building.
- The major advantages of bureaucracy are a division of labor, efficiency of work, ease of administration; rules, and regulations, and consistency and continuity.
- The major demerits of bureaucracy are red tape, rigidity, routine conduct, nepotism, bureaucratic delays, and corruption.
- Niskanen's Budget Maximizing Model hypothesizes that a bureaucrat heading a public administration department or a unit will always try to maximize his department's budget so

that his salary, benefits, status, power, and privilege are also enhanced.

- The policymaking process involves problem identification and agenda setting, where bureaucracy is profoundly engaged in the proper formulation and modeling of public policies. Five factors like information base, knowledge, experience, continuity, and advisory expertise put the bureaucracy at a vital role in the policy formulation stage.
- In their role of policy implementation, the bureaucracy performs an output function. In the process of policy monitoring, the bureaucracy must act like the 'eyes and ears' of the government in collecting policy feedback. policy analysis comprises not only scrutinizing and giving policy improvements, but also evaluating the policy outcomes and policy choices. The policy analysis activity is a highly demanding function. The bureaucrats are often hard-pressed in their daily routines and under the burden of an overload of work.

Key Words			
Bureaucracy	Compartmentalization	Front-end Analysis	Permanent Executive
Bureaucrat	Empire Building	Evaluation Synthesis	Authority Hierarchy
Bureaucratic Elite	Red tape	Policy innovators	Jurisdiction
Impersonality	Nepotism	Bureaucratic rigidity	
Bureaucratic Delay	Niskanen's Model	Corruption	

Questions

A. Quick Check

1. What is Bureaucracy? Discuss.
2. Do you think *Bureaucratic Elitism* helps in good governance?
3. Explain the characteristics of bureaucracy.
4. Discuss Weber's six major principles of bureaucracy.
5. Critically analyze the dysfunctions of bureaucracy.
6. Why do bureaucrats tend to maximize their budgets?
7. What factors favor bureaucracy in policy formulation?

B. Explore

1. Discuss the public perceptions about bureaucracy in India. Comment on the contribution of bureaucracy to India's socio-economic growth during the post-independence period.
2. Critically analyze Niskanen's Budget Maximizing Model in the context of Parliamentary democracy.
3. "Policy formulation, on paper, is the craftsmanship of the legislature." - Discuss

References

- Beteille, Andre (2000). Antimony of Society: Essays on Ideologies and Institutions, Oxford, New Delhi.
- Niskanen, William A. (1968). Nonmarket Decision Making: The Peculiar Economics of Bureaucracy. *The American Economic Review.* 58 (2), 293–305.

Further Reading

- William A. Niskanen, [1971] 1994. Bureaucracy and Public Economics, Elgar. Expanded Ed.

Module III

Public Policy Implementation & Evaluation

Module III: Public Policy Implementation & Evaluation

This module has two chapters:

Chapter 10 Public Policy Delivery and Good Governance
Chapter 11 Public Policy Evaluation

Chapter 10 clearly explains public service delivery, its citizen-centricity, and the governance constraints to service delivery. It discusses good governance and 'SMART' governance. Further, it explains how good governance can be achieved through SMART governance and how 'SMART' Governance leads to e-Governance.

Chapter 11 explains policy evaluation, its types, and barriers to policy evaluation. In addition, it explains the policy evaluation processes and the outcomes of policy evaluation like policy change, reasons for policy change, policy termination, and the reasons for policy termination.

CHAPTER 10

Public Policy Implementation: Public Service Delivery and Good Governance

This chapter aims to glimpse the implementation of public policy in India through public service delivery and good governance. We will first offer a clear understanding of public service delivery, its citizen-centricity, and the governance constraints to service delivery. We then discuss good governance in detail by discussing the excellent governance indicators like voice & accountability, the rule of law, political stability & absence of violence, control of corruption, government effectiveness, and regulatory quality. Continuing with the discussion on good governance, we present a brief on the role of non-government organizations (NGOs) in good governance, followed by a detailed analysis of public-private partnerships (PPP), including the critical characteristics of PPPs, the PPP process, the advantages of PPPs, the role of PPPs in public policy implementation, and the relation between PPPs and good governance. In the subsequent section, we present a detailed description of SMART Governance, including the steps of SMART governance, benefits of SMART governance, features of SMART governance, and the SMART governance models. In the fourth section, we discuss how good governance can be achieved through SMART governance. Finally, this chapter shows how e-governance leads to SMART governance by discussing the e-government functions, barriers to e-governance, and the status of SMART governance in India.

Section 1: Public Service Delivery

Section 2: Good Governance

Section 3: 'SMART' Governance

Section 4: Good Governance through "SMART" Governance

Section 5: 'SMART' Governance to e-Governance

1. PUBLIC SERVICE DELIVERY

Public service delivery is a mechanism through which the local, municipal, or federal governments provide standard services to the citizens.

In the context of public policy, knowing public service delivery is of immense importance. The service the government provides to its citizen is called public service. ***Public service delivery is a mechanism through which the local, municipal, or federal governments provide standard services to the citizens.*** This could be either directly or indirectly. For example, some of the leading public services are necessities like housing, health care, education, food, water supply, electricity, fuel and gas supply, sewage collection and disposal, roads, railways, airports, telecommunications, sanitation, transportation, street lighting, municipal facilities, law enforcement, fire services, and other welfare services to the economically and socially marginalized sections of the society.

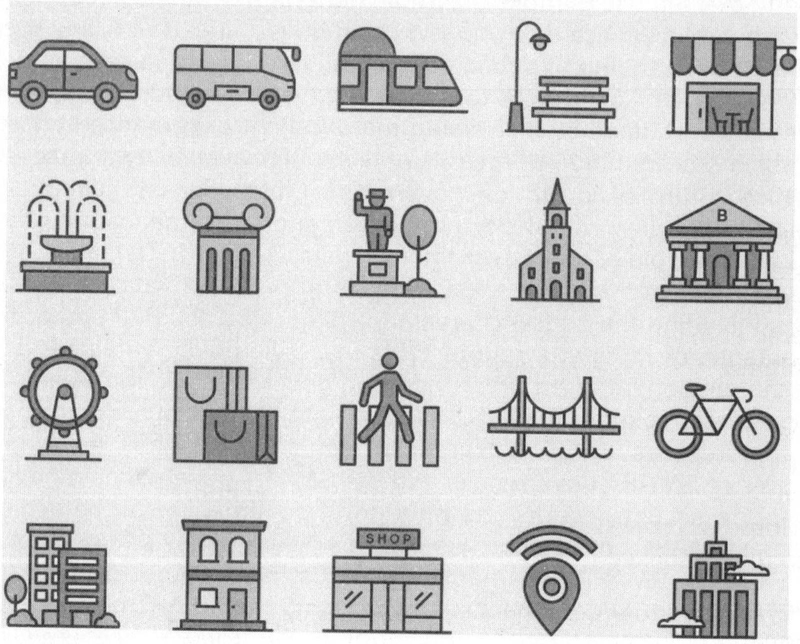

Credit: lesnnik / 123RF

Public service assumes greater importance because its visibility and effectiveness help build the bond of trust between the citizens and the government.

Worldwide, the public sector is the biggest service provider.

In India, public service delivery is so important that one can feel the omnipresence of government in the lives of the citizens. Public service benefits everyone without discrimination in the locality, society, or community. *Public service assumes greater importance because its visibility and effectiveness help build the bond of trust between the citizens and the government.* In addition, public service often lays the strong foundation for nation-building.

The delivery of numerous public services is one of the fundamental obligations of the state. Because of the very nature of public services, the state must provide public services to its citizens despite expanding the market that offers private services. Worldwide, the public sector is the biggest service provider. Every incremental progress in public service delivery greatly influences millions of lives.

What causes poor public service delivery? The reasons for poor quality in public service delivery are many, like corruption, political manipulation, opaqueness in procedures, lack of accountability, absence of citizen and community participation, poor planning, lenient monitoring, improper evaluations, failure to manage change, deficiency of service delivery skills, need for leadership, and lack of adequate resources.

What is required for efficient public service delivery? Some significant measures that make public service delivery more efficient are properly designed concept, political will and commitment to excellence, innovative and robust implementation plans, evolutionary approach, constant capacity development, extensive use of information & communication technologies, citizen-orientation, user public feedback, and good governance.

How to know the resilience of public service delivery? *The four simple tests that help understand whether public service delivery is resilient are the efficacy test, efficiency test, alternate service delivery test, and money's worth test.*

(i) **Efficacy test:** To know the extent to which the public programs meet stated goals.
(ii) **Efficiency test:** To ascertain whether the public services are delivered at least costly for a given quantity and quality of services.
(iii) **Alternate service delivery test:** This test helps us know two things. First, is access to public services expanded with appropriate partnership or contractual relationships within and beyond government? Second, what activities or programs could we outsource in whole or in part to the private or voluntary sectors?
(iv) **Money's worth test:** To know whether the public funds are being put to their best use.

> The four simple to know the resilience of public service delivery are the efficacy test, efficiency test, alternate service delivery test, and money's worth test.

Does government or public expenditure on public services enhance the general delivery service? In developing countries, public expenditure plays a significant role in delivering public services. Education is an essential public service in most developing economies. Public expenditure on education is vital in providing education to the masses. Figure 10.1 compares public expenditure on education in BRICS countries and France, the United Kingdom, and the United States. According to the World Development Indicators (WDI) of the World Bank, India's public expenditure on education was 4.36 percent of GDP in 2018. Brazil is the top public spender with 6.09 percent of GDP. The US public expenditure on education was 4.91 percent of GDP, and the UK spent 5.17 percent of GDP in 2018.

> India's public expenditure on education was 4.36 percent of GDP in 2018

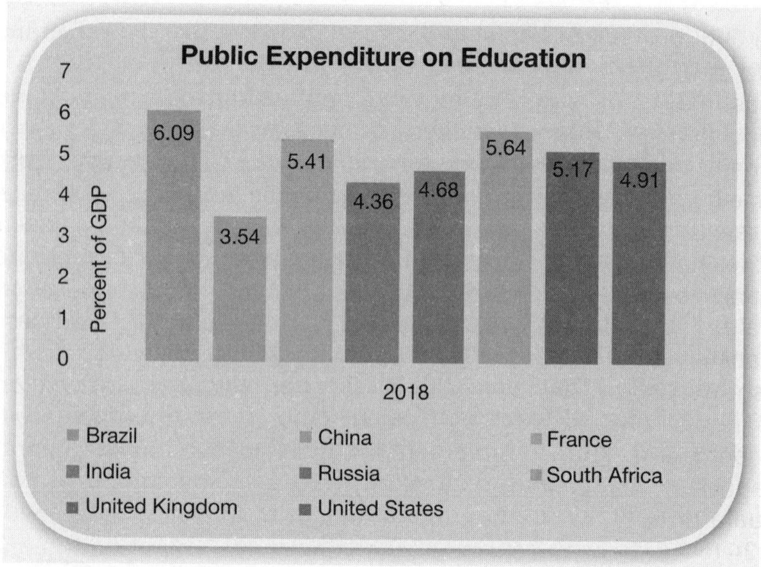

Credit: World Development Indicators (WDI), the World Bank

FIGURE 10.1 A Comparison of Public Expenditure on Education

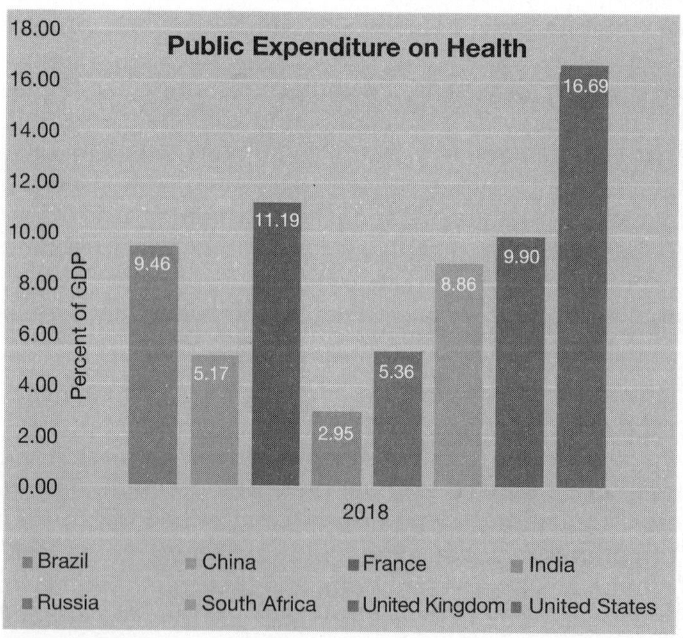

Credit: World Development Indicators (WDI), the World Bank

FIGURE 10.2 A Comparison of Public Expenditure on Health

India's public expenditure on health was a meager 2.95 percent of GDP in 2018.

Why is health care an essential public service? Good health care strengthens human capital and significantly improves productivity and economic performance. Hence, public expenditure on health care assumes significance. Figure 10.2 compares public expenditure on health in the BRICS and other countries. As per the WDI data, the US is the highest public spender on health, with 16.69 percent of GDP in 2018. Contrastingly, India's public expenditure on health was a meager 2.95 percent of GDP. Among all the countries compared here, India has an abysmally low public expenditure on health. Brazil shows the highest public expenditure among the BRICS countries at 9.46 percent of GDP.

Basic drinking water is a necessity. However, across the world, many countries have not provided basic drinking water to many of their citizens. Safe and easily obtainable drinking water is imperative for good public health. The provision of basic drinking water boosts public health and dramatically contributes to vibrant human capital in the country. Figure 10.3 shows the provision of basic water services in India from 2010 to 2020. The population using basic drinking water services has grown from 85.68 percent in 2010 to 90.49 percent in 2020. The Indian government has launched the **Jal Jeevan Mission**, which planned to deliver safe and adequate drinking water through individual household tap connections by 2024 to all households in rural India.

Jal Jeevan Mission is aimed to deliver safe and adequate drinking water through individual household tap connections by 2024 to all households in rural India.

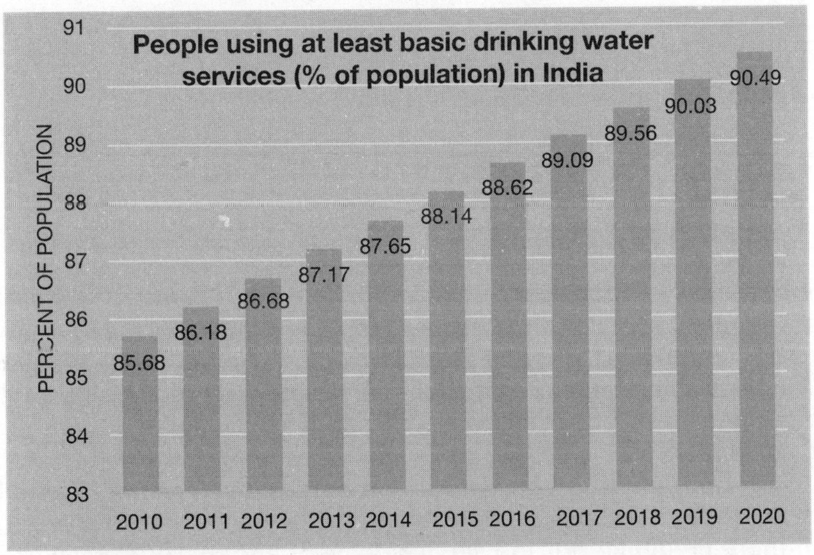

FIGURE 10.3 Provision of Basic Water Services in India

Public health research shows that promoting personal and domestic hygiene improves health outcomes. Maintaining good personal hygiene with basic handwashing facilities helps prevent the spread of diseases. Thus, basic water supply and sanitation can substantially reduce poverty and immensely boost economic growth. Figure 10.4 shows the percentage of the population with basic hand washing facilities in India from 2010 to 2020. As per the WDI data, the basic handwashing facilities in India have improved from 66.90 percent to 67.79 percent of the population. Even though the population with basic handwashing facilities is still increasing, there is a long way to go. The Indian government hopes that its ambitious Jal Jeevan Mission will significantly contribute to achieving higher levels of achievement in this public service delivery.

The basic handwashing facilities in India have improved from 66.90 percent to 67.79 percent of the population during 2010-20.

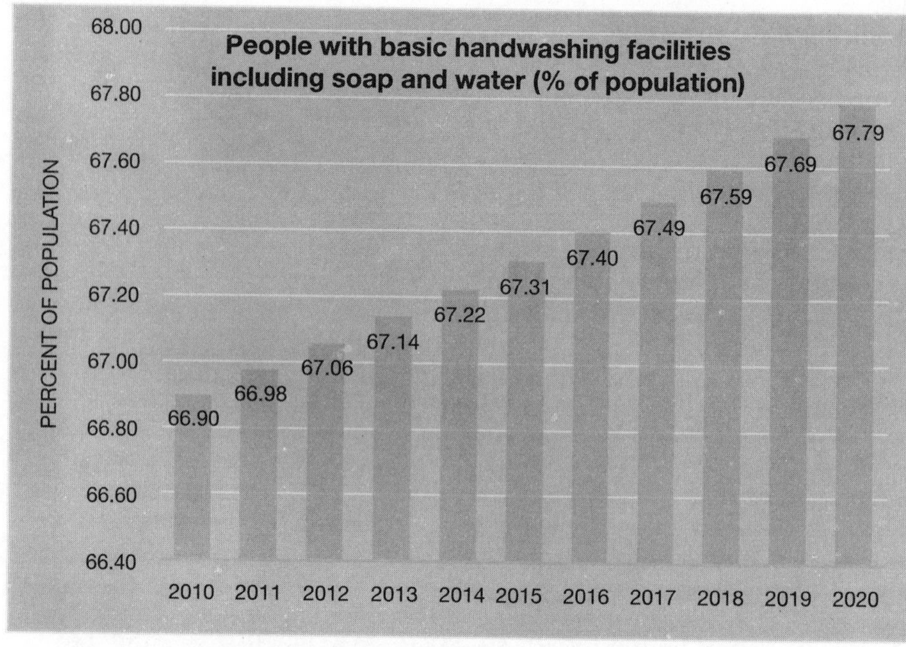

Credit: World Development Indicators (WDI), the World Bank

FIGURE 10.4 Basic Handwashing Facilities in India

'Citizen-centricity' in public service delivery emphasizes that the public services must be designed and provided based on citizens' needs and circumstances.

The governance constraints that affect public service delivery are political market imperfections, policy incoherence, lack of effective performance oversight, collective action challenges, and moral hazard.

1.1 Citizen-Centricity

*The concept of **'citizen-centricity'** in public service delivery emphasizes that the public services must be designed and provided based on service seekers,' i.e., citizens' needs and circumstances.* However, the problem is that in the traditional model of public service delivery, the public services are designed and provided based on service providers' circumstances and conveniences.

How can public service delivery be made citizen-centric? Three factors that can make the public service delivery citizen-centric are (i) to gain more credibility for the service delivery and make it practical and user-friendly, the government or the service delivery agency must incorporate citizen's views, and (ii) Citizens as voters must hold the policymakers accountable during the elections for lapses or inadequacy of public service delivery, (iii) the service delivery agencies should make extensive use of information technology bring ease of use for the citizens, and to raise their concerns.

1.2 Governance Constraints to Public Service Delivery

Research shows that public service delivery, particularly in low-income countries, is plagued with several constraints, particularly corruption, which is cited as the prime cause of the governance deficit. *Broadly, five governance constraints affect public service delivery: (i) Political market imperfections, (ii) Policy incoherence, (iii) Lack of effective performance oversight, (iv) Collective action challenges, and (v) Moral hazard.* Figure 10.5 illustrates the governance constraints on public service delivery.

FIGURE 10.5 Governance Constraints to Public Service Delivery

> Political market imperfections are mainly due to disruptions in the relationships between politicians and citizens.

Political market imperfections are mainly due to disruptions in the relationships between politicians and citizens. These are a lack of credibility in the political promises politicians make to citizens, an absence of information about politicians' performance, and forms of social fragmentation among voters often manifested as identity politics.

These are based on perverse political logic, often patronage or clientelist relationships contributing to short-term, populist policies and biases to visible outputs. Clientelist means the political leaders use authority to maintain their power base or are captured by powerful private interests. Leaders bypass the check and balance institutions and use bureaucracy for patronage.

Policy incoherence indicates the contradictions within policy design, structure, and roles, meaning some part or the entirety of policy design is unimplementable or unimplemented.

Lack of effective performance oversight is the insufficient performance regulation and weak accountability (either top-down or bottom-up) contributing to users exiting the provision.

Collective action challenge is the weak capacity of actors to coordinate their activities and work together productively. It results in groups that fail to act in their collective self-interest.

Moral hazard is a situation that shields the actors from the risks associated with their actions or inaction.

The road to public service delivery revolves around customer-centricity, well-connected government, capacity building, promise delivery, and continuous innovations.

> The success to public service delivery is about customer-centricity, well-connected government, capacity building, promise delivery, and continuous innovations.

2. GOOD GOVERNANCE

As a concept, governance is as old as that of human civilization. The governance mechanisms that existed during the Vedic times are more profound and practical.

Around 400 BC, Kautilya, the great Indian philosopher-statesman and an authority on economics, political science, and governance, in his mega fascinating treatise on economic administrations, state power, and governance – ***'Arthashastra,'*** *premises the concept of governance on two pillars: (i) Nyaya – the justice, and (ii) Dharma – the ethics.* Many scholars, policymakers, and aid donors recognize that good governance is essential to sustain economic development (Kaufmann and Kraay, 2008).

> Governance is how the state acquires and carries out its authority to provide public goods and services to its citizens.

Primarily, ***'governance'*** *is a process of decision-making and implementing them for the benefit of the organization of society.* Governance is how the state acquires and carries out its authority to provide public goods and services to its citizens. We broadly define governance as the governmental authority exercised in a country to effectively frame and implement effective policies duly respecting the citizens and the institutions that are the stakeholders of the economic and social systems (Kaufmann, Kraay, and Mastruzzi, 2009). Governance mechanisms control and operate an organization and are held accountable to the people.

> The elements of governance are ethics, transparency, risk management, compliance, efficiency, and administration.

The ***elements of governance*** include ethics, transparency, risk management, compliance, efficiency, and administration. We see governance in several local, corporate, national, and international contexts.

> Governance consists of the traditions and institutions by which authority in a country is exercised.

According to the World Governance Indicators of the World Bank, "*governance consists of the traditions and institutions by which authority in a country is exercised*." Accordingly, the governance process includes *(i) the process by which governments are selected, monitored, and replaced; (ii) the capacity of the government to formulate and implement sound policies effectively; and (iii) the respect of citizens and the state for the institutions that govern economic and social interactions among them*."

Several actors are involved in governance. One of them is the government. Others vary depending on the context. In rural areas, the governance actors include influential peasant farmers, landlords, cooperatives, and non-governmental organizations. In contrast, in urban areas, the governance actors comprise corporators, mafias, civil society, resident welfare associations (RWAs), social and religious associations, and others.

2.1 What is Good Governance?

Good governance is a normative attribute of governance. According to Mkandawire (2007), 'Good governance' is pro-developmental, democratic, and socially inclusive. Bramwell (2011) defines ***good governance as suitable mechanisms for coordinating collective action.*** On the other hand, the World Bank (2016) describes good governance ***as a mechanism that operates through accomplished, efficient, transparent, all-inclusive, and accountable institutions of governance.*** Put simply; **good governance** assesses how public institutions handle public affairs and govern public resources, guarantee human rights free of exploitation and corruption, and respect for the rule of law.

'Good governance' is pro-developmental, democratic, and socially inclusive.

Good governance is a mechanism that operates through accomplished, efficient, transparent, all-inclusive, and accountable institutions of governance.

Characteristics of Good Governance

Good governance has eight fundamental characteristics. They are (i) participatory, (ii) consensus oriented, (iii) accountable, (iv) transparent, (v) responsive, (vi) effective & efficient, (vii) equitable & inclusive, (viii) compliance to rule of law. Good governance ensures minimizing corruption, regards the minority concerns, and values the voices of the most vulnerable in society during decision-making. It is responsive to the present and future needs of society.

Good governance is responsive to the present and future needs of society.

2.2 Good Governance Indicators

The World Bank has identified six broad dimensions of governance as worldwide governance indicators: *(i) Voice and Accountability, (ii) Rule of Law, (iii) Political Stability and Absence of Violence, (iv) Control of Corruption, (v) Government Effectiveness, and (vi) Regulatory Quality.*

Control of corruption as a governance measure assesses the misuse of how much public power is for private gain.

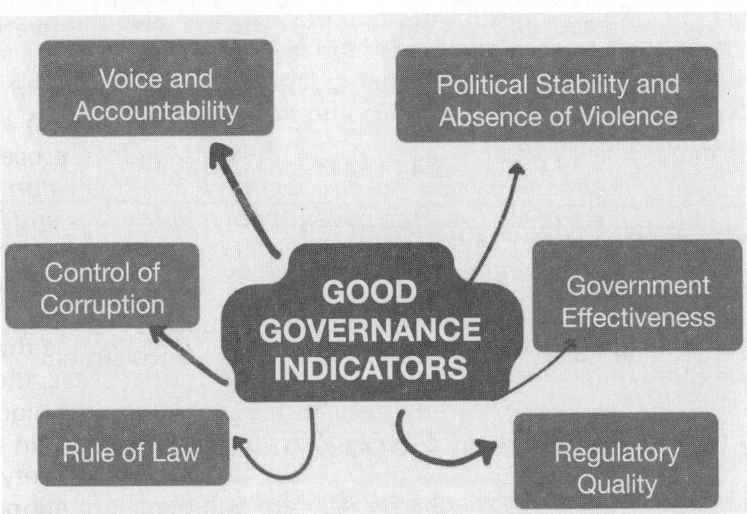

FIGURE 10.6 Worldwide Governance Indicators

2.2.1 Voice and Accountability (VA)

Government effectiveness includes the quality of policy formulation and implementation.

Voice and accountability as a governance indicator capture the views on how much the country's citizens can select their government, freedom of speech, freedom of association, and free media.

2.2.2 Political Stability and Absence of Violence/ Terrorism (PV)

Political stability & absence of violence/terrorism as a governance variable measures the likelihood of political instability due to politically motivated violence and/or terrorism.

2.2.3 Government Effectiveness (GE)

The rule of law as a measure of good governance rates the public perceptions on their trust in and accept the laws of society.

Government effectiveness measures the perceptions of the quality of government-led services for the common public and their credibility. It includes the quality of policy formulation and implementation.

2.2.4 Regulatory Quality (RQ)

Regulatory quality quantifies the perceptions of the government's efficacy in framing and implementing appropriate policies and regulations to promote and regulate the private sector.

2.2.5 Rule of Law (RL)

The rule of law as a measure of good governance rates the public perceptions on their trust in and accept the laws of society comprising the efficient contract enforcement, transfer of property rights, quality of law enforcement agencies like the police and the courts, particularly in controlling crime and violence.

The "gap-filling" role of the NGOs and their independence from the government have allowed them to implement innovative approaches that can serve as models for the government and the public enforcement system.

2.2.6 Control of Corruption (CC)

Control of corruption as a governance measure assesses the misuse of how much public power is for private gain. Corruption results from the failure of accountability relationships in the governance structure.

2.3 Role of NGOs in Good Governance

Non-governmental organizations (NGOs) are voluntary groups of individuals or organizations which are typically not associated with any government and are founded to provide services or advocate a public policy. While some NGOs are for-profit establishments, the vast majority are non-profit organizations. NGOs are vital role in shaping and implementing participatory democracy, thereby contributing to good governance. Mostly, the prominent role of NGOs has been in the enforcement of the provision. Their "***gap-filling***" role and independence from the government have allowed them to implement innovative approaches that can serve as models for the government and the public enforcement system. The NGOs are more effective in educating and sensitizing the public regarding their rights and entitlements under state programs and public services. They attune the official programs to public needs by acting as a conduit for public opinion and local experience.

NGOs are helpful in scaling-up up public service delivery.

NGOs are helpful in scaling-up up public service delivery. They are instrumental in taking the public service to the beneficiaries as they are good at communicating to the public about the public service and mobilizing the required public opinion. In addition, the NGOs' expertise could be used to encourage official aid agencies and government ministries to adopt successful approaches developed within the voluntary sector. Further, establishing operational collaboration of the NGOs with official agencies greatly benefits public service delivery.

The NGOs influence local development policies of local, state, and national governments and international development institutions.

The NGOs are active in influencing local development policies of local, state, and national governments and international development institutions. They help in good governance by helping government and donors fashion a more effective development strategy through strengthening institutions, staff training, and improving management capacity.

2.4 Public-Private Partnerships (PPP)

The unique part of a PPP is that the rights over the facility or system remain with the government, but the private partner has scope for negotiation during project completion.

Public-Private Partnerships (PPPs) aim at financing, designing, implementing, and operating public sector facilities and services. A PPP is an arrangement through an agreement between the government and a private sector partner to undertake a specific project or program. In a PPP arrangement, the government retains ownership of the facility, while the private partner does everything. *The unique part of a PPP is that the rights over the facility or system remain with the government, but the private partner has scope for negotiation during project completion.* The government and the private partners share the profits from the completed project. Generally, PPP projects last for a more extended period than they can last for decades.

A PPP is an agreement between the government and a private sector partner to carry out a specific project or program.

In the Indian context, the Department of Economic Affairs (DEA) of the Government of India defines PPPs as "*PPP means an arrangement between a government or statutory entity or government-owned entity on one side and a private sector entity on the other, for the provision of public assets and/ or related services for public benefit, through investments being made by and/or management undertaken by the private sector entity for a specified time period, where there is a substantial risk sharing with the private sector and the private sector receives performance-linked payments that conform (or are benchmarked) to specified, pre-determined and measurable performance standards.*"

Public-Private Partnerships (PPPs) aim at financing, designing, implementing, and operating public sector facilities and services.

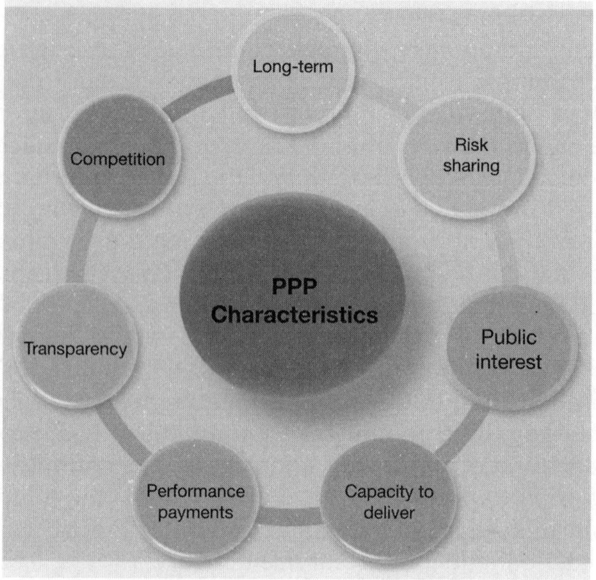

FIGURE 10.7 Key Characteristics of PPPs

The evolution of the PPPs is long-term, risk-sharing, public interest, capacity to deliver, performance payments, transparency, and competition.

2.4.1 Key Characteristics of PPPs

PPPs constantly evolve as a process because the partners seek to refine the collaborative relationship. However, some of the critical characteristics of the PPP framework that continue to guide the evolution of the PPPs are *(i) long-term, (ii) risk-sharing, (iii) public interest, (iv) capacity to deliver, (v) performance payments, (vi) transparency, and (vii) competition.* We briefly describe these characteristics below. Figure 10.7 shows the key characteristics of PPPs.

The PPPs are for a specified long-term and sometimes extend up to 30 years with service provisions.

PPPs focus on the quality of service or performance per the set standards.

Transparency is the hallmark of PPP.

1. ***Long-term:*** Usually, the PPPs are for a specified long-term and sometimes extend up to 30 years with service provisions. However, there are different forms of long-term contracts between the PPP partners.
2. ***Risk sharing and allocation:*** The PPPs provide adequate provisions for optimal risk sharing and allocation among the parties that can manage them. Generally, the risk is transferred to the private partner as it is efficient in risk management.
3. ***Sufficient public interest:*** The PPPs are inbuilt with a proper arrangement between all actors to ensure sufficient public interest in the proposed project by consulting the end-users through the consultation process with end-users.
4. ***Capacity to deliver:*** The PPPs ensures that the private partner has the requisite capacity to manage all the commercial processes and requirements. This is ensured after due consultations with the private partner/s. There is a focus on the quality of service or performance per the set standards.
5. ***Performance payments:*** The PPPs provide provisions that ensure performance-linked payments to the private partner. This entails

suitable human capital and a proper financing framework that underwrites payments to private partners.

6. ***Transparency***: The PPP document is made transparent to ensure that the public and corporate governance guarantee high quality of service and performance to keep the process credible.
7. ***Competition***: One of the significant features of PPP is competition. The very process of PPP begins with encouragement to competition. Because competition is essential to overcome entry barriers.

In addition, introducing new rules, procedures, and guidelines as per needs from time to time is easier despite the organization being large.

Overall, seven essential conditions define a PPP: arrangement, risk-sharing, supply and provision, standards, investment, payments, and a specific period.

Competition is one of the significant features of PPP.

2.4.2 The PPP Process

An overview of the PPP process can be better explained using a PPP Process Map. Figure 10.8 shows the PPP Process Map. Identifying, modeling, and executing a project or a program as a PPP comprises several steps and is shown as a transparent process. The PPP process is split into a succession of broadly four phases – Phase 1, Phase 2, Phase 3, and Phase 4.

The PPP process is broadly categorized into three stages: PPP identification, PPP development pipeline, and PPP operation.

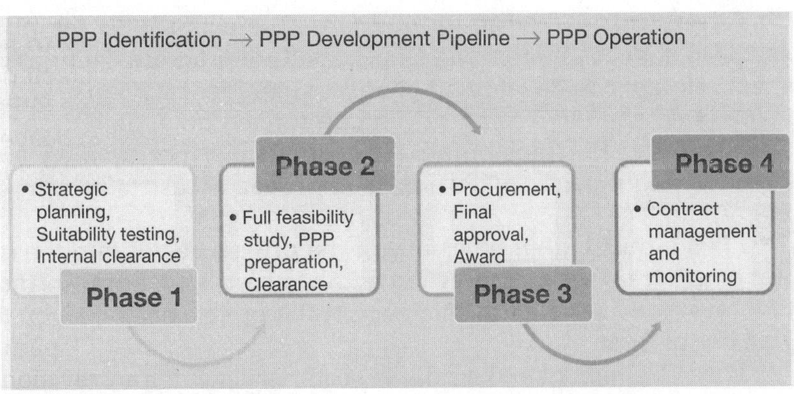

FIGURE 10.8 The PPP Process Map

Phase 1 – PPP Identification

This phase involves project identification, where need analysis, strategic planning, project feasibility, suitability testing, and internal clearances are carried out.

PPP Development Pipeline involves Phase 2 and Phase 3. The 'pipeline' comprises separate projects that have effectively passed the feasibility tests and suitability checks and are internally cleared to proceed with the development as a PPP. These projects are exclusively selected for development as PPPs.

PPP Development Pipeline comprises separate projects that have effectively passed the feasibility tests and suitability checks and are internally cleared to proceed with the development as a PPP

Phase 2: It is the beginning of the *PPP Development Pipeline.* In this stage, they conduct a complete feasibility study to know the suitability of the project or the program. They appraise all the potential PPPs for their suitability for development as PPPs. The suitable ones are studied carefully, and 'in-principle' clearance to continue the project is made.

PPP Operation involves the execution and monitoring of the project.

Phase 3: It is the second stage of the *PPP Development Pipeline.* The procurement process begins at this stage. The application is processed for final approval and award. Detailed negotiations occur with the preferred bidders, and the project is given with technical and financial closure.

Phase 4—PPP Operation

This is the final stage of the PPP process. It involves the execution and monitoring of the project. The private partner executes the project per the PPP agreement, and the public partner meticulously monitors the PPP over the entire life of the contract.

2.4.3 Advantages of PPP

The advantages of PPP include *(i) Access to private sector finance, (ii) Efficiency of the private sector, (iii) Transfer of risk, (iv) Transparency, (v) Focus on the creation of durable assets, and (vi) Reducing total life-cycle costs.*

PPPs enable improved access to investment by transferring the responsibility of funding away from the public sector.

1. ***Access to Private Sector Finance***
   Private sector finance to fund large projects allows the public sector to shift substantial capital expenditure programs' off-balance sheet'. Notably, in developing countries experiencing constraints of inadequate capital, it is an advantage for the governments or the public sector. By transferring the responsibility of funding away from the public sector, PPPs enable improved access to investment.
2. ***Efficiency***
   PPPs induct higher efficiency of the private sector into the project or program execution. When administered well, a well-planned PPP must fully benefit the efficiency of the private sector.

A well-planned PPP benefits the efficiency of the private sector.

3. ***Transfer of Risk***
   The PPPs help gain the private sector skills and transfer the risk to the private sector.
4. ***Transparency***
   The PPPs offer improved transparency in all design, formulation, approval, and execution stages.
5. ***Focus on Creation of Durable Assets***
   The PPPs focus on the enlargement of the focus of the projects or programs from only creating an asset to the delivery of a service to a durable asset of a long operating lifetime that helps the economy or the society.
6. ***Reducing Full Life-Cycle Costs***
   The PPPs broaden the focus to create incentives to cut down the full life-cycle costs of the project or the program.

2.4.4 PPPs and Public Policy Implementation

In public policy execution, pursuing PPPs, particularly in infrastructure sectors, helps the governments capitalize on the risk-management skills of the private sector and achieve effective public service delivery. The PPPs are known to offer guaranteed crucial investments into the public sector, improved infrastructure solutions, efficient public resources administration; faster project accomplishment, better return on investment (ROI), improved risk assessment, cost control, superior quality in public programs or projects, timely delivery of public amenities, reduced government budgets, and private sector know-how.

PPPs offer guaranteed crucial investments into the public sector coupled with improved infrastructure solutions.

Six key measures to ensure successful PPP projects or programs are (i) to keep the credit support ever ready, (ii) continuous, seamless communication between the partners, (iii) establishing transparent accountability practices, and (iv) a proper decision-making hierarchy to overcome frustration, misunderstanding, and delays, and (v) a slackened bureaucracy.

However, the PPPs are not devoid of limitations. Some are inconsistent profits, imperfect competition, compensation to the private sector for shouldering the risk, and sometimes inaccurate costing.

2.5 Good Governance in PPPs

Good governance matters for PPPs because governance failure can jeopardize the delivery of public services. Table 10.1 provides the matrix of good governance and PPP outcome. The matrix considers the principles of good governance: participation, competitiveness, institutional integrity, and transparency. On the other hand, the PPP outcomes are a public good and the market value or business value.

Good governance matrix considers participation, competitiveness, institutional integrity, and transparency.

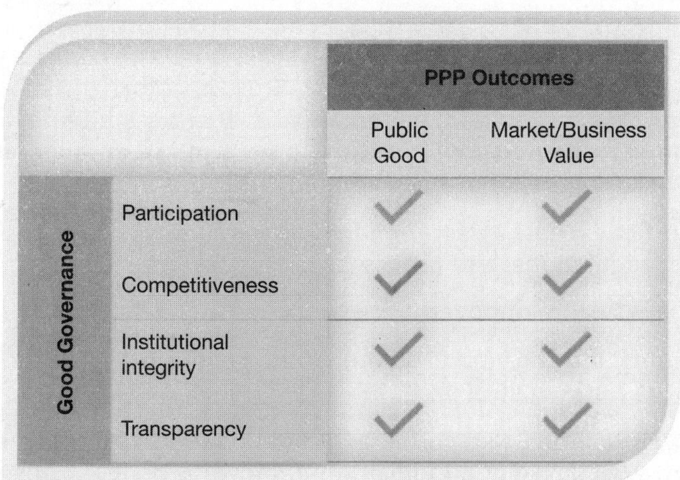

FIGURE 10.9 Matrix of Good Governance and PPP Outcomes

The essential characteristics of good governance in PPPs are putting people first, proper risk-sharing processes, well-designed schedules of payments, suitable legal framework, institutional integrity and accountability, value for money, ensuring affordability, creating competition, and extensive public consultation.

However, some of the essential characteristics of good Governance in PPPs are (i) putting people first, (ii) an honest and impartial tendering process giving an equal chance to all potential bidders, (ii) proper risk-sharing processes, (iv) well-designed schedules of payments, (v) well-supported by a public policy, (vi) suitable legal framework, (vii) institutional integrity and accountability, (viii) value for money, (ix) ensuring affordability, (x) creating competition, (xi) extensive public consultation, (xii) Standardizing commercial principles, (xiii) transparency in contract terms, (xiv) risk-balance among the partners, and (xv) openness of risk allocation.

3. 'SMART' GOVERNANCE

SMART governance is crucial for successful public policy implementation. Because SMART governance helps provide improved information and public service delivery; boosting government transparency for reducing corruption; bolstering political integrity and accountability, and furthering democracy through public involvement and discussion.

SMART Governance uses technology to facilitate and support improved planning and decision-making in the public policy domain.

SMART Governance uses technology to facilitate and support improved planning and decision-making in the public policy domain. It includes improving democratic procedures and transforming the provision of public services.

SMART Governance encompasses E-Governance.

SMART Governance encompasses E-Governance. It aims at the future of public service delivery with superior efficiency, community leadership, mobile technology use, and a sustained thrust in improvement through innovation.

SMART Governance is concerned with furthering democratic procedures and transforming public service delivery.

SMART Governance or E-Governance is the purposive use of technology and innovation to facilitate and espouse superior decision-making and planning within governing departments or agencies. It is concerned with furthering democratic procedures and transforming public service delivery.

SMART Governance is Simple, Moral, Accountable, Responsive, and Transparent governance.

What is SMART Governance? It is **S**imple, **M**oral, **A**ccountable, **R**esponsive, and **T**ransparent governance. It denotes structural changes in Government processes by including a new range of responsibilities for the Legislature, the Executive, and the Judiciary besides the Citizens.

Simple: Citizen expects a user-friendly government with the simplicity of laws, rules, regulations, and processes

Moral: A new system of governance based on moral values.

Accountability: It is the soul of a democratic government and the cornerstone of public administration.

Responsiveness refers to the quality of being attentive to the needs of a commoner. A responsive administration shows urgency in responding to different problems faced by the commoner.

Transparency: - Transparency brings some essential virtues into public life, such as equity, a level playing field, and the rule of law.

3.1 Steps to SMART Governance

The success of SMART Governance lies in properly preparing the people to embrace technology in their lives. The path to SMART Governance begins with a four-step process of transformation comprising Step 1: Safety first, SMART Next, Step 2: Establishing a government cloud, Step 3: Digitization of public service delivery, and Step 4: Public-private participation.

The path to SMART Governance begins with a four-step process of transformation comprising (i) Safety first, SMART Next, (ii) Establishing a government cloud, (iii) Digitization of public service delivery, and (iv) Public-private participation.

Step 1: Safety First SMART Next:

Creating safe living for the public is the priority. We must build SMART governance on the structure of safety where the ordinary person can securely use public services. Ensuring the safety of digital transactions infuses confidence in the public's minds and creates an increased demand for SMART Governance.

Step 2: Setting Up a Government Cloud

The government must collaborate with the private service providers to set up a government cloud in which a healthy collaboration between government departments, private service providers, and citizens ensures the speed and quality of public service delivery. This technological groundwork dramatically helps in setting a successful path towards SMART Governance.

A government cloud can act as an engine of digital transformation with several benefits like (i) shared data across the government departments through service collaboration and expansion, (ii) reducing the costs and complexity of networking, and avoiding resource duplication while maintaining its information technology infrastructure, (iii) securing information against the threats of cyber frauds, and (iv) ensuring scalability and economizing of government service delivery.

A government cloud can act as an engine of digital transformation.

Step 3: Digitization of Public Service Delivery

A committed government can move towards digitization of public service delivery through online mode with pace and quality when the public service delivery is efficiently digitized.

We must develop proper coping strategies for emergent situations while handling online services without hassles. We must aim for ease of government online services operations at better efficacy and less cost, resulting in citizens' satisfaction.

PPP makes government businesses and services more productive and stimulates the economy.

Step 4: Public Private Participation

Public-private participation is a better option for the government to provide digital infrastructure. Private participation in the digitization of infrastructure services dramatically enhances the speed of government functioning and reduces corruption to a considerable extent. This makes government businesses and services more productive and stimulates the economy.

The following measures play a significant role in the path towards SMART Governance.

a) Educating the citizens about government innovations and adequately training the local authorities to handle the technology in service delivery.
b) Hiring skilled professionals to handle the technical processes and deploying the service delivery models.
c) Establishing goals that are accomplishable with smart governance.
d) Setting-up effective strategies to achieve the set goals of governance.
e) Mopping up required capital funding and inviting potential investors for the projects.
f) Launching schemes and programs to encourage public and private collaboration.
g) Updating legislations and policies to help advance innovative governance.

3.2 Benefits of SMART Governance

SMART Governance offers several benefits like reduced corruption, increased public participation and consultation and better democracy.

SMART Governance offers several benefits to society in general, and citizens in particular. It makes the government more efficient. The significant benefits of SMART Governance are as below.

1) Enhanced participation of citizens
2) Access to crucial information
3) Better Democracy
4) Financial and social inclusion

5) Sustainable future
6) Involvement of the private sector
7) Improving internal processes
8) Improved information on public service delivery
9) Increased governmental transparency
10) Reduced corruption
11) Bolstering political integrity, credibility, and accountability
12) Increased public participation and consultation

The Components of SMART Governance include governmental organization, citizen participation, and the use of technology.

3.3 Features of SMART Governance

SMART Governance has several features like (i) Use of Information and Communication Technology, (ii) E-Consultation, (iii) E-Data, (iv) Seamlessness, (v) multi-channel, (vi) responsive, (vii) user-friendly, and (viii) 24x7 accessible. The Components of SMART Governance include governmental organization, citizen participation, and the use of technology. Figure 10.10 shows the components of SMART Governance.

The government is the first building block of SMART governance. *The three characteristics of the government crucial to SMART governance are commitment, responsiveness, and operational management.* According to Przeybilovicz et al. (2017) governmental organization is responsible for "motivation, vision and strategies, attitudes, decision-making, process coordination, and roles and responsibilities, as well as the provision of financial, regulative, technological means and human resources, knowledge management and organizational culture."

The three major characteristics of the government crucial to SMART governance are commitment, responsiveness, and operational management.

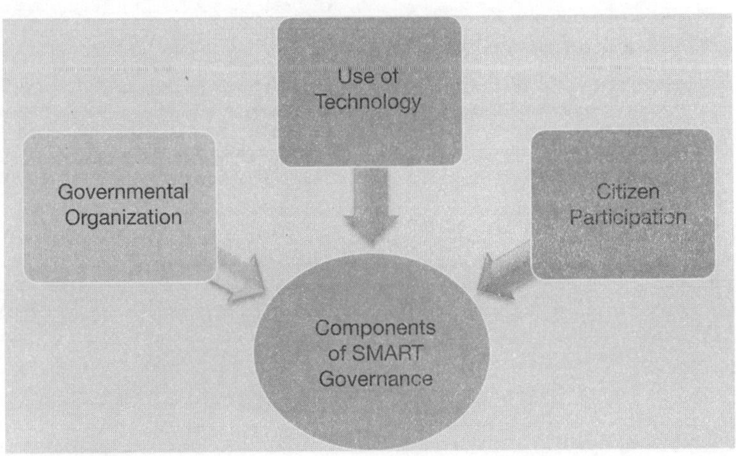

FIGURE 10.10 The Components of SMART Governance

The second building block of SMART governance is Citizen Participation. Citizens are vital in offering valuable and beneficial suggestions to government departments to attain well-informed policy decisions. The relevant components include the degree to which citizen participation is interactive, the representativeness of the participating people, and the motives for citizens to involve themselves.

The government is the first building block of SMART governance.

Citizen Participation is the second building block of SMART governance.

The four models of SMART governance are G2B, G2C, G2E, and G2E.

The use of technology is the third building block of SMART governance. Technological applications, particularly in an increasing diversity of devices, tools, and technologies deployed for various engagements, play a crucial role in governance processes in public policy implementation.

3.4 SMART Governance Models

SMART Governance is essentially a process of using modern technologies and information and communication technologies to make a joint, communication-based, transparent, and sustainable ecosystem for the citizens and the government. Broadly, four models of SMART governance are prevalent:

1. Government to Citizen Model (G2C)
2. Government to Business Model (G2B)
3. Government to Government Model (G2G)
4. Government to Employee Model (G2E)

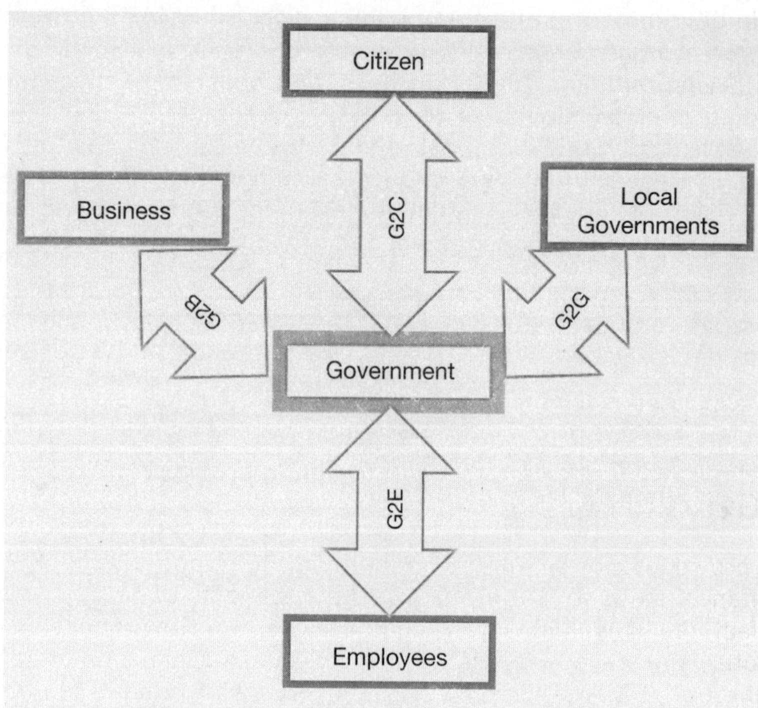

FIGURE 10.11 SMART Governance Models

3.4.1 Government to Citizen (G2C) Model

In this model, the government networks with citizens via communication technologies, news, and print media. The government offers a valuable platform for citizens to voice their opinions and suggestions about government policies and programs.

3.4.2 Government to Business (G2B) Model

The government, in this model, communicates with businesses to boost economic growth. The firms can directly obtain knowledge about new policies and programs of the government, taxes, rules and regulations, and credit services. Besides, the government promotes online business systems to save time and costs; businesses can collect real-time data from the government.

3.4.3 Government to Government (G2G) Model

The government, in this model, establishes a landscape for communication between government and government organizations, agencies, and departments. The purpose is to integrate all governance channels with the help of information and communication technologies (ICT) tools for paperless, corruption-free, and sustainable governance.

3.4.4 Government to Employee (G2E) Model

This model is designed to enable the government to communicate with employees. In a government database, this system stores employees' personal information, such as social security numbers, account numbers, bank details, and other personal details. Government organizations can complete employee-related tasks online, such as payroll, bank loans, medical, and pension plans.

4. GOOD GOVERNANCE THROUGH "SMART" GOVERNANCE

In the previous subsection, we understood the importance of 'SMART' Governance, steps to SMART Governance, benefits of SMART governance, features of SMART Governance, and SMART Governance models. This subsection demonstrates how well they can achieve good governance through 'SMART' Governance. The 21st century has seen a drastic governance shift towards the welfare state. More particularly, democratic governments are increasingly becoming service providers. Good governance is the buzzword among governments and in numerous fora of public discourse. Governments are gradually moving towards SMART governance while making the government machinery to reach citizens to provide essential services more proficiently and equitably.

Democratic governments are increasingly becoming service providers.

SMART governance utilizes modern technologies and information and communication technologies (ICT) to establish a collaborative, communication-based, transparent, and sustainable environment for the citizens and government.

As stated earlier, SMART captures the critical attributes of Good Governance, i.e., Simple, Moral, Accountable, Responsive, and Transparent government. SMART Governance uses newer technologies to facilitate and bolster improved planning and decision-making. It utilizes modern technologies and information and communication technologies (ICT) to establish a collaborative, communication-based, transparent, and sustainable environment for the citizens and government. It focuses on upgrading democratic practices and transforming the delivery of public services. It comprises *e-government with an efficient agenda to make public services more user-friendly and people-centric.*

5. 'SMART' GOVERNANCE TO E-GOVERNANCE

Integrity, transparency, accountability, equality, and equity are the set of principles guides public sector governance.

In the 21st century, significant priorities of the governments are changing towards attaining economic competitiveness, providing citizen-centric affordable digital services, encouraging e-democracy, and supporting e-communities of citizens to move towards E-governance. ***A set of principles guides public sector governance: integrity, transparency, accountability, equality, and equity.*** These five principles of SMART Governance are more appropriate to public sector functioning. Hence, E-governance systems must be designed and built to boost these principles along with SMART principles in practice to ensure the provision of manifold benefits to the public.

E-Governance means 'electronic governance'.

E-Governance can boost e-democracy, citizen participation, citizen's charter to e-governance, and the right to information implementation.

E-Governance *means 'electronic governance' that uses information and communication technologies (ICTs) at different levels of government and the public sector to enhance public governance.* E-Governance is also defined as using information and communication technology (ICT) to offer government services, effective exchange of information, hassle-free transactions, and smooth integration of hitherto existing services and information portals. It includes Wide Area Networks (WANs), the Internet, and mobile computing. *E-Governance* is essentially a concerted step towards SMART governance. The Government of India's vision is to boost citizen-centric design applications in E-Governance. This can boost E-Democracy, citizen participation, citizen's charter to e-Governance, and the right to information implementation. E-governance can be a significant driver for the efficient distribution of the benefits of economic growth through the digitalization of significant segments of society. E-governance emphasizes that government functions can be turbocharged through technology and a citizen-centric approach for a safer, efficient, and sustainable society.

The pillars of e-Governance include people, processes, technology, and resources.

E-Government has emerged as a unique approach for governments to be innovative in using ICTs, predominantly web-based Internet applications, to provide more convenient access to government information and services to citizens and businesses to improve the quality of public service delivery. In a way, E-Governance helps in providing more excellent opportunities for the public to participate in democratic institutions and their processes actively. The pillars of e-Governance include people, processes, technology, and resources.

The objectives of E-Governance include (i) improved service delivery, (ii) shepherding transparency and accountability, (iii) empowering people through information, (iv) enhanced efficiency within governments (i.e., between center-state or inter-states), and (v) expanded governmental interface with business and industry.

5.1 E-Government Functions

The primary purpose of E-government is to effectively disseminate and manage information to citizens and empower the public through ease of access to governmental information and hassle-free participation of the public in policy-making. *The E-government service is also called Digital government services.* E-government services are defined as public service delivery within the government — both between the government and the public — using ICTs. These public digital services include paying taxes online, getting a driving license online, paying the electricity bill, and many more. ***The connotations of e-governance include e-administration, e-services, e-governance, and e-democracy.***

The E-government service is also called Digital government services.

The e-governance connotations include e-administration, e-services, e-governance, and e-democracy.

The following are some of the notable E-government functions.

a) To provide citizens with access to government information.
b) To facilitate general compliance with a set of rules or regulations.
c) To provide access to citizens to personal benefits.
d) To procure, including bidding, purchasing, and payment.
e) To ensure Government to Government information and service integration.
f) To encourage citizen participation.

E-government functions help the government in its efforts towards improved interactions with business, industry, and citizens in its stride towards societal empowerment via access to information, superior management, improved convenience, accelerated revenue growth, significant cost reductions, etc. E-Government typically uses ICT to (i) offer easy access to the public to government information and services, (ii) improve public service delivery by more incredible speed, inclusiveness, and process efficiency, and (iii) deliver citizens with improved access to participate in various democratic processes.

The technology barriers to e-governance are interoperability, maintaining data standards, and legacy systems.

5.2 Barriers to E-Governance

The primary purpose of E-Governance is to provide healthy interaction of government with citizens, public, and private sectors with the efficient use of ICTs in offering public services more effectively and efficiently. However, technology implementation encounters some barriers to overcome. *The significant technology barriers are (i) interoperability, (ii) maintaining data standards, and (iii) legacy systems.* In addition,

The policy barriers to e-governance are citizen privacy, data ownership, and policy implications.

policy barriers to E-Governance include citizen privacy, data ownership, and policy implications. Further, organizational barriers comprise a slow pace of governance reforms, legacy government practices, inadequate management approaches, and technical skills.

'E-Governance barriers' are those characteristics that are either real or perceived in legal, social, technological, or institutional contexts that pose problems in developing e-governance.

Mostly, the evolution of E-Government is through stages of presenting, assimilating, reforming, and morphing. Each of these stages faces several barriers. Eynon and Dutton (2007) define ***'E-Governance barriers' as those characteristics that are either real or perceived in legal, social, technological, or institutional contexts that pose problems in developing E-Governance***. E-Governance barriers impede demand and work as an obstacle for users of E-Government services. They impede supply and act as a disincentive for public sector organizations in providing E-Government services. E-Government barriers are to using ICT for internal administration and external services.

The following are some of the significant barriers to E-Governance.

a) Government culture of secrecy
b) Corruption
c) Culture of seniority
d) Lack of imagination and interest
e) Lack of funding
f) E-Illiteracy

5.3 SMART Governance in India

Digital India Program is the ambitious program of the Government of India for transforming governance into a good governance.

In India, some of the initiatives of the Government of India under its ambitious **Digital India Program** are MyGov, DigiLocker, National Scholarships Portal (NSP), DARPAN, e-Hospital-Online Registration Framework (ORF), PRAGATI (Pro-Active Governance AndTimely Implementation), Common Services Centres 2.0 (CSC 2.0), Mobile Seva, Jeevan Pramaan, National Centre of Geo-informatics (NCoG), and National e-Governance Plan (NeGP).

The nine pillars of Digital India Program are broadband highways, public internet access, information for everyone, early crop harvest, universal access to mobile phones, information technology for all jobs, e-Kranti, e-governance, and electronic manufacturing aimed at net zero import.

The ***Digital India Program*** is built around nine pillars viz., broadband highways, public internet access, information for everyone, early crop harvest, universal access to mobile phones, information technology for all jobs, e-Kranti: electronic delivery of services, e-governance, and electronic manufacturing aimed at net zero import.

In addition, ***e-Kranti: National e-Governance Plan 2.0,*** with 44 mission mode projects, has a vision of transforming e-governance for transforming governance.The thrust areas of e-Kranti are e-Education, PMGDISHA: Pradhan Mantri Gramin Digital Saksharta Abhiyaan, SWAYAM—Massive Online Open Courses (MOOCs) for leveraging e-Education, e-Healthcare, farmers, security, financial inclusion, justice, planning, and cyber security.

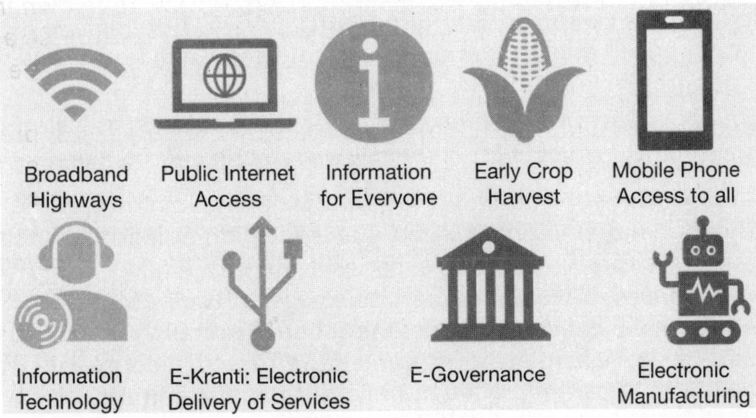

FIGURE 10.12 The Nine Pillars of Digital India Program

- ***MyGov's*** goal is to establish a healthy link between the government and citizens to achieve SMART governance.
- ***Digi Locker*** is a web-based platform to securely empower citizens to store and give direct electronic access to service providers.
- ***National Scholarships Portal (NSP)*** provides a centralized platform for the application and disbursement of scholarships to students under all scholarship schemes.
- ***DARPAN*** is an online tool used for monitoring and analyzing the implementation of high-priority government projects and facilitates the presentation of real-time data on key performance indicators (KPIs) of such projects.
- ***E-Hospital-Online Registration Framework (ORF)*** allows patients to take online outpatient department (OPD) appointments with government healthcare centers.
- ***PRAGATI*** (Pro-Active Governance And Timely Implementation) aims to develop a culture of Pro-Active Governance and Timely Implementation of public policy schemes, bringing e-transparency and e-accountability with real-time presence and exchange among key stakeholders.
- ***Common Services Centres 2.0 (CSC 2.0)*** is aimed at implementing information technology in rural India, under which ICT-enabled kiosks with broadband connectivity provide various services at the doorstep of citizens.
- ***Mobile Seva*** delivers various public services to people through mobile phones. ***The Unified Mobile Application for New-Age Governance (UMANG)*** is a unique all-in-one secure multi-channel, multiplatform, multilingual, multiservice freeware mobile app for accessing more than 2,000 central and state government services.
- ***Jeevan Pramaan*** is an Aadhaar-based biometric authentication service provided for pensioners through which digital life certificates are issued to do away with the pensioners presenting themselves before the pension dispensing authority.

UMANG is a unique all-in-one secure multi-channel, multiplatform, multilingual, multiservice freeware mobile app for accessing more than 2,000 central and state government services.

- ***The National Center of Geo-informatics (NCoG)*** provides support for location-based analytics and decision-making for governments using the geographic information system.
- ***National e-Governance Plan (NeGP)*** encompasses 31 mission mode e-governance projects for collective vision and shared cause.

The Government has instituted the National Government Services Portal hosts various services related to education & learning, health & wellness, electricity, water & local services, money & taxes, jobs, justice, law & grievances, travel & tourism, business and self-employed, births-deaths-marriages-child care, pensions & benefits, transport & infrastructure, citizenship-visas-passports, agriculture-rural development-environment, services-IT-communication, and youth-sports-culture.

National Government Services Portal lists about 13337 government services, including 12321 services of the states.

National Government Services Portal lists about 13337 government services, including 12321 services of the states. Some of the notable schemes are Aadhaar, Kisaan Knowledge Management System, National Agriculture Marketing Portal, Agmarknet Portal, PM-KISAN Samman Nidhi, Pradhan Mantri Bhartiya Janaushadhi Kendra scheme, Pradhan Mantri Ujjwala Yojana (PMUY), Pradhan Mantri Shram Yogi Maandhan Yojana, India's National Single Window System guide for investors, Startup India Seed Fund Scheme, Stand Up India (SUPI), Ayushman Bharat Pradhan Mantri Jan Arogya Yojana, e-Return Filing of income tax, Pradhan Mantri Mudra Yojana (PMMY), Pension Fund Regulatory and Development Authority (PFRDA), ATAL pension yojana, MSME SAMPARK Online Placement Portal, etc.

The National Institute for Smart Government (NISG)

The Government of India has established the NISG to assist Central and State governments in their e-governance initiatives to provide better services to citizens, businesses, and all sections of society. It offers strategic information technology consulting for reducing delivery time of public services, enhanced internal control mechanisms, cost controls in the maintenance of information technology overheads, and increasing the efficiency of employees and others. It helps capacity building and knowledge management using digital services through problem-solving, change management, etc. It also aids in achieving inclusive growth, enhanced citizen-centricity, better investment return for digital citizen services, and improved government productivity.

The National Institute for Smart Government (NISG) assist Central and State governments in their e-governance initiatives to provide better services to citizens, businesses, and all sections of society.

A national e-governance plan has been in place, providing a clear path to achieving smart governance. Some of the initiatives of the states to promote SMART governance are:

- ***Prajavani*** (Andhra Pradesh) is a unique public-private initiative that allows citizens to connect to the government through Information Technology.
- ***Jankari*** (Bihar) is a phone-based right to information (RTI) support system.
- ***Online Land Records*** (Chhattisgarh) is an e-governance program for digitizing land records in the state.
- ***E-city*** (Gujarat) is a one-stop civic shop to provide information about

birth and death registration, building plan, utility services, primary health care, etc.

India has secured the Top-10 position in Global Cybersecurity Index 2020 rankings, published by International Telecommunication. It has scored 97.49 out of 100 among 194 countries. This index is measured using five key pillars viz., (i) legal measures, (ii) technical measures, (iii) organizational measures, (iv) capacity development measures, and (v) cooperation measures.

India stands at the 10th rank in Global Cybersecurity Index in 2020 among 194 countries.

The GovTech Maturity Index (GTMI) developed by the World Bank Group indicates the state of public sector digital transformation. The GTMI is based on the simple average of the normalized scores of four components (i) the Core Government Systems Index (CGSI), (ii) the Public Service Delivery Index (PSDI), (iii) Citizen Engagement Index (CEI), and (iv) GovTech Enablers Index (GTEI). The core aspects of four GovTech focus areas are (1) supporting core government systems, (2) enhancing service delivery, (3) mainstreaming citizen engagement, and (4) fostering GovTech enablers. India is placed in Group A - Very high: GovTech leaders of 43 countries with a score of 0.86. The average GTMI score of 198 countries is 0.52 out of 1 (Dener et al., 2021).

India is placed in Group A - Very high: GovTech leaders of 43 countries with a score of 0.86 under the GovTech Maturity Index (GTMI) developed by the World Bank Group which indicates the state of public sector digital transformation.

The National e-Governance Service Delivery Assessment 2021 Report of the Government of India states that Kerala tops the list of states. The states of India and its union territories are grouped into North-East and Hill States, Remaining States – Group A, Remaining States – Group B, and Union Territories. Nagaland tops the North-East and Hill States, Kerala tops the Group-A, Odisha leads the Group-B, and Jammu & Kashmir leads the union territories.

According to DIGICONNECT of the NISG, India scored the highest ever ranking of 96th rank in the EGDI (e-Government Development Index) in the world in e-governance in the year 2018. The EGDI is a composite measure of three critical dimensions of e-government: provision of online services, telecommunication connectivity, and human capacity. Some parameters include infrastructure, level of promotion of internet access, etc. (NISG, 2022).

Overall, India is progressing rapidly in digitizing its public services to improve good governance through e-governance.

Summary

- Public service delivery is a mechanism through which the local, municipal, or federal governments provide standard services to the citizens. Public service assumes greater importance because its visibility and effectiveness help build the bond of trust between the citizens and the government.
- The reasons for poor quality in public service delivery are many, like corruption, political manipulation, opaqueness in procedures, lack of accountability, absence of citizen and community participation, poor planning, lenient monitoring, improper evaluations, failure to manage change, deficiency of service delivery skills, need for leadership, and lack of adequate resources. The four simple tests that help understand whether public service delivery is resilient are the efficacy test, efficiency

test, alternate service delivery test, and money's worth test.

- The concept of 'citizen-centricity' in public service delivery emphasizes that the public services must be designed and provided based on service seekers,' i.e., citizens' needs and circumstances.
- The five governance constraints that affect public service delivery are political market imperfections, policy incoherence, lack of adequate performance oversight, Collective action challenges, and moral hazard.
- 'Arthashastra,' premises the concept of governance on two pillars: (i) Nyaya—the justice, and (ii) Dharma—the ethics.
- 'Governance' is a process of decision-making and implementing them for the benefit of the organization of society. Good governance is a mechanism that operates through accomplished, efficient, transparent, all-inclusive, and accountable institutions of governance.
- Good governance has eight fundamental characteristics. They are (i) participatory, (ii) consensus oriented, (iii) accountable, (iv) transparent, (v) responsive, (vi) effective & efficient, (vii) equitable & inclusive, (viii) Compliance to rule of law.
- Public-Private Partnerships (PPPs) aim at financing, designing, implementing, and operating public sector facilities and services. The critical characteristics of the PPP framework that guide the evolution of the PPPs are long-term, risk-sharing, public interest, capacity to deliver, performance payments, transparency, and competition.
- The advantages of PPP are access to private sector finance, the efficiency of the private sector, transfer of risk, transparency, focus on creating durable assets, and reducing total life-cycle costs.
- SMART governance is Simple, Moral, Accountable, Responsive, and transparent. It is all about using technology to facilitate and support improved planning and decision-making in the public policy domain. The path to SMART Governance comprises a four-step process of transformation: Step 1–Safety first, SMART Next, Step 2–Setting up a government cloud, Step 3– Digitization of public service delivery, and Step 4–Public-private participation.
- The four models of SMART governments are Government to Citizen Model (G2C), the Government to Business Model (G2B), the Government-to-Government Model (G2G), and Government to Employee Model (G2E).
- E-Governance means 'electronic governance' that uses information and communication technologies (ICTs) at different levels of government and the public sector to enhance public governance.

Keywords

Governance	Voice and Accountability	Wide Area Networks	Jeevan Pramaan
"SMART" Governance	Government Effectiveness	E-Democracy	GovTech Maturity Index
Good Governance	Regulatory quality	e-Administration	e-Government Development Index
e-Governance	Rule of Law	e-Services	Citizen Engagement Index
Citizen-centricity	Government Cloud	e-Illiteracy	GovTech Enablers Index
Public-private partnerships	E-Consultation	Digital India	Public Service Delivery Index
Public service delivery	E-Data	e-Kranti	Core Government Systems Index
Policy incoherence			

Questions

A. Quick Check

1. What is public service delivery? Discuss.
2. What causes poor public service delivery?
3. What is required for efficient public service delivery?
4. How to know the resilience of public service delivery?
5. What is Good Governance?
6. What is the "gap-filling" role of NGOs in good governance?
7. What is the uniqueness of a public-private partnership (PPP)?
8. What is SMART Governance?
9. What are the benefits of SMART Governance?
10. What is E-Governance? What are its objectives?

B. Explore

1. Does government or public expenditure on public services enhance the general delivery service? Discuss.
2. How can public service delivery be made citizen-centric? Discuss.
3. Explain in detail the four models of SMART governance.
4. Explain the barriers to E-Governance.
5. Write a note on the status of SMART Governance in India.

References

- Bramwell, B. (2011). Governance, the state and sustainable tourism: A political economy approach. *Journal of Sustainable Tourism*, 19 (4-5), 459-477.
- Dener, Cem, Hubert Nii-Aponsah, Love E. Ghunney, and Kimberly D. Johns. (2021). GovTech Maturity Index: The State of Public Sector Digital Transformation. International Development in Focus. Washington, DC: World Bank. doi:10.1596/978-1-4648-1765-6. License: Creative Commons Attribution CC BY 3.0 IGO
- Eynon, R, and Dutton, W. H. (2007). Barriers to networked governments: Evidence from Europe, *Prometheus – Critical Studies in Innovation*, 25 (3), 225–242.
- Kaufmann, Daniel., Kraay, Aart., Mastruzzi, Massimo. (2009). Governance matters VIII: aggregate and individual governance indicators 1996-2008 (English). Policy Research working paper; no. WPS 4978. Washington, DC: World Bank. Extracted from http://documents.worldbank.org, accessed on 28.07.2019
- Kaufmann, Daniel., and Kraay, Aart. (2008). Governance Indicators: Where Are We, and Where Should We Be Going? World Bank Research Observer, 23 (1), 1-30 (spring).
- Mkandawire, Thandike (2007). 'Good governance: the itinerary of an idea, *Development in Practice*, 17 (4-5), 679-681. https://doi.org, accessed on 28.07.2019
- NISG (2022) https://www.nisg.org, accessed on 28.07.2019
- World Bank Group (2018). Indicators of citizen-centric public service delivery. Washington DC: World Bank.

Further Reading

- https://ppp.worldbank.org, accessed on 28.07.2019

CHAPTER 11

Public Policy Evaluation

The primary purpose of this chapter is to provide a broad overview of policy evaluation. We begin this chapter by discussing the concept of policy evaluation, the steps in policy evaluation, and how policy analysis differs from policy evaluation. Subsequently, we explain the policy evaluation types: content evaluation, process evaluation, outcome evaluation, impact evaluation, cost-benefit evaluation, experimental evaluation, and personnel performance evaluation. Policy evaluation faces several problems, challenges, dilemmas, and barriers. We then discuss the significant barriers to policy evaluation like goal specification, measurement, targets, efficiency and effectiveness, values and evaluation, politics, information and data, the problem of resources, the optimization dilemma, the equity dilemma, the partisan dilemma, and the unforeseen consequences dilemma.

The following section describes the evaluation process and policy evaluation types. The policy evaluation processes examine six distinct stages; evaluation planning, analytical modeling of evaluation, research design development, data collection and measurement, analysis and data interpretation, and reporting and communication. The five major types of evaluations, internal, external, process, impact, and comprehensive, are discussed. Finally, this chapter discusses the outcomes of policy evaluation like policy change, reasons for policy change, policy termination, and the reasons for policy termination.

Section 1: Policy Evaluation

Section 2: Policy Evaluation Types

Section 3: Barriers to Policy Evaluation

Section 4: Policy Evaluation Process

Section 5: Outcomes of Policy Evaluation

1. POLICY EVALUATION

The policy evaluation process critically studies a public policy program.

We studied in chapter 2 that policy evaluation is the last stage of the public policy process. Policy evaluation is an ongoing activity that follows policy implementation and monitoring. *The policy evaluation process critically studies a public policy program. Policy evaluation aims to collect and analyze information about a program's functioning, features, accomplishments, and outcomes.*

Policy evaluation helps judge a public program's effectiveness (Patton, 1987). As an essential component of the policy process, evaluation aims to know what happens when a policy comes into effect. Policy evaluation addresses the question—***' Does the policy work?'***

Policy evaluation addresses the question—' Does the policy work?'

Policy impact evaluation studies the improvements in the leading indicators of the program from the time of policy implementation and reveals how numerous changes can be attributed to the policy. ***Policy evaluation is a systematic approach to examining a program, policy intervention, or any policy initiative to know how the program goals and objectives are met.*** It helps determine what works well and what we should do to improve the program's performance to meet the set objectives. In addition, evaluation helps demonstrate the policy's impact on the program funders, the public, and the policymakers.

Policy evaluation assumes greater importance because it helps improve the policy design and implementation to meet the policy objectives and benefit the intended or targeted beneficiaries. It promotes accountability in program implementation, improved public policy decision-making, and efficiency in the public sector.

Policy Evaluation is crucial in ascertaining whether the program has met its expectations and achieved the policy objectives per the policy design. It systematically measures program design, implementation process, objectives, and outcomes.

Policy analysis mainly focuses on a pending decision of a program, while policy evaluation is when a program is already implemented.

Does policy analysis differ from policy evaluation? More often, we find the use of terms policy analysis and policy evaluation in place of one another. Even though both are intended to provide the policy makers feedback about a program and help make better decisions, they differ in their use and timing. Policy analysis mainly focuses on a pending decision of a program, while policy evaluation is when a program is already implemented.

1.1 The Concept of Evaluation

Knowing the meaning and purpose of evaluation from the theoretical perspective is quite helpful in understanding the significance of policy evaluation. Gerston (2009) observes that evaluation offers ammunition for future changes and policy refinement in public policymaking. Wholey et al. (1970) explain that policy evaluation is an assessment of the overall effectiveness of a public program in achieving its objectives or assessing the relative effectiveness of two or more similar programs. On the other hand, Wollmann (2007) defines policy evaluation as an analytical tool to investigate a policy program and as a feedback-generating tool for a program in progress.

Rossi et al. (2004) have conceptualized evaluation as a systematic program analysis for assessing the program intervention's utility. According to the well-known public policy expert Thomas Dye, evaluation is a systematic assessment of a policy's short- and long-term effects on both the targeted and non-targeted beneficiaries and measuring its costs and benefits (Dye, 2004).

Generally, we understand that policy evaluation addresses three primary purposes: (i) ***Efficiency Assessment***—knowing whether the policy has worked to attain the intended objectives? (ii) ***Impact Assessment***—gauging the outcomes of the public policy program, (iii) ***Future Action Assessment***—determining whether to continue, amend, or drop the program.

Policy evaluation addresses three primary purposes: efficiency assessment, impact assessment, future action assessment.

Policy evaluation primarily performs four significant functions. First, it offers reliable information for measuring the policy impact and examines the extent to which the policy objectives have been measured. Second, it provides feedback on the policy stages and appraises the policy implementation. Third, it shows whether the policy objectives need restructuring and whether new objectives and novel solutions should be proposed. Fourth, it helps strengthen policy implementation accountability and benefits policymakers or interest groups with the required information about the policy.

1.2 Policy Evaluation Steps

Generally, the policy evaluation process progresses across four steps viz., (i) planning, (ii) implementation, (iii) completion, and (iv) dissemination, and reporting. However, the policy evaluation framework involves steps like (1) recognizing the purposes of evaluation, (2) identifying spheres for evaluation, (3) selecting the evaluation methodology, (4) analyzing the results, and (5) reporting evaluation results.

Policy evaluation offers reliable information for measuring the policy impact and examines the extent to which the policy objectives have been measured.

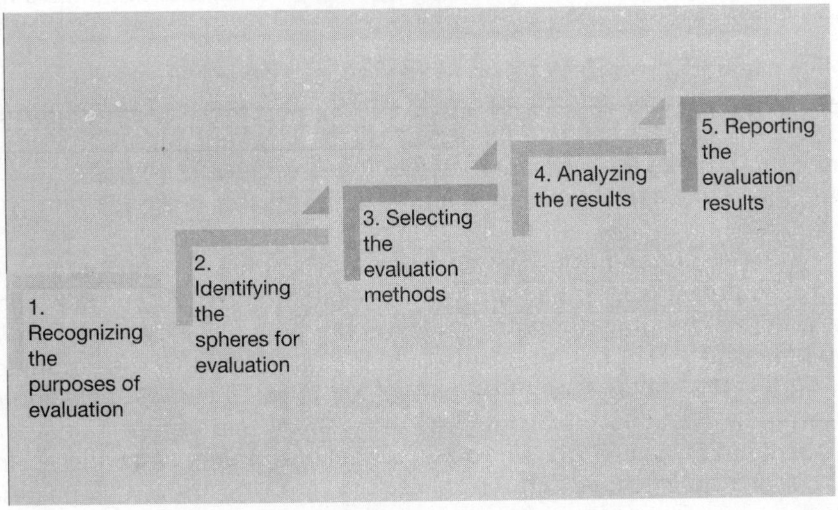

FIGURE 11.1 Policy Evaluation Steps

Policy evaluation covers two aspects: policy program, and evaluating personnel.

The first step is identifying the purposes of the evaluation—Why should evaluation be carried out? What purposes are to be covered? What should be the scope of evaluation? The second step focuses on domains of evaluation—What are the broad areas of evaluation? What is required from the evaluation process? The third step is choosing the proper evaluation methods—which evaluation techniques or methods should be employed to find the correct outcomes? How best the evaluation method will suit the evaluation process? Does the evaluation process suit the program under evaluation? The fourth step analyzes the evaluation results—Arranging the results according to the program objectives, highlighting the unique outcomes, analyzing the reasons for such outcomes, and suggesting policy improvements based on the results. Finally, the fifth step is about communicating the evaluation results—The results should be reported to the policy stakeholders like the government agency, policymaker, public, interest groups, and others. This is a crucial step where transparency matters supreme. This helps build trust and win the policy stakeholders' confidence to refine the program further if required and replicate the program if found successful.

Policy evaluation covers two aspects: (i) the policy program—assessment of the policy and its impact on the targeted beneficiaries, and (ii) the evaluating personnel—choosing the right personnel suitable for policy implementation.

Why is policy evaluation necessary? Policy evaluation is imperative because of the following reasons: (i) documenting policy design, (ii) detailing and apprising policy implementation, (iii) assessing backing and compliances in the existing policies, (iv) Expounding the policy impacts and policy worth, (v) Demonstrating an evidence base, (vi) Providing feedback for future policies, and (vii) confirming accountability for the invested resources.

2. POLICY EVALUATION TYPES

Policy evaluation must focuses on formative evaluation and summative evaluation.

Policy evaluation must focus on (i) ***Formative Evaluation***–measuring the policy achievement against its goals, and (ii) ***Summative Evaluation***–assessing the actual effects of the policy on the targeted and non-targeted population. While the formative evaluation is called the implementation evaluation, the summative evaluation is called the program outcome evaluation.

Policy evaluation employs evaluation principles and procedures to study the policy content, policy implementation, and policy impact. It is the activity through which we comprehend a policy's advantages, costs, and benefits.

Figure 11.2 shows the policy evaluation types: (i) content evaluation, (ii) process evaluation, (iii) outcome evaluation, (iv) impact evaluation, (v) cost-benefit evaluation, (vi) experimental evaluation, and (vii) personnel performance evaluation.

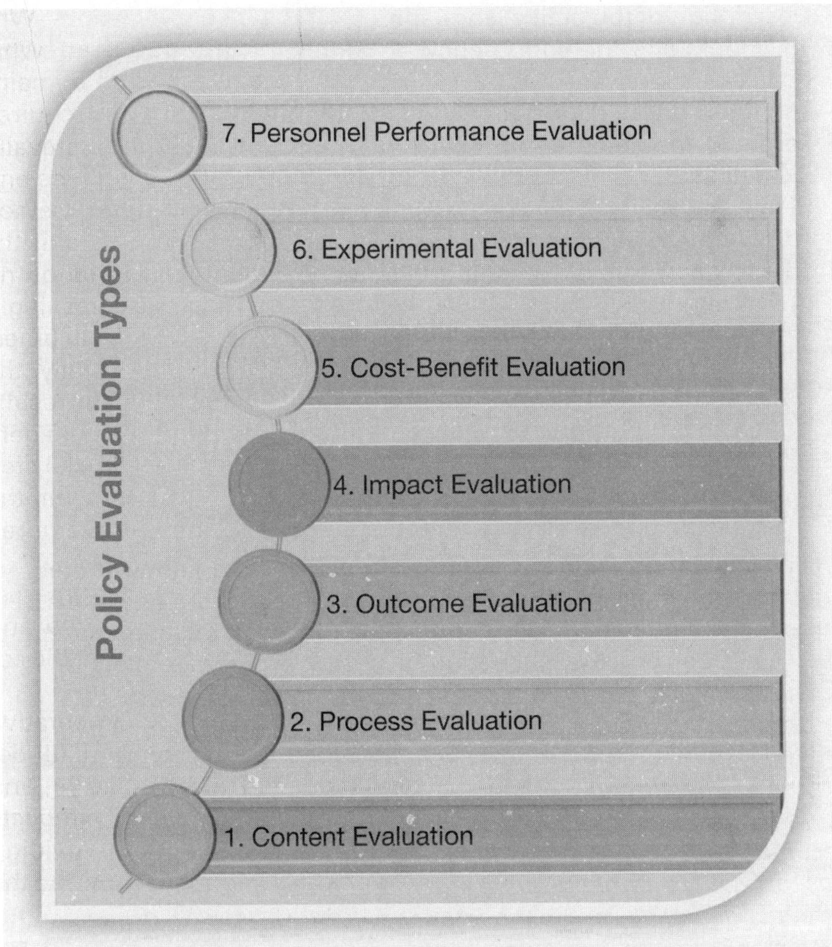

FIGURE 11.2 Types of Policy Evaluation

2.1 Policy Content Evaluation

Policy content evaluation studies the substantive information in a policy vis-à-vis its requirements, its resemblance to other policies, and the context of policy design and development. Policy content evaluation has several purposes: (i) recognizing the level to which the subject matter of the policy visibly communicates the requirements, (ii) Comparing the policies among communities to recognize critical resemblances and variances, and (iii) Knowing the process of policy selection and consent, (iv) Enhancing the implementation of policy and development of future policy, and (v) Notifying the growth and expansion of policy implementation and impact assessment. One of the critical aspects of policy content evaluation is articulating the pertinent dimensions and components of the policy. Policy content evaluation involves several variables, such as.

> Policy evaluation comprehends a policy's advantages, costs, and benefits.

Policy content evaluation studies the substantive information in a policy vis-à-vis its requirements, its resemblance to other policies, and the context of policy design and development.

a) Description of the policy language.
b) To understand the consistency or variance with other comparable policies.
c) To assess policy complexity and its components.
d) To know the steps and timeline between policy authorization and execution.
e) Scope and ability of the policy to influence the adjoining communities.
f) Arrangement of policy structure.
g) To reckon the level of political influences and other stakeholder pressures.

Overall, policy content evaluation tries to know whether the content of the policy lucidly articulates the policy logic, goals, implementation, and intended change.

2.2 Policy Process Evaluation

Process evaluation verifies the program activities to know whether we implement them as envisioned and whether outputs are as per expectations. One should periodically conduct the process evaluation during the policy life. Does process evaluation help track program implementation-related questions like *(i) To whom is the program intended? (ii) What is the program's outcome so far? (iii) When did the program activities occur? (iv) Where did the program activities happen? and (v) What are the barriers to implementation?*

Policy process evaluation provides the required information about the barriers to policy implementation and facilitating factors that help in the process.

Policy process evaluation is crucial because evaluating the policy outcomes with proper knowledge and info concerning the policy goals, aims, objectives, target groups, and target areas helps determine whether the public policy serves the intended purpose. It looks broadly at two aspects: (a) whether we implement the policy as per the goals directed at specified target groups or target areas set during the policymaking? (b) Are the policy implementation strategies executed per the policy design to achieve the planned outcomes? Moreover, policy process evaluation provides the required information about the barriers to policy implementation and facilitating factors that help in the process.

2.3 Policy Outcome Evaluation

Before explaining the policy outcome evaluation, ***it is desirable to clarify the difference between the outcome and output of policy intervention.*** *Output is the measure of policy activities, mostly quantifiable results. In contrast, the outcome is the impact of a policy on the targeted beneficiaries in terms of the intended behavioral change.* The policy outcomes are important because the outcomes determine the accomplishment of the policy due to the policy intervention. Policy outcome evaluation measures the policy intervention effects on the targeted beneficiaries by evaluating the improvement in the expected outcomes according to the policy or the program goals.

The outcome evaluation helps in assessing the effectiveness of a policy and knowing whether the policy worked at the desired level and achieved the anticipated results. It measures the policy effects and ascertains whether envisioned outcomes were attained. In a way, it compares the conditions of the targeted beneficiaries before and after participation. An example of policy outcome evaluation could be an evaluation undertaken to determine a policy's outcome to dissuade people from smoking. The policy outcome evaluation essentially seeks to know whether the program or the policy succeed in making people cease smoking.

Output is the measure of policy activities, mostly quantifiable results. In contrast, the outcome is the impact of a policy on the targeted beneficiaries in terms of the intended behavioral change.

2.4 Policy Impact Evaluation

Policy impact evaluation is about knowing whether the policy has produced the impact per the policy's intended aims and purpose. We can evaluate the policy impact of three situations: short-term, medium-term, and long-term. The impact can be either positive or negative. Understanding the policy impact and attributing it to the policy must be careful to ascertain whether the impact is due to the policy intervention effect or other factors. Given this, the evaluator's questions determine the quantification of output and outcome are crucial. The following are the questions commonly asked during policy impact evaluation.

a) What was the change after the policy intervention?
b) Are the measured changes attributable to the policy intervention?
c) How much did the policy contribute to the outcomes?
d) What are the negative consequences due to policy intervention?
e) What contextual factors influence the level of impact?
f) What was the economic impact of the policy intervention?
g) Was the policy intervention cost-effective?

Understanding the policy impact and attributing it to the policy must be careful to ascertain whether the impact is due to the policy intervention effect or other factors.

The impact evaluation process envisages the consequences or impacts of changes due to the policy intervention. It is an amalgam of procedures, measures, methods, and tools used to assess the potential effects of a policy or program, or project on the targeted beneficiaries within the population and the indirect impact on the remaining population.

2.5 Policy Cost-Benefit Evaluation

Cost-Benefit evaluation emphasizes comparing the costs and benefits associated with the policy intervention. It is an analytical method that profoundly influences policymaking, particularly in the public sector. Also called the Cost-Benefit Analysis (C.B.A.) technique, this approach proposes that we should quantify all elements in a policy decision to expound logical reasoning for policymaking. Often, the C.B.A. evaluation is preferred because actual real-world costs are easy to ascertain, quantify, assess, contrast, and compare against various metrics or other policies/programs. There is little doubt about the profound contribution of C.B.A. However, it is not free from criticism that quantification is merely politics spruced up in techniques. Moreover, intangible costs and benefits

Cost-Benefit evaluation compares the costs and benefits associated with the policy intervention.

associated with the policy intervention are exceptionally complex to calculate.

2.6 Experimental Evaluation

Experimental evaluation offers more convincing evidence by demonstrating a causal connection between the program and its impact.

The primary purpose of an experimental evaluation is to determine whether a policy intervention or a program is more effective than the present situation by randomly consigning the participants to a treatment group and a control group. This approach offers more convincing evidence by demonstrating a causal connection between the program and its impact.

Many policy experts opine that experimental evaluation is quite suitable for gauging the impact of public policy programs. As this evaluation is carried out in the post-implementation stage of the policy intervention, it seeks to estimate the gross and net effects of policy intervention. Dye (2004) makes a strong case for experimental evaluation, as it is advantageous in more scientifically capturing the impact of policy intervention. Palumbo (1987) refers to summative evaluation as an impact evaluation carried out at the post-implementation stage of the policy as an experiment that seeks to examine a problem before and after policy intervention.

The gender of the participating poor undoubtedly affects the outcomes of financial inclusion programs.

For example, using experimental evaluation, Swamy (2014) examined the significance of the gender dimension in financial inclusion through microfinance in the economic upliftment of poor households in India. Using household survey data from selected states of India, the study answers the question—"In the context of gender dimension, what is the evidence of the impact of the financial inclusion programs on poor households represented by women relative to that represented by men?" By constructing a good counterfactual and comparison group and employing the difference-in-difference estimator approach, the study uses panel least squares and generalized methods of moments using standard errors for a robust analysis. The findings reveal that the compounded annual growth rate of income (net of inflation effect) was 8.40% for women as against 3.97% for men, signifying that the gender of the participating poor undoubtedly affects the outcomes of financial inclusion programs.

2.7 Personnel Performance Evaluation

The idea behind the personnel performance evaluation is that evaluation of the performance of the personnel involved in policy implementation can ensure better policy outcomes.

Interesting to note that policy evaluation also involves the evaluation of the performance of the personnel responsible for policy implementation at all the key levels. The idea behind the personnel performance evaluation is that evaluation of the performance of the personnel involved in policy implementation can ensure better policy outcomes. Governmental agencies or non-governmental agencies can carry out this evaluation.

The media, researchers in private and public think tanks, academic institutions, policy research bodies, public commissions, and public-interest organizations all evaluate programs and policies that have a greater or lesser impact on public officials.

3. BARRIERS TO POLICY EVALUATION

As the state's role is widening, there is increasing pressure on the public sector to perform with efficiency and effectiveness. Given this, policy evaluation becomes even more crucial and a source of conflict. Evaluation research has recently become a significant industry with many consulting firms, universities, and organizations. Too many adverse outcomes of the policy evaluations could damage public policymaking. Hence, it is vital to ensure the content of policy evaluation is neutral and objective so that the policy assessment does not affect policy performance. Theodoulou and Kofinis (2004, pp. 163-174) observe that there are enormous possibilities of these evaluating organizations imposing their perspectives on what is right and wrong in policy and will bring those values with them when they undertake policy evaluation.

It is vital to ensure the content of policy evaluation is neutral and objective so that the policy assessment does not affect policy performance.

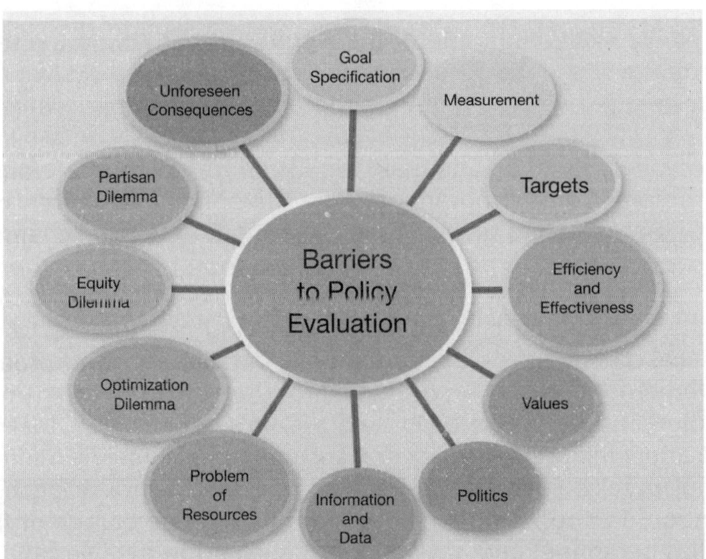

FIGURE 11.3 Barriers to Policy Evaluation

Policy evaluation faces several problems, challenges, dilemmas, and barriers. Public policy experts like Peters (1988), Nagel (1990), and Rossi et al. (2004) observe several barriers to policy evaluation. The major barriers to policy evaluation are (i) goal specification, (ii) measurement, (iii) targets, (iv) efficiency and effectiveness, (v) values and evaluation, (vi) politics, (vii) information and data, (viii) problem of resources, (ix) the optimization dilemma, (x) the equity dilemma, (xi) the partisan dilemma, and (xii) the unforeseen consequences dilemma.

Policy evaluation faces several problems, challenges, dilemmas, and barriers

3.1 Goal Specification

Goal specification is affected by political bias, information asymmetry, confusion about the nature of the problem, individual value bias, the plurality of competing interests, and deficiency in recognizing potential alternatives.

Often, political bias, information asymmetry, confusion about the nature of the problem, individual value bias, the plurality of competing interests, and deficiency in recognizing potential alternatives are some of the limitations that affect the stages of problem identification and policy formulation. Such shortcomings lead to vague, confusing, contradictory, unrealistic, or unachievable policy goals. Hence, the policy evaluation stage faces several problems due to goal specification vis-à-vis policy outcomes.

The ambiguous language of the policy instrument with vague policy goals often affects the policy evaluation. In addition, due to inadequate budgetary support, policy programs face 'displacement of goals.' Goal specification suffers because public programs targeting poverty, employment, health care, education, and public utilities mostly remain political propaganda when adequate funds are not released on time. In such situations, policy evaluation becomes a futile exercise.

3.2 Measurement

Setting proper yardsticks for measuring policy performance is necessary for practical policy evaluation.

During policy evaluation, one of the significant barriers is the measurement problem due to the absence of well-identified measures/variables for the performance evaluation of the program. Setting proper yardsticks for measuring policy performance is necessary for practical policy evaluation.

The availability of an adequate time span for policy evaluation is another problem. Some programs require the policy evaluation to be carried out immediately after policy implementation, while others require some time gap after the program implementation to capture the benefits of the policy adequately. Because some demonstrate immediate short-term benefits and others take a long term to indicate the impact/results.

Political compulsions, manipulations, and distortions also affect policy implementation, causing problems for the outcome measurement of policy intervention. In addition, the program's beneficiaries' characteristics also affect the policy impact measurement. Because the beneficiaries might not precisely reveal the benefits or adverse effects of the policy intervention. Further, problems like lack of adequate competency of the evaluation personnel and cooking up of evaluation data seriously affect the policy evaluation.

3.3 Targets

The achievement of policy goals is directly dependent on the targets set out in the policy.

The performance measurement relies on the procedural efficiency of the evaluation process.

The achievement of policy goals is directly dependent on the targets set out in the policy. So, policy targets are crucial in the process of policy evaluation. Stringent criteria for admission of the beneficiaries might directly affect the attainment of policy targets. Sometimes, the policy implementing officials misreport the out-of-target population (selecting beneficiaries who need little help rather than those who are significantly in need of help) as beneficiaries and misleadingly declare the policy's success that it has achieved the target. Such a false sense of success in a policy affects policy evaluation.

3.4 Efficiency and Effectiveness

A program's efficiency depends on how the costs are assigned to the program implementation activities and the policy outcomes. Difficulties arise when such costs are not spelled out in the policy and when they are unrealistic. Further, such problems also lead to problems in measuring effectiveness. More often, the performance measurement relies on the procedural efficiency of the evaluation process.

3.5 Values and Evaluation

The values and perceptions of the policy evaluators also pose problems in policy evaluation, particularly in evaluating the policy outcomes. When the policy evaluator measures the unintended effects against the intended policy outcomes, the values and perceptions of the policy evaluators greatly matter. In the case of external policy evaluation agencies, that agency's philosophy, agenda, and ideology significantly affect the outcomes of policy evaluation. Such problems can be overcome only when the evaluators are of high integrity and professional to the core.

> The problems due to values and perception can be overcome only when the evaluators are of high integrity and professional to the core.

3.6 Politics

Politics has become omnipresent and hence affects policy evaluation as well. It affects policy evaluation as an obstacle to fairness and an unbiased approach. The political context also affects policy evaluation because political interests influence the evaluation process. Sometimes the data is manipulated to suit the interests of the political dispensation during the evaluation process to claim the credit for the policy's success. Quite often, politics influences policy evaluations to go for short-term outcomes of the policy and report positive findings. On the other hand, there are possibilities that if the evaluators are of opposition ranks, the findings might be adversely reported to construe the policy as a failure. Thus, political considerations during the policy evaluation significantly affect the policy evaluation process.

> Political considerations during the policy evaluation significantly affect the policy evaluation process.

3.7 Information and Data

Accurate information and reliable data are the two eyes of an evaluation exercise. Quality data greatly matters in any evaluation. Hence, before we begin the policy evaluation process, we need to ascertain the data type, quality, suitability, reliability, qualitative data, quantitative data, data formats, and related aspects. On the face of it, though data collection looks like a simple exercise, it is an important activity that needs a careful approach to ensure appropriate data collection for evaluation. Further, problems in collecting information and data due to the non-availability of proper records or accurate data sources and lack of desired data formats pose limitations to policy evaluation.

3.8 Problem of Resources

The problems in collecting information and data due to the non-availability of proper records or accurate data sources and lack of desired data formats pose limitations to policy evaluation.

In developing countries, the most common problem is a lack of financial resources and a shortage of human and infrastructural resources. The lack of resources causes a severe impediment to the policy evaluation process. There has been a rising demand for policy evaluation, but there is commensurate funding from the government or corporations. Hence, the problem of resources continues to bother the process of policy evaluation, more particularly in developing countries.

3.9 The Optimization Dilemma

Policy optimization entails adopting a policy that optimizes or maximizes the anticipated policy goals under distinct conditions, constraints, and challenges instead of emphasizing forecasting exclusively. Primarily, evaluation reports convey the association between policies and goals. Nagel (1990) states, "The optimization dilemma encompasses whether we must be concerned solely with prediction and causation or with prescription and possibly policy optimization." Society needs prescriptive requirements rather than predictive findings and the relationship between policies and goals.

3.10 The Equity Dilemma

The equity dilemma in policy evaluation arises due to the recurrent conflict between equity and efficiency in policy goals.

The equity dilemma in policy evaluation arises due to the recurrent conflict between equity and efficiency in policy goals. According to Nagel (1990), "the vital point is not the technical aspect of the approach taken to equity of benefits, equity of costs, and efficiency, but the conscious consideration of these criteria. Hence, policy evaluators should, however, discuss these issues explicitly in policy evaluation."

3.11 The Partisan Dilemma

Policy evaluators, mostly government employees, often dance to the tunes of their political masters rather than going about their job of evaluation unbiasedly.

The fundamentals of objectivity, commitment to the public interest, and resistance to complex political and other pressures are much required in policy evaluation. However, the problems of a partisan approach creep into policy evaluation. Policy evaluators, mostly government employees, often dance to the tunes of their political masters rather than going about their job of evaluation unbiasedly. The dilemmas in policy evaluation may vary from country to country, dependent on mostly eight factors: (i) the nature of the political system, (ii) the party system, (iii) interest groups, (iv) media, (v) citizenry, (vi) administrative capability, (vii) the competence level of human resources, and (viii) the level of economic development.

3.12 The Unforeseen Consequences Dilemma

The evaluators come through many unforeseen consequences during the evaluation process, which they had never conceived of. Generally, while confronting unforeseen consequences, the policy evaluator operates by the data and the well-tested methodology. This might primarily affect the policy evaluation report. Hence, contingency models in such cases would enable the evaluation report to reflect the realities more emphatically.

To summarize, policy evaluation is a crucial stage in the public policy cycle. Political will is necessary to make the policy evaluation system more effective. In addition, the support and coordination of administrative departments of the government, research organizations, academic institutions, think tanks, and external consultants are essential to minimize the problems in policy evaluation and make it a practical exercise and a success.

Political will is necessary to make the policy evaluation system more effective.

4. POLICY EVALUATION PROCESS

The policy evaluation process is a critical activity that needs a careful approach. In general, policy evaluation processes examine six distinct stages: *(i) Evaluation Planning, (ii) Analytical Modeling of Evaluation, (iii) Development of Research Design, (iv) Data Collection and Measurement, (v) Analysis and Data Interpretation, and (vi) Reporting and Communication.* While these stages mirror the common policy evaluation steps, depending upon the nature of the policy and the program, the evaluation stages can be modified to suit the needs of the evaluation. Figure 11.4 shows the stages sequentially in the evaluation process.

The policy evaluation processes examine six distinct stages: evaluation planning, analytical modeling of evaluation, development of research design, data collection and measurement, analysis and data interpretation, and reporting and communication.

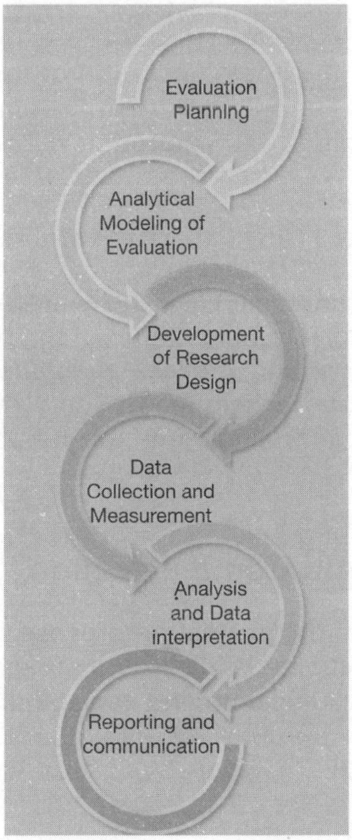

FIGURE 11.4 Stages in the Evaluation Process

4.1 Policy Evaluation Process

4.1.1 Evaluation Planning

The evaluation planning stage of the planning process involves the scheduling of evaluation activities like identifying the goals and objectives of the program, measuring the variables, and comprehension of the outcomes vis-à-vis the mission statement. One of the key considerations during this stage is prioritizing short- and long-term goals, determining data collection methods, assessing the feasibility of the policy/program, and identifying the target audience.

4.1.2 Analytical Modeling of Evaluation

This stage of the evaluation process involves the construction of an analytic model of the program expectations, which includes a set of theoretical propositions about means-ends relationships.

4.1.3 Development of Research Design

In this stage of the evaluation process, evaluators develop a research design to distinguish program or policy goals vis-à-vis outcomes.

One of the key considerations during evaluation planning stage is prioritizing short- and long-term goals, determining data collection methods, assessing the feasibility of the policy/program, and identifying the target audience.

4.1.4 Data Collection and Measurement

This stage begins with the implementation of the evaluation process. It may vary from program to program, mainly using appropriate data collection techniques to collect the required data and its measurement.

4.1.5 Analysis and Data Interpretation

In this stage of the evaluation process, the evaluators complete the evaluation activity. Depending upon the nature of the program, the evaluators concentrate on formative and process evaluation strategies. The analysis uses the appropriate techniques to know the long-term outcomes and impacts. Further, the findings are interpreted vis-à-vis the program objectives.

The five types of policy evaluation are internal evaluation, external evaluation, process evaluation, impact evaluation, and comprehensive evaluation.

4.1.6 Reporting and Communication

This is the final stage of the evaluation process, wherein the evaluators tell the story more effectively. While doing so, they use the most appropriate methods of communication and disseminate the findings to reach the target audience.

4.2 Policy Evaluation Types

In the field of public policy, there are several evaluation types in practice. The purpose of all these evaluations is to evaluate the policy outcomes. However, each of the evaluation types has a specific focus. *Broadly, we notice five types of policy evaluations (i) Internal Evaluation, (ii) External Evaluation, (iii) Process Evaluation, (iv) Impact Evaluation, and (v) Comprehensive Evaluation.* We briefly describe them here below.

4.2.1 Internal Evaluation

The internal evaluation is a policy evaluation carried out in-house by the implementing agency or the institution. It is a kind of self-evaluation generally practiced in the Weberian bureaucratic model using hierarchical oversight based on regular reporting. However, evaluation research emphasizes monitoring and evaluating the programs using performance evaluation indicators (Wollmann 2003).

4.2.2 External Evaluation

External evaluation, on the other hand, is initiated or funded by outside sources generally contracted out by an agency or actor outside the operating or administrative unit. Parliaments have shown an interest in external evaluations to use the evaluation to oversee the policy implementation by the administration. Similarly, courts of law and government ministries also use external evaluations to shed light on the effectiveness of the administrative mechanisms.

> External evaluation is initiated by outside agency or actor outside the operating or administrative unit.

4.2.3 Process Evaluation

Process evaluation is an evaluation that seeks to know whether we implement a specific policy as per the guidelines set during policymaking. First, it focuses on whether the policy aims rightly at the appropriate target group or area.

Second, it seeks the policy interventions and implementation practices per the policy design. More often, program managers employ process evaluation to know whether the policy implementation process for service delivery supports the policy objectives planned during policymaking. It helps determine why a program or policy is performing at current levels, identify problems, develop solutions to process problems, and enhance policy performance by suggesting how solutions must be implemented and assessed.

4.2.4 Impact Evaluation

The impact evaluation undertakes to evaluate policy goals' positive and negative changes.

The impact evaluation undertakes to evaluate policy goals' positive and negative changes. In this evaluation, a review of the conditions of the target population before and after the implementation of the policy is made. It requires developing a proper design that allows the investigator to demonstrate the changes attributable to the policy intervention and its treatment.

4.2.5 Comprehensive Evaluation

A comprehensive evaluation is a blend of process and impact evaluation. It brings to light the policy outcome, possibility, and drawbacks. It also seeks to know how policy implementation could usher in improvements. From the public policy perspective, a comprehensive evaluation is more beneficial than either process or impact evaluation.

5. OUTCOMES OF POLICY EVALUATION

The outcomes of that policy determine the success of a policy.

The primary purpose of policy evaluation is to know whether the policy has achieved the policy goals in terms of outcomes. Outcomes are the measures of program effects on the target population that assist in assessing policy effectiveness. The outcomes of that policy determine the success of a policy. When the outcomes are measured during policy evaluation, there are three options for the policy owners to decide: (i) maintaining the status quo if the policy is performing as intended, (ii) if not satisfied with the policy outcomes, adjust the policy, i.e., make changes to policy, and (iii) if the policy needs an overhaul, terminate the program, or repeal the policy.

5.1 Policy Change

Policy change does not happen in a vacuum.

Policy change occurs when a policy is replaced, modified, or repealed.

What is Policy Change? Policy change occurs when a policy is replaced, modified, or repealed. Policy change does not happen in a vacuum. Change is inevitable on various occasions, as often, for various factors, the policies are not maintained as planned during policymaking.

Once a policy is implemented, it becomes the subject of criticism of all political tones, thus raising the need for policy change in tune with the new realities. Thus, the policy cycle continues again, like formulation, adoption, implementation, evaluation, reformulation, and re-implementation.

According to Theodoulou and Kofinis (2004), policies constantly evolve, so the policy cycle is an ongoing process. In essence, the proposed changes go through some modifications of the policy stages, like agenda setting, policy formulation, decision making, implementation, and evaluation (Howlett and Ramesh, 2003).

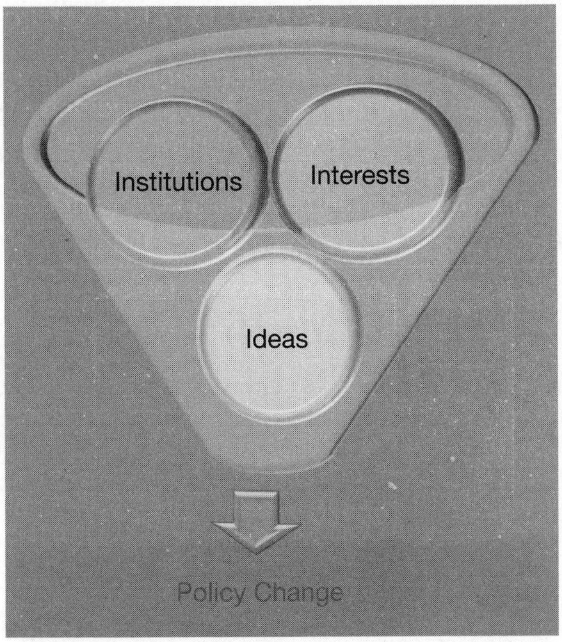

FIGURE 11.5 The '3Is' Policy Change Framework

Policy change comprises policies both at the legislative and organizational levels. For instance, institutionalizing reforms, decrees, resolutions, mandates, and regulations are policy change actions. According to Walt (1994), ***policy change frameworks are gathered into three critical elements known as the '3Is': (i) institutions (processes, context), (ii) interests (actors, power), and (iii) ideas (content, evidence, values).*** Figure 11.5 illustrates the '3Is' Framework of Policy Change.

In summary, policy change replaces existing policies with one or more new ones. Policy change can be through adopting new policies, changing existing ones, or terminating them (Lester and Stewart, 1996).

> The three critical elements of policy change framework known as 3Is are institutions, interests, and ideas.

5.2 Reasons for Policy Change

Several factors necessitate a policy change, like changes in societal dynamics, the problem being solved, the legality of the policy being challenged, apparent policy defects, rejection by the target beneficiaries, and new policies invalidating the existing policy. Some drivers of policy change are lack of public support or public anger, constitutional validity issues; technological changes; discoveries or revelations; change in economic conditions; change in political conditions; power shifts; and managerial inefficiency of implementing agencies. We briefly them here below.

5.2.1 Lack of Public Support or Public Anger

Public opinion has a powerful influence on public policy because, invariably, public support lends greater credibility to a policy. Without public support, it is impossible to pursue a public policy. Policy change becomes necessary when there is a lack of public support or public anger. For example, the Government of India withdrew the three farm bills in India due to some farmers' agitation and anger leading to policy change.

5.2.2 The Constitutional Validity Issues

In a democracy, without public support, it is impossible to pursue a public policy.

We must frame all public policies within the ambit of law and should align with the spirit of the constitution. When a policy is challenged in a court of law about its legality or constitutionality, it becomes difficult to pursue the policy. The policy change will be inevitable if the policy fails to stand the test of the law.

5.2.3 Technological Changes

In recent decades, technologies have been fast evolving. Rapid technological changes also result in a more significant impact on public policies by altering their feasibility or relevance. The governments must adjust the policies to be in tune with the changing technologies. Failure to align the policies to the changing technologies will lead to policy failure calling for policy change.

5.2.4 Discoveries or Revelations

Discoveries or Revelations change the consumption and behavior patterns of the target beneficiaries and hence can impact the effectiveness of existing policies.

Discoveries of economic resources change the consumption patterns of the public, and their consumption behavior and hence can impact the effectiveness of existing policies. Similarly, revelations also affect consumer behavior and alter public support for the policies, thus demanding policy change.

5.2.5 Change in Economic Conditions

Economic conditions significantly impact policy change. Economic factors like income distribution, economic structure, costs of information, and transaction costs affect the implementation of public policies. Because the target beneficiaries might not get involved in the policy acceptance process due to the changed economic levels in their livelihoods, economic conditions are potent influencers on public policy. Under adverse conditions, governments prioritize economic growth and jobs over expensive public programs.

5.2.6 Change in Political Conditions

Political conditions exert a considerable influence on policy change. Factors like governance structures (domestic political institutions and international organizations) and their political ideology, values, beliefs, and philosophy cause policy change. Political parties participate in policy design and can cause policy change (Howlett et al., 2009).

5.2.7 Power Shifts

Power shifts owing to new elections often cause policy change, as the ruling parties intend to implement their political ideology and manifesto. The power allocation or characteristics of the institutions involved in policy design also affect policy change. The new power structures change the policies according to their party philosophy.

The power allocation or characteristics of the institutions involved in policy design also affect policy change.

5.2.8 Managerial Inefficiency of Implementing Agencies

Lack of skills with the implementing agencies also often affects the successful implementation of the policy. Sometimes such institutions cannot manage the policy implementation due to a lack of appropriate managerial competencies. Hence, managerial inefficiency and lack of skill with the implementing agencies cause policy change.

5.3 Policy Termination

Policy termination means the abolition of all policy-linked activities and related public financing. However, new public policy and policy termination are rare because the policy is most likely transformed into a 'new' policy in the process of succession. ***Why is a policy terminated?*** The primary reason for policy termination is that a policy problem is solved or the policy measures are ineffective in addressing the problem. Sometimes policy termination is because of budget cuts, changing governments, and public sentiments (Geva-May, 2004). One example could be the first Schroder government's withdrawal of pension reforms announced by the Kohl-Government in Germany.

The policy termination is rare because it is cheaper to retain the program than to terminate it.

Why is policy termination so rare? Because it is cheaper to retain a program functioning than to terminate it. Some programs must subsist because of the constitutional provisions. Generally, people prefer the existing policy to continue with modifications rather than its termination, as there is resistance to change. And some political actors or public opinion bat for the continuation of the existing policies.

5.4 Reasons for Policy Termination

Policy termination occurs due to several reasons like (i) The problem is no more relevant, (ii) Failure to attain policy objectives, (iii) Budgetary constraints, and (iv) Ideological reasons. We will briefly discuss these factors here below.

5.4.1 The Problem is No More Relevant

Policy termination becomes necessary when the problem identified for the existing policy no more exists or the problem has become irrelevant. In such situations, there is no point in continuing the policy. Policy relevance is directly related to the problem that is targeted. Hence, when the problem is solved, the policy is deemed to have achieved its relevant goals. Sometimes, the problem gets resolved independently due to social, economic, and technological changes; hence, policy termination becomes essential.

5.4.2 Failure to Attain Policy Objectives

Policy failure occurs when a policy fails to attain its stated objectives.

Policy failure happens when a policy fails to attain its stated objectives. It could be because of several reasons: ineffective policy implementation, lack of coherence in policy design and implementation among the policy implementing agencies, inaccurate identification of target beneficiaries, and inefficiency on the part of the human capital involved in program implementation. In such situations, policy termination becomes inevitable.

5.4.3 Budgetary Constraints

Policy termination sometimes occurs due to budgetary constraints. During extraordinary times of distress, governments resort to cutting the budgetary support to the programs that are not essential and provide support only to those crucial for helping the public. Without budgetary support, it becomes challenging to continue a public policy. Thus, budgetary constraints on many occasions compel policy termination.

5.4.4 Ideological Reasons

Competitive politics in some countries or states sometimes leads to a situation where a new ruling party decides to terminate a policy that is not in alignment with its political ideology. For example, in India, On 5 August 2019, the National Democratic Alliance (N.D.A.) government revoked Article 35A, which provided special rights and privileges to the citizens of Jammu & Kashmir.

Because Article 35A was against the ideology of the N.D.A., which advocates for the unification of India without any discrimination, the Jawaharlal Nehru Cabinet brought in article 35A in 1954.

Policy evaluation is quite complex and challenging.

In summary, policy evaluation is a crucial exercise in the policy cycle. However, policy evaluation is quite complex and challenging. It becomes still more challenging when (i) the policy is addressing a large section of the population; (ii) lack of coherence among the policy implementors; (iii) the policy is quite complex, and (iv) when some individuals in the targeted beneficiaries have control over their treatment status.

Summary

- Policy evaluation aims to collect and analyze information about a program's functioning, features, accomplishments, and outcomes. It addresses three primary purposes: efficiency assessment, impact assessment, and future action assessment.
- The policy evaluation types include content evaluation, process evaluation, outcome evaluation, impact evaluation, cost-benefit evaluation, experimental evaluation, and personnel performance evaluation.
- The primary purpose of an experimental evaluation is to determine whether a policy intervention or a program is more effective than the present situation by randomly consigning the participants to a treatment group and a control group. This approach offers more convincing evidence by demonstrating a causal connection between the program and its impact.
- Policy evaluation is a crucial stage in the public policy cycle. Political will is necessary to make the policy evaluation system more effective. It faces several problems, challenges, dilemmas, and barriers. The significant barriers to policy evaluation are goal specification, measurement, targets, efficiency and effectiveness, values and evaluation, politics, information and data, the problem of resources, optimization, equity, partisan, and unforeseen consequences dilemma.
- The support and coordination of administrative departments of the government, research organizations, academic institutions, think tanks, and external consultants are essential to minimize the problems in policy evaluation and make it a practical exercise and a success.
- The policy evaluation process is a critical activity that needs a careful approach. Policy evaluation processes examine six stages: evaluation planning, analytical evaluation modeling, research design development, data collection and measurement, analysis and data interpretation, and reporting and communication.
- The purpose of policy evaluations is to evaluate the policy outcomes. Broadly, there are five types of policy evaluations: internal, external, process, impact, and comprehensive.
- The primary purpose of policy evaluation is to know whether the policy has achieved the policy goals in terms of outcomes.
- Policy change occurs when a policy is replaced, modified, or repealed. Policy change does not happen in a vacuum. Change is inevitable on various occasions, for various factors, as the policies are not maintained as planned during policymaking.
- The '3Is' Policy Change Framework involves three critical elements known as (i) institutions (processes, context), (ii) interests (actors, power), and (iii) Ideas (content, evidence, values).
- Policy termination means the abolition of all policy-linked activities and related public financing. The primary reason for policy termination is that a policy problem is solved or the policy measures are ineffective in addressing the problem.

Key Words

Policy evaluation	Formative evaluation	Cost-benefit evaluation	Equity dilemma
Policy analysis	Summative evaluation	Experimental evaluation	Partisan dilemma
Efficiency assessment	Content evaluation	Evaluation research	Policy change
Impact assessment	Process evaluation	Policy optimization	Policy termination
Future action assessment	Outcome evaluation		

Questions

A. Quick Check

1. Explain the meaning and purpose of policy evaluation.
2. Does policy analysis differ from policy evaluation?
3. Explain the four primary functions of policy evaluation.
4. Describe the policy evaluation steps.
5. Why is policy evaluation necessary?
6. What is the difference between process evaluation and content evaluation?
7. Differentiate outcome evaluation and output evaluation.
8. What is unique about experimental evaluation?
9. What is an equity dilemma?
10. Explain the five evaluation types.

B. Explore

1. Explain with examples the policy evaluation types.
2. Discuss in detail the policy evaluation barriers.
3. What is policy change? Discuss the '3Is' Framework of Policy Change.
4. Discuss with examples the drivers of policy change.
5. Why is a policy terminated? Elaborate with some examples.

References

- Dye, T. (2004). *Understanding Public Policy* (11th Education. ed.). Delhi, India: Pearson.
- Gerston, L.N. (2009). *Public Policymaking in a Democratic Society* (2nd ed.). New Delhi: PH1 Learning.
- Geva-May, Iris (2004). Riding the Wave of Opportunity: Termination in Public Policy. *Journal of Public Administration Research and Theory*: J-PART, Vol. 14, No. 3 (Jul. 2004), pp. 309-333.
- Howlett, Michael., and Ramesh, M (2003). Studying public policy: policy cycles and policy subsystems. 2nd Edition |Toronto, Canada: Oxford University Press, 2003.
- Howlett, Michael, M. Ramesh, and Anthony Perl (2009). Studying Public Policy: Policy Cycles and Policy Subsystems. 3rd Ed, Oxford University Press. 298 pages.
- Lester, J., and Stewart, J. (1996): Public Policy. An Evolutionary Approach.: West Publishing Company.
- Nagel, Stuart S. (Ed.) (1990). *Policy, Theory, and Evaluation: Concepts, Knowledge, Causes, and Norms*. Greenwood, New York.
- Palumbo, D. (Ed.) (1987). *The Politics of Programme Evaluation*. Newbury Park, California: Sage.
- Peters, B. Guy (1988). *American Public Policy: Promise and Performance*. Aff. East-West Press, New Delhi.
- Rossi, P.H., Lipsey, M.W. & Freeman, H. (2004). *A Systemic Approach* (7th ed.). California: Sage.
- Swamy, Vighneswara (2014). Financial Inclusion, Gender Dimension, and Economic Impact on Poor Households. *World Development* 56 (April), 1–15.

- Theodoulou, S. Z., and Kofinis, C. (2004). *The art of the game: Understanding American public policymaking*. Recording for the Blind & Dyslexic.
- Walt G, Gilson L. (1994). Reforming the health sector in developing countries: the central role of policy analysis. Health Policy and Planning 9: 353–70.
- Wholey, J.S.et al. (1970). *Federal Evaluation Policy*. Washington: Urban Institute.
- Wollmann, H. (2003). Evaluation in Public-Sector Reform. Towards a 'third wave' of evaluation. In H. Wollmann ed., Evaluation in Public-Sector Reform, Cheltenham: Edward Elgar, pp. 1-11.
- Wollmann, H. (2007). Policy Evaluation and Evaluation Research. In F. Fischer, G.J. Miller &M.S. Sidney (Eds.). *Handbook of Public Policy Analysis*. Boca Raton: C.R.C. Press.

Further Reading

- Frank Fischer, Gerald J. Miller, and Mara S. Sidney (ed.) (2007). *Handbook of public policy analysis: theory, politics, and methods.* Taylor & Francis Group. Boca Raton | London | New York.
- Peter H. Rossi, Mark W Lipsey, Howard, E Freeman. (2004). *Evaluation: A Systematic Approach*—Seventh Edition. Sage Publications, Thousand Oaks | London | New Delhi.
- Peters, B Guy., and Jon, Pierre. (2006). *Handbook of Public Policy*. Sage Publishing, Thousand Oaks, CA.
- Peters, B Guy (2019). *Policy Problems and Policy Design*. Edward Elgar Publishing.

Module IV

Public Policy Reforms in India

Module IV: Public Policy Reforms in India

This module has two chapters:

Chapter 12 Public Policy—Institutional Problems & Police Reforms
Chapter 13 Public Policy—Regulatory Reforms

Chapter 12 provides an overview of institutional problems and police reforms in India. It explains the evolution of the Indian administrative system, the hallmarks of Indian civil services, administrative structure—at the Centre, states, and districts, the new challenges to the administration, reforms in public sector institutions, First Administrative Reforms Commission (1st ARC), Commissions & study groups in the post-ARC period, Second Administrative Reforms Commission (2nd ARC), administrative reforms outcomes, education policy reforms in India, the industrial policy reforms in India and the way ahead.

Chapter 13 explains the public policy—regulatory reforms in India, the main concerns, the need for regulatory reforms, the typology of regulation in India, and the significant regulations in India. It presents an interesting discussion about the judicial reforms, the police reforms, and the ease of doing business reforms in India.

CHAPTER 12

Public Policy Reforms in India

This chapter introduces the administrative system, the civil service system, administrative reforms and educational reforms implemented in India. The first part of this chapter presents the administrative system prevailing in India at the centre, state and district levels. It is followed by a section on Civil services system in India. Administrative reforms implemented in India and details of 1st and 2nd Administrative commission reports are given in the third section. Education sector reforms and recommendations of various commissions are given in the fourth section with details on National Educational Policy 2020. Industrial policy reforms implemented since 1991 are given in the last section with special focus on recent policy changes.

India follows a federal form of governance with central and state governments. However, the federal system in India is different from that of the USA and other countries. The constitution of India envisages India as a quasi-federation with a strong centre and weak states, unlike the USA, where states are more powerful. The constitution of India demarks powers between the centre and state.

When the constitution was adopted in 1950, India was declared as a " Union of States" with the following types of states.

Part A States: Former governor provinces of British India

Part B States: States governed by a president appointed "Rajpramukh" and with an elected legislature.

Part C States: States governed by the chief commissioners appointed by the president of India.

Part D States: States administered by central government appointed Lieutenant Governor.

Later, as a country with diverse cultures, languages and religions, the Government of India created more states based on linguistic basis and culture. Soon after the independence, the Government of India realised the need to reorganise the state boundaries as the states formed during the British period were not suitable for effective governance. The Congress party was in favour of creating states based on the linguistic

Federalism is the basic structure of Indian constitution.

basis as it would reduce the problems of linguistic diversity. The chairman of the constituent assembly Dr Rajendra Prasad has constituted the Linguistic Provinces Commission (aka Dhar Commission) to decide whether to reorganise states on linguistic basis. The commission was not in favour of linguistic states and recommended forming provinces based on geographical contiguity, financial self-reliance, administrative viability, and potential for development. In 1948, congress appointed JVP (Jawaharlal Nehru, Vallahbhai Patel, Pattabhi Sitaramayya) committee to consider the issue of formation of linguistic states. Later in 1953, Fazl Ali Commission was formed to reorganise states. The Fazl Ali Commission (State reorganisation commission) submitted its report in 1955 in favour of forming states based on linguistic and cultural homogeneity. Dr. B R Ambedkar also favoured creating states based on linguistic considerations. The state reorganisation act was passed in 1956 by forming states based on the recommendations of the Fazl Ali commission. Some states that existed in 1956 are not there in 2022, and new states have been created based on public sentiment and other considerations.

Andhra State was the first state formed on a linguistic basis after the death of Potti Sreeramulu, a congress leader who died after undertaking a fast- unto- death for the formation of a state for Telugu-speaking people in Madras province. However, in 2022 we have Andra Pradesh and Telangana as Telugu-speaking states after the formation of Telangana in 2014. At present, India has 28 states and 8 Union territories. In 2016, the Government of India withdrew the statehood of Jammu and Kashmir and formed two Union territories- Jammu and Kashmir and Ladakh.

1. THE ADMINISTRATIVE SYSTEM IN INDIA

An effective administrative system at various levels is essential for the timely delivery of services to the citizens and responsive governance. India's administrative system has three levels: central, state and district administration.

1.1 Central Administration

The president of India is the head of the Indian republic. The prime minister of India is the head of the government

The Government of India is the chief administrative authority of the Republic of India. The President of India is the head of the Indian republic and the commander in chief of the armed forces. The Prime minister heads the government and council of ministers. According to the constitution of India, the president appoints the prime minister. The president appoints the members of the council of ministers on the prime minister's advice. The size of the council of ministers can be up to 15% of the members of the house of people.

1.1.1 Cabinet Secretariat

The cabinet secretariat is responsible for the administration of the Government of India (Transaction of Business) Rules, 1961 and the Government of India (Allocation of Business) Rules 1961. It provides secretarial assistance to various ministries and committees for smooth decision-making and implementation of the decision. The cabinet secretariat works directly under the prime minister, and the cabinet secretary is the head of the cabinet secretariat. "This Secretariat provides Secretarial assistance to the Cabinet and its Committees, and also assists in decision-making in Government by ensuring Inter-Ministerial co-ordination, ironing out differences amongst Ministries/ Departments and evolving consensus through the instrumentality of the standing/ Adhoc Committees of Secretaries".

Cabinet secretariat provides secretarial assistance to various central ministries.

1.1.2 Council of Ministers

The Government of India follows the portfolio system, and each member of the council of ministers is in charge of a ministry. Each ministry has a specific set of businesses under the Government of India (allocation of business) rules in 1961. The decision-making in the Government of India is as per the Government of India (transaction of business) rule 1961. The cabinet secretariat is known as the custodian of Government of India (transaction of business) rules 1961 and Government of India (allocation of business) rules 1961. According to the constitution of India, the council of ministers is collectively responsible to the parliament of India.

1.2 State Administration

As mentioned in the second administrative commission report, citizens interact closely with state and district administration as it provides various services most needed in their life. State governments perform essential functions like maintaining law and order, distributing ration cards, maintaining land records, implementing employment guarantee schemes, and distributing drinking water and electricity. An efficient state administration is vital in a nation like India, which is on a fast development path.

Governor is the head of State and the government is headed by the Chief Minister.

Each state is headed by the Governor, appointed by the President of India. The chief executive of the state is the chief minister. Governor appoints the council of state ministers based on the Chief Minister's advice. The size of the council of ministers in a state is restricted to 10 to 15% of the size of the state legislature.

1.2.1 State Secretariat

The state secretariat is the centre of state administration and is headed by the state's chief Secretary. State secretariat functions are similar to cabinet secretariat- providing secretarial services to smooth decision-making in various state government departments and ministries.

1.3 District Administration

District administration is headed by district collector. He performs the duties of district magistrate also.

The district administration in India is headed by a civil service officer known as a District collector. Also called district magistrate (DM), he is in charge of general administration, discharges the duty of senior most executive magistrate and is in charge of revenue collection. Mr Warren Hastings introduced the office of district collector in India in 1772.

The district administration, headed by the district collector, performs the following functions.

1. **Regulatory functions**- The district collector administers regulatory functions in the district, such as land revenue, law and order, excise, treasury, etc. The district collector also oversees the government's agriculture, primary and secondary education and animal husbandry departments.
2. District / sub-district level offices of the state government departments and their agencies such as PWD (Public Works Department), health irrigation, etc. These offices are directly under the state governments, and district collector has fewer roles in their functioning.
3. Local bodies (Panchayati Raj Institutions and Municipal bodies)-These institutions came into force with the constitution's 72nd and 73rd amendments, and they cater for the needs of people at the local level.

1.3.1 Roles of District Collector

The following are the functions of district collectors in India:

1. **Revenue Administration**: All matters related to land reforms and revenue administration.
2. **Executive Magistracy and Maintenance of law and order**: District collector exercises powers under various provisions of the CRPC, and he is in charge of law and order of the district.
3. **Disaster Management**: District collector supervises the disaster management wing of the district.
4. **District election officer**: District collector coordinates the entire election proceedings in the district.
5. Coordinates the activities of various government offices in the district
6. Census officer of the district.
7. Preparation of district development plans.
8. Apart from this, the district collector plays an essential role in economic development, welfare activities of the government department, Human resource development and rural development. However, the role of the district collector in these functional areas varies in different states.

1.4 Division of Powers Between Centre and States

The constitution of India demarks the powers of the central and state governments of India. In the seventh schedule of the constitution (Article 246), three lists are included- the Union list, state list and concurrent list. The union list (list I of the seventh schedule) includes 97 areas under the central government's jurisdiction. The state list (list II of the seventh schedule) comprised of 66 items (where states can execute power), and the concurrent list (list III of the seventh schedule) included 47 items. The concurrent list includes areas where both state and central governments have powers.

2. CIVIL SERVICE SYSTEM IN INDIA

India has a unified civil service system.

The civil service system in India helped the nation to maintain continuity in administration, irrespective of the political situation prevailing in the country. Civil service officers are well trained and are capable of advising political executives on various aspects of decision-making. The civil service officers also ensure that the decisions of the political executives are being implemented.

2.1 Significant Landmarks in the History of Civil Service in India

- The British East India Company introduced the civil service system in India. Initially, the civil servants were nominated by east India Company directors and trained at Haileybury College in London before sending them to India.
- Merit-based system of civil service in India was introduced in 1854, as per the recommendations of Lord Macaulay's Report of the Select Committee of British Parliament. Lord Macaulay's report recommended replacing the patronage-based system with a merit-based one. It also recommended to conduct a competitive examination for the selection of civil servants.
- Civil service commission was set up in 1854, and the first Civil service examination was conducted in 1855 in London.
- Satyendranath Tagore, brother of Rabindranath Tagore, was the first Indian to clear the civil service examination.
- From 1922 onwards, the Indian civil service examinations are conducted in India and later Federal Public Service Commission was set up for this.
- After independence, the Federal Public Service Commission was converted into the Union Public service commission.
- Article 312 of the constitution empowers the government to set up an all-India service.

- The civil service in India has undergone many changes in the nature of selection and training. The first Administration reforms committee of 1966, the Kothari committee and the second Administration reforms committee of 2005 have given several recommendations to strengthen the all-India service in India.

Many scholars and committees have recommended further reforms in civil service to make it more professional and outcome-oriented. While addressing the newly recruited civil service officers in 2019, the World Bank Group President David Malpass suggested strengthening the civil service system in India, keeping pace with the country's economic development and social changes. He said that "India's civil service needs to shift from a focus on enforcing compliance and meeting minimum requirements of service delivery to finding ways to ensure high-quality services and regulation... (Civil service officers) need to build the institutional capacity to deliver broad-based growth and a thriving private sector"(Malpass,2019).

3. ADMINISTRATIVE REFORMS IN INDIA

3.1 Need for Administrative Reforms

Administrative reforms are required in most developing countries to improve service delivery and ensure good governance. Most developing countries like India inherited a colonial administration that needs to be reformed to create a well-developed democratic society with a responsive administrative system. Administrative reforms are required in response to innovations, technological changes and changes in demand for services and service quality from the citizens.

Since independence, the Government of India has taken serious steps to implement administrative reforms in the country.

3.2 First Administrative Reforms Commission

The Government of India constituted the first administrative reform commission on January 1966 under the chairmanship of Morarji Desai. The commission has submitted 20 reports with 580 recommendations.

3.2.1 Major Recommendations

> The first administrative reforms commission was formed under the chairmanship of Morarji Desai

- Establish an inter-state council to discuss issues between states under article 263 of the constitution.
- Establish the Department of Administrative Reforms and Department of Personnel.
- The commission's interim report recommended to set up the State planning board in all states.

- The commission recommended that the prime minister should not be the chairman of the central planning commission. However, the government has rejected this recommendation.
- The commission recommended introducing performance budgeting in all departments involved in program implementation.

3.3 Second Administrative Reforms Commission

The second administrative reforms commission was constituted on 31st August 2005 under the Chairmanship of former Karnataka Chief minister Veerappa Moily. In reply to a question in LokSabha, the Government of India stated that the second administrative commission was asked to suggest measures to " achieve a proactive, responsive, accountable, sustainable and efficient administration for the country at all levels of the Government"(LOK SABHA Q&A session document 2015).The main areas of consideration of the commission were the government's organisational structure, ethics in governance, strengthening the financial management systems, ensuring effective state, district and local level administration, Citizen centric administration, promoting e-governance, etc.The commission has submitted 15 reports to the government on various issues.

The second administrative reforms commission was appointed in the year 2005 under the chairmanship of Veerappa Moily

Reports of the Second administrative reforms commission

Report	Title of the reports
1	Right to Information: Master Key to Good Governance
2	Unlocking Human Capital: Entitlements and Governance
3	Crisis management
4	Ethics in governance
5	Public order
6	Local administration
7	Capacity building for dispute resolution
8	Combating Terrorism - Defending Through Religion
9	Social capital - shared destiny
10	Personnel Administration & Scaling New Heights
11	Promoting e-governance
12	Citizen centric administration
13	Organisational Structure of the Government of India
14	Strengthening the financial management system
15	State and District Administration

Source: Department if Administrative Reforms & Public Grievances. Ministry of Personnel, Public Grievances and Pensions. ARC Reports. @Government of India. Accessed from https://darpg.gov.in on May 23, 2023.

3.3.1 Major Recommendations of the Commission

1. The official secrets act 1923 should be repealed and substituted by provisions in the National Securities Act.
2. As an affirmation of transparency in public life, ministers should take the oath of transparency along with the oath of office.
3. Set up regional offices of the Central Information Commission.
4. All states should appoint a state information commission(SIC), and larger states should start regional offices of SIC.
5. Regarding the rural employment guarantee scheme, funds should be transferred directly from the centre to the districts.
6. The contribution of the state to REGS(Rural Employment Guarantee Scheme) should be restricted to 10% of the cost.
7. Government ministries should be reorganised, and the meaning of ministry should be redefined. Ministry should consist of various interrelated departments. Page 160 of the 13th report states, "A Ministry would mean a group of departments whose functions and subjects are closely related and is assigned to a First or Coordinating Minister to provide overall leadership and coordination"(report of second administrative commission).
8. Regarding the Union government, the commission recommends focusing more on Rationalising the Functions of Government, Recasting the Allocation of Business Rules, concentrating more on Policy analysis, policy evaluation, Creation of Effective Executive Agencies, etc.
9. The state government's size should be restricted, and the size of the ministry (number of ministers) can be 10 to 15% of the strength of the legislature.
10. All states should have a Vigilance Commission/ Commissioner on the patterns of a central vigilance commissioner.
11. Redefine the role of the district collector. The district collector should "concentrates on the core functions such as land and revenue Administration, maintenance of law and order, disaster management, public distribution and civil supplies, excise, elections, transport, census, protocol, general administration, treasury management and Coordination with various agencies/ departments".
12. The gap between government budget "estimates" and "actual" should be minimised, and it should be evaluated at the end of each year.
13. Government expenditure follows "Skewed Expenditure Pattern - Rush of Expenditure towards the End of the Financial Year". A Monthly Expenditure Plan (MEP) should be worked out to reduce the skewed pattern of government expenditure.
14. An Office of the Chief Internal Auditor (CIA), directly responsible to the Secretary of the Department, should be set up in each ministry for internal auditing.
15. Along the lines of SIAFI of Brazil, a robust financial information system should be created in government.

16. To promote citizen-centric governance, all government agencies should create a single window agency concept to minimise delay and maximise the convenience of citizens.
17. Increase participation of citizens in planning, implementation and monitoring of all programs, and social audit should be mandatory for all programs.
18. Increase participation of women and physically challenged persons in various government policies and programs.

3.4 Right to Information (RTI) Act, 2005

The Right to information act, 2005, was a revolutionary step in the history of independent India. The RTI act aimed to empower citizens and promote government transparency and accountability. The act empowers the citizens by asking the government and various utility service providers questions. Further, this made citizens more informed about the working of the government and informed citizen strengthens the democratic system. The act mandates that any Indian citizen is entitled to get any information (which is supposed to be public knowledge) from different offices and departments of the government. All government offices and departments should make arrangements for the timely processing of RTI applications.

The RTI Act aimed at promoting transparancy and accountability in government

3.4.1 What is "Information?"

Guide of RTI 2005 defines Information as any material in any form. It includes records, documents, memos, e-mails, opinions, advice, press releases, circulars, orders, logbooks, contracts, reports, papers, samples, models, data material held in any electronic form. It also includes information relating to any private body which can be accessed by the public authority under any law for the time being in force".(GOI 2005)

4. EDUCATION REFORMS IN INDIA

The role of education in the progressive transformation of society has been well recognised in India. The leaders of the freedom struggle have given much importance to promoting education in India. Even the princely state rulers have given preference to education. It is evident from the fact that the King of Travancore made an unsuccessful attempt to appoint Albert Einstein as the first Vice-chancellor of the University of Travancore in 1936 for a monthly pay of Rs.6000.

After independence, the new Indian government has given much importance to reforming the education system in India. The Government of India has established several commissions to examine the problems and prospects of the education system in India.

4.1 University Education Commission 1948

The Government of India appointed the University education commission in November 1948 under the chairmanship of Dr. S. Radhakrishnan, a noted educationist. The commission was asked to make recommendations on the Finance of universities, medium of instruction of universities, the need for more universities in India, qualifications, salaries, and terms of service of teachers, the standard of admissions to university courses, maintenance of high standard of teaching and examinations, etc. The main features of this report are:

1. **Aim of the education system:** The commission mentioned that "The outlines of the social philosophy which should govern all our institutions, educational as well as economic and political, are indicated in the preamble to our Draft Constitution".(page 31, Report of University education commission 1948)
2. **Classification of teachers:** the report recommended classifying teachers as professors, Readers and lecturers.
3. **Medium of education:** The medium of education, English, should be replaced by the Indian language as early as practically possible. Regarding the dominance of English as a medium of instruction and political communications, the reports say that "National pride legitimately felt hurt at the idea of an alien language occupying a dominating position in the field of national culture".
4. **Financing of the Universities:** The commission recommended giving government grants to universities and colleges, encouraging donations by the private sector by providing income tax concessions, etc., and setting up a University Grand commission.

Dr. S Radhakrishnan was the chairman of University Education commission(1948)

4.2 Secondary Education Commission 1952–53

The Government of India constituted the secondary education commission under Dr. A. Lakshmanswami Mudaliar, then Vice-Chancellor of Madras University. The commission's terms of reference include examining the current position of the secondary education sector and suggesting measures for reorganising the secondary education sector.

4.2.1 Main Recommendations of the Commission Are:

1. Seven years of secondary education(the Middle or Senior Basic or Junior Secondary stage of 3 years, and (b) the Higher Secondary stage of 4 years).
2. Merge class 11 with secondary education and class 12 with the graduation.
3. Establishment of multipurpose schools.
4. Establishment of technical schools as part of the multipurpose schools separately.
5. Establishment of central technical institutes near industrial centres.

6. Introduction of "Industrial Education Cess' on industries to finance technical education.
7. Establishment of residential schools in rural areas.
8. Separate schools for girls whenever required.
9. The mother tongue should be the medium of instruction throughout the secondary stage.
10. English and Hindi should be introduced at the end of the Junior Basic stage.
11. Two languages should be taught at the high and higher secondary stage, and one of them must be a regional language or mother tongue.

4.3 Kothari Commission 1964-66

The Government of India appointed a commission under the chairmanship of Prof. D. S. Kothari to advise the government on the pattern of education and policies for development at all stages of development of the education sector. The commission has formed 12 task forces to review the education system at different levels. These include task forces on school education, higher education, technical education, adult education and teacher education. Kothari commission has conducted comprehensive consultations with noted educationists in India and abroad and submitted its report. Based on the Kothari commission recommendations, the Government of India adopted a national education policy in 1968. The main points of the policy are as follows

1. Free and Compulsory Education up to the age of 14 as per the directive principles of state policy.
2. Policies regarding Status, Emoluments and Education of Teacher: Special efforts will be made to improve teachers' salaries and other evolvements, including grants for research.
3. Three-Language Formula: State governments would adopt a three-language formula in secondary schools. This includes English, Hindi and a regional language.
4. The government would ultimately aim to implement the 10+2+3 pattern of education. This includes merging pre-University courses with schools as suggested by the Kothari commission.
5. The government should promote Part-time education and correspondence courses.

4.4 National Policy of Education 1986/92

Realising the need to restructure the education system in India to cater for the needs of the country, the Government of India announced the National Policy of Education in 1986. The government has appointed 23 task forces to frame a comprehensive action plan.

4.4.1 Early Childhood Care Education (ECCE)

Children achieve rapid physical and mental growth in their early childhood days. Keeping this in mind, the government announced the National Policy of Children in 1974 and has started the Integrated Child development program, balwadis and daycare centres, Pre-primary schools run by state governments, etc.

Nation policy of education recommends to

1. Improve the child-worker ratio in ECCE centres
2. Improve the quality of personals in ECCE
3. Increase the remuneration of workers in ECCE
4. ECCE will be directed to the most underprivileged groups of the society like slum areas, ecologically fragile areas, working children in the unorganised sector, etc.
5. Establish modest ECCE in all tribal development blocks and blocks having substantial tribal populations.
6. Adding health and nutritional component to ECE(Early Childhood education) centres, Anganwadis, pre-primary schools and balwadis

4.4.2 Elementary Education

The policy focuses on the following three thrust areas in elementary education:

1. Universal access and enrolment
2. Retention of children up to the age of 14
3. Improve the quality of elementary education

Children have different levels of learning skills, and they learn in different ways. Hence, a child-centric approach would be followed, and first-generation learners would be given their own pace for learning. This is aimed at reducing the child drop out in elementary education. The policy aimed to improve school facilities by ensuring a minimum number of teachers and learning aids in all schools.

4.4.3 Secondary Education

The government would focus on increasing the enrolment of girls, SC, and ST students in secondary education. Secondary education boards need to be restructured by adding eminent persons to these boards. Providing computer literacy to secondary school children was another area of focus.

4.4.4 Higher Education

Higher education plays a vital role in society as it provides the necessary opportunity to reflect on humanity's critical social, economic, cultural, moral and spiritual issues. Also, higher education institutions produce human resources with specialised skills required for economic development and provide teachers for higher educational institutions. The National Policy of education lays particular focus on higher education and recommends the following changes

1. Autonomous colleges would be promoted to provide academic freedom and promote accountability.
2. Redesign the existing courses to cater for the needs of the industry
3. Efforts will be made to improve the teaching methods using modem audio-visual methods.

4.5 National Education Policy 2020

National Education Policy(2020) aimed at making India a knowledge superpower

The Narendra Modi government announced its ambitious new education policy in 2020 to ensure equitable and inclusive quality education and promote lifelong learning opportunities as envisaged in the Sustainable development goals. To achieve this government recognises the need to reconfigure the entire education system based on the ethos of the rich learning culture of India. The government wants to build the gap between the current learning outcome and what is required by reforming the education system based on Indian value-based education. The world is changing rapidly, and the knowledge landscape needs to be strengthened by incorporating the latest developments in the area such as big data, artificial intelligence, machine learning, etc. The National education policy (NEP) aims to create an educational system which ensures equitable opportunities for all learners irrespective of their socio-economic background. The guiding light of this policy is the ancient Indian knowledge and thoughts.

4.5.1 The Vision of the Policy

The National education policy's main objective is to make India a knowledge superpower. "An education system rooted in Indian ethos that contributes directly to transforming India, that is Bharat, sustainably into an equitable and vibrant knowledge society, by providing high-quality education to all and thereby making India a knowledge superpower" (page 6 of NEP 2020). The curriculum should be developed in such a way that it instils a sense of pride in being Indian and develops respect for fundamental duties and constitutional values.

4.5.2 Principles of the Policy

The following are the basic principles of NEP given in the policy statement:

NEP 2020 follows a multidisciplinary approach

1. Learners will have the freedom to choose their learning trajectories and programs according to their interest

2. Ensuring the integrity and unity of knowledge: No hard separations between science, arts and other subjects between vocational and academic education
3. Multidisciplinary and holistic education
4. Emphasis on conceptual understanding rather than learning for examinations
5. Encourage logical decisions making and innovation through developing critical thinking
6. Instil ethics and constitutional values among the students
7. Develop life skills (for e.g., teamwork, communication, resilience, etc.)
8. Equity and inclusion
9. Regular formative assessment for learning
10. Teachers and faculty at the heart of the learning process
11. 'light but tight' oversight and regulatory system to ensure integrity and transparency

4.5.3 Changes in Curricular and Pedagogical Structure

The new policy proposed to change the existing 10+2 structure of education. In the present structure, students start education at six and the 3-6 age group is not covered in the current system. This system gives less importance to early childhood care education (ECCE). However, the brain development of a child happens before age 6. Hence, the new policy envisages building a robust EECE system. To strengthen the ECCE, a National Curricular and Pedagogical Framework for Early Childhood Care and Education for children up to the age of 8 will be developed by NCERT. The policy also wants to strengthen the current ECCE system by improving physical infrastructure. The policy intends to ensure that every child moves to a "preparatory class" or "Balavatika" with an ECCE-qualified teacher.

The policy envisages changes in the curricular structure from the current 10+2 to 5+3+3+4 design.

As per the new structure, there will be four stages of education

1. **Foundational stage:** This covers ages 3 to 8 of the child, and this stage has two parts, ie three years of Anganwadi or preschool and two years of primary school in classes 1 and 2. The foundational stage will have flexible, multilevel, play/activity-based learning and the curriculum and pedagogy of ECCE.
2. **Preparatory stage**: In 3 years of the preparatory phase, the student will be introduced to light textbooks with more formal but interactive classroom learning. This stage would build solid groundwork across subjects including writing, reading, speaking, arts, mathematics, science, etc.
3. **Middle stage:** The middle age education will be designed on the foundations of the preparatory phase, and specialised teachers will be introduced to explain abstract concepts in each subject. Experimental learning will be promoted, and students will be encouraged to

explore interlinkages among different subjects. More specialised subjects and teachers will be introduced at this stage.

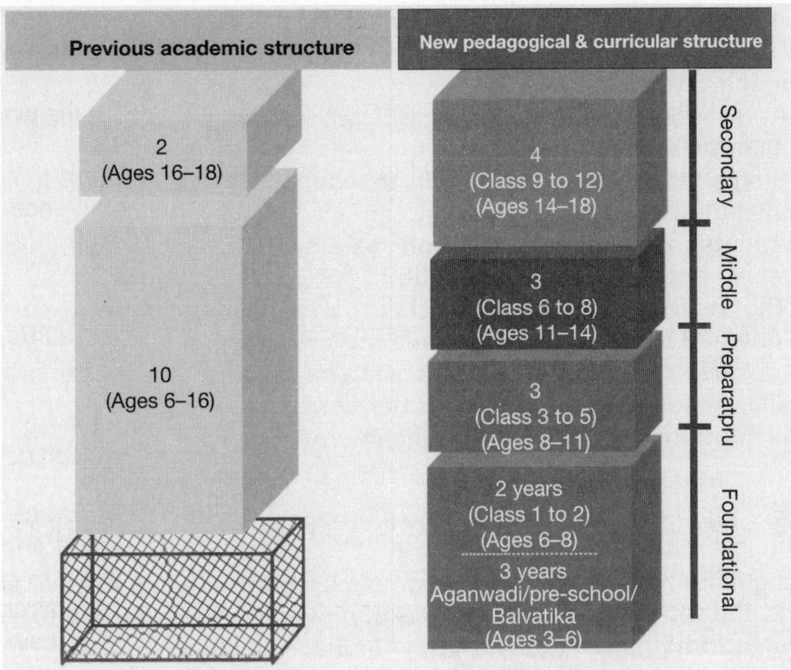

FIGURE 12.1 Current Curriculum structure and the proposed structure in

4. **Secondary stage:** The secondary stage will be multidisciplinary in nature and will be on the foundations of middle-age schooling. In this stage, the focus will be on greater critical thinking, greater attention to life aspirations, and greater flexibility and student choices. Students will have the option to exit after grade 10 and reenter classes 11 and 12 later.

4.5.4 Higher Education System

Higher education is crucial in a nation's socio-economic and political environment. Highly trained human capital produced by the higher education system is the key to achieving the economic development of a country. The higher education system should be vibrant and dynamic to create the talent required for the modem world. The NEP envisages restructuring the higher education system and suggests the following.

1. Transform higher education institutions into multidisciplinary universities, colleges, and HEI clusters/ knowledge hubs with at least 3000 students.
2. The NEP defines a university as "a multidisciplinary institution of higher learning that offers undergraduate and graduate programmes,

with high-quality teaching, research, and community engagement". The NEP envisage three types of universities/ institutions: Research intensive Universities, Teaching intensive Universities and Autonomous degree-granting colleges.

3. HEI must become multidisciplinary by 2030 and have more students in the 1000s by 2040.
4. At least one multidisciplinary HEI will be started in every district or near the district by 2030.
5. Single-stream institutions will be converted into multidisciplinary institutions.
6. An integrated higher education system will be created with professional and vocational education.
7. The present complex nomenclature of HEIs in the country, such as 'deemed to be university, 'affiliating university, 'affiliating technical university', 'unitary university, shall be replaced simply by 'university' on fulfilling the criteria as per norms.
8. Institutions need to focus on the internationalisation of education

4.5.5 Change in the Regulatory System of Education

The regulatory system in India is complex, with multiple bodies of regulations and too many concentrations of power in the hands of a few and conflicting interests. Regulatory bodies have to perform four different duties: Regulations, accreditation, funding, and academic standard setting. To ensure transparency and integrity in the system, the NEP envisages a 'light but tight' oversight and regulatory system. NEP proposes to set up the **Higher Education Commission of India (HECI)** with four verticals for regulation, accreditation, funding and academic standard setting. The following four institutions will be under the umbrella of the **Higher Education Commission of India (HECI)**

1. National Higher education regulatory council(NHERC)-a single point regulator for education except for the medical and legal education sector
2. National Accreditation Council (NAC) will supervise and oversee accrediting institutions.
3. Higher education Grant Council (HEGC)- Responsible for funding and financing of the higher education sector.
4. General Education Council(GEC)- A National Higher Education Qualification Framework (NHEQF) will be set up under GEC, and it will be in sync with National Skills Qualifications Framework (NSQF) for better integration between vocational and higher education.

National education policy 2020 is considered as a game changer in the education sector. Integration of advanced technology in the education system is crucial to make the system more dynamic and improve the outcome of education. The NEP proposes to set up the National Educational Technology Forum (NETF) to facilitate decision-making regarding the induction, deployment and use of technology.

5. INDUSTRIAL POLICY REFORMS

When India gained independence, we envisaged a socialistic development pattern with an active government role. However, following the changes in the world economy, India adopted the policy of liberalisation and privatisation in the 1990s. The primary purpose of this policy was to change the state's role by reducing the state's role in some sectors and increasing it in others. As noted by former governor of RBI Dr. C Rangarajan, "The new economic policies followed by India in the post-1991 years aim to create a 'different government' with 'more market' rather than 'less government..."(Rangarajan 2012). As part of the new economic policies, the India government introduced a new industrial Policy in 1991. The government has opened up new sectors for private participation and allowed foreign direct investment in many sectors.

The India Government announced the New Economic policies in 1991.

The Government of India announced the new industrial policy in 1991, focusing on liberalising the economy from bureaucratic hassles and integrating the economy with the world economy.

The government has made the following significant changes in its 1991 policy

Liberalisation, Privatisation and Globalisation are the basic features of the new economic policy announced in 1991.

1. **Abolition of the industrial licensing system**: Industrial licensing system was introduced as part of the planning process for efficient allocation of resources to different sectors of the economy. However, the licensing system has discouraged the private sector from investing and increased bureaucratic control over the economy. In 1991 Government of India abolished the industrial licensing system.
2. **Changing role of the public sector**: As per the industry policy resolution of 1956, 17 industries were reserved for the public sector. The Government of India has reduced this to 8 core sectors, and private participation was allowed in 9 more sectors. Later in 1993, two more sectors were opened up for private participation, and in 1998-99 another two sectors were removed from the list of reserved sectors for the public sector.
3. **Abolition of MRTP act: The** MRTP act 1969 restricted large firms from investing. These firms were allowed to invest only after getting government approval. The government has amended this act and given more freedom for firms to take investment decisions. The government amended the MRTP act in 1991, and as per the amendment, prior permission from the government is not required for firms to invest.

Recent policy changes

5.1 National Manufacturing Policy 2011

As Mihir Swarup Sharma of the Observer Research Foundation pointed out, "the objective of 1991 reform was to increase the size of the industrial sector". However, in the late 1990s and 2000, the growth of the service sector increased, and the share of Industry in GDP declined. Mr Mihir Swarup Sharma further explains that this was because of the third industrial revolution led by the information and communication technologies, which helped India to increase growth led by the service sector.

The new Manufacturing Policy aimed at increasing the share of manufacturing in India's GDP.

The manufacturing policy statement of 2011 highlighted this point. It noted that the share of manufacturing in GDP in 2010 was 16%, less than that in many Asian countries. A country with such a large population can't generate enough employment opportunities without developing the manufacturing sector. With this view, the Indian government introduced the new manufacturing Policy in 2011.

The New manufacturing Policy 2011 had the following objectives

1. To increase the share of the manufacturing sector in GDP to 25% by 2022
2. Create 100 million jobs in the manufacturing sector by 2022
3. Increase value addition in manufacturing and technological depth
4. Improve domestic competitiveness
5. Achieve inclusive growth through improving skill sets among migrant workers and urban poor.
6. Ensure sustainability of growth
   - The policy focuses on rationalisation and simplification of business operations to promote investment and employment opportunities.
   - The policy offers exit options to sick units by protecting the interest of labour
   - Incentives for technology development, including green technology
   - Creation of National Investment and Manufacturing Zones (NIMZs) to promote aggregation and cluster of industries.

5.1.1 Performance of National Manufacturing Policy 2011

Despite the constant efforts by the government to push industry-friendly policy changes, the national manufacturing Policy 2011 could not achieve its targets. Chakraborty, J., & Nagaraj, R. (2020) noted that the share of manufacturing in employment in most of the district has remained unchanged since 1991. This shows that the New manufacturing Policy has not made much progress in developing the manufacturing sector.

1) **Share of manufacturing in GDP**
   a. NMP 2011 aimed at increasing the share of manufacturing in GDP to 25% by 2022. However, the share of manufacturing declined over this period, and manufacturing contributed 15.2% of GDP.
2) **On job creation**
   a. The second objective of NMP was to create 100 million jobs by 2022. But Kujur and Goswamy(2021) noted, "The Indian manufacturing sector experienced a net job loss of 14,70,000 between 2010–11 and 2017–18. Within manufacturing, the labour-intensive industries, which were considered the potential employment generators, witnessed job destruction to 17, 31,000 and 6, 07,000, respectively".
3) **Growth of skilled workers and training institutes**
   a. However, during this period, the number of industrial training institutes has increased in India from 9,404 in 2010 to 15,154 in 2019. However, this has not resulted in a substantial increase in vocationally trained workers.

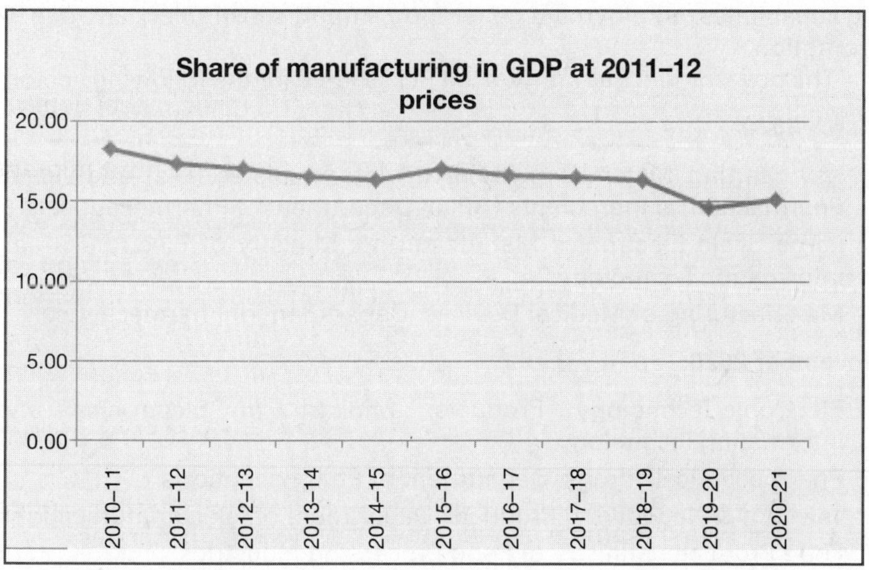

FIGURE 12.2 Share of Manufacturing in GDP(2011-12 prices)

5.2 Make in India Scheme

On 25th September 2014 Prime Minister Narendra Modi announced the NDA government's ambitious "Make in India" scheme to foster innovation, design and investment in India to make India a global manufacturing hub. The make in India project aimed at job creation and skill enhancement in 25 sectors of the economy. Later Make in India 2.0 was announced, and the government focused on 27 industries in this program. The make in India program includes steps to improve the ease of doing business, a set of campaigns in foreign countries to showcase the investment potential of India and changes in public procurement system to give preference for products manufactured in India.

5.3 Production Linked Incentive(PLI) Scheme

PLI scheme provides incentives for local manufacturing

The production Linked incentive Scheme was launched in March 2020 to attract FDI and encourage local manufacturing. As per the scheme, firms producing in India are entitled to get financial incentives from the government on their incremental sales. Both foreign and domestic firms are eligible for incentives under this scheme. Under this scheme, domestic firms can expand their production capabilities to get incremental benefits. Initially, the scheme was announced for three sectors and later extended to 13 sectors. These schemes aimed to increase manufacturing capabilities, employment generation, import substitution, and export promotion.

The government has announced PLI scheme for the following sectors

March 2020

- Key Starting Materials (KSM)/Drug Intermediates (DIs) and Active Pharmaceutical Ingredients (APIs): Department of Pharmaceuticals
- Large Scale Electronics Manufacturing: Ministry of Electronics and Information Technology
- Manufacturing of Medical Devices: Department of Pharmaceuticals

November 2020:

- Electronic/Technology Products: Ministry of Electronics and Information Technology
- Pharmaceuticals drugs: Department of Pharmaceuticals
- Telecom & Networking Products: Department of Telecommunications
- Food Products: Ministry of Food Processing Industries
- White Goods (ACs & LED): Department for Promotion of Industry and Internal Trade
- High-Efficiency Solar PV Modules: Ministry of New and Renewable Energy
- Automobiles & Auto Components: Department of Heavy Industry
- Advance Chemistry Cell (ACC) Battery: Department of Heavy Industry
- Textile Products: MMF segment and technical textiles: Ministry of Textiles
- Specialty Steel: Ministry of Steel

September 2021

- Drones and Drone Components: Ministry of Civil Aviation

PLI scheme for various sectors

Sector	Total outlay
Automobile and Auto Components sectors.	INR 25,938 cr
Drones and drone components	INR 120 cr
Chemicals	INR 18,100 Cr
Large Scale Electronics Manufacturing and	INR 40,951 cr
IT Hardware	INR 7,325 cr
Food processing	INR 10,900 cr
medical devices	18420 Cr
Metal and Mining	INR 6,322 cr
Starting Materials (KSMs)/Drug Intermediates (DIs) and Active Pharmaceutical Ingredients (APIs)	INR 6,940 crores
Pharmaceuticals d (PLI 2.0)	INR 15,000 crore
High Efficiency Solar PV Modules	INR 24,000 cr
Telecom & Networking Products sector	INR 12,195 cr
Textiles Products	INR 10,683 cr
White Goods	INR 6,238 Cr

6. REFORMS: THE WAY FORWARD

- The economic reforms initiated in 1991 have accelerated the growth of the Indian economy. India followed a holistic and gradual approach towards reforms. As observed by Ahluwalia (2016), the reform agenda was homegrown, and it was the "logical culmination of internal rethinking that started well before the 1991 crisis" (page 41).
- According to Ahluwalia, the reform process started in the 1980s as the government realised the need to promote the private sector for export growth. The government moderated the bias against the private sector in the 1980s and even flexibly implemented the MRTP act provisions. In the mid-1980s, the government started the liberalisation process at a low pace by increasing the MRTP limit from 20 crores to 100 crores, delicensed 30 industries, etc.
- The world economy is experiencing the fourth industrial revolution. However, the Indian economy consists of sectors with different characteristics. Indian economy consists of industries with features of the

first industrial revolution (small enterprises using basic technology), second industrial revolution(advanced firms in steel and automobile) and third industrial revolution(world-class information technology firms). And in some industries, firms are leading the fourth industrial revolution (Jio, etc.) Hence the future reform should energise all the four types of firms existing in the Indian economy

- Mihir Swarup Sharma suggests the following reforms.
  a. Factor markets need to be energised. Even though the government introduced the labour code, it needs more flexibility with the social security net
  b. Land reforms- allow free buy and sell of agricultural land to avoid the domination of middle man and government bureaucrats in the land market
  c. Judicial reforms are required for the proper implementation of the bankruptcy code
  d. India faces the issue of skill deficit, and skilling of labour should be a priority to reap the benefits of the 4th industrial revolution.
  e. Administrative reforms are not complete. Government need to strengthen the regulatory institutions for dispute resolution.

Montek S. Ahluwalia suggests the following reforms in the near future

> India needs to implement more structural reforms to reap the benefits of 4th industrial revolution.

a. India needs to strengthen its infrastructure; for this, we need institutional reforms to solve the problems in the PPP model. This includes creating a legal framework within which PPP projects would be attempted. Also, the government must establish a dispute resolution system relating to PPP project-related issues.
b. More investment is required in health and education, and more important is the delivery system's efficiency at the state and local levels. We need to strengthen the state-level implementation system of health and education projects through the political process.
c. Implementing GST is an essential step in the right direction but needs to fix the problems of multiple GST rates and the exclusion of certain items from GST.

Summary

- India follows a federal form of government with a Union government at the Centre and State governments. However, the federal system in India is different from the United States, where states have more power. In India, we follow a quasi-federal system where the centre has more power.
- India's administrative system is at three levels- Centre, state/UT and District administration. The President of India is the head of the Indian republic and the commander in chief of the armed forces. The Prime minister heads the Government of India and the council of ministers. India has 28 states, and each state has a state administration. Governor is the head of the state, and the chief minister is the head of the state government. The district collector heads the district administration. The district

collector oversees the functioning of various state government departments and performs the duties of the district magistrate.

- India has a well-organised civil service system, and the civil service officers are selected through a rigorous process. Civil service officers are well trained and are capable of advising political executives on various aspects of decision-making. The civil service officers also ensure that the decisions of the political executives are being implemented.
- Most developing countries like India inherited a colonial administration that needs to be reformed to create a well-developed democratic society with a responsive administrative system. The Government of India has appointed different commissions to implement administrative reforms in India. The first administrative reform commission was appointed on January 1966 under the chairmanship of Morarji Desai. The second administrative reforms commission was constituted on 31st August 2005 under the Chairmanship of former Karnataka Chief minister Veerappa Moily
- The Right to information act 2005 was a revolutionary step in the history of independent India. The RTI act aimed to empower citizens and promote transparency and accountability in governance
- After independence, the new Indian government has given much importance to reforming the education system in India. The Government of India has established several commissions and announced various policies to promote the education system in India. These include the University Education Commission(1948), secondary education commission(1952-53), Kothari Commission(1964-66), National Policy of Education (1986/92) and New Education Policy 2020.
- When India gained independence, we envisaged a socialistic development pattern with an active government role. However, following the changes in the world economy, India adopted the policy of liberalisation and privatisation in the 1990s. The primary purpose of this policy was to change the state's role by reducing the state's role in some sectors and increasing it in others.
- The Government of India has announced several steps for the development of the Industrial sectors of India. These include the New manufacturing Policy 2011, and Make in India scheme; the Production Liked Incentive scheme, etc.

Keywords		
The administrative system in India	President of India	Civil Service in India
Central Administration	Prime Minister of India	District Magistratrate
State Administration	Chief Minister of India	Administrative reforms
Central Secretariat	Cabinet Secretary	First Administrative reforms commission
State Secretariat	Chief Secretary	Second administrative reforms commission
District Administration	District collector	Education reforms
New Education Policy 2020	Industrial policy reforms	New economic policy
New manufacturing policy	Make in India scheme	PLI scheme

Questions

1. Explain the administrative system prevailing in India
2. Explain the recommendations of the second administrative reforms commission.
3. Explain the features of National Education Policy 2020
4. What are the characteristics of Economic reforms implemented in India since 1991
5. What measures were taken by India's government to develop the industrial sector?

References

Ahluwalia, M. S. (2019). India's economic reforms: Achievements and next steps. Asian Economic Policy Review, 14(1), 46-62.

GOI(2005). Guide on the Right to Information Act, 2005 - updated Version, No. 1/32/2013-IR

LOK SABHA document (2015). Response to a question on ADMINISTRATIVE REFORMS COMMISSION ON PUBLIC REFORMS, dated 18/03/2015

Malpass, David (2019). Strengthening Indian civil service towards efficient service Speech to members of India's civil service Kevadiya, Gujarat, India delivery

National Education Policy(2020). Ministry of Human Resource Development Government of India. https://www.education.gov.in, accessed on 16.12.2018

Rangarajan, C(2012). "economic Reforms do not take away the role of the state", The Hindu, OCTOBER 09, 2012

Report of second administrative commission (2009a). Organisational Structure of Government of India, 13th report.

Report of second administrative commission (2009b). STATE AND DISTRICT ADMINISTRATION, 15th report

Sharma, Mihir Swarup (2021). Completing the 1991 agenda: Reforms for the Fourth Industrial revolution, https://www.orfonline.org, accessed on 16.12.2018

THE REPORT OF THE UNIVERSITY EDUCATION COMMISSION (1949). https://www.educationforallinindia.com, accessed on 16.12.2018

Website of cabinet secretary, https://cabsec.gov.in

CHAPTER 13

Public Policy – Regulatory Reforms

1. NEED FOR REGULATIONS IN THE ECONOMY

According to the classical school of thought, the market functions efficiently and ensures consumer value. However, in practice, markets fail to ensure maximum social welfare because of the concentration of market power in the hands of a few and externalities. Hence, regulating the market participants to ensure fair practices became necessary.

The need for regulations and regulatory institutions has increased globally since the 1970s when many economies embraced neo-liberal economic policies and redefined the State's role in the economy. Countries have opened up more sectors for private participation; in many countries, several sectors were reserved for public sector enterprises. This raised the fear concentration of market power in the hands of few private players and the resultant exploitation of consumers and labour.

The early decades of 20th century saw the rising role of state globally

The early decades of the 20th century saw the rising role of the State in every sector of the economy backed by political ideologies like the communist movement, and new economic thinking started with Keynesian economics. The emergence of Marxists and socialist thought has resulted in significant government presence in the redistribution of income functions which the classical economist was not concerned with much. The classical economist was in favour of a minimalist state and focused more on the allocative function of the State. Socialistic thinking has resulted in adopting the Soviet Union model planning system in many countries, including India. This has resulted in the emergence of mixed economies where the State played a proactive role in running business enterprises, and many sectors were reserved for the public sector. In addition to socialistic thinking, Keynesian economics also supported government intervention in the economy. This has resulted in large-scale public investment in infrastructure, welfare programs and large-scale investment in the public sector to generate employment opportunities, etc.

However, this trend changed in the 1970s and 1980s, and a regulatory State in many countries replaced the interventionist state. There are several reasons for the fall of the interventionist state: Lack of accountability, politicisation of public sector enterprises, poor economic performance, rising unemployment and inflation (Mojone 1997). Public expenditure and welfare schemes were seen as a reason for poor economic performance in many countries, especially in Europe. This led to the fall of interventionist state and saw the emergence of regulatory states in Europe. Mojone (1997) observed, "Strategic adaptation to the new realities has resulted in a reduced role for the positive, interventionist state and a corresponding increase in the role of the regulatory state: rulemaking is replacing taxing and spending". The European states transformed themselves from an interventionist nature to regulatory nature in the 1970s.

1.1 Changing Role of the Indian State: from Interventionist to the Regulatory State

India followed a socialistic pattern of development after gaining independence

Soon after becoming an independent nation, the Government of India followed a socialistic path and adopted the soviet model of economic development. India adopted the economic development planning process and started the first five-year plan in 1951. According to the directive principles of state policy of the Indian constitution, "The State shall strive to promote the welfare of the people by securing and protecting as effectively as it may a social order in which justice, social, economic and political, shall inform all the institutions of the national life". Even though the Government of India is not liable to implement the directive principles, these principles are fundamental in governance in India.

The Government of India followed welfare-oriented policies since independence and developed strong presence of public sector enterprises in strategic sectors of the economy. Most strategic sectors were reserved for the public sector enterprises, and private sector participation was restricted. The MRTP act in 1969 prohibited the growth of large private enterprises. At the time of independence, India had just 5 Central Public sector enterprises, which increased to 84 in 1969, 176 in 1980 and 244 in 1990. The Government of India established many green field public sector enterprises in the 1950s and 1960s. Also, the government nationalised many private sector enterprises during the 1950s and 1960s. The Government of India nationalised Air India in 1953, which the TATA group owned. Later, the State bank of India was established after nationalising the Imperial Bank of India. Bank nationalisation took place in 1969 and 1980 under the leadership of then Prime Minister Ms Indira Gandhi. Hence, India also expanded the role of the State in the economy till the 1980s. Former RBI governor Dr Y V Reddy mentions, "This happened as a reluctant concession to realities by market economies, as a commitment to ideology by socialist systems, and as a pragmatic approach by mixed economies like ours" (Reddy 1996). However, the Indian government started implementing reform policies in the mid-1980s to change the State's role in the economy.

After independence, the Government of India has nationalized the strategic industries in India and started public sector undertakings

In 1991, the Government of India announced its reform policies based on Liberalisation, Privatisation and Globalisation. This was a historical year in independent India as it marked the starting point of making India a regulatory state from the interventionist state.

The 1991 New industrial policy opened up many of the sectors reserved for the public sector for private anticipation. Dr. Y V Reddy mentions that in the "nineties, most, if not all, economies have launched on a policy of redefining and reducing overall the role of the State vis-à-vis the market. This phenomenon signifies the new trade-off between 'State failures' and 'market failures' or what may be termed as the new realities in the relationship between the State and the market". So until the 1990s, the world was more concerned about market failure and followed interventionist state policies. From the 1990s onwards, we recognised the State failure in managing the economy and relying on the market to maximise social welfare.

India also followed this process through the 1991 reforms and opened up many sectors for private participation, which were earlier reserved for the public sector. Hence, the public sector lost its monopoly position in many sectors of the economy. "The steady displacement of public sector production by private entities in these sectors has inevitably required redefining the role of the State as a regulator to ensure competition on a level playing field" (Som and Naru 2017). Hence, from 1991 onwards Indian government created new regulatory institutions in different sectors of the economy or reformed the currently existing regulatory mechanism.

2. TYPOLOGY OF REGULATIONS IN INDIA

Regulations in India can be classified into the following types

> Regulations in India can be classified into Economic regulations and Social regulations.

2.1 Economic Regulations

According to Joskon and Rose(1989), "Economic regulation refers to the direct legislation and administrative regulation of prices and entry into specific industries or markets. It follows conventional treatment in distinguishing economic regulation from other forms of government intervention in markets, including the social regulation of environmental, health and safety practices, antitrust policy, and tax and tariff policies". Hence the main objective of economic regulation is to prevent market failure. A competitive market is the best way to protect consumer and producer interests. Economic regulations aim to preserve competitive markets and avoid market failure by regulating the market and distorting participants' behaviour.

Examples of economic regulation in India include the Competition Commission of India(CCI), SEBI, etc.

2.2 Social Regulations

Social regulations are "requirements for firms to comply with, safeguard values and rights, and address negative market externalities". These types of regulations include liability law, Labor market regulations, Bankruptcy Law, Intellectual property regulation, Product quality and safety regulation, Worker health and safety regulation, Information security regulation, and environmental regulations. India has enacted several laws to ensure labour safety, information protection and others.

2.2.1 Environmental Regulations

Economic activities cause environmental pollution and pose a severe threat to the ecology. Environmental regulations refer to restrictions on human and business activities to protect and sustain the environment. According to the UN environment report 2019, there has been 32 fold increase in environmental laws in the world since 1972. This is in response to the growing consensus on the need to protect the environment and achieve sustainable development.

The Government of India enacted the Environment Protection Act in 1986 under article 253 of the constitution. The Government of India set up National Green Tribunal (NGT) in 2010 to further strengthen India's environmental regulations.

3. MAJOR REGULATIONS AND REGULATORY BODIES IN INDIA

The following are the important regulatory bodies in India

3.1 Securities and Exchange Board of India (SEBI).

SEBI is a regulatory body for capital markets in India.

The parliament passed the Securities and Exchange Board of India Act (1992) to give statutory powers to the Securities and Exchange Board of India (SEBI), which was established in 1988 as an executive body. The SEBI act was passed to protect the interest of investors in securities and to regulate and develop the securities market in India. The SEBI board consists of Chairman, three full-time members and four part-time members. The Government of India appoints the Chairman and members of the board.

According to the SEBI act, the duty of the board is "Subject to the provisions of this Act, and it shall be the duty of the Board to protect the interests of investors in securities and to promote the development of, and to regulate the securities market, by such measures as it thinks fit"(SEBI act chapter 5)

SEBI performs the following functions

a) Regulate the stock exchanges and other financial markets in India
b) Registration and regulation of the working of stock brokers, portfolio managers, investment advisors and other intermediaries of the securities market in India

c) Registration and regulation of foreign institutional investors, depositories and securities custodians, credit rating agencies, etc.
d) Prohibition of insider trading, fraudulent and unfair trade practices in Indian securities market
e) Regulation of mutual funds, venture capital funds, take over of companies

The Government of India widened the powers of SEBI in 2014 through the Securities Laws (Amendment) Act, 2014, which provided additional powers to SEBI to present fraudulent financial schemes and establish a special fast-track court.

3.2 Companies Act 1956 and 2013

The formation, functioning, financing and dissolution of companies in India are governed by the Companies Act 1956, the new Act passed in 2013 and related amendments. The companies act 1956 was enacted on the recommendations of the Bhaba Committee, which was constituted in 1950. The companies act 1956 repealed the Companies Act 1913 and provided a new basis for corporate sector operations in India. The companies act 1956 allowed the registration of companies under 11 categories. As per the 1956 act, the wind-up of companies is under high courts' jurisdiction.

In response to changing realities of the global economic environment, the Government of India has amended the companies act several times. Significant amendments happened in 1988(based on the Sachar committee), 1998, 2000 and 2002. The Government of India has constituted the JJ Irani committee to review the company law in India. Based on this report, the parliament has repealed the Companies Act 1956 with the Companies Act 2013.

The Companies Act (2013) has replaced the Companies Act(1956).

Features of Companies Act 2013

a) **Corporate Social Responsibility:** Companies with more than Rs.50 million net profit or Rs.10 billion turnover or 5 billion net worth have to spend 2% of the last three years net profit on corporate social responsibility.
b) **National Company Law Tribunal (NCLT):** National Company Law Tribunal (NCLT) was constituted in 2016 as a quasi-judicial body to deal with corporate disputes arising under the Companies Act with civil nature. Initially, 11 branches were set up in various cities; currently, NCLT has 16 branches. The NCLT considers matters related to merger approval, corporate reorganisation, capital reduction, etc.

NCLT is a quasi-judicial body to deal with corporate disputes with civil nature.

c) **National Financial Reporting Authority (NFRA):** As per the Companies Act(2013), NFRA was constituted in 2018 to recommend accounting and auditing policies and standards adopted by companies and as an authority to monitor and enforce compliance with accounting standards.
d) As per the 2013 Act, a private company can have 200 members.
e) Uniform financial year for all companies ending 31st March.

f) Introduction of One Person Company(OPC)
g) Allowed merger of Indian companies with foreign companies if RBI approves

The Companies Act(2013) was amended in 2015, 2017, 2019 and 2020.

3.3 Competition Commission of India(CCI)

CCI is created as regulatory body for promoting competition and to protect the interests of consumers.

The Government of India established the competition commission of India(CCI) in October 2003. The competition Commission of India (CCI) was proposed in the competition act 2002 "as a commission to

- prevent activities harming competition,
- to promote and sustain competition in the markets,
- to protect the interest of the consumers, and
- to ensure freedom of trade carried on by other participants in the markets, in India and,

for matters connected therewith or incidental thereto" (Competition Act 2002). The competition commission has seven members, including the Chairman appointed by the Government of India.

3.4 Telecom Regulatory Authority of India (TRAI)

TRAI is the regulatory body for telecom sector in India.

The Government of India enjoyed monopoly in the telecom sector till mid-nineties with three State-owned service providers- the Department of telecommunications, MTNL (Mahanagar Telephone Nigam Limited) and Videsh Sanchar Nigam Ltd. (VSNL). The telecom sector in India undergone significant reforms in the 1990s with the announcement of the National telecom policy in 1994 and the NewTelecom Policy in 1999. With these reforms, private sector participation allowed in providing telecom services in India and the Government of India established a regulatory body for the telecom sector in 1997 with an act of parliament called Telecom Regulatory Authority of India Act 1997.

Some of the objectives of TRAI include

a) Ensure a fair and transparent policy environment for creating a level playing field in the Indian telecom sector
b) Protect the interest of consumers
c) Monitoring of quality of service(QoS) offered by various service providers
d) Increase tale-density and ensure access to telecom services at affordable prices
e) Migration to digital addressable systems in broadcasting.
f) Re-balancing ofTariffs to meet the dual objectives of affordability and operator viability

3.5 IRDA (Insurance Regulatory and Development Authority)

IRDA was established in 2000 as a regulatory body for India's insurance and re-insurance sector through the IRDA act 1999. The insurance sector in India was reopened for private participation in the 1990s ending the decades-old monopoly of public sector enterprises. The life insurance sector was a monopoly for The Life Insurance Corporation (LIC) since its incorporation in 1956. LIC enjoyed the monopoly status in the industry till the 1990s, when the Government of India decided to reopen the sector for private participation.

IRDA was established in 2000 as a regulatory body for insurance and reinsurance sector.

Duties, Powers and Functions of Authority

Section 14 of the IRDA act (1999) specifies the following as the primary duties, powers and functions of IRDA. IRDA act mentioned that "the Authority shall have the duty to regulate, promote and ensure orderly growth of the insurance and re-insurance business." (IRDA Act 1999)

Powers and functions of the authority include

a) protect the interest of policy holders regarding assigning of policy, claim settlement, insurable interest, etc.
b) Issue of registration, re-registration, renew, cancel or modify, withdraw, suspend or cancel such registration
c) specifying requisite qualifications, code of conduct and practical training for intermediary or insurance intermediaries and agents
d) Specify required qualifications and code of conduct for intermediaries and agents.
e) Training of intermediaries and agents
f) Promoting efficiency in the insurance sector

3.6 Insolvency and Bankruptcy (IBC) Code, 2016

Insolvency and Bankruptcy Code, 2016 (Code) is a much-awaited reform in India. The IBC code aimed to protect both creditors' and shareholders' interests and ensure the timely reorganisation of insolvent firms. The IBC intended to provide time-bound resolution of insolvency and solve the banking system's fundamental debt problems.

IBC (2016) ensures timely resolution for insolvency

The primary objective of IBC is "to consolidate and amend the laws relating to reorganisation and insolvency resolution of corporate persons, partnership firms and individuals in a time bound manner for maximisation of value of assets of such persons, to promote entrepreneurship, availability of credit and balance the interests of all the stakeholders including alteration in the order of priority of payment of Government dues and to establish an Insolvency and Bankruptcy Board of India, and for matters connected therewith or incidental thereto" (IBC Act 2016)

As per the Act, the insolvency procedure has to be completed within 180 days; for small companies, it should be completed within 90 days. This can be extended if the creditors have no objection. The IBC can be applied if the default amount is more than one crore rupee. Both financial and operational creditors can file an application for the Corporate Insolvency Resolution Process (CIRP) or liquidation of the corporate debtor under the IBC. The Corporate Insolvency Resolution Process (CIRP) includes steps to revive the insolvent company by raising funds or finding a buyer to take over the company. If the CIRP fails, the company will be liquidated to recover the creditor's money.

According to the IBC code, the following is the insolvency procedure in India

a) **Stage 1-Approaching NCLT for CIRP**: The financial creditor, operational creditor or corporate debtor approaches the NCLT for the CIRP process if the debtor is a company. Once the NCLT gets an application for CIRP, it has to call both parties for a hearing within 14 days.
b) **Appointment of IRP by NCLT**: Once the NCLT finds merits in the application for CIRP, the NCLT will appoint an interim resolution personal (IRP). Once the insolvency commences, the powers of the board of corporate debtor are suspended and the powers exercised by the IRP and later resolution professional. The IRP would constitute a committee of creditors (CoC), and the committee of creditors appoints the Resolution Professional in its first meeting. The Committee of Creditors consists of all financial creditors and operational creditors.
c) **Moratorium**: The moratorium period will continue until the CIRP process ends within 180 days, and the NCLT can extend it by another 90 days. The moratorium ensures that the debtor is not burdened with additional stress and gets protection from all suits, legal proceedings, and recovery actions.
d) **Resolution plan**: The IRP or RP would verify the creditors' claims and announce to the public that the corporate debtor is undergoing the CIRP process. Also, the IRP would invite a resolution plan from all stakeholders. Once the RP gets resolution plans, it evaluates these plans and submits them before the CoC for consideration.
e) **The decision of the NCLT**: The NCLT can reject or accept the resolution plan submitted by the CoC. If the NCLT approves the plan, the same is binding to all stakeholders. However, the company will undergo a liquidation process if the NCLT does not accept the plan.
f) **Liquidation**: Liquidation is defined "as a process by which the life of a company is brought to an end in legal terms, after which it will be properly administered by a liquidator for the benefit of its creditors, members, and other stakeholders"(IBBI 2020)

Flow chart of the CIRP Process in India

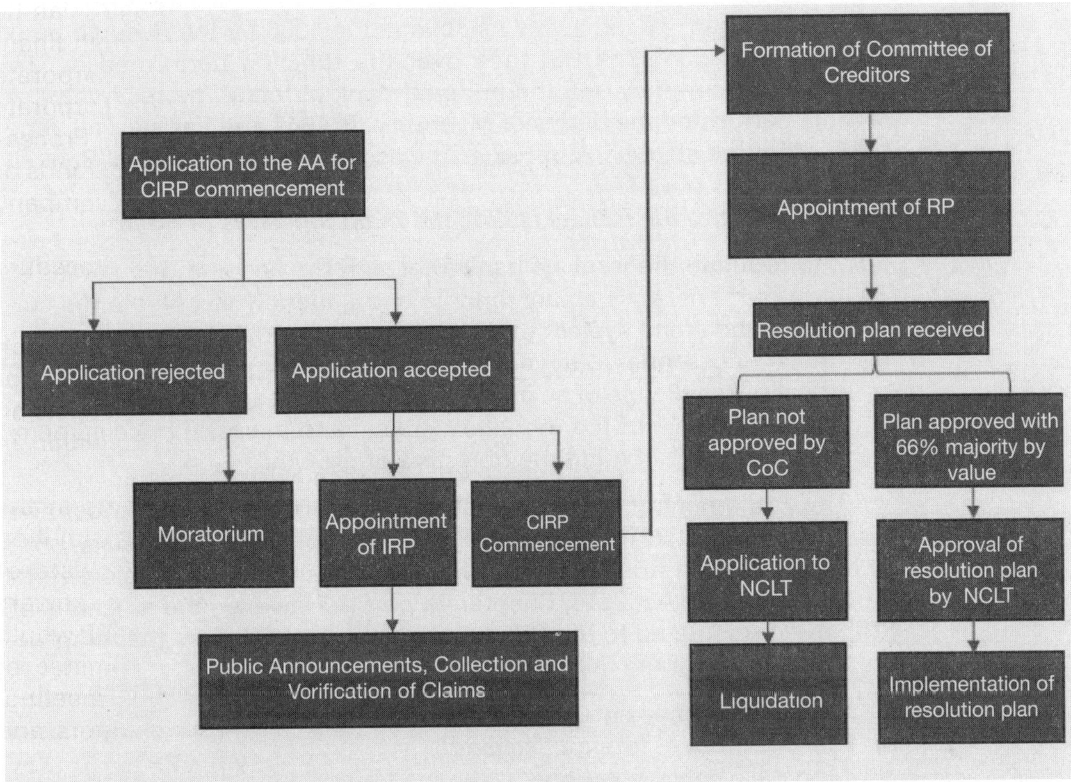

3.7 Insolvency and Bankruptcy Board of India (IBBI)

IBBI oversees the insolvency procedure in India

The IBBI was established in 2016 under section 188 of the Insolvency and Bankruptcy Act 2016 as a corporate body regulating insolvency professionals and transactions conducted. It is headquartered in New Delhi and consists of Chairman, three central government officers representing Ministries of Finance, Corporate Affairs, and Law, ex-officio, one member nominated by RBI and five other members appointed by the central government. Among these, three are full-time members. Section 196 of the IBC mentions the following as the powers and functions of IBBI;

a) Act as a regulator for the market process and practices related to CIRP, liquidation, and individual insolvency and bankruptcy.
b) As a regulator in charge of registration and regulation of service providers in the insolvency process in India
c) enforcement of rules for service providers and adjudication
d) professional development of expertise of service provider
e) professional development of expertise of service provider

3.8 Reserve Bank of India (RBI)

As a central bank of India RBI oversees the banking operations in India

The reserve bank of India was established in 1935 by the Reserve bank of India Act (1934). The RBI took over the function performed by the Controller of currency and the imperial bank of India. The reserve bank of India performed the duties of Myanmar till 1947 and Pakistan till June 1948, when the state bank of Pakistan was constituted as central Bank of Pakistan.

According to the RBI act (1934), the main functions of RBI are;

(i) "to regulate the issue of banknotes and the keeping of reserves to secure monetary stability in India and generally to operate the currency and credit system of the country to its advantage, and

(ii) that it is essential to have a modern monetary policy framework to meet the challenge of an increasingly complex economy and the primary objective of the monetary policy is to maintain price stability while keeping in mind the objective of growth."

The Parliament of India has amended the RBI act (1934) through the India Finance Act(2016) and added that the objective f monetary policy is "to maintain price stability while keeping in mind the objective of growth" (Finance Act 2016, Chapter VII part I). However, the functions of RBI are not restricted to the RBI act and various other Acts that empowers RBI to perform the following functions.

a) Issue of currency notes in the country-
b) Management of foreign exchange
c) Monetary Policy functions
d) Public Debt functions
e) Regulation and Supervision of NBFCs
f) Regulation & Supervision of Co-operative banks
g) Regulation of Derivatives and Money Market Instruments
h) Payment and Settlement Functions
i) Consumer Protection and promotion Functions

MPC formulates monetary policy in India since 2016.

Monetary policy Committee (MPC): A significant reform in the monetary policy framework: According to the India Finance Act (2016), the parliament has constituted the Monetary Policy Committee (MPC) to formulate the monetary policy. As per this amendment, RBI follows an inflation targeting policy and the inflation target is set by the Government of India in consultation with RBI. It will be revised every five years.

The monetary policy committee will have six members given as follows;

a) RBI governor –Chairman of the committee
b) Deputy Governor in charge of the monetary policy
c) One officer of the board to be nominated by the central board
d) Three members nominated by the central government

The constitution of MPC aims to introduce a modern monetary policy framework followed internationally and to ensure transparency in bank's decision-making. The MPC has to meet at least four times a year, and RBI has to publish the minutes of the monetary policy committee meeting. RBI is liable to provide all relevant information to the committee members for achieving the inflation targeting. If the bank fails to reach the inflation target, it has to submit a report to the central government explaining the reason for failure, remedial measures and the time frame to achieve the target.

3.9 National Green Tribunal (NGT)

The National Green Tribunal was established in 2010 under the National Green Tribunal (NGT) Act(2010) to dispose of cases related to environmental protection and conservation of forests and natural resources. The NGT act says that "effective and expeditious disposal of cases relating to environmental protection and conservation of forests and other natural resources including enforcement of any legal right relating to the environment and giving relief and compensation for damages to persons and property and matters connected therewith or incidental thereto"(GOI 2010).

NGT deals with all civil cases with substantial questions related to environmental issues involved.

1. **Jurisdiction and powers of the NGT**
 Jurisdiction: the NGT can consider all civil cases where substantial questions related to environmental issues are involved

2. **Powers of the tribunal:**

a) The tribunal can issue orders about compensation and relief to the victims of pollution and other environmental damage
b) It can issue orders related to the restitution of property damaged and restitution of the environment in such areas.
c) The tribunal approves or disapproves environmental clearance for industries.

3.10 Real Estate Regulatory Authority (RERA)

The Real estate Regulatory Authority (RERA) is established underThe Real Estate (Regulation and Development) Act, 2016, as a regulatory body for the real estate sector to ensure transparency in real estate transactions and protect the consumers' interests. As per the Act, state governments must issue notification for establishing RERA within one year.

The RERA act mentions the objective of establishing RERA as "regulation and promotion of the real estate sector and to ensure the sale of plot, apartment or building, as the case may be, or sale of real estate project, efficiently and transparently and to protect the interest of consumers in the real estate sector and to establish an adjudicating mechanism for speedy dispute redressal and also to establish the Appellate Tribunal to hear appeals from the decisions, directions or orders of the Real Estate Regulatory Authority and the adjudicating officer and for matters connected therewith or incidental thereto" (RERA Act 2016)

RERA was established to ensure transparancy and growth in real estate sector.

The following are the RERA compliance for builders under the Act;

1. Registration of the project with RERA is mandatory, and create a webpage in authority explaining details of the project
2. While giving advertisements and doing other promotional activities, the webpage of the authority and details given should be mentioned
3. While issuing the allotment letter or time of booking, the promoter has to say the approved plan and timeline for project completion.
4. The promoter is not allowed to take advance payment before agreeing to the sale
5. The promoter has to complete the project as per the approved plan

Rights and duties of the allottees

1. They are entitled to get all information related to sanctioned plan by the competent authority, layout plans and any other information provided in the Act or sale agreement.
2. Entitled to know the progress in stage-wise completion of projects
3. Allottee is entitled to get a refund in case of non-completion of the project within the stipulated time.

Other regulatory bodies operating in India

Regulatory Body/ Act	Areas
FEMA(foreign Exchange Management Act) (1999)	Foreign exchange dealings
Electricity Regulatory Commissions (ERC's) in center and states	Power sector
The Petroleum & Natural Gas Regulatory Board (PNGRB)	Oil and Natural Gas
Tariff authority for Major Ports (TAMP),	Ports
Director general of Civil Aviation(DGCA) and Airport Authority of India(AAI)	Airports
UGC, AICTE, Indian medical Council	Higher education
Pension Fund Regulatory and Development Authority (PFRDA)	Pension schemes like national Pension Scheme and Atal Pension Yojana
FSSAI(Food safety and standard authority of India)	Food safety and public health
Bureau of Indian Standards(BIS)	Standards and certification

4. JUDICIAL REFORMS IN INDIA

India has an independent and reliable judicial system. Judicial independence means the legislature and executive organs of the government are not interfering in the functions of the Judiciary. In India, the constitution ensures Judicial independence, which is the strength of Indian democracy. The judicial system in India safeguards the constitution, interprets the law, safeguards citizen's fundamental rights, and resolves disputes between citizens, between states and between centre and states. India has a unified judicial system, and the Supreme Court of India is the Apex court of India. Even though the Judicial system in India is independent and reliable, it suffers from a few drawbacks.

India has an independent and reliable Judicial system

a) The considerable number of pending cases
b) Long time for trials
c) Lack of transparency in the appointment of Judges

Figures 1, 2 and 3 show the number of cases pending in India's Supreme Court, High Courts and Subordinate courts. In 2021 almost 70 thousand cases were pending in Supreme Court against 55 thousand cases in 2010. The number of pending cases in High Courts was 42 lakh in 2010 and 56 lakh in 2021. Almost four crore cases are pending in subordinate courts in 2021 against 2.8 crore cases in 2010.

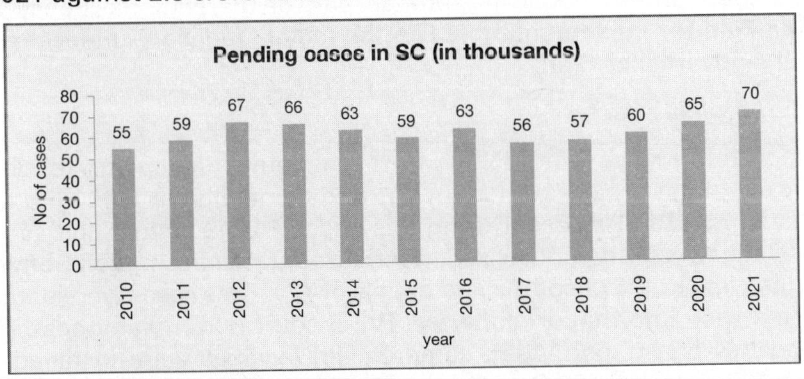

FIGURE 13.1 Pending cases in Supreme Court.

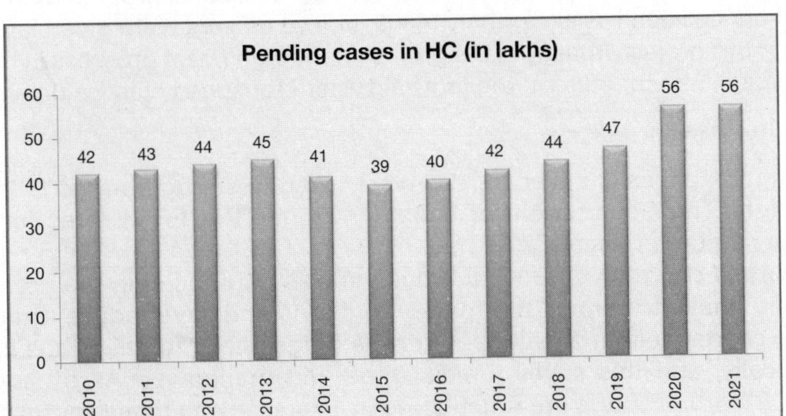

FIGURE 13.2 Pending cases in High Court

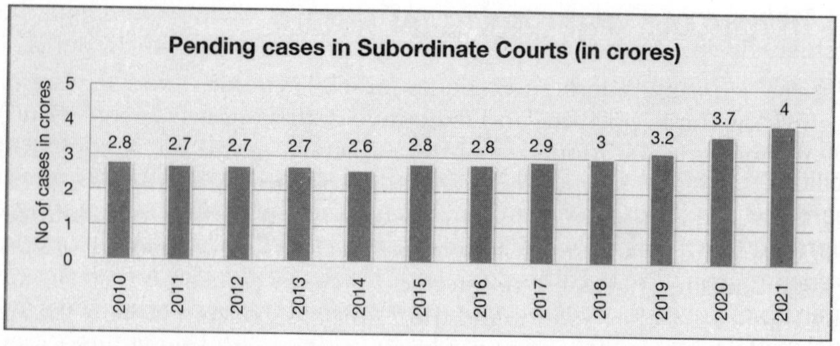

FIGURE 13.3 Pending cases in Subordinate courts.

The Government of India and the Supreme Court has taken many reform measures to ensure timely delivery of Justices and improve accountability and transparency in the judicial system. The Supreme court has approved the implementation of the E-Court project in India to integrate ICT into the function of the Judiciary.

4.1 E-Court Project

E-Court project is part of National e-governance plan.

The E-court project began in 2007 as part of the National Policy and Action Plan for Implementing ICT in the Indian Judiciary under the national e-governance plan.

E-court project phase I:

National Informatics Centre(NIC) was the implementing agency for phase I. Phase I of the project started in 2011 and completed in 2015 with total outlay of Rs.639.41 crores. During this phase 14,249 district and sub-ordinate courts were computerised. Centralized Case Information Software was installed in 13672 courts, and details of 7.2 crores cases were entered into the case information software. The E-court portal was operational during this phase, and Video conferencing facilities were installed between 347 Jails and 493 Courts.

National Judicial Data Guild (NJDG) was started to provide details of pending/ decided cases. Further, 14309 judicial officers were given laptops during this project. Phase I of the project made significant progress in building digital infrastructure in the judicial system for speedy justice delivery.

E-court Phase II:

During the phase II, several steps were taken to strengthen the IT infrastructure. The Government of India sanctioned Rs. 1670 crores for the Phase II of the project in 2015.

Virtual courts: A virtual court system was introduced in the project's second phase to reduce the footfall in courts and save judges' time. In these courts, neither the litigant nor the judges need to attend the court physically, and this saves judicial time and manpower. As of August 2022, 21 virtual courts are functioning in 17 states, and these courts have handled 1.79 crores.

Mobile apps: During phase II two mobile apps were launched- JustIS exclusively for judicial officers and e-Courts Services- for litigants, lawyers and judges.

Installation ofVideo conferencing facilities in more courts: During the second phase, 3240 courts and 1272 jails are equipped with Video conferencing facilities. Since the COVID-19 lockdown started, 2.19 crore cases have been heard in India through Video conferencing in the district and high courts. Supreme Court heard 2, 61,338 hearings till 13.06.2022 through Video conferencing. Hon'ble Supreme Court of India gave an order on 6th April 2020 regarding the hearing of cases through Video conferencing, which provided legal sanctity and validity to court hearings through Video conferencing.

Live Streaming of Court proceedings: Live streaming of court procedures started in Gujarat, Orissa, Karnataka, Jharkhand, Patna and Madhya Pradesh. This ensures more transparency in the working of the Judiciary. In 2018, the Supreme court allowed live streaming of constitutional cases and cases of national importance. In July 2021, the Gujarat High court became the first court in the country to live stream proceedings.

E-Court Phase III:

The E-committee of the Supreme Court has released a vision document for phase III of the E-court project. Phase III will be based on the following building blocks.

a) a set of core values,
b) a whole-of-system approach,
c) a focus on the adoption of technology by users, and
d) a robust governance framework.

4.2 National Judicial Appointments Commission (NJAC) Bill 2014

Article 124 of the constitution deals with the appointment and removal of Supreme Court judges, and article 217 deals with the selection of high court judges. A "collegium system appoints the high court and Supreme Court judges" in India. The "collegium" consist of the Chief Justice of India and four senior judges of the Supreme Court. Hence, many Jurists have criticised the "Judges appoint Judges System" practised in India.

The parliament of India passed the National Judicial Appointments Commission (NJAC) bill 2014, the 99th constitutional amendment Bill, to constitute National Judicial Appointment Commission for appointing judges in the high court and Supreme Court. As per the NJAC Act 2014, judges will be selected by a commission consisting of the Judiciary, legislature and Civil society members. The NJAC would have five members.

> The parliament of India passed the NJAC bill in 2014 to replace the collegiums system of Judicial appointments in India

> In 2015, the Supreme court declared that the NJAC bill is unconstitutional

- Chief Justice of India as Chairman
- Two senior Judges of the Supreme Court
- Union Law Minister
- Three members of the civil society nominated by a committee consisting of the Prime Minister of India, the Leader of the opposition and the CJI.

However, the Supreme Court declared the National Judicial Appointments Commission (NJAC) bill 2014 unconstitutional in 2015. The Supreme Court observed that NJAC Act interferes with the independence of the Judiciary, which is the base of the constitution.

Some of the proposed reforms are as follows

4.3 National Judicial Infrastructure Corporation (NJIC)

Former CJI NV Ramana proposed to constitute National Judicial Infrastructure Corporation (NJIC) to ensure infrastructure in trial courts. According to a survey conducted by the office of CJI, many of the trial court premises lack basic infrastructure facilities, and 620 court complexes operate from rented buildings. There are 24,280 judicial officers in trial court, but only 20,143 court halls are available. Hence, there is a need to improve the infrastructure facilities in trial courts. NJIC's role would be confined to infrastructure development, and it won't involve appointing judges or other functions.

4.4 Regarding the Post-Retirement Appointment of Judges

After retirement, judges are appointed by the government to various committees and other important offices. Many legal experts have questioned this on the grounds of judicial independence. Hence, many legal experts favour restricting post-retirement appointments for judges. Justice Yatindra Singh, former Chief Justice of Chhattisgarh High Court, says that "If due to age, a person is not suitable to continue as a judge, and then it is not understandable, how is he suitable for another post"

5. POLICE REFORMS

Law and order is a state subject in India and each states has their own police forces.

In India, police and public order are part of the state list in the constitution and come under the state government. Each state government has their police forces, and crime prevention, detection, investigation and prosecution are functions of the state government. However, the central government gives intelligence and other support to state governments in maintaining law and order in the country.

5.1 Various Commissions Constituted for Police Reforms

1. **National Police Commission (NPC) 1977:** NPC has submitted eight reports, and significant recommendations of the commission are the amendment of the Code of Criminal procedure 1973, revision

of syllabus for IPS probationers trainees, and a new bill for regulation of private security agencies have been implemented by the government.

2. **Ribero Committee(1998):** Ribero Committee was appointed under the directions of the Supreme Court to examine the progress in implementing NPC recommendations. This committee has endorsed the recommendations of NPC.
3. **Padmanabhaiah Committee(2000):** The Ministry of Home Affairs document says that 154 recommendations of the committee can be implemented without structural changes.
4. **Malimath Committee on Reforms in the Criminal Justice System (2000):** This committee was under the chairmanship of f Dr. (Justice) V.S. Malimath, former chief justice of Kerala and Karnataka High court. This committee has given 158 recommendations, including setting up a State security commission(SSC), separation of investigation and law and order wing in police, etc.
5. **MHA(Ministry Of Home Affairs) committee:** The MHA constituted a committee to review the recommendations of various police reform committees and identified 49 recommendations crucial for creating a professional and service-oriented police force in the country. The MHA has sent these recommendations to state governments for action.

5.2 Supreme Court Directions on Police Reforms in India and its Implementation

In 2006, in the Prakash Singh case, the Supreme Court of India asked the state governments to implement reforms in police. SC has asked the state governments to implement six reforms in state police forces. The following are the directions for SC.

> In 2006, the Supreme Court of India has asked the States to implement reforms in state police forces.

a) **Constitution of State Security Commission(SSC) in all states:** This is to reduce the undue influence of political "supervision" and "control" over the police forces. The State security commission would consist of the minister in charge of the home, the Leader of the opposition, other elected representatives, experts, and credible members of civil society. The SSC is supposed to prepare policing policy, performance criteria of police personnel and evaluate the performance.

b) **Selection and Security of Tenure for the DGP**: The chief minister of the State would choose an officer for the post of DGP from a list of three senior-most officers prepared by the Union Public Service Commission. This is to ensure certainty in position and tenure.

c) **Minimum tenure for officers**: The SC directs the State to ensure that officers (from the SHO level) get a minimum tenure of two years to avoid unnecessary transfers and punishments.

d) **Separation of Investigation and Law and Order wings within Police:** There should be two wings within state police- one for investigation and the second for law and order. This would help in the specialisation of skills, and further, the court directs that there should be proper coordination between these two wings.

e) **Police Establishment Board**: A police establishment board should be set up in every State to decide the transfer, promotion and other service matters of officers. The board consists of DGP and senior officers.

f) **Police Complaints Authority:** The police complaint authority should be established at the state and district levels to investigate complaints against police officers.

5.3 Progress of Implementation of SC Recommendations

Recently, Commonwealth Human Right Initiative released a study on state government compliance with the Supreme Court directions on police reforms (CHRI 2021). The following are the findings of the survey regarding the compliance with the SC directions

a) **Constitution of State Security Commission(SSC):** 27 state governments have constituted the state security commission. However, only 20 states have included the opposition leader in the SSC. So no state is fully complying with the recommendations regarding the composition of SSC.

b) Only five states have implemented the directions regarding the appointment of DGP in the State.

c) 17 states have implemented the direction of 2 years minimum tenure for officers, and seven states are Compliant with it completely

d) **Regarding the separation of investigation and law and order wing**: Only 16 states have taken measures to separate investigation and law and order wing within the police. Twelve states have not done anything about the separation of duties. Mizoram has implemented it as per Mizoram police Act 2012

e) **Police establishment board:** 25 states have constituted the police establishment board. But only in 14 states, this board gives recommendations regarding transfer and promotion.

f) 12 states have constituted state police complaint authority, and only six have constituted the district-level Police Complaint authority.

5.4 Model Police Act (2006)

The Union government has prepared the model Police Act (2006) to replace the Police Act 1861. The police forces in various Indian states were structured according to the Police Act (1861). The model police Act (2006) is broader in scope, and MHA has requested all state governments to take necessary action on Model Police Act (2006).

Current status of Police Acts/Amendments in Various states and UTs

	States	Police Act/Amendments passed after SC Judgment-2006 and Model Police Act(2006)
1	Assam	**Assam Police Act 2007**
2	Andhra Pradesh	**Andhra Pradesh Police Reforms (Amendment) Act 2014**
3	Bihar	**Bihar Police Act 2007**
4	Chhattisgarh	**Chhattisgarh Police Act 2007**
5	Gujarat	**Bombay Police (Gujarat Amendment) Act 2007**
6	Haryana	**Haryana Police Act 2007; Haryana Police (Amendment) Act 2014**
7	Himachal Pradesh	**Himachal Pradesh Police Act 2007**
8	Karnataka	**Karnataka Police (Amendment) Act 2012**
9	Kerala	**Kerala Police Act 2011**
10	Maharashtra	**Maharashtra Police (Amendment and Continuance) Act 2014**
11	Meghalaya	**Meghalaya Police Act 2011**
12	Mizoram	**Mizoram Police Act 2011**
13	Punjab	**Punjab Police Act 2007**
14	Rajasthan	**Rajasthan Police Act 2007**
15	Sikkim	**Sikkim Police Act 2007**
16	Tamil Nadu	**Tamil Nadu Police (Reforms) Act 2013**
17	Tripura	**Tripura Police Act 2007**
18	Uttarakhand	**Uttarakhand Police Act 2007; Uttarakhand Police (Amendment) Act 2018**
19	Arunachal Pradesh	**Police bill drafted but not tabled in the legislature**
20	Goa	**Goa Police Bill 2008 introduced in state legislature, and referred to a Select Committee for review. This Bill lapsed in 2012. The state government is reportedly drafting a revised Police Bill.**
21	Jammu and Kashmir	**Jammu and Kashmir Draft Police Bill 2013, made public for feedback but no progress since then.**
22	Odisha	**Odisha Police Bill 2015 passed by state assembly, sent to Governor for approval but returned back to assembly with comments.**
23	West Bengal	**Police Bill drafted in 2007 but not tabled. No progress since.**
In Jharkhand, Madhya Pradesh, Manipur, Nagaland, Uttar Pradesh and the newest State of Telangana, efforts have been made to draft Police Bills which to date have not moved further.		
		Union territories
1	Chandigarh	**Adopted the Punjab Police Act 2007 in 2010**
2	Delhi	**Police Bill drafted in 2010-11 but no progress made. Delhi Police Act 1978 in force.**
Other UTs–Daman and Diu, Lakshadweep, Andaman and Nicobar Islands, Dadra and Nagar Haveli, and Puducherry–continue to be governed by the Police Act of 1861.		

Source: adapted from the government compliance with Supreme Court directives on police reforms: An Assessment, prepared by The Commonwealth Human Rights Initiative (CHRI)

6. REFORMS FOR EASE OF DOING BUSINESS

In 2014, India ranked 142 in Ease of doing business, and in 2020, the latest ranking India's rank was 63, a significant 79 rank improvement.

The World Bank discontinued the Ease of doing business ranking in 2021 due to internal irregularities.

In 2014, India ranked 142 in Ease of doing business, and in 2020 India's rank was 63, a significant 79 rank improvement. However, the World Bank discontinued the Ease of doing business ranking in 2021 due to internal irregularities.

The Department for Promotion of Industry and Internal Trade (DPIIT) of the Government of India is publishing monthly newsletters and other reports on the business climate in the country. The Worldbank Ease of Doing Business ranking was based on ten parameters: Starting a Business, Registering Property, Dealing with Construction Permits, Getting Electricity, Getting Credit, Paying Taxes, Trading Across Borders, Protecting Minority Investors, Enforcing Contracts and Resolving insolvency.

Some of the important steps taken by the Government of India in improving the Ease of doing business are as follows.

6.1 Starting a Business

The government has simplified the business procedure by introducing new registration forms- SPICe+ and AGILE PRO forms. This has reduced the length of documents for company incorporation and simplified the procedure. Further, the introduction of GST replacing VAT reduced the time for completing procedure from 7-10 days to 3 days in Mumbai and Delhi.

6.2 Getting Credit

The government established the Central Registry of Securitisation Asset Reconstruction and Security Interest of India (CERSAI) in 2011 to provide a geographically unified electronic registry for all registration types. The CERSAI allows the registration of securities interest created on all types of companies. This is considered under the "strength of the legal rights index" of the ease-of-doing business of the World Bank.

6.3 Paying Taxes

The following measures were taken to decrease the effective 'total tax and contribution rate' calculated as a profit percentage.

a) Corporate taxes reduced from 30% to 25% for midsized companies
b) Effective from July 2017 Good and Service(GST) law subsumed and replaced 12 different types of indirect taxes. This has reduced the mandatory payments to 10 from 13
c) GST law allows input tax credit, reducing the effective "Tax and contribution rate."

d) Introduction of Electronic facilities for GST payment reduced the time required for preparation, filing and payment of taxes from 105 hours to 36 hours annually.
e) By using modern technology, the income tax department has reduced the time taken for tax filing

6.4 Resolving Insolvency

The IBC Act (2016) ensures the Corporate Insolvency Resolution Process ('CIRP') for insolvent companies in a time-bound manner. This has simplified the insolvency procedure and improved the recovery rate.

6.5 Construction Permit

Online Building Permission System (OBPS) introduced and simplified the procedure for NOCs from DPCC, Fire and Director of Factories. The OBPS would forward the NOCs to DPCC, Fire and the Director of Factories. This and other related procedural changes reduced the time for completing the procedure no one from 47 days to 15 days.

6.6 Electricity Connection

Various state governments and power companies have simplified the procedure for getting the electricity connection, which has reduced the time taken to get electricity connections for firms.

6.7 Registering Property

The government has released a model sales deed in editable format. Citizens can use for preparing documents for property registration. This reduces dependence on middle man, document writers, and other technical experts. This has simplified the procedure for property registration and reduced the deed preparation cost to zero from 1%.

6.8 Enforcing Contracts

a) A new Case Management System was introduced in Delhi and Mumbai district courts and High courts, and cases are assigned to judges randomly using the software.
b) Electronic cases filing was introduced in district courts
c) E-court program of the government aimed at improving the Judiciary's functioning and ensuring speedy justice.

6.9 Trading Across Borders

a) Traders can file trade documents online at a single point using India Customs Electronic Gateway (ICEGATE)

b) Central Board of Indirect Taxes and Customs allowed advance Bill of entry(Advanced imports declaration)

c) e-SANCHIT- a platform for exporters and importers to submit clearing documents online at a single point.

All these reforms have reduced the number of documents, time documentary compliance, and the cost of imports and exports.

6.10 Business Reform Action Plan (BRAP)

The Department for Promotion of Industry and Internal Trade (DPIIT) started Business Reform Action Plan (BRAP) in 2014 to engage State and Union Territories in improving the business climate. This program encourages states and UTs to improve the business climate and promote "competitive federalism". In 2020, the DPIIT has identified 15 reform areas and 301 sub-reform points.

6.11 Start-Up Ranking of States

India is the third largest start-up ecosystem in the world. To further improve the start-up ecosystem in the country, the Government of India started the start-up ranking of states in 2018. The State's start-up ranking 2021 considered the following reform areas; **Institutional Support,** Fostering Innovation and Entrepreneurship, Access to Market, Incubation Support, Funding Support, Mentorship Support, and Capacity Building of Enablers. The 2021 ranking categorises states into Best performers, Top performers, leaders, aspiring leaders and emerging start eco ecosystem.

State start-up ranking 2021

Category	States
Best Performers	**Gujarat, Karnataka and Meghalaya**
Top performers	**Kerala, Maharashtra, Odisha, Telengana and Jammu and Kashmir**
Leaders-	Utharakhand, Assam, Tamil Nadu, Uttar Pradesh, Andaman and Nicobar Islands, Arunachal Pradesh, Punjab and Goa
Aspiring leaders-	Madhya Pradesh, Delhi, Chandigarh, Nagaland, Dadra and Nager Haveli and Daman and Diu
Emerging start up ecosystems-	Bihar, Andra Pradesh, Mizoram, Ladakh

Credit: ImageFlow / Shutterstock

FIGURE 13.4 States' Startup Ranking 2021

Summary

- The need for regulations and regulatory institutions has increased globally since the 1970s when countries embraced neo-liberal economic policies and redefined the State role in the economy.
- In 1991, the Government of India announced its reforms based on Liberalisation, Privatisation and Globalisation. This was a historical year in independent India as it marked the starting point of making India a regulatory state from the interventionist state.
- In India three types of regulations are present namely- Economic regulations, Social regulations and Environmental regulations
- India government has constituted number of regulatory institutions in India. These include Securities and Exchange Board of India (SEBI), Companies Act 1956 and 2013, Competition Commission of India(CCI), Telecom Regulatory Authority of India (TRAI), IRDA (Insurance Regulatory and Development Authority), Insolvency and Bankruptcy (IBC) Code, 2016, Insolvency and Bankruptcy Board of India (IBBI) , Reserve bank of India (RBI), National Green Tribunal (NGT), Real estate Regulatory Authority (RERA), FEMA Act(1999), Electricity Regulatory Commissions (ERC's) in center and states, Petroleum & Natural Gas Regulatory Board (PNGRB), Tariff authority for Major Ports (TAMP), Director general of Civil Aviation(DGCA) and Airport Authority of India(AAI), Food safety and standard authority of India and Bureau of Indian Standards(BIS), etc.
- The judicial system in India safeguards the constitution, interprets the law, safeguards fundamental rights of citizens, and resolves disputes between citizens, between states and between centre and states.

- The Government of India with the approval of Supreme Court of India is implementing the E-court project to improve the efficiency of Judicial system in India.
- The Government of India and various state government have taken number of steps to reforms the police system in India. These include appointment of National Police Commission (1977), Ribero Committee (1998), Padmanabhaiah Committee (2000), Malimath Committee on Reforms in the Criminal Justice System (2000), etc.
- India has made significant progress in improving the business environment. In 2014, India ranked 142 in Ease of doing business. In 2020, India's latest ranking was 63, a significant 79 rank improvement. However, the World Bank discontinued the Ease of doing business ranking in 2021 due to internal irregularities.
- **Start-Up ranking of States-India started the states' start-up ranking in 2018.** The state' start-up ranking 2021 considered the following areas; **Institutional Support,** Fostering Innovation and Entrepreneurship, Access to Market, Incubation Support, Funding Support, Mentorship Support, and Capacity Building of Enablers. The 2021 ranking categorises states into Best performers, Top performers, leaders, aspiring leaders and emerging start eco ecosystem.

Keywords		
Interventionist state	SEBI	Competition Commission of India(CCI)
Regulatory State	RBI	NCLT
Neo-liberal view	RERA	IBBI
Regulatory reforms	TRAI	National Green Tribunal (NGT)
Economic regulation	IRDA	Judicial reforms
Social regulation	IBC	E-Court
Environmental regulation	Companies Act	Police Reforms
Model Police Act	Start up ranking	Ease of doing business

Questions

1. Explain the need for regulatory reforms.
2. Which are the regulatory bodies operating in India?
3. Explain the types of regulations prevailing in India.
4. Explain the E-Court project.
5. Explain the reforms implemented in the police system in India.

References

CHRI(2021). Government Compliance With Supreme Court Directives On Police Reforms an Assessment, https://www.humanrightsinitiative.org, accessed on 08-Dec-2021.

Competition Act (2002). Ministry of Corporate Affairs. https://www.mca.gov.in, accessed on 08-Dec-2021.

Finance Act (2016). https://www.indiabudget.gov.in, accessed on 17-April-2022.

GOI(2018). Status Note on Police Reforms in India, https://www.mha.gov.in, accessed on 17-April-2022.

GOI(2010). National Green Tribunal Act 2010. https://greentribunal.gov.in, accessed on 17-April-2022.

IBBI(2020). Understanding the IBC KEY JURISPRUDENCE AND PRACTICAL CONSIDERATIONS- A HANDBOOK, IBBI.

IRDA Act(1999). Insurance Regulatory And Development Authority Of India Act, 1999, https://www.irdai.gov.in, accessed on 17-April-2022.

Joskow, P. L., & Rose, N. L. (1989). The effects of economic regulation. Handbook of industrial organisation, 2, 1449-1506.

Justice Yotindra Singh(2020). Appointment of Judges and Judicial Reforms: need of the hour. https://theleaflet.in, accessed on 17-April-2022.

Kapur, Davesh (2018). India's public sector enterprises: Where do we go from here?, The print. https://theprint.in, accessed on 17-April-2022.

Majone, G. (1997). From the positive to the regulatory State: Causes and consequences of changes in the mode of governance. Journal of public policy, 17(2), 139-167.

RBI Act (1934). Reserve bank of India Act. https://rbidocs.rbi.org.in, accessed on 17-April-2022.

Reddy YV (1996). Public Enterprises and Economic Reforms, Golden Jubilee Endowment Lecture by Dr. Y. V. Reddy, Deputy Governor, at the Osmania University Department of Commerce on 27th December, 1996, at Hyderabad

RERA Act(2016). THE REAL ESTATE (REGULATION AND DEVELOPMENT) ACT, 2016, https://legislative.gov.in, accessed on 17-April-2022.

Som, lalitha and Faizal Naru(2017). Regulatory policy in India: Moving towards regulatory governance, OECD Regulatory Policy Working Papers No. 8

State's Start-up India Ranking(2021). https://www.startupindia.gov.in, accessed on 17-April-2022.

Tanzi, M. V. (1997). The changing role of the State in the economy: a historical perspective. International Monetary Fund.

TRAI(2017). A Twenty-Year Odyssey 1997-2017. https://www.trai.gov.in, accessed on 17-April-2022.

Module V

Contemporary Topics in Public Policy

Module V: Contemporary Topics in Public Policy

This module has two chapters:

Chapter 14 Data Science and Public Policy
Chapter 15 Current Trends in Public Policy

Chapter 14 discusses the contemporary topic of data science in the context of public policy and covers topics like data science lifecycle; data science-led governance, ai and public policy, data use for social equity, data science for social good, data science as a planning tool, improving transparency, mapping public utilities, public policy analytics, text analytics for policy analysis, solving complex service-delivery puzzles, and policy research & development.

Chapter 15 captures the current trends in public policy like Internationalization of Public Policy, Gender as a Critical Component in Public Policy, Public Policy: Beyond Government, Innovations and Social Change, and Planning the Future World: The Sustainable Development Goals.

CHAPTER 14

Data Science and Public Policy

This chapter presents the role of data science in public policy. Section 1 introduces the concept of data science and its sub-fields like Artificial Intelligence, machine learning and deep learning. The data science life cycle is explained in section 2. Data science also influences the public policy cycle; we presented this in section three. Section four offers the influence of data science on governance. Data science is a powerful tool for building an inclusive society; we present this in section five. Data science is used to improve public utility services, which is explained in section 6. We also show the role of data science as a planning tool in section 7, followed by a section on public policy analytics. Data science governments also pose serious challenges, and the privacy issues with data science are presented in section 9.

The fourth industrial revolution is making significant changes in the life of people, and the functioning of firms and governments. Artificial Intelligence and Machine learning drive the fourth industrial revolution. Artificial Intelligence and other data science techniques offer many opportunities to the world to change how we live, work or interact with others. Similarly, it will change how governments formulate policies, implement, and evaluate them. Governments can extract actionable information from the vast data available.

> Artificial Intelligence and Machine learning drive the fourth industrial revolution.

The first industrial revolution happened during the 18th and 19th centuries, driven by the steam engine and mechanization of production. The second industrial revolution helped the world in mass production with electric motors. The second industrial revolution started in the 1870s and ended in 1914. The third one started in the 1980s with the introduction of internet technologies, which have transformed the world into a more connected one. The fourth industrial revolution is driven by Artificial Intelligence, the Internet of things (IoT), big data and cloud computing.

According to World Economic Forum, the fourth industrial revolution is distinct: velocity, scope, and systems impact, not merely a continuation of the third industrial revolution. The speeds at which changes happen today have no historical precedent and affect every economic sector, transforming production, management and governance systems.

1. DATA SCIENCE

The digitalization process, use of a smartphone, and Increase in computing power and storage capacity have create a large amount of data. In 2018, 33 Zettabytes (ZB) of data were made, which grew to 59ZB in 2020, reaching 173 ZB by 2025(Vopson 2021). Data science is extracting information from this data for an actionable purpose by combining mathematics and Statistics with technology. According to IBM, "Data science combines math and statistics, specialized programming, advanced analytics, artificial intelligence (AI), and machine learning with specific subject matter expertise to uncover actionable insights hidden in an organization's data."

1.1 Artificial Intelligence, Machine Learning and Deep Learning

Data science combines Mathematics and statistics, Computer programming and Domain knowledge.

Artificial Intelligence has grown significantly in recent years, and many companies and governments have adopted Artificial intelligence to improve performance and decision-making. Alan Turing, the British mathematician and logician, is known as founding father of artificial intelligence. Even though he has not used the term "Artificial intelligence", he asked, "Can machines think". John McCarthy of Stanford University, who first used the term Artificial intelligence, defines AI as "the science and engineering of making intelligent machines, especially intelligent computer programs. It is related to the similar task of using computers to understand human Intelligence. However, AI does not have to confine itself to methods that are biologically observable."

The following are some of the examples of technologies based on AI

a) Various websites for customer interaction offer chatbots. These chatbots respond to customers' queries instantly without human help.
b) **Alexa**- Amazon introduced Alexa, for digitalizing home appliances, shopping sites, etc. It helps decipher speech and allows us to use voice commands for online shopping and home appliances.
c) **Siri**- Apple's assistant

Machine learning is a sub-field of Artificial Intelligence, and *deep learning* is a sub-field of machine learning. Machine learning is the art of Artificial Intelligence but is not equal to Artificial Intelligence. Deep learning is a part of Machine learning where human interference is not required for machines to take decisions. In machine learning, machines learn from structured data sets with labelled data, and human interference is necessary to label the data. However, in deep learning, learning occurs from the unstructured and unlabelled database, where human interference is significantly less.

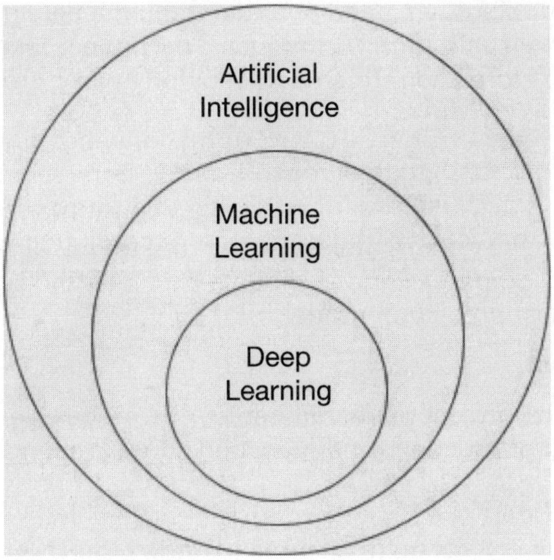

2. DATA SCIENCE LIFECYCLE

The Data Science Life cycle explains various stages of a data science project. Various organizations give different data science life cycles. Here we present the data science life cycle referred by Microsoft.

According to the Team Data Science Process (TDSP) of Microsoft (2022), the following are the stages to be followed in a data science project.

1. Business understanding
2. Data acquisition and understanding
3. Modelling
4. Deployment
5. Customer Acceptance

1. Business Understanding

This is the starting stage of the project. In this stage, we need to understand the customer's specific requirements. The project team, along with the project's customer or other stakeholders, identifies the business problem and then formulates questions to define the business problem. The project team also needs to identify the variable that needs to predict in the project. The project team assigns a specific target to each member and finalizes the success matrix of the project. The team also identifies variables used in the project, the data available, and the data needed.

2. Data acquisition and understanding

In this stage, the team transfers data from source locations to the locations where analytics takes place. Before analyzing the data, we need to clean the data and should have a better understanding of the data. Once we get the clean data after removing repeated values and taking care of missing values, we need to understand the data using data summarization and visualization techniques. The project team will create a data pipeline to store and refresh data regularly while progressing in the project.

3. **Modelling**

In this stage, the team will set optimal features of the machine learning model and then create a model to predict the target variables. The data analytics team compares various models based on the success rate and identifies the best prediction model.

4. **Deployment**

At this stage, the project team will deploy the model identified with the data pipeline to production for application consumption.

5. **Customer Acceptance**

In this stage, the project team ensures that the project outcome satisfies Customer needs. Customers will validate whether the project outcome meets their business needs or not. If the customer accepts the project outcome, the project team exits the project.

3. DATA SCIENCE AND PUBLIC POLICY CYCLE.

AI plays crucial role in all stages of public policy cycle.

AI changes the way government functions.

Adopting data science, especially Artificial Intelligence, changes the way government functions. It can bring more accuracy in identifying the problems where policy action is required, formulation of policy to address the issue, policy implementation, and evaluation. Boston Consulting Group(BCG) has formulated a public policy cycle with AI adoption. Public policy lifecycle with AI adoption has five stages and AI can play a significant role in all five stages of the public policy cycle.

The following are the give stages of Public policy lifecycle with AI adoption.

1. Identification
2. Formulation
3. Adoption
4. Implementation
5. Evaluation

1. **Identification**

In this stage, government and its departments identifies the problem, which requires a policy response. When we use data science in policy-making, we can use Artificial Intelligence to analyze a large amount of data to identify patterns. In this way, we can identify problems more accurately. Once we identify issues from the data patterns, we can further assess the various aspects of this problem using artificial Intelligence.

2. **Formulation**

In this stage, the government formulates appropriate policies to address the issue identified in stage 1. Sometimes, one policy for the entire population may not work, and different approaches for people from diverse socioeconomic backgrounds is required for successful policy formulation. AI can give information on various sections of people using a large amount of data. Large amounts of information and details of the problem can help policymakers to get more insights into multiple aspects of the problem and formulate better policy.

3. **Adoption**

In this stage, the legislature adopts the policy formulated by the government in power. Well-informed members of the legislatures can make better laws for the country. Artificial Intelligence(AI) can provide more infromations to the members of the lesgislature and this can help them while participating in the discussions related to the policy. Hence, AI can help the legislature in the process of policy adoption.

4. **Implementation**

In the policy implementation stage, the government and other agencies will undertake a series of activities to achieve the goals and targets mentioned in the policy statement(Bullock and Lavis, 2019). Policy Implementation is a challenging state in the policy cycle as coordinated efforts of various departments and agencies required at this stage. Good policies fail because of poor implementation by the government departments and agencies. Artificial Intelligence can help in implementation based on feedback from the ground.

5. **Evaluation**

Evaluation of policy is a crucial stage in the policy life cycle, and at this stage, we analyze whether the policy has achieved its declared objectives or not. Evaluation is conducted at various levels to examine the effectiveness of the policy. Artificial Intelligence(AI) based software offers the government many data tools to evaluate policy effectiveness at different levels and cross sections. This helps the government make a proper evaluation of the policy and make necessary corrections if required.

Adoption of AI in government in different countries

Adoption of Artificial Intelligence in Government in Various countries.

Facial Recognition technology(FRT)

- Interpol has introduced INTERPOL Face Recognition System (IFRS) in which facial images of persons from 179 countries are added and it is a global criminal database. When facial image is entered into this system, the IFRS system will compare the facial image with the images already there in data base and identify the persons. As per the Interpol database almost 1500 terrorist, criminals, persons of interest or missing people have been identified since the launch of this system.

- Recently Europe has announced the introduction of a Facial Recognition system to keep track of the movement of criminals across the boarders.
- In India various state police forces including Delhi Police uses FRT technology

AI based cameras for traffic

Traffic congestions and traffic rule violations are a major problem in many of the Indian cities. Now Indian cities use Artificial Intelligence based cameras for traffic management and detection of traffic rule violations. These cameras can detect overspeeding, reluctance to wear seat belt, helmet, triple riding in two wheelers, etc. Vehant Technologies, a start up, incubated in Indian Institute of Technology (IIT)-Delhi is a pioneer in AI based Physical Security, Surveillance and Traffic Monitoring & Junction Enforcement Solutions in India.

Application of AI(Artificial Intelligence) in Legislature

Various legislatures around the world has introduced AI based solution to improve the functioning of legislature.

- United States of America: The US House of Representatives is using a AI based tool to analyse difference between the bills, amendments and current laws by using Natural language processing based tool.
- The Parliamentary reporting office of the House of representatives in Netherland has introduced a system called 'Speech2Write' to convert speech to text and even translate to different languages.

4. DATA SCIENCE AND GOVERNANCE

Ensuring efficiency in service delivery is one of the challenges faced by the governments and public sector units. The government and public sector can use modern technologies to improve service delivery efficiently and smartly. According to Kupi et al. (2021), digital transformation in government is about the systematic collection, evaluation, linking and application of data to provide better public governance. Governments have access to a large amount of data, which can analyze systematically to make actionable policy suggestions. Data analytics can help the government in various aspects of public governance. Boston Consulting Group (BCG) reports that "AI will not replace policymakers, but it can enable a comprehensive, faster, and more rigorous approach to policy-making in the short run. More broadly, AI can deliver on the promise of a future government that is more responsive and leaves no one behind. "(Patel et al 2021)

"AI will not replace policymakers, but it can enable a comprehensive, faster, and more rigorous approach to policy-making in the short run. More broadly, AI can deliver on the promise of a future government that is more responsive and leaves no one behind. "
BCG report

4.1 Challenges for Applying AI in Governance

The application of AI in governance faces several challenges. Some of these are as follows.

1. **Insufficient infrastructure**: The application of AI requires IT infrastructure with advanced computing power. Such infrastructure is not available in many government departments and public sector units.
2. **Capacity building**: There is a massive demand for data scientists worldwide. The corporate sector pays heavily for data scientists. The availability of data scientists is another challenge faced by governments and the public sector in implementing AI-based governance.
3. **Resistance to AI**: AI may reduce employment opportunities in the government sector. In many countries, youth rely on the government as a primary source of employment. Hence, resistance to AI from the public is another challenge for the government.

5. DATA SCIENCE FOR BUILDING A MORE INCLUSIVE SOCIETY

Governments across the globe are fighting socio-economic inequities and inequities in access to public services. Minorities and other disadvantaged communities or races are out of the public service delivery system, which needs to be corrected. The fruits of economic development need to reach all sections of society, which is a challenge we face in the policy formulation and implementation stages. In many cases, lack of data or an insufficient amount of data about disadvantaged sections of people makes them out of focus on the policy formulations. Hence, poor people's issues are not adequately addressed in public policies, which is a challenge for policymakers.

The COVID-19 pandemic has worsened the inequalities across the countries and within countries as it hit the poor or disadvantaged sections the most. According to the World Bank, the lowest 40% of the population's average income is 6.7% less in 2021 compared to there income in the pre-pandemic period. However, for the highest 40% of people, the income was down 2.8%. The difference is that the poor sections have not started recovering from their income losses. The difference in response like this is because of the inequalities in capabilities. The World Bank advocates for shared prosperity: "increasing the incomes and welfare of the bottom 40 per cent of society wherever they are, be it in the poorest of nations or thriving middle-income countries."

> Data science can help policymakers to take more accurate policy decisions to address disparities and inequities across different sections of people.

Agencies worldwide are facing the issue of a lack of adequate data to assess the effectiveness of projects funded in addressing inequalities. Inadequate data availability makes it difficult for international funding agencies to select projects addressing the inequalities projects and evaluate these project in terms of the objectives achieved. Data science can help policymakers to take more accurate policy decisions to address disparities and inequities across different sections of people. Clifford Stein of the Data Science Institute(DSI), Columbia University, USA, says that an interdisciplinary approach is required to fight social injustice and create a more inclusive society. The adoption of technologies for automated decision-making can reduce bias due to human bias, emotion, fatigue, faults, years of experience, etc. Data scientist can collaborate with domain experts in other disciplines, particularly social scientists , to design multifaceted, human-centred, and ethical policy solutions to address the inequality issue.

Tech-based solutions can help governments to identify "hard-to-survey" areas while conducting socioeconomic surveys or census. Identification of "hard-to-survey areas" can help the survey agency find tailor-made solutions to address the low response rate towards surveys these areas while conducting the survey.

The following are some of the technology applications in improving the database or providing solutions using data science.

1. **Response Outreach Area Mapper(ROAM)**

This is an application developed for identifying "hard to survey areas" while conducting the American Community Survey (ACS) by the US Census Bureau. The census Bureau is crafting tailor-made strategies to address the problems in "hard-to survey areas" identified through ROAM.

2. **Data Science for Good: Center for Policing Equity.**

This is a project from Kaggle, a data scientists community of Google. Organizations with extensive data sets can approach Kaggle to solve their problems using the data set. In the "Data Science for Good" project, the data scientists use policing and census data to address the issue of racism in policing. Data scientists identify the police deployment areas where racism still exists, and policing agencies can take appropriate steps to reduce racism in policing. A solution like this requires combining different datasets such as police data, census-level data, and other socioeconomic factors. When the dataset is not normalized since different federal states follow different data standards for policing data, the service of data scientists with adequate expertise is required to find solutions like this.

3. **Minneapolis Police Department Project: Center for Policing Equity**

In this project, the data scientists have analyzed the "use-of-force incidents by police" data and identified districts where more such accidents happen. The use of Police data combined with census and other socioeconomic characteristics shows that use of force incidents on Blacks was three times that of whites—72% of the incidents are targeted at blacks, whose population is less than 20%. Asian population is 1.5% while 6.5% incidents targeted Asian population. They use police vehicle stops data and combine it with the population data of the areas to understand the racial disparities in policing.

Equality: equality means equal access to resources or opportunities irrespective of the capabilities of individuals or section of people.

Equity: Equity recognises the difference in capabilities or circumstances among individuals or sections of people and provides resources or Opportunities to reach same level of income.

6. MAPPING PUBLIC UTILITIES USING DATA SCIENCE

Utilities like water, electricity, gas, drainage, etc., are essential in the daily life of citizens. In most countries, the public sector provides these services. These services are kept under state monopoly because of the advantages of economies of scale, enormous capital cost involved and the need for maintaining the excess capacity to meet peak demands. However, in countries like USA, utility sector is completely privatized. In many other countries, both private sector and public sector enterprises are allowed to participate in this sector. Utility firms have assets in different locations and a large part of their expenditure is for asset management. Modern data tools can help the utility firms to better manage assets and reduce the asset management expenditure.

Data science can help to improve the functioning of Public Utility system.

Provision of Utilities is like the nerves and veins in urban areas; any disturbances in the supply of these utilities affect the urban life. Hence, well-functioning utility services are essential for economic and social development, especially in Urban areas. According to the World Bank, "A well-performing utility can be characterized as one that permanently provides services to all customers in full compliance with applicable quality standards (both for supply and commercial services), and that operates efficiently across all business areas within a framework of financial sustainability"(World Bank 2020).

Data science tools are extensively used in different parts of the world to develop a well-functioning utility system. Large amounts of real-time and near real-time data are available with these utility providers. Data science can help them to integrate these real-time and near real-time data with historical data to improve the functioning of these utility firms by optimizing the cost and usage.

6.1 Big Data and Utility Firms

Utility firms get a large amount of data due to intelligent transformations of the industry by installing smart meters, mobile phones, sensors, cloud computing technologies, wireless, power planning, and network communication. These changes produce a large amount of data, and the firms can use it to arrive at actionable insights to improve their operational efficiency.

Utility companies have a large amount of geospatial data, and geospatial analytics can provide more insights about using assets in different locations, etc. Geospatial data refers to information on features, objects, events and classes on the earth's surface or even in space. These objects can be static in the short run and dynamic in some other cases. Integrating these data with census data and another dataset can provide valuable inputs for utility firms.

6.2 Use of Blockchain

Blockchain includes a chain of transactions about assets. These assets can be money, maps, datasets, etc. Blockchain technology can help power distribution, water supply, and other companies to improve operational efficiency and asset management.

Big data, Block Chain and Artificial Intelligence can help Utility firms in the following way

1. **Asset management:** Proper asset management is one of the issues facing Utility companies, especially public Utility companies. Lack of proper maintenance of assets like the power grid, power plants, waste recycling plants, etc., leads to additional costs for Utility firms and can cause supply failure. Further, timely asset maintenance is essential for these assets' safety, reliability, longevity, and proper utilization. In the electricity sector, Power failure causes massive

losses to the economy by disrupting economic activities and public life. Blockchain technology can help Utility firms in asset management, reduce maintenance costs, and avoid supply disruptions.

2. **Inventory management:** Utility firms store large amounts of inventories like spare parts, etc., to avoid risk. Additional inventory stock causes extra costs for these firms affecting their profitability. Multiple firms are involved in the supply chain of these spare parts. Blockchain technology can help these firms connect, and share real-time data, and this could avoid overstocking and understocking of inventories.
3. **Power generation planning:** power generation planning can help the firms to reduce power outrage and other disturbances. Predictive analytics can help firms properly plan power generation using data from multiple sources.
4. **Forecasting power renewable energy supply**:The supply of renewable energy like solar and wind energy depends on the weather conditions. Predictive analytics using data from different locations can help power firms predict the renewable energy supply.
5. **EV Charging stations**: Large investments are required in EV charging stations all over the world. This causes a challenge for governments, power generation and distribution firms. Blockchain-based EV charging ecosystem can help individuals share their charging infrastructure with needy customers and make more income by adequately utilizing these infrastructures.

7. DATA SCIENCE AS A PLANNING TOOL

Formulating futuristic policies and preparation of urban planning requires accurate prediction of future population, future requirements of different locations, traffic flow and the possibility of congestion, immigration from rural areas, housing demand, etc. An accurate forecast of traffic flow in a particular area can help the municipality to develop road infrastructure to reduce possible traffic congestion. Further, this is important in preparing the urban plans as we need to build infrastructure keeping future needs in mind. Urban planners use traditional methods to predict the population in an area, traffic flows and utility requirements. In many cases, these predictions can go wrong, leading to faulty plans and inefficient allocation of scarce resources. Inadequate urban planning is evident in many cities around the world, especially in developing countries. Inadequate planning causes prolonged traffic congestion, improper drainage facilities, water logging on rainy days and the growth of slums because of lack of housing infrastructure, etc. Can we use data science as a planning tool?

GIS helps the urban planners.

Geographical Infromation System(GIS) data can help urban planners with actionable insights from spatial thinking. GIS provides more detailed information from satellite images, areal photography and sensors. By analyzing these information, GIS professionals can give actionable insights into land use and infrastructure availability in a particular area. Such actionable insights can help urban planners in

1. Reviewing the existing plan
2. Accurate prediction of population and plan housing facilities in urban areas
3. Analyze the existing road infrastructure and identify areas where additional infrastructure is required.
4. Mapping of Utility delivery
5. Assess the environmental impact and protection of forest areas.

8. PUBLIC POLICY ANALYTICS

According to a Brooking Report(2020), understanding two different trends in data science is essential in understanding the role of data science in public policy. The first is the development of new statistical methods and the availability of new data set that may give more actionable insights into public policy analysis. These are predictive analytics, text analytics, image analysis, etc. The second is the set of tools and formalization standards in the data science field, such as the emergence of cloud computing, better infrastructure and data visualization techniques, etc.

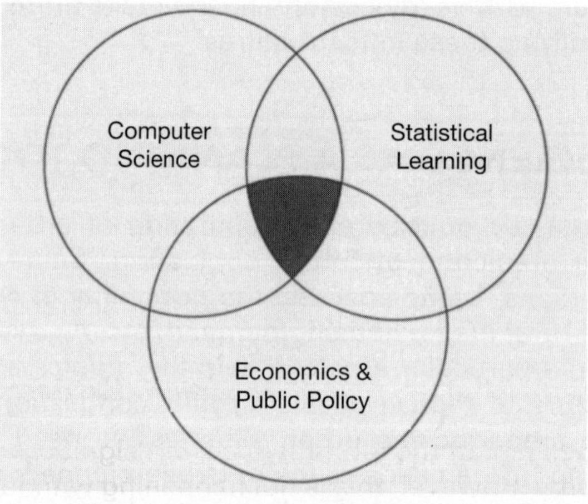

Data science overlaps computer science, statistical analysis and domain knowledge. It overlaps public policy and economics, computer science and statistical methods in our context.

8.1 Predictive Analytics

Predictive analytics is a branch of data science which use historical data combined with statistical methods and machine learning to make predictions. In the context of public policy, predictions are significant concerning population, Utility demand, and traffic flows, etc. These predictions can help policymakers in urban planning.

8.2 Clustering

Clustering is a machine learning technique used to cluster the data into different subgroups with similar data characteristics. Hence, clustering allows us to understand the features of subgroups within the population and is helpful in public policy analysis.

8.3 Big Data

Big data refers to the availability of a large amount of data, and it isn't easy to process this data with traditional statistical methods. Big data has four main properties: Volume, Velocity and Variety. Volume: Much information is available, which may be structured, unstructured or semi-structured. Variety: Different types of data are available, and velocity means these data are generated in less time.

8.4 Geospatial Analytics

Data with timing and location information is available with the geospatial dataset. In geospatial analytics, data with location and timing are visualized on a map, which can help Utility firms and urban planners.

8.5 Text Analytics

Unstructured and structured texts can transform into actionable inputs using text analytics. Natural language processing or text analysis can help us understand readers' sentiments, classify texts, convert text into quantitative data, etc.

9. DATA SCIENCE AND PRIVACY ISSUES

Data science is reshaping the world by causing significant disruption in the global economy. However, this is not happening without cost. Human rights activists and others have raised concern over citizens' privacy while collecting, storing and using the data.

Increased use of data causes serious data privacy issues.

Many governments collect data on their citizens to issue identification cards and store a large amount of data. In India, Aadhar is widely used as an identity card for various government programs. Many activists have warned that this causes a risk to data privacy to the citizens. What is data privacy? Data privacy differs from the fundamental right of "right to privacy" ensured by the constitutions in many countries. **Data privacy** is about "*appropriate and permissioned use and* governance of data", as per the World Bank. This "means that data should only be accessed, processed, or shared by and with authorized users for pre-specified purposes that have been agreed in advance"(World Bank 2010)

Many of the datasets include personally identifiable information(PII)-which can be used to identify a person, including name, identity number, location data, and any other information related to the physical, genetic, racial, economic or cultural identity of that person. Big data poses the risk of misusing this Personally Identifiable Information (PII) and is a threat to the citizens. Risk to personal data arises at different stages: data collection, storage, and data sharing and disposal of data. The following are the main risk associated with personal data.

1. **Cyber attacks**: Cyber criminals may access vast amounts of data and may misuse these data.

2. **Functional creep**: Collecting information for one purpose and using it for another. For example. Data on COVID 19 patients collected to track the spread of COVID 19 is transferred to the private pharmaceutical company and used for a different purpose.
3. **Surveillance**: Personal information may be misused to track the activities of individuals by government agencies or private agencies.
4. **Discrimination or persecution**: In some cases, the big data and the algorithm used is discriminatory and may lead to persecution.
5. In corporate, some of the data security types are as follows.

   Accidental sharing: Sometimes, employees may share data accidentally through mail or other ways. Here there is no criminal intent to share these data with outsiders, but it happens because of carelessness.

   Because of corrupt employees: Sometimes dishonest employees may share information with outsiders against bribes. In 2020, Amazon fired an employee for leaking customer information to a third party.

Facial Recognition technology(FRT) and privacy issues

The use of Facial Recognition technology by law enforcement agencies and intelligence agencies has raised public criticism. In many countries, this is used to track different communities, races and groups of people opposing the government. Recently many companies have taken stand against the use or development of this technology.

- In June 2020, IBM announced that the company would stop offering FRT software as it is widely used for abuse and misuse.
- In 2020, Amazon declared a one-year moratorium on selling its Facial recognition Software- **Rekognition**. The company urged the US government to pass adequate legislation to regulate the use of Facial Recognition technology.
- Microsoft president Brad Smith said that his company would not sell Facial recognition Technology to police until the government passes legislation for the regulation of technology.

Summary

- Data science development has been changing the way public policy is made.
- Data science combines computer technology, statistical and mathematical theory and domain knowledge.
- Artificial Intelligence is a sub-field of data science, machine learning is a subfield of Artificial Intelligence, and deep learning is a part of machine learning. Machine learning requires human interference to a limited extent,

whereas deep learning does not require any human interference.

- There are different data science life cycle theories. According to the data science life cycle suggested by Microsoft, data science life cycles has five stages namely-business understanding, data acquisition and understanding, modelling, deployment and customer acceptance
- Data science has influenced the public policy cycle and has impact on all the stages of public policy life cycles. Data science can be used in various stages of the public policy cycle, such as problem identification, policy formulation, policy adoption, implementation and evaluation. Data science makes more actionable input for the policy makers using a large amount of data, which helps the public policy-making process.
- Governments have been using data science and related technology to improve the efficiency in service delivery, transparency and accountability in government.
- Data science can be used to create a more inclusive society. Artificial Intelligence and machine learning make more data available about the disadvantaged sections of society and help the policy makers formulate policies based on accurate information.
- Big data, Artificial Intelligence and Blockchain technology, are used in Public Utility companies to improve service delivery.
- Various data science techniques are used in public policy analytics. These include predictive analytics, clustering, bid data, text analytics, etc.
- The use of data sciences is not free from security issues. Data use poses serious privacy issues for citizens. Cyber attacks, surveillance by private and government agencies, functional creep, accidental data leakage, etc. are the major issues.

Keywords

Data Science	Artificial Intelligence	Machine Learning
Deep learning	Blockchain	Predictive Analytics
Clustering	Data life cycle	Facial recognition technology
Public Utility firms	Cyber attacks	Functional creep

Questions

1. What is data science? What are the sub-fields of data science? Explain
2. Explain the data project life cycles.
3. Explain the effect of data science on the Policy life cycle
4. Can we use data science to build a more inclusive society? Explain
5. What is Public Policy Analytics? Explain

References

Bullock, H. L., & Lavis, J. N. (2019). Understanding the supports needed for policy implementation: a comparative analysis of the placement of intermediaries across three mental

Vopson, Melvin M(2021). The world's data explained: how much we're producing and where it's all stored. The Conversation. https://theconversation.com, accessed on 15-Jan-2020.

Microsoft(2022). The Team Data Science Process lifecycle, https://learn.microsoft.com, accessed on 17-April-2022.

Patel et al (2021). AI Brings Science to the Art of Policymaking. https://www.bcg.com, accessed on 17-April-2022

Worldbank(2020). What lessons can we learn from IEG evaluations in the energy and water sectors?. https://openknowledge.worldbank.org, accessed on 17-April-2022

Hadoo (2018). Big Data & Analytics in the Energy & Utilities industry. https://www.hcltech.com, accessed on 17-April-2022

Brookings Report(2020). What all policy analytics need to know about data science. https://www.brookings.edu, accessed on 17-April-2022

Worldbank(2019). ID4D Practitioner's Guide, https://documents1.worldbank.org, accessed on 17-April-2022

Health systems. *Health Research Policy and Systems, 17*(1), 1-13.

CHAPTER 15

Current Trends in Public Policy

This chapter introduces the current trends in public policy. The internationalisation of public policy in the context of globalisation. Section 2 of this chapter explains the gender component of public policy, followed by a section on Public policy beyond government. We present the role of non-state actors in this section. Role of innovation in making Social Change is presented in section four. Sustainable Development Goals(SDGs) are presented in section five.

1. INTERNATIONALISATION OF PUBLIC POLICY

Today's global economy is much more connected and integrated than the economy in the last century. The liberalisation wave that started in the 1980s has led to massive changes in economies around the world. Globalisation has created a much more integrated economy with eco nomic, financial, cultural, and Political globalisation. Further, it has led to the globalisation of markets, competition, companies and industries. Political globalisation has integrated the political systems around the world by adopting the democratic form of government in most countries. The disintegration of the Soviet Union has aggravated this process, and many of the former soviet countries have adopted a democratic form of government.

Public policy-making in a globalised world is much more challenging.

Globalisation has influenced all aspects of human life and changed the nature of nation-states and governments. Public policy-making in a globalised world is much more challenging as the policymakers have to look at the international environment while framing the policies. Globalisation has made several changes in the working of the State. States have joined the globalisation process at the cost of sovereignty and the democratic demands of the people. On the public policy front, policy-making has been subject to privatisation, deregulation and internationalisation (Lodhi 2021). In short, states have compromised their sovereignty for the benefits offered by globalisation and become a manager and organisers in a globalised world motivated by global capitalist interests(Lodhi 2021).

The changing role of the State in a globalised world has transformed the policy-making process within nation-states.

Colin Hay, a professor at the University of Birmingham, lists the following changes in public policy-making.

a. Globalisation has reduced the policy-making capacity of institutions' by reducing national states' autonomy. Globalisation has transferred the functions of public institutions to quasi-public institutions like regulatory bodies. Hence, state intervention in many sectors of the economy reduced, and regulatory bodies are formulating policies to control these sectors. Further, globalisation has taken away the policy-making powers of national governments, as international organisations like WTO, IMF, World Bank, etc., formulate policies in many sectors of the economy. Federal governments have to follow these policies because of the commitments in international agreements like WTO agreements, etc.
b. International organisations like WTO, IMF and the World Bank, the leading advocates of globalisation, call for the depoliticisation of central bank decision-making and privatisation of the economy. This reduced the democratic nature of public policy as policy-making. Functions of central banks are not subject to democratic scrutiny directly and is done by professionals without direct interference from political actors. For example, In India, a professional committee called Monetary Policy Committee(MPC) formulates the monetary policy, and the decision-making process is depoliticised, upholding the central bank's autonomy. However, this makes policy-making more accountable and transparent by using the service of professionals in decision making.
c. Globalisation favours free flow of capital, and national governments try to create investor-friendly policy environments in the economy. This happens through reduction in tax rates and relaxation regulations for the free flow of capital. Hence, globalisation reduced the "fiscal space" in the economy which funds public policy.

1.1 Policy Learning, Policy Transfer and Internationalisation of Public Policy

Policy transfer is the process in which policies and programs are transferred from one political system to develop policies and programs in another.

The primary objective of public policy is to solve a socio-economic problem. Different nation-states may face similar issues, which provides opportunities for policymakers to learn from the experience of other nation-states. The problems of a state depend on the demographic, cultural, and political characteristics, and nations' problems would be unique. However, policymakers can learn how their counterparts in other countries respond to the problems with appropriate policy responses.

Policy transfer is the process in which policies(goals, content and instruments) and programs are transferred from one political system to develop policies and programs in another. This happens within nations between state governments, state and federal governments. Policy transfer occurs in varying degrees:

a. **Coping**: In this case, the entire policy will be copied
b. **Emulation**: In Emulation, the entire policy is not copied, but the idea behind the policy is copied to another political system
c. **Combination**: this involved mixture of several different programs or policies
d. **Inspiration**: A successful policy or program in one political system may inspire another political system to adopt the same policies with different outcomes.

Globalisation opens new avenues for policymakers to learn from other political systems and adopt policies or programs from other countries or states. Globalisation increased the speed at which information spread among people and improved communication. More information about policies, their success and failure in different countries are available in a globalised world, which helps the policy transfer between countries. Policy transfer leads to policy convergence across nations, and globalisation provides a platform for policy convergence. Further, governments worldwide face common problems like climate change, global warming, inequality, etc. Addressing these issues requires unified and coordinated policy efforts by different governments. International organisations like United Nations, UNDP, etc., encourage governments to adopt similar policies to address these global issues.

2. GENDER COMPONENT OF PUBLIC POLICY

Ensuring gender equality is critical in achieving an inclusive society. The constitution of India guarantees equality of citizens and ensures the absence of discrimination based on Gender. Gender equality is a central objective of public policy deliberations around the world. The current social order in many countries, especially in developing countries, give more representation to men in political structures and more influence to men in the decision-making process. In many countries, girls have fewer education opportunities and lag behind boys in educational attainment. These disparities reflect the inequality in economic opportunities between men and women. Gender equality offers significant economic benefits to the world economy. In 2015 a McKinsey Global Institute (MGI) study found that if women were allowed to participate identically to men, the global economy could contribute $28 trillion more to annual GDP by 2025. Achieving gender equality is essential in attaining sustainable development goals(SDGs), as the 5th SDG is Gender Equality. The United Nations considers says that gender equality is " not only a fundamental right but necessary for a prosperous, peaceful and sustainable future.

> The constitution of India guarantees absence of discrimination based on Gender.

Public policy is a powerful tool for creating a gender-neutral society. Public policies like education, healthcare, microfinance, MSME, and Startup policies can effectively address gender issues. The government's commitment toward gender equality may reflect in the national or State plans, programs, budgets, etc.

> Achieving gender equality is essential in attaining sustainable development goals(SDGs)

2.1 Gender Mainstreaming

Gender mainstreaming is a globally accepted strategy for achieving gender equality.

Gender mainstreaming is a globally accepted approach to policy-making considering gender aspects. Nairobi World Conference on Women, in 1985, discussed the concept of Gender mainstreaming for the first time. Later in 1991, the Fourth United Nations World Conference on Women in Beijing adopted Gender mainstreaming as an approach to policy-making. Gender mainstreaming is a strategy for achieving gender equality. It involves ensuring gender perspectives as the central them of policy development, Research, legislation, resource allocation, planning and implementation of programs and projects.

2.2 Gender Responsive Budget

Gender Responsive budget allocates resources to all sections of society, men, women, girls and boys, to promote gender equality.

The budget statement shows the intent and priorities of the government in the forthcoming financial year.

Gender-responsive Budget does not mean that government prepares a separate budget for women and girls. Gender Responsive budget allocates resources to all sections of society, men, women, girls and boys, to promote gender equality. Hence the gender-responsive Budget considers gender aspects while allocating resources to various projects and programs and allocating resources.

2.3 Government of India's Initiative for Gender Equality

The Government of India has initiated several schemes and programs to empower women and girls. The following are some of the important among them

- **Beti Bachao Beti Padhao**: *Beti Bachao Beti Padhao* is a national campaign to avoid discrimination against girls and focuses on 100 districts with the lowest Child Sex Ratio. This scheme, launched in 2015, has three objectives: (1)prevent gender-biased sex selective elimination, (2) Ensure survival & protection of the girl child, and (3) ensure education and participation of girl child.
- **Sukanya Samriddhi Yojna(SSY):** This is part of Beti Bachao Beti Padhao scheme. SSY is a deposit scheme for the girl child and offers high-interest rates and tax-free withdrawal. As per this scheme, an SSY account can be opened in the name of a Girl child before age 10, and the money can be withdrawn for education or marriage purpose of the girl.
- **Mahila Shakti Kendra (MSK)**: MSK Scheme was announced in the 2017-18 budget to empower rural women with skill development and training.
- **Mahila Police Volunteers Scheme: T**his scheme was launched to reduce crime against women and increase the reporting of crimes. As

per this scheme, the Home department of states and U.T.s appoint women who are socially and voluntarily committed to women and girl empowerment as Mahila Police Volunteers(MPV). MPVs report to the Circle of Police and help the police authority report crimes against women like domestic violence, dowry-related violence and harassment, child abuse, trafficking, etc. MPVs also improve awareness about government schism for the welfare of women and children.

- **Political Participation:** The government reserves 33% of seats in urban and Local bodies for women in India with the 74th constitution amendment in 1992. Later many states increased the reservation for women to not less than 50%. States like Andhra Pradesh, Assam, Bihar, Chhattisgarh, Gujarat, Himachal Pradesh, Jharkhand, Karnataka, Kerala, Madhya Pradesh, Maharashtra, Odisha, Punjab, Rajasthan, Sikkim, Tamil Nadu, Telangana, Tripur a, Uttarakhand and West Bengal reserve 50% of the seats in panchayat Raj institutions to women.
- **Gender Budgeting:** Government expenditure on various schemes affects men and women differently, and recognising this, the Government of India introduced gender Budgeting in 2005. The Gender Budget of Government lists expenditure on schemes exclusively for women and prominently for women. In 2021-22 government spent Rs.166182.71(revised estimate) crores under the gender budget, which increased to Rs.171006.47 crore in the 2022-23 budget.

Innovative Practices for Gender Equality

Women-ReBoot: This is a scheme introduced by a Software Skill net, an enterprise-led skills network, in Ireland in collaboration with the technology companies to increase women's participation in the tech workforce by enabling qualified women to re-enter the workforce after a career break. Under this scheme, a four-week training program is organised to prepare the participant for job market re-entry.

Girls as Engineers! and Girls as Science: Poland Government has initiated this policy to introduce science and technology studies to high school girls to motivate them to join technology-related jobs.

Cooks without Home: This is an initiative of Homelike (Jako doma), an NGO in Czech Republic. This scheme encourages homeless women to cook and sell food at low prices. This scheme empowers homeless women by providing support through social contacts and safe working spaces.

Cleo-Patria Women's and Neighbourhood Studios: These are places for safe meeting places and learning environments for migrant women from all nationalities in Netherland. Cleo-Patria Foundation has initiated it, and this scheme targets migrant women who are isolated, illiterate and speaks Dutch language poorly.

3. BEYOND GOVERNMENT: ROLE OF NON-STATE ACTORS IN PUBLIC POLICY

Civil society can provide helpful information to government agencies about the effectiveness of public policy and the issues faced by various sections of people.

The role of the State has changed dramatically in the economy and policy-making process. Policy-making is not a monopoly of State or government in 21st century. Non-government actors like Civil society play crucial roles in the policy-making process. The World Bank defines Civil society as "*the wide array of non-governmental and not-for-profit organisations that have a presence in public life, express the interests and values of their members and others, based on ethical, cultural, political, scientific, religious or philanthropic considerations.*" The World Bank engages with civil society through information sharing, policy dialogue, strategic consultation etc. Example of Civil Society organisations include Amnesty International, the World Wide Fund for Nature (WWF), Greenpeace, etc.

Civil society can provide helpful information to government agencies about the effectiveness of public policy and the issues faced by various sections of people. Public policy influences different racial and cultural groups differently, and engagement with civil society organisations can help the government formulate appropriate public policy. According to World Economic Forum, Civil society..." can express controversial views; represent those without a voice; mobilise citizens into movements; build support across stakeholders, and bring credibility to the political system by promoting transparency and accountability. In terms of policy formulation, civil society is a valuable partner in providing deep subject-matter expertise based on first-hand experience, trialling and scaling up innovations in social services and facilitating citizen engagement." (World Economic Forum, 2013)

3.1 Policy Advocacy and Civil Society

Civil society organisations bridge the gap between citizens and policy-making institutions.

Policy advocacy includes various activities like campaigns, education, litigation, lobbying, protest, etc., to influence the policymakers. Civil society organisations can use and generate evidence on policy issues to influence policymakers. Civil society organisations bridge the gap between citizens and policy-making institutions. In many countries, policy-making actors are unaware of the fundamental problems of citizens. Civil society organisations that work closely with people can help the policy makers by providing vital information about the sections of society they engage in or the issues they address.

International Organisation for Public Advocacy lists four methods adopted by NGOs for policy advocacy.

a. **Advising**: Think Tanks involved Research to develop new ideas and evidence on existing policies. These research reports would help in influencing policymakers.
b. **Media campaigning**: Civil society organisations are active in social media and have good relations with mainstream media. Sometimes

they involve in media campaigns to create public opinion toward new policies.

c. **Lobbying:** Sometimes face to face meeting with policymakers or influential people helps the civil society groups generate interest among the policymakers to change the policies.

d. **Activism:** Civil society groups are also involved in political activities like demonstrations, poster campaigns, petitions, etc., influencing the policymakers.

3.2 Policy Transfer and Non-State Actors

As mentioned in section 1 of this chapter, Policy transfer is the process in which policies(goals, content, and instruments) and programs are transferred from one political system to develop policies and programs in another. Non-state actors play an essential role in the policy transfer process across the nations. Non-state actors, called "policy entrepreneurs", play a crucial role in policy transfer. Policy entrepreneurs or policy brokers include consultants, banks,Think tanks, international organisations, law firms, etc. Policy entrepreneurs have necessary marketing and selling skills and can influence the policymakers to adopt the policies they suggest (Nainggolan 2017).

> Policy entrepreneurs or policy brokers include consultants, banks,Think tanks, international organisations, law firms, etc.

Policy entrepreneurs keep close contact with political actors, especially political executives, which helps them influence policy-making. Political entrepreneurs provide new ideas and information on various issues, allowing political actors to win the elections. Policymakers are always sceptical about the possible risk of adopting new policies.The expert opinions given by policy entrepreneurs can help the policy makers to create adequate public support for adopting new policies (Anderson, DeLeo, and Taylor 2019). Hence, policy entrepreneurs set the legislative agenda, which is vital for policy change through legislation.

4. INNOVATION AND SOCIAL CHANGE

Positive transformations in the social structure over time are essential in creating a modern, inclusive society. Urbanisation, industrialisation and, more recently, digitalisation have shaped this transformation in social structure. Innovations and, more notably, social innovations are essential in social change. "Social innovation refers to those social processes of innovation that address unmet social needs by reconfiguring established social relations"(Vadrot, 2020). Catalytic innovations, a subset of disruptive innovations primarily focusing on social change, can help societies solve social problems(Christensen et al. 2006). Disruptive innovations also may lead to social change, but the primary objective of disruptive innovation is not social change. Disruptive innovations are not intended for social change; on the other hand, they focus on business opportunities that may cause social change.

> Catalytic innovations, a subset of disruptive innovations primarily focusing on social change, can help societies solve social problems.

Some of the catalytic innovations that promote social change are as follows

Toynovo: Toynova is a B company focusing on children's early childhood development and promoting play in vulnerable communities in Columbia. Playing with peer group is essential for children's physical and psychological development. However, children from vulnerable communities lack the tools for learning through play. Primarily, plastics are used for making toys; over 80% of the toys end up in landfills. Toynovo recycles and repairs these toys and makes them available to children from vulnerable communities.

Microfinance: Traditional bankers are reluctant to lend to poor households because of a lack of collateral. Microfinance institutions fill this gap by lending money to needy households at a lower interest rate. Grameen bank in Bangladesh is a pioneer in this field, and similar organisations work in different countries.

Child and family clinics: The healthstore Foundation(HSF) runs Child and family Clinics in Kenya, Rwanda and Ghana to provide quality healthcare at an affordable rate. The healthcare foundation follows the franchise model in healthcare and provides "e*ffective*-Quality Care (EQC)" in developing countries at the cost of $4.5, which is the price Starbucks charges in USA.

Kickstart International: Kickstart International is a non-profit social enterprise which helps small-scale farmers in Kenya by designing and marketing climate-smart irrigation technologies. This irrigation equipment helps the farmers to increase yield and income and allows them to come out of poverty.

Women Moving Millions: Women Moving Millions is a community of individuals who donates or pledge to donate $1 million towards the upliftment of women and girls to achieve gender equality.

200 million artisans: 200 million artisans is a Non-governmental organisation working creatively for artisans in India. They raise funds and use these funds to improve the living standards of artisans and their families. They have raised funds worth $30000 and given scholarships worth $8750 for the artisans' children.

SUSTAINABLE DEVELOPMENT GOALS

The Sustainable Development Goals(SDGs) or Global Goals are a collection of 17 goals set by the United Nations General Assembly in 2015.

5. PLANNING THE FUTURE WORLD: THE SUSTAINABLE DEVELOPMENT GOALS

The Sustainable Development Goals(SDGs) or Global Goals are a collection of 17 goals set by the United Nations General Assembly in 2015. The United Nations has set a target of 2030 to achieve these goals. In 2015, the United nation general assembly passed a resolution, and these 17 goals were part of that resolution. The U.N. set a 15 years target to achieve these goals primarily aimed at ending poverty, saving the planet, and protecting the lives of everyone and everywhere. These 17 goals are interlinked, and fulfilling each is essential in achieving development by balancing economic, social, and environmental sustainability.

The following are the 17 Sustainable Development Goals or Global Goals.

5.1 Goal 1: End Poverty in All Foams Everywhere

Globally 10% of the population lives in poverty(less than $1.90 per day) in 2015. This was against 36% in 1990, and the world has made remarkable progress in reducing the poverty level. However, almost 700 million people lives in poverty in 2015 with inadequate access to proper food, safe drinking water, sanitation, health services, etc. The following are the goal 1 targets.

- Eradicate extreme poverty by 2030 for all people everywhere, currently measured as less than $1.25 per day
- Reduce poverty by half the proportion of men, women and children of all ages by 2030.
- Implement social protection programs and measures for all poor and vulnerable by 2030.
- Ensure that both men and women, particularly the poor and vulnerable, have equal rights to economic resources by 2030
- Ensure resilience to the poor and vulnerable and reduce their exposure to climate-related extreme events and other socio-economic shocks.

5.2 Goal 2: Zero Hunger

In 2015, 690 million people suffered from hunger -measured by the prevalence of undernourishment, and this constitutes 8.7% of the world population. The world food program estimates that almost 135 million people suffer from hunger because of climate change, man-made disasters and economic crises. The specific targets are as follows

- End hunger by 2030 and ensure safe, nutritious and sufficient food for all, particularly the poor and live in vulnerable situations.
- By 2030, end all forms of malnutrition and, by 2025, achieve internationally accepted targets of stunting and wasting in children under five years of age. Address the nutritional needs of adolescent girls, pregnant women and older persons.
- By 2030, double the agricultural productivity and income of small-scale food producers.
- By 2030, Ensure sustainable food production systems and resilient agricultural practices to address the challenges posed by climate change
- By 2020, maintain the genetic diversity of seeds, cultivated plants and farmed and domesticated animals and their related wild species

- Increase investment in rural infrastructure, agricultural Research, extension services, and technology development.
- Prevent and correct trade restrictions and distortions in world agricultural markets
- Ensure proper functioning of agricultural markets

5.3 Goal 3: Health

The world has made significant progress on the health front by improving life expectancy and eradicating some diseases related to child and maternal mortality. Further improvements health front are required by ensuring access to physicians, improving health systems, sanitation, hygiene, etc. The specific targets under this goal are as follows

- By 2030, reduce global maternity mortality rates to 70 per 100,000 population.
- By 2030, end preventable death of newborns and children under age 5, reduce neonatal mortality to 12 per 1000 live birth and under 5 mortality to 25 per 1000 live birth.
- By 2030, end AIDS, tuberculosis, malaria, and combat hepatitis, water-borne diseases, and other communicable diseases.
- Strengthen the prevention treatment of substance abuse
- By 2030, halve the number of death and injuries due to road accident
- By 2030, ensure universal access to sexual and reproductive health services

- Strengthen the healthcare systems, particularly in developing countries, by increasing health funding and recruiting healthcare professionals.

5.4 Goal 4: Education

The world has made significant progress in student enrolment, particularly for girls. However, in 2018, 260 million children are out of school and more need to be done to meet the minimum proficiency standards. The following are some of the specific targets to be achieved by 2030:

- Ensure free , equitable and quality primary and secondary education for all boys and girls
- Ensure that all boys and girls have access to quality early childhood development, care and pre-primary education
- Ensure accessible and quality technical, vocational and tertiary education for all men and women.
- Build and upgrade education facilities

5.5 Goal 5: Achieve Gender Equality and Empower All Women and Girls

The united nations consider gender equality a prerequisite for a peaceful, prosperous and sustainable world. Eventhough the school enrolment of girls has increased, and a substantial decrease in child marriages were seen in different countries, more needs to be done to achieve gender equality. Discriminatory laws, social norms, low representation of women in political establishments, violence against women, etc., need to be addressed immediately. The specific targets include

- End all forms of discrimination and violence against women and girls everywhere
- Eliminate child, early and forceful marriages and female genital mutilation
- Recognise and value unpaid care and domestic work
- Ensure equal opportunities and effective participation in decision-making bodies
- Ensure equal rights for women in ownership of property and other economic resources

5.6 Goal 6: Ensure Access to Water and Sanitation for All

Lack of access to drinking water, sanitation facilities and open defecation are major problems in many parts of the world. One out of three persons in the world faces the issue of lack of access to water, and two out of five persons do not have access to a primary handwashing facility with water and handwash. Similarly, 673 million people practice open defecation. Most of these populations live in Central and Southern Asia, Eastern and Southeast Asia and Sub-Saharan Africa. Open defecation threatens people's health and well-being, especially women and girls. Some of the specific targets under goal 6 are as follows

- By 2030, ensure equitable and affordable access to drinking water for all
- End open defecation and provide hygiene and sanitation facilities to all
- Improve the quality of water by controlling pollution and promoting the reuse and recycling of water
- By 2030, improve the water use efficiency and implement integrated water resource management at all levels.
- Protect and restore water related ecosystems

5.7 Goal 7: Ensure Access to Affordable, Reliable, Sustainable and Modern Energy

The world economy is shifting towards renewable energy by reducing the dependence on fossil fuels. There are significant improvements in energy efficiency and electrification in developing countries. Reducing reliance on fossil fuels and shifting focus on renewable energy is the key to fighting environmental challenges and climate change. However, 13% of the world population lack access to electricity and 3 billion people rely on traditional cooking and heating. Combustible fuel for household energy caused 4.2 million deaths; more than 60% of these include women and girls. The specific target for 2030 under Goal 7 include

- Ensure universal access to reliable, affordable and modern energy for all
- Achieve a substantial increase in the share of renewable in the global energy mix
- Improve the energy efficiency levels.
- Promote international cooperation and investment in renewable and green energy infrastructure and Research.

5.8 Goal 8: Promote Inclusive and Sustainable Economic Growth, Employment and Decent Work to All

COVID-19 and related issues cause challenges in achieving inclusive economic growth and employment opportunities. Even before the COVID-19, the economic growth rate started declining in the world economy, and COVID made it worse. COVID-19 poses challenges to the workforce as more than 61% of the workers live in the informal sector. The situation is complicated in sub-Saharan Africa and Central and Southern Asia, with more than 85% of labour working in the informal sector. Inequality in wages and labour participation between men and women workers is another challenge. Men's labour participation rate is 94% against 65% for women globally, and the gender pay gap is 23%. Besides this, globally, women continue to do 2.6 times more unpaid care and domestic work than men. The following are some of the specific targets for 2030 under Goal 8

- Sustain 7% per capita income growth in less developed countries
- Increase the productivity level through diversification, technological progress and innovation.
- Achieve full and productive employment for men and women and equal pay for work of equal value
- Protect the rights of labour and provide a safe work environment

5.9 Goal 9: Build Resilient Infrastructure, Promote Sustainable Industrialisation and Foster Innovation

Growth in the manufacturing sector can generate more employment opportunities and income. Promoting innovations and technological progress in the industrial sector can solve many challenges the world economy faces, like environmental pollution. Innovation needs substantial investment in Research and development activities, and developing countries spend less in these areas. Globally 1.7% of the GDP spend on R&D, and in less developed countries, this is less than 1%.

The following are some of the important specific targets for 2030

- Develop quality, resilient and sustainable infrastructure to support economic development
- Promote inclusive and sustainable industrialisation
- Provide financial services, including affordable credit and access to markets for small and medium enterprises
- Improve the Research and development infrastructure and increase the number of research and development workers per million.

5.10 Goal 10: Reduce Inequality Within and Among Countries

Various forms of inequality persist worldwide despite serious efforts undertaken by international agencies. Among the persons with disabilities, only 28% of the persons get disability benefits, and 80% of the persons with disabilities stay in developing countries. Women in rural areas of developing countries are three times more likely to die while giving birth compared to women in urban areas.

Specific targets under Goal 10 include

- By 2030, achieve and sustain income growth of the bottom 40% of the population at a rate higher than the national average.
- Promote the socio, economic and political inclusion of all
- Adopt more policy measures to reduce inequality
- Improve the regulation and monitoring of global financial markets
- Formulate planned migration policies for safe and responsible migration and mobility of people.

5.11 Goal 11: Make Cities Inclusive, Safe, Resilient and Sustainable

Urban areas constitute 3% of the earth today, and more than 50% of the population lives in this 3% of the earth's area. More than 60 to 80% of energy consumption and 75% of the carbon emissions. By 2030, more than 5 billion people will live in cities against 3.5 billion today, and 95% of the urbanisation will happen in developing countries. Almost 50% of the urban population in Sub-Saharan Africa and Central and Southern Asia live in slums, which is another challenge for the governments. Hence, the cities need to be more inclusive, safe and sustainable. The following are some of the targets for 2030 under goal 11.

- Ensure affordable and safe housing facilities for all and upgrade the slums
- Develop affordable, safe and sustainable transport systems, especially public transportation
- Reduce the city's per capita environmental impact by improving air quality and maintaining proper waste management systems
- Develop inclusive and sustainable urbanisation

5.12 Goal 12: Ensure Sustainable Consumption and Production Patterns

The global population will be 8.5 billion by 2030 and 9.7 by 2050, as per current estimates. This is going to cause more challenges for resource use. Less than 0.5% of the available water is fresh(drinkable), and ensuring drinking water for the 8.5 billion population is challenging. Polluting the water bodies makes the problem severe as the rate of pollution is more than nature's capacity to recycle the water. Another challenge is regarding the availability of food grains. The world faces issues such as degradation of soil fertility, land degradation, overfishing and degradation of the marine environment. These factors restrict the food supply capacity of the economy. Further, 1.3 billion tons of food grains are getting wasted yearly due to related transportation and harvesting issues. To address these challenges, Goal 12 has the following targets for 2030.

- Halve the per capita food waste at consumer and retailer levels and reduce food losses at production and supply chain levels.
- Ensure efficient use and sustainable management of natural resources
- Encourage large companies to adopt sustainability practices and sustainability reporting
- Promote a nature-friendly lifestyle and provide information and awareness about sustainable development

5.13 Goal 13: Climate Action: Take Urgent Action to Combat Climate Change and Its Impacts

Globally, especially in developing nations, challenges related to climate change and carbon emissions are having an impact on people's social and economic well-being. Life is in danger due to the rise in sea level, the rise in temperature, and extreme weather conditions. Agriculture output is greatly threatened by climate change, and farmers around the world are negatively impacted. The Intergovernmental Panel on Climate Change estimates that a 1% increase in global temperature results in a 5% decrease in grain yield. Due to the warmer climate, the yield of maize, wheat, and other important crops decreased by 40 megatons annually between 1981 and 2002. Because of this, farmers' livelihoods and food production are both threatened by climate change. The Paris Agreement in 2015 offers the chance for the international community to strengthen the global response to climate change. This calls for urgent global action to tackle climate change. With this background, the U.N. set the following targets under goal 13

- Climate change-related measures should be integrated into national policies and strategies of all countries
- Strengthen the adaptive capacity and resilience measures to climate change
- Improve education and awareness about climate change-related issues
- Take steps to mobilise 100 billion annually from developed countries, to support developing countries in mitigating climate change

5.14 Goal 14: Conserve and Sustainably Use the Oceans, Seas and Marine Resources

Oceans play an essential role in sustaining the planet as the rainwater, climate, etc., depend on oceans directly or indirectly. Oceans cover three fourth of the earth's surface and 97% of the water resources. Acidification, Ocean warming and oxygen loss due to carbon emission is a threat to the planet and the life of millions of people depending on oceans. Over

200 million people are employed in the marine fishery, and over three billion depend on coastal biodiversity for livelihood. Hence, we need to conserve oceans and save the lives of millions of people depending on the seas. Some of the specific targets under this goal are

- by 2025, Reduce marine pollution, minimise and address the impact of acidification of oceans
- By 2020, Manage and protect marine and coastal ecosystems
- Prevent overcapacity and overfishing, illegal, unreported and unregulated fishing activities
- Ensure that small-scale fishers have access to marine resources

5.15 Goal 15: Sustainably Manage Forests, Combat Desertification, Halt and Reverse Land Degradation, Halt Biodiversity Loss

According to the U.N., 75% of the earth's surface is altered due to human activity, posing a threat to the forest cover and wildlife. According to a report, 1 million animals and plant species are facing the danger of extinction worldwide. The world is facing deforestation, desertification, land degradation, etc. Land degradation has reduced productivity in 23% of the terrestrial areas and caused a fall in food production. From 2010 to 1015, we lost 3.2 crore hectares of forest areas. When we encroach the fragile ecosystems, the chances of zoonotic diseases(diseases transmissible between men and animals) increase.The following are the essential specific targets set under goal 15.

- By 2030, Prevent desertification, restore degraded land and soil
- By 2020, Promote the Implementation of sustainable management of forest
- By 2020, Ensure conservation, restoration and sustainable use of terrestrial and inland freshwater ecosystems
- Mobilise financial resources for the preservation of biodiversity

5.16 Goal 16: Promote Just, Peaceful and Inclusive Societies

The United Nations considers that conflict, injustice and weak institutions cannot ensure sustainable development. Increasing levels of injustice, different types of disputes and attacks against human rights activists are causes of concern in creating an inclusive society. According to U.N. Human Rights Commission(2019), 70 million people got displaced in 2018 due to war, persecution and conflict, which is the highest in 70 years. Birth registration with proof of identity is significantly less in some areas; in sub-Saharan Africa, less than 44% of births are registered. From 2010 to 2019, globally, one in every four births is unregistered(U.N. 2020).

To create a just, peaceful and inclusive society, U.N. set specific targets. Some of the important among them are as follows

- Promote the rule of law at the international and national level and ensure justice for all
- Prevent violence and violence-related death everywhere
- Prevent abuse, torturing, and trafficking of children
- By 2030, reduce the illegal financial and arms flows across the borders
- By 2030, ensure that everyone gets a legal identity and registers the birth
- Promote responsive, inclusive, and participatory decision-making at all levels.

Reduce corruption and bribery in all forms

5.17 Goal 17: Partnership for the Goals

17 PARTNERSHIPS FOR THE GOALS

The U.N. want to promote international cooperation to achieve the Sustainable Development Goals(SDGs). Most of the issues we face today are global, and international collaboration is required to address these issues. Developing countries lack the financial resources to realise their developmental goals, and the international community needs to contribute to developing countries. However, declining global aid and economic crisis in developed countries due to the pandemic are the significant issues we face in financing the SDGs. Some of the specific targets of Goal 17 are as follows

- Strengthen the domestic resource availability in developing countries through international assistance and increased tax revenue
- Developed countries need to fulfil their international development assistance commitments
- Assist developing countries in attaining debt sustainability
- Encourage the development, transfer, dissemination and diffusion of environmentally friendly technologies
- Promote universal, non-discriminatory
- Promote policy coordination and coherence for global macroeconomic stability

Summary

- Globalisation has changed the role of the State and even altered the policy-making process too. Globalisation has reduced the fiscal space and policy autonomy of government. Many of the functions of the State are transferred to quasi-federal regulatory bodies with less political interference. The formation of quasi-federal regulatory bodies brought professionalism to decision-making.
- Globalisation facilitates policy learning and policy transfer. Policy transfer is the process in which policies(goals, content and instruments)

and programs are transferred from one political system to develop policies and programs in another.

- Another feature of public policy in the current world is the focus on gender equality in policy-making. Public policy should benefit men and women equally, and Gender mainstreaming and gender-responsive budgeting are globally accepted approaches for achieving gender equality.
- Gender mainstreaming involves ensuring gender perspectives as the central them of policy development, Research, legislation, resource allocation, and planning and implementation of programs and projects. Gender Responsive budget allocates resources to all sections of society, men, women, girls and boys, to promote gender equality.
- The Government of India has taken several policy measures to promote gender equality in India. This includes Beti Bachao Beti Padhao program, Sukanya Samriddhi Yojna(SSY), Mahila Shakti Kendra (MSK), Mahila Police Volunteers Scheme, etc.
- Non-state actors like non-government Organisations, international organisations, Think Tanks, etc., play a crucial role in policy-making. Non-state actors like "policy entrepreneurs" facilitate the policy transfer across borders.
- Social change is a process of transforming the social structure of society to make it more inclusive. Catalytic innovations play a crucial role in this process, and many NGOs or other organisations are involved in changing social order and improving the lives of socially disadvantaged sections.
- Sustainable development Goals or Global goals are 17 goals approved by the United Nations in 2015, and U.N. has set 2030 as a deadline to reach these goals. These 17 goals are interlinked, and fulfilling each is essential in achieving development by balancing economic, social, and environmental sustainability.

Keywords

Internationalisation of Public Policy	Globalisation
Policy Transfer	Policy learning
Policy Entrepreneur	Gender equality
Gender mainstreaming	Gender-responsive budgeting
Civil society	Policy Advocacy
Innovation	Social Change
SDGs	Global Goals

Questions

1. Explain the effect of globalisation on the policy-making process
2. What are policy learning and Policy Transfer? Explain the role of Policy entrepreneur in policy transfer
3. Can we achieve social change through innovation? Explain
4. What is Gender mainstreaming? How it ensures gender equality?
5. What are the different SDGs? Explain

References

Anderson, S. E., DeLeo, R. A., &Taylor, K. (2020). Policy entrepreneurs, legislators, and agenda setting: information and influence. Policy Studies Journal, 48(3), 587-611.

Eóin Young & Lisa Quinn(2012). Making Research Evidence Matter A Guide To Policy Advocacy InTransition Countries, Open Society Foundation.

IPBES(2019). Global Assessment Report on Biodiversity and Ecosystem services. https://ipbes.net, accessed on 24-Mar-2021.

Lodhi, I. (2021). Globalisation and public policy: bridging the disciplinary and epistemological boundaries. Policy and Society, 40(4), 522-544.

Madgavkar, A., Elingrud, K., & Krishnan, M. (2016). The Economic Benefits of Gender Parity. *Stanford Social Innovation Review.* https://doi.org/10.48558/4G9Z-RG27

Moran, M., Rein, M., & Goodin, R. E. (Eds.). (2008). *The Oxford handbook of public policy.* Oxford University Press.

Nainggolan, A. H. (2017). Key dynamics of internationalisation of public policy in the context of policy transfer. Jurnal Politik, 3(1), 5-20.

Nainggolan, A. H. (2017). Key dynamics of internationalisation of public policy in the context of policy transfer. *Jurnal Politik, 3*(1), 5-20.

U.N. Human Rights Commission(2019), Worldwide displacement tops 70 million, U.N. Refugee Chief urges greater solidarity in response. https://www.unhcr.org, accessed on 17-April-2022.

U.N. (2020). Progress towards the Sustainable Development Goals Report of the Secretary-General https://sustainabledevelopment.un.org, accessed on 17-April-2022

World Economic Forum,(2013). The Future Role of Civil Society. https://www3.weforum.org, accessed on 17-April-2022

Glossary

Administrative man It refers to the traditional bureaucratic decision-making approach that focuses on achieving organizational goals through rational, orderly, and efficient processes, while often overlooking the complex social and political dynamics of policy implementation and the diverse needs and perspectives of stakeholders.

Adverse selection It refers to the tendency of individuals or groups with a higher risk of negative outcomes to seek out or be more likely to use a public service or policy, potentially undermining the effectiveness and efficiency of the policy.

Agenda setting It is the process of determining which issues or topics are given attention, by whom, and how they are presented in the media and public discourse.

Aggregationism It refers to the idea that public policies should be designed to maximize social welfare by aggregating individual preferences or interests, often through democratic processes or market mechanisms.

Anarchy It refers to a state of disorder, absence of government, and breakdown of social order, where individuals and groups may pursue their own interests and goals without regard for public goods and collective welfare.

Aristocracy It refers to a social and political system in which power and privilege are held by a small, privileged elite based on birth, wealth, or other exclusive criteria, which may have implications for public policy decisions and outcomes.

Artificial Intelligence It refers to the development and use of computer-based systems and algorithms that can perform tasks that typically require human intelligence, and is increasingly being considered by policymakers as a tool for addressing public policy challenges in areas such as healthcare, transportation, and public safety.

Asymmetric information It refers to a situation where one party has more or better information than the other party, potentially leading to unequal bargaining power, adverse selection, and moral hazard problems, and requiring regulatory or market-based interventions to mitigate these issues.

Authoritarianism It is a form of governance characterized by centralized and non-democratic decision-making, limited political freedoms, and the use of coercion and control to enforce compliance with government policies and goals, often leading to violations of human rights and social justice.

Autocracy It refers to a form of government in which political power is concentrated in the hands of a single ruler or a small elite group, with limited or no input from the general public, and public policy decisions are made without democratic deliberation or accountability.

Bicameral system It refers to a government style with two separate divisions within the legislative branch of government.

Blockchain It is a decentralized, tamper-resistant digital ledger that allows for secure and transparent record-keeping of public policy decisions and transactions.

Bounded rationality It refers to the limited cognitive capacity of policy-makers and their reliance on heuristics, biases, and incomplete information in making decisions about public policies, which can result in suboptimal outcomes and unintended consequences.

Capitalization policies These refer to the set of rules and practices that govern the management, allocation, and financing of public infrastructure assets, such as transportation, water supply, and energy systems, aimed at maximizing their long-term value and benefits to the society.

Citizen-centricity It is a principle of designing policies, services, and systems that prioritize the needs, perspectives, and experiences of citizens.

Citizenry It refers to the collective body of citizens who are members of a community, nation, or state and have rights, responsibilities, and interests in public policy processes and outcomes.

Civil society It refers to the collective space of voluntary and non-governmental organizations and individuals that operate independently from the government and engage in advocacy, public participation, and social action to promote the common good and hold the government accountable.

Co-advocacy It refers to the joint efforts of multiple individuals, organizations, or interest groups to promote a common policy agenda and achieve policy goals through collaboration and collective action.

Coercive power It refers to the authority of the government to use force, sanctions, or penalties to enforce compliance with laws, regulations, or policies, and deter individuals or groups from engaging in behaviors deemed harmful or illegal.

Common information bias It refers to the tendency of decision-makers to rely on readily available or commonly shared information, rather than seeking diverse or independent sources of information, which can lead to flawed policies and decision-making.

Common Law It refers to the body of legal principles and doctrines developed through judicial decisions and precedents, rather than statutes or codes, that shape the interpretation and application of public policies in many countries, especially those with a common law legal system.

Consequentialism It is a normative ethical theory that evaluates the morality of an action or policy based on its consequences or outcomes, with the goal of maximizing overall social welfare or utility.

Conservatives These are people who generally oppose government intervention or regulation in the economy and support individual freedom of choice in all areas of life.

Data science It involves using statistical analysis and machine learning techniques to extract insights from large datasets, informing evidence-based decision making and policy development.

Decision criteria These refer to the standards or measures used to evaluate alternative policy options or solutions based on their effectiveness, efficiency, equity, feasibility, and other relevant factors, in order to make informed and justified decisions in the public interest.

Decision leaders These are individuals or groups who have the authority, expertise, or influence to make critical decisions and take actions that shape the policy agenda, policy choices, and policy outcomes.

Deep learning It refers to a type of artificial intelligence that uses neural networks to analyze and make predictions based on large and complex data sets, which can be applied to various policy areas such as healthcare, transportation, and public safety to inform decision-making and improve outcomes.

Delphi method It is a structured and iterative process of gathering and synthesizing expert opinions and knowledge to support decision-making in the development, implementation, and evaluation of public policies.

Democracy It is a form of government in which the power and authority are vested in the people, who exercise their rights and responsibilities to participate in the decision-making processes of public policy and hold their leaders accountable for their actions.

Democratic dilemma It refers to the tension between competing values of democracy, such as individual rights, popular sovereignty, and minority representation, which can present challenges in designing and implementing public policies that are inclusive, effective, and legitimate.

Dictatorship It refers to a form of government in which a single individual or a small group holds absolute power and makes decisions without democratic input or accountability, often leading to limited or no public policy development and implementation.

Diplomacy It means the profession, activity, or skill of managing international relations, typically by a country's representatives abroad.

Distributive policies These refer to public policies that involve the allocation of benefits or resources to specific individuals or groups, such as welfare programs, education grants, and tax credits.

Doctrine of Precedent It refers to the legal principle that courts are bound to follow previous decisions or judgments in similar cases, establishing a consistent and predictable legal framework for policymaking and implementation.

Downsian competition It is a model of party competition that assumes that parties formulate policies aimed at winning elections in that parties try to maximize their votes and that the median voter theorem applies.

Economic man It is a theoretical construct that assumes individuals behave rationally and self-interestedly in their economic decisions, often used in the analysis and design of public policies that aim to influence or incentivize individual behavior.

Electoral bond It refers to a financial instrument introduced by the Indian government as a mode of anonymous donation to political parties, aimed at promoting transparency and reducing the use of black money in electoral funding, and is a policy tool to regulate political financing.

Empire Building It is a term used to describe the act of increasing the size, scope, or power of an organization, often at the expense of others.

Equity dilemma It refers to the challenge of balancing the interests and needs of different groups or individuals, often with competing priorities, in a fair and just manner.

Expert opinions These refer to the informed and authoritative perspectives of individuals or groups with specialized knowledge, skills, or experience, which can provide valuable insights and recommendations to policymakers in shaping policy decisions.

Expert power It refers to the ability of an individual or group to influence public policy decisions based on their knowledge, expertise, and credibility in a particular field or issue area.

Externalities These refer to the unintended spillover effects, positive or negative, of an economic activity or policy on third parties who are not involved in the activity or transaction, creating market failures and justifying public policy interventions.

Functional creep In context of public policy it refers to the phenomenon where a program or policy's scope expands beyond its original intended purpose, resulting in unintended consequences and potential inefficiencies.

Functionalism It is a theory that emphasizes the role of government in achieving functional efficiency and rationality in delivering public goods and services, and in balancing competing interests and values in society.

Gender mainstreaming It refers to the process of integrating a gender perspective into all aspects of public policy, planning, and decision-making to promote gender equality and improve the lives of both women and men.

Goal orientation It refers to the individual or organizational focus on achieving specific objectives or targets through actions, strategies, and resources.

Government policy It refers to the set of principles, laws, regulations, and guidelines established by government bodies to address issues of public concern and achieve their goals.

Groupthink It refers to the tendency of group members to conform to a consensus opinion, suppress dissenting views, and ignore alternative perspectives, often leading to flawed decision-making and policy outcomes.

Impeachment It refers to the legal process by which a public official, such as the president or a judge, can be charged with and removed from office for committing high crimes or misdemeanors, often with significant implications for public policy and governance.

Impossibility theorem It refers to the mathematical proof that shows it is impossible to construct a voting system that satisfies all desirable criteria, such as fairness, accuracy, and consistency, under certain conditions.

Informational power It refers to the ability of individuals or organizations to influence policy decisions and outcomes by providing or withholding information, expertise, data, or analysis that shapes the perceptions, priorities, and choices of policymakers and stakeholders.

Judgmental heuristics These refer to mental shortcuts or rules of thumb used by policymakers to simplify complex policy issues and make decisions based on limited information, experience, and cognitive biases.

Judicial activism It refers to the approach of judges in interpreting and applying the law in a manner that promotes their own policy preferences, rather than deferring to the legislative or executive branches of government, potentially shaping or influencing public policy outcomes.

Judicial activism It refers to the willingness of judges to interpret and apply the law in a broad and expansive manner to address social or political issues, even if it requires going beyond the traditional limits of judicial authority, and can have a significant impact on public policy.

Judicial anarchy It is sometimes used to describe a situation where the judiciary oversteps its bounds and becomes too powerful, leading to a breakdown in the rule of law.

Judicial restraint It refers to the judicial philosophy that judges should defer to the other branches of government and avoid interfering with their policy decisions, except when necessary to enforce constitutional limits or protect individual rights.

Judicial review It is the power of the courts to review and potentially invalidate government actions or policies that are deemed to be inconsistent with the constitution, laws, or other legal standards, and is an important tool for ensuring accountability and protecting individual rights in the public policy process.

Jurisdictional dilemmas It refers to situations where different levels or branches of government have conflicting interests or responsibilities, resulting in policy fragmentation, coordination challenges, and accountability issues.

Jurisprudence It refers to the philosophy of law and the study of legal systems.

Legitimacy It refers to the perceived authority, trustworthiness, and fairness of the policy-making process and its outcomes, as judged by stakeholders and the broader society.

Legitimate power It refers to the authority or influence that a government or public institution has over citizens or stakeholders, based on their recognition of the legitimacy of the government's legal and moral authority.

Liberals These are people who generally support government intervention or regulation in the economy and support individual freedom of choice in personal matters.

Lobbying It refers to the activities of individuals, groups, or organizations aimed at influencing the development, implementation, or outcomes of public policies by communicating with government officials, legislators, or other stakeholders.

Lobbyist An individual or organization that engages in advocacy and communication activities to influence the decisions and actions of government officials, policymakers, or legislators in favor of a particular policy or interest group.

Machine learning It refers to the use of algorithms and statistical models to analyze and learn from data in order to inform decision-making processes that address social, economic, and environmental challenges.

Majority rule It is a decision-making process that gives each member of a group or society an equal vote, and the decision is made by the majority of the votes.

Median Voter This theorem is a political theory that states that in a two-party system, if voters are distributed along a single left-right spectrum and if parties want to maximize their vote, they will converge towards the median voter's position.

Meritocracy It refers to a system in which individuals are selected, promoted, or rewarded based on their merit or achievement rather than their social status, wealth, or connections.

Moral hazard It refers to the risk that individuals or organizations may engage in risky behavior or take advantage of policies or regulations, knowing that they will not bear the full costs or consequences of their actions.

Moral hazard It refers to the risk that individuals or organizations may take excessive risks or engage in undesirable behavior due to the expectation that they will be protected or bailed out by the government or other actors, leading to unintended consequences and costs.

Neoliberalism It is an economic and political philosophy that emphasizes the role of the private sector, market-based solutions, and limited government intervention in public policy.

Nepotism It is the practice of showing favoritism to relatives or close friends, especially by giving them jobs or other opportunities.

Nirvana fallacy It refers to the flawed logic of comparing a realistic policy option to an idealized, perfect solution, often leading to the rejection of feasible options that can still make a positive impact in the real world.

Niskanen's Model It is a theory of bureaucracy that suggests that government agencies will seek to maximize their budgets and power, rather than efficiently carrying out their stated objectives.

Oeconomy It is an archaic spelling of "economy" and refers to the management and regulation of economic affairs in a society, including the allocation of resources, production, distribution, and consumption, which are critical elements of public policy.

Oligarchy It refers to a system of governance in which power and decision-making are concentrated in the hands of a small group of elites, often with significant influence over public policy.

Organizational policy It refers to the set of rules, procedures, and guidelines that govern the operations and behavior of an organization, including its employees, stakeholders, and processes.

Pareto property It is a concept in economics that refers to the idea that an economic system is Pareto efficient if no one can be made better off without making someone else worse off.

Partisan dilemma It refers to the challenge of balancing political ideology and loyalty to one's political party with the need to make policy decisions that effectively address the issues and needs of the public.

Perfect rationality It refers to the assumption that policymakers have complete information, can accurately forecast the consequences of their decisions, and always choose the option that maximizes the expected utility, which may not reflect the actual behavior of policymakers in the real world.

Personal policy It is a set of individual beliefs, values, and principles that guide an individual's decisions and actions in their personal and professional life.

Plural executive It is a system of government in which the executive power is vested in a group of individuals with equal authority, rather than in a single person for a set period of time.

Plutocracy It refers to a system of governance in which the wealthy elite exert disproportionate influence or control over public policy, often to the detriment of the common good or the interests of the broader population.

Policy actors These are individuals, groups, or organizations that have an interest, stake, or influence in the development, implementation, or outcomes of public policies, including government officials, interest groups, citizens, experts, and international organizations.

Policy advocacy It refers to the process of promoting or opposing specific policy proposals or decisions, often by mobilizing public opinion, engaging with policymakers, and building coalitions to influence the policy-making process.

Policy entrepreneur An individual or group who identifies and promotes innovative solutions to public policy problems, working to change the agenda and mobilize support for their proposals.

Policy environment It refers to the political, economic, social, and institutional factors that influence the development, implementation, and outcomes of public policies in a given context.

Policy goals These are specific and measurable outcomes that a public policy is designed to achieve, often reflecting the values, priorities, and needs of the society or community it serves.

Policy incoherence It refers to a situation where different policies, strategies or actions pursued by a government or organization contradict or undermine each other, resulting in ineffective or counterproductive outcomes.

Policy instruments These are the specific tools and methods used by governments and other organizations to implement and achieve policy goals, including regulations, incentives, sanctions, and information campaigns.

Policy learning In the context of public policy it refers to the process of acquiring knowledge and expertise through experience and analysis to inform and improve the development and implementation of policies.

Policy life-cycle It refers to the stages of development, implementation, evaluation, and revision of public policies over time.

Policy model It is a simplified representation of the complex social, economic, and political reality that enables policymakers and analysts to understand, predict, and evaluate the potential effects of policy interventions.

Policy players It refer to the individuals, groups, organizations, and institutions that are involved in the policy-making process, including government officials, politicians, interest groups, experts, media, and the public.

Policy science It refers to the interdisciplinary study of public policy, drawing on theories, methods, and insights from various fields, such as political science, economics, sociology, law, and management, to inform policy analysis, design, and evaluation.

Policy transfer In public policy it refers to the process of adopting and adapting policies or practices from one context to another, either within the same country or across different countries, to address similar or related policy challenges.

Political economy It refers to the study of the interaction between politics and economics, and how this interaction affects the distribution, regulation, and management of resources, wealth, and power in society.

Political finance It refers to the funding of political campaigns, parties, and activities, and the rules, regulations, and practices governing the sources, uses, and disclosure of such funds, which can have significant implications for the transparency, accountability, and integrity of public policy.

Political inequality It refers to the unequal distribution of power, resources, and opportunities among different groups in society to participate in the policy-making process, influence policy decisions, and hold policymakers accountable, which can affect the fairness and effectiveness of public policies.

Political money It refers to the financial contributions made to political candidates, parties, or interest groups by individuals, corporations, unions, or other organizations, which can have a significant impact on the formulation and implementation of public policies.

Power It refers to the ability of individuals, groups, or institutions to influence policy decisions, outcomes, and implementation, often based on their access to resources, information, and social networks.

Predictive analytics It refers to the use of data mining, statistical modeling, and machine learning techniques to analyze past and current data and make predictions about future outcomes or trends that can inform policy decisions.

Private good It refers to a product or service that is excludable and rivalrous, meaning that it is only available to those who pay for it, and its consumption by one person reduces its availability for others.

Problem definition It refers to the process of clearly and accurately defining a problem, issue, or challenge that needs to be addressed or solved.

Public advocacy It refers to the active support or promotion of a particular policy, cause, or issue by individuals or groups, aimed at influencing public opinion, policy decisions, and social change.

Public choice It refers to the application of economic principles and models to the analysis of political and social decision-making processes, including the behavior of individuals, groups, and institutions involved in public policy formulation and implementation.

Public finance It refers to the study of how governments raise and spend funds to provide public goods and services, redistribute income, and stabilize the economy, while ensuring fiscal sustainability and accountability.

Public good It refers to goods or services that are non-excludable and non-rivalrous in consumption, meaning that their benefits are available to all and the consumption of the good by one person does not reduce its availability for others.

Public interest It refers to the common good, welfare, or benefit of the general public, often based on values, principles, and goals that reflect the needs and aspirations of a society or community.

Public opinion It refers to the attitudes, beliefs, and preferences held by a diverse group of citizens on various policy issues, which may influence the development, implementation, and effectiveness of public policies.

Public opinion It refers to the views, attitudes, beliefs, and preferences of the general public or specific groups on policy issues, which can influence policy decisions and implementation.

Public policy It is the set of principles, laws, regulations, and guidelines established by government bodies to address issues of public concern.

Public property It refers to assets, resources, or facilities that are owned by the government and are intended for public use or benefit, such as parks, roads, public buildings, and utilities.

RadicalsThese are people who generally support extreme changes in the political, social, or economic systems.

Rational choice It refers to the approach that assumes individuals and organizations make decisions based on a careful analysis of costs, benefits, and risks, and that policies should be designed to incentivize desirable behaviors and outcomes.

Rational ignorance It refers to the decision by individuals to remain uninformed or underinformed about public policy issues or decisions when the costs of acquiring information outweigh the perceived benefits or impact of their participation.

Rational irrationality It refers to the behavior of individuals who act in a seemingly irrational manner due to the high cost or low probability of their individual actions affecting public policy outcomes, even if they recognize the potential collective benefits of alternative policies.

Rationality It refers to the use of evidence-based, logical, and systematic thinking to inform policy decisions that are based on clear goals, adequate information, and an understanding of the potential benefits, costs, and trade-offs of different policy options.

Red tape It refers to bureaucratic procedures, rules, and regulations that are considered excessive, burdensome, and time-consuming, often hindering the efficiency and effectiveness of public policy implementation and delivery.

Redistributive policies These refer to public policies aimed at reducing economic and social inequalities, through various mechanisms such as taxation, social welfare programs, and public services.

Referent power It refers to the ability of an individual or group to influence policy decisions based on their perceived expertise, credibility, and legitimacy in a particular domain or issue area.

Regulatory policies These are a set of government rules, standards, and requirements that are designed to regulate the behavior and conduct of individuals, organizations, or industries, in order to achieve specific public policy goals, such as safety, health, environmental protection, or consumer protection.

Regulatory State It refers to a government model where regulatory agencies play a prominent role in setting and enforcing rules and standards to promote public welfare, safety, and other policy objectives.

Reward power It refers to the ability of policy makers to influence the behavior of individuals or organizations by providing incentives or rewards for compliance or desirable actions.

RIsky shift It refers to the phenomenon where a group's decision-making process leads to riskier or more extreme decisions than an individual member would have made, which can have implications for public policy decision-making and implementation.

Rule of Law It is the principle that everyone, including governments and individuals, is subject to and accountable to the same set of laws, which are enforced fairly and impartially.

Screening It refers to the process of identifying individuals or groups who are eligible or qualified for a particular program, service, or benefit, based on specific criteria and information.

Selectorate It refers to the group of individuals or organizations that have the power to influence or determine policy outcomes, including elected officials, interest groups, experts, and other stakeholders.

Self-advocacy It refers to the active and assertive participation of individuals or groups in advocating for their own rights, interests, and needs, and influencing the policy decisions and outcomes that affect them directly or indirectly.

Signaling It refers to the use of policy decisions or announcements to convey information to the public, stakeholders, or other governments, often with the aim of influencing expectations, behavior, or outcomes.

Social choice It refers to the process of making collective decisions that reflect the preferences and values of individuals or groups in a society, often involving trade-offs and compromises among different policy options and stakeholders.

Social dilemma It refers to a situation where individual incentives conflict with the collective interest, leading to suboptimal outcomes, and where policy interventions may be necessary to align individual and social goals.

Stare decisis It refers to the legal principle of following precedent and relying on past court decisions when making future judicial rulings, which can influence the development and implementation of public policies.

Substantive policies These refer to public policies that directly address a specific problem or issue and provide solutions or interventions to achieve specific outcomes or goals, as opposed to procedural policies that define rules and procedures for implementing policies or managing government operations.

Superior decisions These refer to those that are based on rigorous analysis, empirical evidence, stakeholder engagement, ethical principles, and public values, and are effective, efficient, equitable, and sustainable in addressing public problems and achieving policy goals.

Theocratic It refers to a form of government or policy-making that is based on religious principles, beliefs, or authority, often with religious leaders playing a significant role in policy decisions and implementation.

Titular executive It is a person in an official position of leadership who possesses few, if any, actual powers.

Totalitarianism It is a political system characterized by centralized and authoritarian control of all aspects of society, including political, economic, social, and cultural life, often resulting in the suppression of individual rights and freedoms and the promotion of a single ideology or party.

Transitivity It refers to the property of a relationship between three elements such that if the relationship holds between the first and second elements and between the second and third elements, it also holds between the first and third elements.

Tribalism It refers to the tendency of individuals or groups to prioritize their own interests, values, or identities over the common good, leading to polarization, conflict, and inefficiency in the policy-making process.

Unicameral system It refers to a legislative body consisting of a single chamber, often used in small or homogeneous countries, which can have advantages such as efficiency and lower costs but may also pose challenges for representation and diversity of perspectives.

Unitary It refers to a form of government organization or decision-making process that is centralized, with ultimate authority and power resting in a single entity or actor, such as the national government.

Welfarism It refers to the belief that the government should take an active role in promoting social welfare and ensuring the well-being of its citizens, often through policies aimed at reducing poverty, inequality, and discrimination.

Index

D

R

Credits

Description	Credits
Text According to Statista©2020, … was 12137 (Page 34)	Annual lobbyist salaries in the United States as of September 27, 2021, by percentile (in 1,000 U.S. dollars), https://www.statista.com/, © Statista 2022
Table 2.2 Types of Political Action Committees (Page 36)	Federal Election Commission of the USA. Extracted from https://www.fec.gov/
Figure 2.3 Political Action Committees (PAC) contributions in the US from 2017 to 2018 (Page 37)	Data sourced from the Federal Election Commission, www.fec.gov, (c)Federal Govt. of USA, accessed Jan. 2023
Figure 2.3 Political Action Committees (PAC) contributions in the US from 2017 to 2018 (Page 37)	dedek / Shutterstock
Figure (Page 39)	alphaspirit / 123RF
Figure 3.9 Index of Economic Freedom-2022 (Page 70)	Data compiled by author from 2022 Index of Economic Freedom, https://www.heritage.org/index/about
Figure 3.10 Top Command Economies in 2022 based on Index of Economic Freedom (Page 72)	Data compiled by author from 2022 Index of Economic Freedom, https://www.heritage.org/index/about
Figure 3.11 Government Spending as % of GDP (Page 73)	Data compiled by author from World Development Indicators of World Bank Data
Figure 3.13 Changing Size of Government Spending as % of GDP (Page 77)	Data compiled by author from World Development Indicators of World Bank Data
Figure (Page 82)	aurielaki / Shutterstock
Figure 5.6 Political Inequality Index 2016 (Page 136)	Graph made by author based on: Choi, Gwangeun. Political Inequality Index. Ann Arbor, MI: Inter-university Consortium for Political and Social Research [distributor], 2019-12-01. https://doi.org/10.3886/E101268V3 , released under CCBY 4.0 International license
Figure 5.8 Political finance through electoral bonds in India (Page 139)	Association for Democratic Reforms (ADR)
Appendix 5.1 Political Inequality Index: 1990-1998 (Page 143)	Table made by author based on: Choi, Gwangeun. Political Inequality Index. Ann Arbor, MI: Inter-university Consortium for Political and Social Research [distributor], 2019-12-01. https://doi.org/10.3886/E101268V3 , released under CCBY 4.0 International license

Description	Credits
Appendix 5.2 Political Inequality Index: 1999-2007 (Page 144)	Table made by author based on: Choi, Gwangeun. Political Inequality Index. Ann Arbor, MI: Inter-university Consortium for Political and Social Research [distributor], 2019-12-01. https://doi.org/10.3886/E101268V3 , released under CCBY 4.0 International license
Appendix 5.3 Political Inequality Index: 2008-2016 (Page 145)	Table made by author based on: Choi, Gwangeun. Political Inequality Index. Ann Arbor, MI: Inter-university Consortium for Political and Social Research [distributor], 2019-12-01. https://doi.org/10.3886/E101268V3 , released under CCBY 4.0 International license
Figure 7.9 A Template for Performance Management System in Government (Page 194)	Adapted from Second Administrative Reforms Commission's Tenth Report, 2008
Figure 7.10 A suggested Model of Performance Management in Government (Page 195)	Report of the Committee on Performance Management in Government
Table 7.1 Critical Issues in Performance Management in Government (Page 196)	Report of the Committee on Performance Management in Government. https://darpg.gov.in/sites/default/files/Performance_Management.pdf
Figure 8.1 Four Features of The State (Page 202)	Lee Yiu Tung. Shutterstock
Figure 8.2 Mann's Overlapping and Intersecting Socio-spatial Networks of Power (Page 204)	Lee Yiu Tung. Shutterstock
Image Public Service Delivery (Page 240)	Lesnnik / 123RF
Figure 10.1 A Comparison of Public Expenditure on Education (Page 242)	World Development Indicators (WDI), World Bank
Figure 10.2 A Comparison of Public Expenditure on Health (Page 242)	World Development Indicators (WDI), World Bank
Figure 10.4 Basic Handwashing Facilities in India (Page 244).	World Development Indicators (WDI), World Bank
Figure (Page 256)	Creative Stall / Shutterstock
Figure Flow chart of the CIRP Process in India (Page 327)	Adapted from Understanding the IBC Key Jurisprudence And Practical Considerations- A Handbook, Ibbi
Figure 13.4 States' Startup Ranking 2021 (Page 341)	ImageFlow / Shutterstock
Figures (Pages 373–381)	The United Nations Sustainable Development Goals, (c) United Nations, all rights reserved. Used with permission. The content of this publication has not been approved by the United Nations and does not reflect the views of the United Nations or its officials or Member States. UN SDG goals available at: https://www.un.org/sustainabledevelopment/ , accessed March 2023